SECRETS
of the
GOLDEN AGE PRINCE
FRANCIS BACON

SECRETS
of the
GOLDEN AGE PRINCE
FRANCIS BACON

ELIZABETH CLARE PROPHET

SUMMIT UNIVERSITY PRESS®
Gardiner, Montana

SECRETS OF THE GOLDEN AGE PRINCE: FRANCIS BACON
by Elizabeth Clare Prophet
Copyright © 2024 The Summit Lighthouse, Inc. All rights reserved.

Except for a single copy for your personal, noncommercial use, no part of this work may be used, reproduced, stored, posted or transmitted in any manner or medium whatsoever without written permission, except by a reviewer who may quote brief passages in a review.

For information, contact
The Summit Lighthouse, 63 Summit Way, Gardiner, MT 59030 USA
Tel: 1-800-245-5445 or 1 406-848-9500
info@SummitUniversityPress.com
SummitLighthouse.org

Library of Congress Control Number: 2023951302
ISBN: 978-1-60988-438-3 (softbound)
ISBN: 978-1-60988-439-0 (eBook)

SUMMIT UNIVERSITY ꙮ PRESS®

The Summit Lighthouse, Summit University, Summit University Press, ꙮ, Church Universal and Triumphant, Keepers of the Flame, and *Pearls of Wisdom* are trademarks registered in the U.S. Patent and Trademark Office and in other countries. All rights reserved.

27 26 25 24   1 2 3 4

CONTENTS

A Note to the Reader   xi

Part 1   A Sacred Mystery   1
  A Marvelous Being Is Born   8
  Out of Darkness   9
  A Mystic History   11
  A Violent Break   14
  The Rise of the Virgin Queen   17
  Prince Francis   20
  The Education of a Prince   25
  A Prince at Cambridge   29
  The Reformation of the Whole Wide World   31
  The Fairie Queen   40
  A Dread Secret Revealed   43
  A Celestial Visitation   47
  The Parisian Court   49
  The Rose of France   54
  Esoteric France   58
  Secret Wisdom   64
  Birth of Works Immortal   69
  Calling the Wits Together   76
  The Knights of the Helmet   80
  Arcadia   81
  Shake-Speares   83
  The Shakespeare Notebook   86
  The Actor and the Adept   87
  A Member of Parliament   93
  Brothers United   95
  The Rose Cross   97
  Secret Mysteries of Francis and the Brethren   100

The Mysterious Spirit of Francis   102
Baconian Gardens   103
Portia and Belmont   105
The Northumberland Manuscript   106
Times Perilous   108
The Second Son   113
A Prince Ensnared   121
Now Cracks a Noble Heart   127
The Mystery of the Ring   134
A Philosopher's Death   138
The Murder of the Queen   139
Celestial Portents   145
The Changeling Becomes King   149
The Founding Vision of America   154
The Upward Trek   157
The College of Invisibles   161
Genius of the Ancient Pile   163
The Breaking Storm   165
The Fate of the Conspirators—Karma Descends   175
The Gemini Brothers—Twin Works   178
The Six Days Work   185
Poison, Parliament, and the Pen   190
A Phoenix from the Ashes   193
The New Atlantis   198
The Mystery of the Second Shakespeare Folio   201
Uncivil War   202
The Execution of the King   203
Reformation and Liberty   204
The Mystery of the Book of Emblems   205
The Revelation of Apollo and the Great Assizes   206
The Rosicrucian Path   208

Part 2 A Holy Brother 217

    The Ascension of the Golden Age Prince 219
    The Ascending Arc: A Cosmic Romance 221
    The Mystery of the Personal Ascension 224
    Saint Germain: Ascended Master, Alchemist and Mystic 231
    A Morning in Transylvania 233
    The Wonderman of Europe 235
    The House of Rakoczy 242
    Early Travels 244
    The Court of Versailles 245
    A Tale of Two Countries 252
    Foundations of Freedom 252
    Francis and Friends in America 254
    The Mystical Origins of America 256
    The Legend of the Anointing 257
    The Professor and the Starry Flag 263
    Old Glory 269
    The Speech of the Unknown 269
    Son of the Republic 274
    A Nation Is Born 280
    The Brewing Violence 281
    The Reign of Terror 291
    The Music of Freedom 292
    A Farewell 294
    Hope for a United Europe 295
    An Initiation of Power 297
    The Force of Anti-Freedom 301
    Karma, Destiny and Free Will 308
    A New Cycle for Humanity 310
    The Masters of Wisdom 312
    The Path of the Fiery Heart 317

The Magic Presence   328
Unveiled Mysteries   330
The Violet Transmuting Flame   332
The Power of the I AM   336
Keeping the Flame   339
A Living Master   344
Light Is the Alchemical Key   351
The Inheritance   359
The Age of the Seventh Angel   363
Your Own Holy Brother   365

Appendices   370
Notes   371

DEDICATION

To Pallas Athena,
the Goddess of Truth and Wisdom,
priestess of the Sacred Fire and elder sister of cosmic art—
she who is the muse and patroness of Francis Bacon,
who came in her name to shake her spear
and pierce the veil of ignorance.

A NOTE TO THE READER

> *Greater love hath no man than this,*
> *that a man lay down his life for his friends.*
> ~ John 15:13

Francis Bacon lived every day of his life for humanity, not just in his own time but for all ages to come. In his writings, his plans and hopes stretch far beyond his own day, touching us in the here and now. With his "muse of fire" and his ever-unfolding works, Francis wove the threads for us to follow out of the maze of human ignorance. He implores us to share in his vision and to be enfired with *love in action*. Francis did not just dream of a golden age, he created an entire culture and system that *is* leading humanity to self-transcendence and global enlightenment. Our choice is "to be or not to be" a partner in the enlightenment of civilization.

By studying his works and decoding his ciphers, friends of Francis Bacon have been in a conversation with him that has lasted centuries. The soul of Francis, as that of Jesus and Gautama Buddha, is now an ascended master, a living Spirit. He works with each one who follows the inner connection. He is the loving teacher who, with a glint of humor in his eyes, begins a game of hide-and-seek that gives the seeker not only the secrets of his life but also the understanding and ability to seek and find divine Truth hidden within creation.

Peter Dawkins, an expert Baconian scholar and student of ancient wisdom, wrote of Francis Bacon as a *living* master:

> Different people come to find this Master and his work in different ways. Sometimes the finding is dramatic: it is always momentous....
>
> Sir Francis Bacon, Baron Verulam, Viscount St Alban (1561–1626) was acknowledged by the poet laureate Ben Jonson and others as one of the greatest of Masters to appear in our world for many ages—a Socrates, Plato and Orpheus all rolled into one—an Apollo, leader of the Choir of Muses, and a Solomon, wisest of the wise....

Like Elias or John the Baptist, Bacon referred to himself as the herald or harbinger of a new age—an age of universal enlightenment. Like Orpheus he was a renovator or reviver of the ancient and original wisdom teachings taught via the Mysteries and based on love—a "music" by means of which all things can be brought to a harmonious perfection.

Bacon is not a dead Master but a living Master. His work was designed for the benefit not just of our generation but of generations and ages to come. His Spirit imbues it all, and his soul overlights and guides all those who draw close and take part.[1]

This book is simply a signal light, illuminating the way to this wonderful master. It is for those hearts who have kept the flame of Francis's Great Instauration, or Great Restoration, some doing so without any outer memory of their heart-friend of old. More than four centuries ago, Francis and his friends kindled the flame of wisdom and freedom that is behind the Coming Revolution in Higher Consciousness. The time for that brightening illumination of the world and all of humanity is now.

As you embark on this journey of discovery, filled with new potential, you step over a secret threshold into new environs, strange yet somehow familiar. In a rarefied place, you move forward in beauty, peace, and his presence. Awakening to an inner thread that has always been there, it can now be sensed as it is, clothed with his voice, poetry, and brotherhood.

The key to the new era is a golden thread—if we can but follow it.

~The editors of Summit University Press

Secrets of the Golden Age Prince: Francis Bacon

— PART 1 —

A Sacred Mystery

May God the Maker, the Preserver, the Renewer
  of the Universe
of his love and compassion to man protect and guide
  this work
both in its ascent to His glory, and its descent to the
  good of man,
through his only Son, God with us.

~ Francis Bacon, *Abecedarium Naturæ*

The Dark Ages were ending. The sacred secrets of the hidden mystery schools were coming again to the surface of thought, culture, and philosophy. The warm light of the Renaissance was beginning to gleam in the hearts of spiritual seekers once again. The entire world waited for the coming of a true teacher, a master, to light that spark.

In November 1572, a supernova flashed out of the constellation Cassiopeia, startling the world. As bright as Venus, it caused great speculation and had royalty from Britain to China questioning their astrologers.

Tycho Brahe, who first recorded the supernova's appearance, wrote in his *Introduction to the New Astronomy* that "some great light is now at hand which shall enlighten and by degrees expel the former darkness."[1]

Its appearance in Cassiopeia held great mystical meaning. "Cassiopeia means 'the Enthroned Lady' or 'Celestial Queen.' She represents

the Virgin Queen and Mother of the Christ Child (or children)....
Each new star that appears within her basic star pattern signifies the
birth of a new Christ impulse or 'Child of Light' that will influence
and manifest itself on Earth. Cassiopeia is the 'Woman with Child'
of Revelation, and was also called by the Druids, *Llys Don,* meaning
the 'Court of the Lord.' Each star in her bosom is a 'Child of Don,'
a sun-son of the Supreme Lord."[2]

The constellation also signifies the Elohim Cassiopea who holds a focus of great illumination on behalf of the Godhead. This cosmic being assists in raising the consciousness of the entire planet in preparation for the golden age.

The supernova came with an upwelling of cultural reformation and signified the appearance of a soul who would lay the foundations for a new age. For centuries, scientific experimentation in Europe had been virtually nonexistent, except in the alchemical laboratories of the mystics. The spirit of intellectual discovery had been snuffed out during the thousand-year reign of a despotic Church and State. Alfred Dodd, a biographer of Francis Bacon, explains:

> In 1561 England was slowly awakening from the death-like trance into which she had fallen, in common with the rest of Europe, through the spells of the Holy Catholic Church. For upwards of a thousand years this Church had reigned supreme over an entire Continent. The Pope was the Dictator not only of the religious life of the nations but he also controlled all

intellectual activity. Men and women had no right to think outside the narrow bonds of an enervating theology.

... All search for Truth from the third century onwards ended in a pre-ordained cul-de-sac—orthodox dogma. Theology led men away from the great thinkers of Greece and Rome and from the Ethical Rituals of the Mysteries that had once displayed their Secret Dramas in Sacred Temples on the banks of the Nile. It trampled on the Pagan Schools of Thought and ground their teachings into the dust with cries of "heresy." It scoffed at secular learning. Under the leadership of the priest, civilization plunged blindly forward into the abyss of the Medieval Era.[3]

The corruption of the Roman Catholic Church had reached astounding extremes in the practice of indulgences for crimes.* If you could afford to pay the Church, they promised God would forgive you for crimes such as incest, perjury, and even murder, which was in fact the least expensive to absolve. Its corruption was topped only by its use of violence to control populations. Under the chief inquisitor of the Spanish Inquisition, Torquemada, "10,220 persons were burned alive, 97,321 being punished with confiscation of property."[4]

In terms of literature in Europe and England, Alfred Dodd points to similar suffocating effects of both Protestant and Catholic religious dogma. "The Reformation did little to aid Free Thought. The English Puritans made great bonfires of everything Popish, destroying Art and glorying in their depredations. Luther called Copernicus, 'this fool who wishes to reverse the entire system of astronomy.' Puritans and Romanists alike were united in their persecution of philosophy and their hatred of secular knowledge for the common people."[5]

This was a dangerous environment for independent thinkers. But the appearance of the supernova in the constellation Cassiopeia heralded a remarkable change in Europe and England—a change wrought by the secret Brotherhood of adepts, saints, and masters by hidden means and great courage. The sudden intellectual revolution

---
indulgence: a distinctive feature of the penitential system of both the medieval and Roman Catholic Church that granted full or partial remission of sin

Dante and His Poem
Florence Cathedral, Florence, Italy
Painting by Domenico di Michelino, 1465.

of the sixteenth century was born from the seeds planted by those such as Dante and Roger Bacon, who hid liberating spiritual truths within their writings that were anathema to the Roman Catholic Church.

Historian Alfred North Whitehead, in his book *Science and the Modern World,* wrote that this resurgence of learning "bequeathed formed systems of thought touching every aspect of human life. It is the one century which consistently, and throughout the whole range of human activities, provided intellectual genius adequate for the greatness of its occasions."[6]

Those in power tried to control this new renaissance of thought and the coming birth of a new world by reinforcing the oft misunderstood and misused ideal of the divine right of kings—Philosopher-King or Holy Emperor. But the corrupt power structures of Europe were far from this ancient ideal of rulers who have the greatest attainment of the God consciousness and the greatest mastery of the physical universe—individuals who are accomplished in the sciences, in economics, in government, as well as in religion. Many new thinkers no longer had faith in their rulers, seeing little of the divine in their politicking. Mystics and philosophers across Europe were now inspired by the belief of a coming golden age governed by wisdom, love, and the divine rights of each individual.

Peter Dawkins, a Baconian scholar, writes about this time period:

> Many looked to a rebirth of Christianity according to its original model, before the "Roman" takeover and domination of what should have been a free and personal religion. Movements aiming to reform the Church, to return to the first principles of religion and religious life, to study and comprehend the original and true sources of Christian thought and inspiration, spread like wild-fire.... The invention of the printing press enabled the new gospel—the new learning—to be spread. Renaissance colleges, academies, schools and universities raised the level of education, not only amongst the more wealthy and privileged, but amongst the poorer classes of society too....
>
> Amongst the better educated, moderate and beautiful humanistic thought developed, both mystic and scholarly, surrounded on one side by the mediaeval and conservative dogmas of Roman Catholicism and on the other by new and radical dogmas of various reforming movements. The pendulum was swinging from one side of tyranny and oppression, to another side that was proving to be equally violent and aggressive, in Reformation and Counter-Reformation.[7]

This division and warring between theologies threatened to destroy the true reformation that was beginning to take place, but for the coming of one man who took up the cause for freedom and enlightenment. The coming of the supernova coincided exactly with the dawning of a century of genius in science and literature, which was initiated by "the greatest of mankind," Sir Francis Bacon of England.

How could one person usher in a new age? It was only possible because Francis Bacon came to earth with soul mastery that took lifetimes to achieve. This is the story of a wonderful man who became a spiritual adept and a living master. This is a being who personified the Christic light and embodied the Higher Self. Francis's soul journey is like our own. Each soul is here to fulfill her own spiritual destiny.

Francis blazes ahead and shows us the way.

A Marvelous Being Is Born

O, he sits high in all the people's hearts,
And that which would appear offense in us
His countenance, like richest alchemy
Will change to virtue and to worthiness.

~ *Julius Ceasar,* act 1, sc. 3

The "great light," Francis Bacon, was born in 1561. He incarnated the true expression of *noblesse oblige* and never failed to follow the inner teaching of the heart.

The supernova appeared above Francis at the dawn of his age of reason. Even at twelve, Francis saw the shortcomings of civilization and discovered tangible pathways toward their improvement. As a boy, he possessed cheerfulness, great wisdom, and a practicality that enabled him to succeed in the projects he set before himself.

Jesus the Christ, the avatar or master of the Piscean age, publicly lived the example of the sacred mysteries of the crucifixion, the resurrection, and the ascension. Francis Bacon, as the future avatar for the Aquarian age, lived the example of the inner ancient mysteries. Like Solomon, he built the temple, but his was an inner temple of the spirit. His life was the enfolding and revealing of Truth, a life that exemplifies the edict of God for mankind to find the living Truth concealed in the Matter cosmos.

To be a follower of the way that Jesus taught is to be the living flame of love in action; it is to be God's charity at work—to sacrifice your life for others. This is what Francis Bacon did. He dedicated his life to creating a culture of true brotherhood and a reformational foundation of principles, education, law, government, culture, and theology. He worked to save a people in ages beyond his own. He strove against great odds to create a world where personal Christ-hood and freedom could thrive.

Traditional historians state that Francis was the son of Sir Nicholas and Lady Anne Bacon, but there was a secret to his birth. Though these two raised Francis and gave him love, inspiration, and education, they were not his parents by blood. For Francis was a true Tudor prince, the firstborn son of Queen Elizabeth I.

Out of Darkness

Out of this nettle, danger,
We pluck this flower, safety.

~ Henry IV, part 1, act 2, sc. 3

Court intrigue, murder, treachery, fear, and suspicion paint a disturbing pattern in medieval England. The monarchs ruled with tyrannical power, Machiavellian lords manipulated and committed murder for power, the merchant guilds stripped the craftsman of any protections, and the laborers and common people lived as serfs in hovels. The wisdom of the ancients was unknown to the illiterate populace and a heresy to the controlling factors of Church and State. Though even then, in England, there were bright lights such as Sir Thomas More, who formed a secret spiritual society that believed in the coming of a special soul and the true reformation of the world.

Francis's grandfather was the tempestuous King Henry VIII. The birth of Henry's elder brother, Arthur, unified the two warring royal houses of York and Lancaster. At age fifteen, Arthur married sixteen-year-old Catherine of Aragon and was the hope of the British nation, but in 1502, only five months later, the two newlyweds came down with the "sweating sickness."* Catherine survived but Prince Arthur did not.

Catherine stayed on in the English court, and when Arthur's younger brother, Prince Henry, ascended the throne, the previous marriage of Catherine to Arthur was annulled by the pope. Henry and Catherine married in 1509. They were married for over twenty years and had one child, Princess Mary Tudor.

After the thirty long years of dynastic civil war that England had just endured, King Henry knew he needed a strong line of succession. Dissatisfied that his marriage to Catherine produced no male heir, and infatuated with a younger courtier, Anne Boleyn, Henry appealed to Pope Clement to have his marriage to Catherine annulled. The pope

---

*A mysterious and contagious disease that struck England and later continental Europe in a series of epidemics beginning in 1485, with the last outbreak in 1551. The onset of symptoms was sudden, with death often occurring within hours.

King Henry VIII, by Hans Holbein

refused and in a regal power play, King Henry defied the Church and the pope by assuming supremacy over all religious matters in England. This was unprecedented in European history.

At first glance, King Henry's defiance seems to be completely ruled by self-interest, not by law. However, he asserted the primacy of British Christianity over the Vatican as lawful precedent. His ascendancy, he claimed, was founded on the historical fact that Britain was the first Christian kingdom and the early refuge of Joseph of Arimathea and Jesus' disciples. It is interesting to note that the Vatican had accepted the primacy of the British Church for hundreds of years before Henry VIII.[8]

A Mystic History

Thou met'st with things dying,
I with things newborn.

~ *The Winter's Tale*, act 3, sc. 3

For generations, the British monarchy had been trying to rid itself of Roman papal control. Rome had never been able to conquer the entirety of Britain with military tactics and force, so they sent in the Roman Church to convert the Anglo-Saxons. The corruption of the Roman Catholic Church began as early as the Council of Nicaea in the year AD 325. It was then that Christianity became a universal religion based on the ambitions of Rome and a Roman emperor. Thus Christianity has descended as a Roman religion, not as a religion of Jesus. Despite its claim, Saint Peter and Saint Paul were never bishops of Rome; they were apostles whose work extended to all people and not confined to location.

Hugh Paulinus Cressy,* an Anglican turned Benedictine priest and close relative through marriage to Francis Bacon, wrote that Britain received "beams of the Sun of Righteousness before many other countries nearer approaching the place where He first rose." In his history of Christianity in Britain, he wrote:

> Now the most eminent of the *Primitive Disciples,* and who contributed most to this heavenly building, was *S. Joseph of Arimathea,* and eleven of his companions with him, among whom is reckoned his *Son,* of his own name. These toward the latter end of *Nero's* raign, and before *S. Peter* and *S. Paul* were consummated by a glorious Martyrdom, are by the Testimony of ancient *Records* said to have entered this Island, as a place for the retirednes of it, the benignity of the *Brittish Princes,* and the freedom from *Roman Tyranny,* more opportune, and better prepar'd for entertaining the Gospell of Peace, then almost any Countrey under the *Romans.*[9]

---

*Hugh Paulinus Cressy became Serenus de Cressy after he converted to Catholicism while living in Europe.

In his *Ecclesiastical Annals,* a sixteenth-century work, Cardinal Caesar Baronius, a historian and librarian to the Vatican, stated that those who accompanied Joseph were: "the two Bethany sisters, Mary and Martha; their brother Lazarus; Saint Eutropius; Saint Salome; Saint Cleon; Saint Saturninus; Saint Mary Magdalene; Marcella, the maid of the Bethany sisters; Saint Maxim or Maximin; Saint Martial; Saint Trophimus; Restitutus, the man who was born blind." And he also says that "Mary the mother of Jesus undoubtedly was not left behind."

So in many of the early historical accounts, Joseph of Arimathea then carries the Holy Grail west, in most cases to Britain, usually to Glastonbury. When Rome, through Augustine, tried to place its authority over the Bishops of the British Church, they answered him saying, "We have nothing to do with Rome. We know nothing of the Bishop of Rome in his new character of Pope. We are the British Church, the Archbishop of which is accountable to God alone, having no superior on earth."[10]

Francis Bacon knew well this history and the ancient mysticism of the original British Church. He wrote:

> The Britons told Augustine they would not be subject to him, nor let him pervert the ancient laws of their Church. This was their resolution, and they were as good as their word, for they maintained the liberty of their Church five hundred years after this time, and were the last of all Churches in Europe that gave up their power to the Roman Beast, and in the person of Henry VIII, that came of their blood by Owen Tudor, the first that took that power away again.[11]

Though the Roman Church was finally successful in taking over the isle, the British Church never died out. Instead, it hid its mysteries until a time when Rome's control would crack.

King Edward III had started the process in the 1300s. He held King Arthur as his ideal and refounded the British Order of St. George. King Arthur, a descendant of Joseph of Arimathea, had first founded

> an Order of Chivalry based on the traditional pattern adopted by Jesus and his disciples—the Zodiacal Round Table (*i.e.* Christ,

the "Sun," surrounded by 12 Apostles or "Signs"). Each Christian community was established on this same pattern, each Apostle representing the Christ and presiding over one or more "Round Tables" of disciples, with a Bishop as chief or head of each Twelve (and being one of those Twelve). With the ideal and example of St. George brought into the Christian symbology, it became possible to translate the priestly office to that of a knight for those of the fighting, chivalrous ilk. Thus the Holy Grail of the priest-priestess could become, at another level of expression, the Holy Grail of the knights and their ladies. This was no new idea, but a revival of ancient traditions and systems of initiation. Arthur called his Order of Chivalry, "The Order or Society of St. George and the Round Table," and he adopted (or was allowed to adopt) the Cross of St. George (*i.e.* the Rose Cross) as his personal banner.[12]

The Rose Cross was first given to the ancient British hero, Caradoc, by Joseph of Arimathea along with the title "Defender of the Faith." It is in fact older than the symbol of the crucifixion, which did not come into use until the seventh century.

It is interesting to note the pattern of a soul's work, for as Merlin, Francis's soul was in embodiment for this rejuvenation of ancient mysteries. "Merlin or *Myrrdin,* meaning 'Wise Man,' was a title given to Ambrosius (*i.e.* Merlin Ambrosius), who was also known as 'the Prince of the Sanctuary' because of his holiness and wisdom.... It is quite possible and in keeping with Ancient British practice that Uthyr's son Arthur was adopted by Ambrosius, raised and initiated by him into the Mysteries."[13]

A part of the Arthurian legend deals with the quest for a vessel of great sanctity, the Sangreal, the "Grail." Camelot as a mystery school became the quest for the vessel of Christ, in other words, one's own true being. This quest took the outer form of conquering all that was less than the qualities and virtues of Christ within ourselves. It took the form of defending the people against injustice and every force that was anti-Grail. To deny the vessel is to deny the very content of the vessel. The Grail, then, is seen as the community, as the mystery school, as the individual that, somehow in the mystery, merits bearing the light or containing the essence of God.

In refounding this order under the name "The Most Noble Order of St. George and the Garter," Edward III created a "society, fellowship and college of knights" for the purpose of "Good Fellowship."[14] He obtained a papal bull from Pope Clement VI, which declared the Chapel of the Knights of the Order of St. George and the Garter as free of the jurisdiction of the archbishop of Canterbury. This Chapel with its college was the first religious foundation in England to be free of Roman control since the fall of the British Church.

This order was also known as "The Knights of the Blue Garter" and has included women since its founding. The garter and its symbolism go back to Druidic teaching. The Druids' battle cry was "Truth against the World." The blue garter tied around or slightly below the knee, held the druidic meaning to "represent unity amongst a fellowship who never fled from living, proclaiming or defending the Truth."[15]

A Violent Break

*So every bondman in his own hand bears the power
to cancel his captivity.*
~ *Julius Caesar,* act I, sc. 3

History cycled forward and two hundred years later, the pope excommunicated the upstart English King for England's final break with Rome. King Henry VIII defied the pope and proceeded to exercise sole religious power in England, including confiscation of Church properties and the destruction of monasteries. In 1533, as head of the new Church of England, he dissolved his own marriage with Catherine and married Anne Boleyn. Unfortunately, with this dramatic shift of power came the cost of innocents and wise men. The mystical author, philosopher, and judge Sir Thomas More was beheaded, and many monks and nuns lost their lives.

Princess Elizabeth was born to Anne and Henry, but by the time she turned three, she was motherless. With Henry no longer in love and still seeking a male heir, Anne was accused of adultery, incest, and treason and sent to the Tower. While Anne awaited her fate, Henry had their marriage annulled, making Elizabeth illegitimate. On May 19, 1536, Anne was beheaded.

After Henry's third wife, Jane Seymour, gave Henry the long-awaited male heir, he declared Elizabeth legitimate once more by an act of Parliament in 1543. She was raised with her half brother and a succession of stepmothers. Under the care of her final one, Katherine Parr, Princess Elizabeth was given an education far surpassing many women of that time. She could speak in French, Italian, Spanish, and Dutch as well as write in Greek, Latin, French, and Italian.

After long being ill, King Henry VIII died January 28, 1547. His young son, Edward VI, took the throne. Elizabeth became the ward of Katherine Parr and her new husband, Thomas Seymour (Jane Seymour's brother). Thomas's elder brother was Lord Protector and Regent to the young King Edward, and as such he held power over the throne, which Thomas wanted. Once ensconced in the same household as Elizabeth, Thomas showed inappropriate attention to her. As a fourteen-year-old, she would have had little recourse against the forty-five-year-old Lord of the house.

At the same time as he was pursuing Elizabeth, Thomas bought the wardship of Jane Grey, the great granddaughter of Henry VII, thus gaining control of two of the four women who could inherit the throne. Katherine, who was in love with her husband, did not see anything wrong at first. It was only when his actions became undeniable that Elizabeth was sent away. This parting was hard for both women.

When Katherine died, Seymour set about not only trying to marry Elizabeth but to overthrow his brother as well. When his plans for a coup were discovered, he even tried to kidnap the young king.

When Thomas Seymour discovered that Elizabeth was with child, he told her to kill her baby. Francis wove the story of his life into multiple types of cipher, hidden in his literary and scientific works. In his biliteral cipher, he wrote about Seymour: "He, by disownei'g the child, subjected the princely heart to ignominie, and co'pelled Elizabeth to murder this infant at the very first slight breath."[16] In his word cipher, he gives a poetic version of this secret history as his foster mother had told it to him. Anne Bacon, who had been a young unmarried Anne Cooke at the time, served Elizabeth and could give Francis her firsthand account of what truly happened: When Princess Elizabeth confessed her condition to Anne and begged her for help, Anne had her feign illness and keep to her bed to conceal her pregnancy.

> *That here she liest till at last*
> *The swelling infant, ripe,*
> . . . .*
> *From the fortress built by nature*
> *With fury sprung selfborn,*
> *And yet unborn.*
> . . . . .
> *This sweet soul in speechless death*
> *Lie'st in bed as in a grave.*
> *I was not skill'd enough*
> *To play the nurse, open the rotten bands*
> *And aid the poor child*
> *From the impervious case*
> *Which keeps it from breathing native breath.*
> *So unhallowed, unmuzzled, it passed in silence*
> *To the fountain of final causes,*
> *Namely, God.*[17]

This tragic account paints the picture of two frightened young women facing a complicated birth alone. To call a doctor could have been to forfeit Elizabeth's life. Afterward, Anne attempted to bury the infant in secret but was seen and her actions were reported to the King. Upon the arrest of Seymour, Elizabeth and her two servants were detained and questioned. Elizabeth convinced her questioners that she had nothing to do with Seymour's plots for the throne, swearing that she would never think of marrying someone without the permission of the King.

Only six years after his reign began, King Edward VI died at the age of fifteen (whether by poison or disease). Lady Jane Grey was named queen by Parliament and her father-in-law, John Dudley, who had replaced Seymour's brother as the late king's Chief Advisor. She was not even officially crowned before Henry VIII's oldest daughter,

---
*This represents the omission of a full line or of several consecutive lines within a quoted poem or drama in verse. *(Chicago Manual of Style)*

Mary, a Catholic from birth, overthrew her. Elizabeth rode to London with her half sister amidst cheering crowds. One can only imagine Princess Elizabeth's thoughts as she rode through the throngs.

The Rise of the Virgin Queen

We were not born to sue, but to command.

~ *Richard II*, act 1, sc. 1

Elizabeth's life remained in turmoil. In the first year of Mary's reign, Wyatt's Rebellion sought to stop her from marrying the Catholic King Philip of Spain with the undeclared objective to put Elizabeth on the throne. When it failed, Elizabeth was arrested and placed in the Tower, but Lady Jane Grey, her husband, and father-in-law were put to death. Mary could not afford to have figureheads for rebellions to rally around.

After this failed uprising, Mary became more ruthless in her dedication to restoring Catholicism in Britain. During her short reign, she condemned over 280 Protestant dissenters to be burned at the stake and gained the epithet "Bloody Mary." She endeavored to return to the monasteries the land that her father had confiscated but was blocked by Parliament, which was made up of the Lords who would have to give up their newly obtained properties.

While being held in the Tower, Elizabeth fell in love with Robert Dudley, Lady Jane Grey's young brother-in-law, who was also being held in the Tower. Although Robert Dudley was already married, a passionate relationship sprang up between them. Both Elizabeth and Robert believed they were likely to lose their lives and were not in a mind to waste any time they had. She was in one tower and he in another with a connecting walk between them. They would exchange letters, delivered by one of the children also imprisoned there. Eventually Robert, through subterfuge, persuaded a Catholic priest to perform a secret marriage ceremony.

After two months, on the anniversary of her own mother's execution, Elizabeth was suddenly released from the Tower and taken to the Palace of Woodstock in Oxfordshire to live under house arrest. After almost a year, she was brought back to court and spent a few months at Mary's side while the Queen thought herself pregnant. After this, Mary allowed Elizabeth her own household away from court. When Mary realized that she was not pregnant but dying, and would leave no heir except Elizabeth, she tried to persuade her half sister to follow in her footsteps as a Catholic, but Elizabeth refused.

When Mary died, English Protestants rejoiced at the crowning of Queen Elizabeth. Many marveled that she looked like the Old King with her fiery red hair and youthful power. The Catholics in the country worried about how the new Queen would treat them.

As her first royal act, the new Queen appointed Robert Dudley as her Master of the Horse and then anointed him Earl of Leicester. During the early years of Elizabeth's reign, she and Robert Dudley were inseparable. Elizabeth gave Robert all the honors he wanted, poured wealth upon him and put power into his hands. No one doubted that she loved him passionately.

What the court didn't know in those early years was how far her love went. Elizabeth was not only a secret wife but she became a mother as well. At that time, Robert's wife, Amy, met with a fatal fall, and three weeks later, the Queen remarried Robert in a secret ceremony at the house of Lord Pickering. A young prince was born just four months after Elizabeth and Robert's second marriage. Meanwhile, the British Kingdom was at great risk. The powerful Catholic countries of France and Spain sought total control and revenge for the actions of Henry VIII.

Elizabeth's honor, public image, and the security of the throne were tenuous early in her reign. She could not let it be publicly known that she had married and had a son at all, let alone with a man who was already married. Her power with foreign sovereigns lay in the fact that she might marry one of them. She posed as the Virgin Queen even while in secret she lived as wife and mother. From the day of her coronation, twenty-two-year-old Queen Elizabeth was faced with court intrigue, dangerous incursions and spies from Spain, Scotland, and the Vatican. Symbolically, her people saw her as the personification of Astrea, the Virgin Queen. This was vital for

Elizabeth at her coronation

her, for it was an image that was acceptable to both the English Catholics and Protestants. With the religious wars tearing France apart, Elizabeth knew how quickly religious differences could induce countrymen to massacre each other. In the imaginations of her people, she had to be the "Faerie Queen on the throne of Merry Old England." The supernova in the constellation of Cassiopeia helped cement this imagery and its importance.

The true lineage of her son became a state secret, although many members of her court learned of it and the common people suspected it. It became a criminal offense to mention the obvious. It meant certain death or mutilation to speak slander about the Virgin Queen. Mistress Anne Dowe of Brentwood gossiped that the Queen had given birth. She was burned to death. Robert Brookes of Devizes was sent to prison for reviving the report. And in 1570, Mr. Marsham, a gentleman of Norfolk, had his ears cut off for having said, "My Lord of Leicester had two children by the Queen."

Prince Francis

The golden age prince was born on January 22, 1561. Queen Elizabeth had her lady-in-waiting and trusted friend, Lady Anne Bacon née Cooke, with her. Anne pleaded with the Queen to spare this very inconvenient new baby's life. She had faithfully kept the princess's secret and now would keep the queen's living son. She offered to christen and raise the young prince as her own. Lady Anne took the baby boy home that same day in a little "round, painted box."[18]

Anne had been expecting a child herself and planned to simply announce the birth of twins. But a week later, Anne's baby was stillborn, and Elizabeth's baby was introduced to the world as Anne's son, Francis Bacon.

The baptism of Francis was recorded in the church of St. Martin-in-the-Fields on the twenty-fifth of January 1561. Historians have been puzzled by his registered name, "Mr. Franciscus Bacon," an unusual title of respect for a newborn.

The universe had provided the young infant with a perfect place to grow and thrive. Francis grew up in an atmosphere full of learning, wit, and wordplay. His childhood was spent at the Bacon's York House by the Thames River, and Gorhambury, their country estate near St. Albans. The Lord Keeper Nicholas Bacon welcomed the notable minds of the time to his home—statesmen, scholars, patriots, and poets. Francis gained a love for the ancients, for myth and fairytales, logic and classical literature.

Lady Anne was known throughout England as a deeply religious woman whose accomplishments were many and varied. As the daughter of Sir Anthony Cooke, the tutor to both Elizabeth I and Edward VI, she was well versed in classical and modern languages and was respected in Europe for her translations from Latin and Italian.

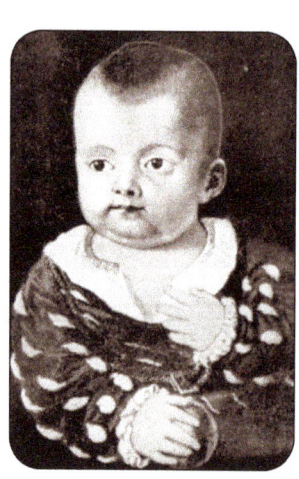

Francis Bacon as a young child

York House, the Bacons' home in London

Francis loved her "passionately," calling her "God's own saint," and even in his middle years he often returned home to be with her.

As an expert in coded ciphers and a secret author himself, his foster father, Lord Keeper Bacon, gave Francis the key to publishing secret truth and a love of ancient wisdom. Sir Nicholas Bacon with Sir Thomas More had founded the college for the "Advancement of Learning and Training of Statesmen" during the reign of Henry VIII. Long before Francis's birth, Sir Nicholas Bacon had joined the Sir Thomas More spiritual fraternity that focused on the coming age of spiritual light.

It can only be seen as the work of divine wisdom that the boy destined to "change the face of the world" would be fostered by a man whose passion and works were laying the foundations for that path.

During this time, young Francis was constantly with the Queen and Lord Leicester at court, during her regular visits to Gorhambury, and at Burghley House, the country seat of the Cecil's, where plays and pageants were often performed.

Leicester was the first man to receive a royal license for the performance of plays in England. His band of players was organized the year after Elizabeth was enthroned, and he maintained them all

Sir Nicholas and Lady Anne Bacon

his life. Leicester's theater was the first to be built in England, and until the 1580s, it was the only one. He had tremendous force of will and is said to have possessed remarkable literary ability.

Queen Elizabeth possessed genius administratively and intellectually. She was literary "to the fingertips." She and Mary were the first queens of England to rule in their own right. The fact that Elizabeth not only survived but held a long, successful reign is a testament to her mind and spirit.

Francis himself was not cut from the common mold. From an early age, he showed touches of genius. His natural talents were enhanced by a palace education "fit for a king." The Queen demanded that Francis receive the same caliber education as she had and, rather prophetically, called him "baby Solomon." His young heart was full of the fire of the new science and the new era that he felt and knew in his very soul.

As a child Francis was remarkable for his precocity and understanding. Alfred Dodd wrote, "If ever a man was born for power, a man on whom there shone a beam of God's splendour from the cradle to the grave, a man sent out from the World Unseen to do things —great things—to re-create England, the Continent, the World— *'Born to set it Right'*—that man was Francis Bacon."[19]

Lord Leicester, Queen Elizabeth and Francis Bacon miniatures by Hilliard

He was a favorite with the servants that made up the Bacons' two households as well as with the nobility. The Queen often invited Francis to accompany Sir Nicholas to court. Dr. Rawley, later Francis's chaplain, wrote:

> His first and Childish Years were not without some Mark of Eminency; at which time he was endued with that pregnancy and towardness of Wit, as they were Presages of that deep and universal Apprehension which was manifest in him afterward, and caused him to be taken notice of by several Persons of Worth and Place, and especially by the Queen; who (as I have been inform'd) delighted much then to confer with him, and to prove him with Questions; unto whom he delivered himself with that Gravity and Maturity above his years, that Her majesty

would often term him, *The young Lord Keeper.* Being asked by the Queen how old he was, he answered with much discretion, being then but a Boy, *That he was two years younger than Her Majesties happy Reign;* with which Answer the Queen was much taken.[20]

Francis's home with the Bacons was the perfect chrysalis for his exceptional mind. "In many respects 'Mr. Francis' was fortunate in being reared in the household of a great civil servant... where quips, jests and wordplay were part of the mental atmosphere. He slowly developed into a little philosopher, but he was a 'Laughing Philosopher' and not a grave one of severe mien. The academic picture that he was from his cradle a solemn little prig is ludicrously false.... The real truth is well expressed by Dr. Abbott: 'Francis was probably indebted to Sir Nicholas for his placid self-control and *his rich humour.*'"[21] He was full of joy and could rarely pass up an opportunity for a good jest with his foster brother and dearest friend, Anthony.

The high spirits of her two boys often worried and exasperated the pious Lady Anne, especially when they slipped away from prayers in the family chapel for a visit to the stables, preferring a lively chat with the grooms and stable boys to serious conversation with God.

When Francis was five, Queen Elizabeth had a second son with Lord Leicester. He, too, was secretly brought up by courtiers close to the Queen. Named Robert Devereux, he became the Earl of Essex when he inherited his foster father's title and estate. Virginia Fellows writes,

> Lettice, a granddaughter of Mary Boleyn (Ann Boleyn's sister) and therefore a cousin to Elizabeth, had been married for some time to Walter Devereux, viscount of Hereford.... When the boy baby was born, supposedly the first son of Walter and Lettice Devereux, he was not named, as was the custom, after his supposed father, but he was given the name Robert (after Lord Leicester?). It was the next son of the family who was given the name Walter.
>
> Another oddity about Robert's birth was that one finds no record of such a birth in the parish register. The births of the other three Devereux children—Penelope, Dorothy and Walter—are

duly recorded, as one would expect, at their estate of Chartley. Only the birth of Robert was left unrecorded (as the birth of Francis had been).[22]

After the death of Lord Walter Devereux (possibly poisoned), Robert Devereux became a ward of Elizabeth's Chief Advisor and Master of the Court of Wards, William Cecil. At the age of nine, he joined the Cecil household at Burghley House, among other aristocratic young men. Robert Devereux and the other wards to the Crown were frequent companions of Francis and Anthony Bacon. These were the "golden lads" of Queen Elizabeth's young reign.

The Education of a Prince

For all knowledge and wonder (which is the seed of knowledge) is an impression of pleasure in itself.

~ Bacon, *The Advancement of Learning*, Book I, 1, 3

As a boy, Francis longed to know and understand everything. Books were rare and difficult to obtain. He loved reading his foster father's famous classical library, full of philosophers and playwrights of ancient Greece and Rome and the Church Fathers—Augustine, Origen, Jerome, and Clement. For fun, he read the novelists of Italy and the satires of Erasmus.

Everything was worthy of his attention, and books were Francis's greatest treasures. "You know," he later wrote to his uncle Lord Burghley, "that from my earliest boyhood I have followed a course of study which has embraced all subjects. I have made myself acquainted with all knowledge which the world possesses. To enable me to do this I mastered all languages in which books are written. . . . My powers are not to be measured by my years. This I will say, I am no vain promiser but I am assured that I can accomplish all that I contemplate."[23]

Francis was fortunate—or divinely ordained—to have access to rare books, brilliant minds, and esoteric treasures at a time when books were scarce and expensive.

Lord Burghley's mansion Theobalds

Francis's education was supervised by the Queen herself. Taken to court when quite young, he was patted publicly on the head by Queen Elizabeth and called "My Little Lord Keeper." His foster grandfather, Sir Anthony Cooke, oversaw Francis's and Anthony's early education. They had other tutors in French, Italian, religion, fencing, and music. When they went to college, both could write fluently in Latin, Greek, Italian, French, and Hebrew.

Francis also had access to the legendary mystical library at Mortlake collected by Queen Elizabeth's famous astrologer and tutor, Dr. John Dee. When Dr. Dee's request to the earlier king to establish a royal library had been denied, Dee began his collection of manuscripts, rare books, and art from all over Europe. Dr. Dee established a center of universal learning, an academy. He had over 4,000 books while the University of Cambridge had only 451 books listed in 1582.[24] And, most key, Dr. Dee was under the "special protection" of the Queen.

This mysterious library included nearly every known magical, mystical, or occult treatise written in any Western language since the time of Plato. These writings were from the divinely inspired pre-Chrisian authors such as Hermes Trismegistus, Zoroaster, Orpheus, Pythagoras, and Plato.

John Dee performing an experiment before Queen Elizabeth I
Oil painting by Henry Gillard Glindoni
Attribution-NonCommercial 4.0 International (CC BY-NC 4.0).
Source: Wellcome Collection. https://wellcomecollection.org/works/nydjbrr7

Dr. Dee was called a "Religious Hermeticist," which is precisely the spiritual philosophy that the Great Instauration was to be founded upon.

Francis read the esoteric books as eagerly as the classical literature. His later writings are filled with references to the great mystics and poets of the ages. But, as Dr. Rawley stated, "I have been induced to think, That if there were a Beam of Knowledge derived from God upon any Man in these Modern Times, it was upon him: for though he was a great Reader of Books, yet he had not his Knowledge from Books, but from some Grounds and Notions from within himself."[25] Francis had direct access to the inner Divine Presence.

The Queen visited Gorhambury in July 1572 when Francis was eleven, just before the supernova graced Cassiopeia with a "new star." She visited again in March 1573, which led to Francis, together with his foster brother, Anthony, and the Bacon ward, Edward Turell, entering Cambridge that Easter.

By the time Francis had reached the age of twelve, "his great, fixed, and methodical memory, his solid judgment, his quick fancy, his ready expression, gave high assurance of that profound and

An old engraving of Gorhambury

universal knowledge and comprehension of things which then rendered him the observation of great and wise men, and afterwards the wonder of all."[26]

Richard Ince, in his historical fiction on the life of Francis Bacon, recounts a story relating the spirit of that time when the Queen and her court would travel to the great houses, and Francis and his friends would write and perform masques for them:

> When he was twelve years old he wrote a play and took it to Mr. Cottwin. The play was in Latin and smacked strongly of Plautus. It was called "Rex Philosophus"—The Philosopher King....
>
> A FORTNIGHT later on a warm afternoon in June, freshened by a breeze from the river, the Queen and Leicester and Lord Burghley and his Lady,... and many other members of the nobility, were gathered in the shady gardens of York House to see a little Mask called "Rex Philosophus,"... acted by Master Anthony and Master Francis Bacon, assisted by Mistress Betty Cecil, Master Robert Cecil, and sundry little Arundels and Pembrokes, and stage-managed by Mister Edward Cottwin, M.A., and Mister John Cosgrave of Lord Leicester's Company of Players.
>
> The stage was the green lawn that spread, like a thick carpet, between the wings of the long two-storied house, with its prick-eared gables and tall chimney stacks. A massive oak seat, spread with rugs, served as a throne for the Queen. Lord Leicester and the Earl of Pembroke stood on either side of her....

Francis was the Philosopher-King, splendid in his little suit of scarlet and cloth of gold, with large pink roses on his pointed shoes. It was the first time Francis had taken part in a real masque, with grown-ups for an audience, and at first his voice was rather low. But when Mr. Cottwin from behind the laurel bushes, shouted in a stage whisper, "louder! louder!" the Philosopher-King sprang as it were to life. His words were spoken with clear enunciation, rising at times to an urgency of passion, strange in a child so young. All whispers died; all eyes were fixed upon him.

"And I say to you, great Kings and Princes, be philosophers; and to you, Philosophers, I say, be Kings—Kings of yourselves, and so will you lead all men captive. For the King who knows not his own heart will never read the hearts of his subjects, and the philosopher who lives only in his mind, forever turning this problem and that, will never find the Key of escape, climb the golden tree, or gather the apples of the Hesperides."[27]

One Baconian researcher has put forward the theory that Francis published plays during his youth under the pseudonym Ulpian Fulwell, as proven by the ciphers within the plays. Three plays were published under this name, the first when Francis was only seven, named *Like Will to Like*.[28] It portrays the idea that like attracts like, that the vile will end poorly and the virtuous will gain everlasting glory. In it can be found the type of wordplay and puns known to be enjoyed by Francis and his foster father as well as the use of simple cipher. This play could easily be an example of how Sir Nicholas taught Francis and Anthony cipher with a love of literature and humor.

A Prince at Cambridge

Knowledge is the wing wherewith we fly to heaven.
~ *Henry VI*, part 2, act 4, sc. 7

With the supernova shining above him in the sky, twelve-year-old Francis started at Cambridge as an undergraduate at Trinity College on April 6, 1573. He and Anthony only studied till the end of 1575 before asking to leave. Though both were placed directly in the charge of the Master of Trinity, one of the Queen's private chaplains, and made lasting friends with writers such as Edmund Spenser, John Lyly, and Gabriel Harvey, they soon felt that Cambridge had little more to give them.

Universities in the Elizabethan era were not scenes of high-minded study. Though some students may have attended in order to learn and better themselves, overall the universities had deteriorated into unattended lectures and useless arguments, with drinking and debauchery being the main employment of many students. The curriculum consisted of the studies of Aristotle and, in imitation of him, the application of "dialectic" to countless questions, or "topics." These questions concerned theology almost exclusively. An occasional discussion of ethics might occur, but the natural sciences were not considered important.

The dialectic was studied alongside grammar and rhetoric as part of the study of language and communication. It was considered the backbone of the educational process.

But early in the fifteenth century, there was a revision of the dialectic handbook at Cambridge. The educational "reformers" responsible for the change preferred legalistic debate and opposed what would become Renaissance ideals of revealing truth. Their method relied on empty intellectual argument that produced no change or improvement in the conditions of life.

Francis reacted to this "reformed dialectic" with a determination to challenge the entire intellectual establishment and propose his own method for the advancement of learning.

He noted that the old form of science "whereby the principles of sciences may be pretended to be invented, . . . is utterly vicious and incompetent: wherein their error is the fouler, because it is the duty of art to perfect and exalt nature; but they contrariwise have wronged, abused, and traduced nature."[29]

Many years after he left Cambridge, Francis published his famous book, *Novum Organum*, as a replacement for reformed dialectic and a way of recommending the method of induction as the "great method" of learning. This "great method" was the genesis of the modern scientific method and the way of thought that instigated the scientific revolution.

The Reformation of the Whole Wide World

*For charity itself fulfills the law,
And who can sever love from charity?*

~ *Love's Labour's Lost,* act 4, sc. 3

Amidst the ignorance at Cambridge and the injustices perpetuated on the common man throughout Britain, Francis found his life's calling: a secret vision held in his heart. He refused to let mankind waste away in ignorance and want, and so discovered a way to light the world on fire with wisdom. From his dream of universal illumination, Francis conceived of "The Universal Reformation of the Whole World." This was to become his Great Instauration, a renaissance of learning, and he would build the foundations upon which the world could climb out of its current darkness.

This great aim became the light by which Francis viewed his life. He not only infused this work into his writings, he lived it. Every decision, every friendship made, every judgment, every law proposed or defended, every action he took was for the building of a wiser, more just and loving world. He had been born to bring light.

Trinity College, Cambridge

Francis saw that it was time to bring Jesus the Christ's teachings into the practical philosophy of society. If a golden age was to come, the words of Christ had to live beyond the pulpits and private prayer books, they had to be love in action. He knew that if humanity could set aside the hatreds and judgments ingrained in them and truly develop hearts full of fervor and oneness with Jesus, following the true path of mercy, compassion, and charity, those hearts could turn around a world. For he knew, as the ancient mystics knew, that when you have this fire of love for God, then you and God are one and you walk together, and he will speak through you, and you will find your own Christ Self truly one with God in your temple of self. Francis knew that he and his friends could be those hearts. The work would never be the same.

The historian Spedding wrote about this moment of revelation for Francis:

> It seemed that towards the end of the sixteenth century men neither knew nor aspired to know more than was to be learned from Aristotle; a strange thing at any time; more strange than ever just then, when the heavens themselves seemed to be taking up the argument on their own behalf, and by suddenly lighting up within the very region of the Unchangeable and Incorruptible, and presently extinguishing, a new fixed star as bright as Jupiter (the new star in Cassiopeia shone with full lustre on Bacon's freshmanship) to be protesting by signs and wonders against the cardinal doctrine of the Aristotelian philosophy. It was then that a thought struck him, the date of which deserves to be recorded, not for anything extraordinary in the thought itself, which had probably occurred to others before him, but for its influence upon his after-life. If our study of nature be thus barren, he thought, our method of study must be wrong: might not a better method be found? The suggestion was simple and obvious. The singularity was in the way he took hold of it. With most men such a thought would have come and gone in a passing regret.... But in him the gift of seeing in prophetic vision what might be and ought to be was united with the practical talent of devising means and handling minute details. He could at once imagine

like a poet and execute like a clerk of the works.... From that moment he had a vocation which employed and stimulated all the energies of his mind, gave a value to every vacant interval of time, an interest and significance to every random thought and casual accession of knowledge; an object to live for as wide as humanity, as immortal as the human race; an idea to live in vast and lofty enough to fill the soul forever with religious and heroic aspirations.[30]

Here is the spiritual adept at work to remake society in the divine image. Francis's plan to change the "whole wide world" crystallized into an outline in which he proposed a renewal of art, science, literature, religion, and ethics. His concept, in essence, became the blueprint for the English Renaissance. He took the truths he had learned from the classical ancient mysteries, the Druidic path, and British Christian mysticism, and fashioned works of literature, societies of brotherhood, and new methods of science that can, when fully understood and practiced, lift the world into a true golden age—an age in which people understand that they are destined to become God-conscious, that they are meant to follow the footsteps of Jesus and become one with Christ in the mystical union of their soul to their own immortal Christ Self. Francis set the foundation for a culture that supported and mentored higher consciousness in all people.

Francis understood that without Truth, people could never achieve such an age. If civilizations continued to simply impose their own ideas onto reality, they would never see or understand God's creation. In his own words:

> The sciences are confined to certain and prescribed authors, and thus restrained are imposed upon the old and instilled into the young; so that now (to use the sarcasm of Cicero concerning Caesar's year), the constellation of Lyra rises by edict, and authority is taken for truth, not truth for authority.... For we create worlds, we direct and domineer over nature, we will have it that all things *are* as in our folly we think they should be, not as seems fittest to the Divine wisdom, or as they are found to be in fact; and I know not whether we more distort the facts of

nature or our own wits; but we clearly impress the stamp of our own image on the creatures and works of God, instead of careful examining and recognising in them the stamp of the Creator himself.... If therefore there be any humility towards the Creator, any reverence for or disposition to magnify His works, any charity for man and anxiety to relieve his sorrows and necessities, any love of truth in nature, any hatred of darkness, any desire for the purification of the understanding, we must entreat men again and again to discard, or at least set apart for a while, these volatile and preposterous philosophies, which have preferred theses to hypotheses, led experience captive, and triumphed over the works of God; and to approach with humility and veneration to unroll the volume of Creation, to linger and meditate therein, and with minds washed clean from opinions to study it in purity and integrity.[31]

In his address to the king in the beginning of the first part of *The Advancement of Learning,* Francis defends the search for knowledge against those who would equate it with the original sin through the misreading of Solomon and Saint Paul. True knowledge, he states, must be gained with humility and charity. One must approach God's creation with awe and seek Truth, knowing that the human mind and senses cannot comprehend it all. There can be no true understanding of creation's secrets without charity, which is love in action.

> This corrective spice, the mixture whereof maketh Knowledge so sovereign, is Charity, which the Apostle immediately addeth to the former clause: for so he saith, *Knowledge bloweth up, but Charity buildeth up;* not unlike unto that which he delivereth in another place: *If I spake,* saith he, *with the tongues of men and angels, and had not charity, it were but as a tinkling cymbal....* And as for that censure of Salomon, concerning the excess of writing and reading books, and the anxiety of spirit which redoundeth from knowledge; and that admonition of St. Paul, *That we be not seduced by vain philosophy;* let those places be rightly understood, and they do indeed excellently set forth the true bounds and limitations, whereby human knowledge is confined and circumscribed; and yet without any such

contracting or coarctation, but that it may comprehend all the universal nature of things; for these limitations are three: the first, *That we do not so place our felicity in knowledge, as we forget our mortality*: the second, *That we make application of our knowledge, to give ourselves repose and contentment, and not distaste or repining*: the third, *That we do not presume by the contemplation of nature to attain to the mysteries of God.*

For as touching the first of these, Salomon doth excellently expound himself in another place of the same book, where he saith: *I saw well that knowledge recedeth as far from ignorance as light doth from darkness; and that the wise man's eyes keep watch in his head, whereas this fool roundeth about in darkness: but withal I learned that the same mortality involveth them both.* And for the second, ... all knowledge and wonder (which is the seed of knowledge) is an impression of pleasure in itself: but when men fall to framing conclusions out of their knowledge, applying it to their particular, and ministering to themselves thereby weak fears or vast desires, there groweth that carefulness and trouble of mind which is spoken of. ... And as for the third point, it deserveth to be a little stood upon, and not to be lightly passed over: for if any man shall think by view and inquiry into these sensible and material things to attain that light, whereby he may reveal unto himself the Nature or Will of God, then indeed is he spoiled by vain philosophy: for the contemplation of God's creatures and works produceth (having regard to the works and creatures themselves) knowledge, but having regard to God, no perfect knowledge, but wonder, which is broken knowledge. And therefore it was most aptly said by one of Plato's school, *That the sense of man carrieth a resemblance with the sun, which, as we see, openeth and revealeth all the terrestrial globe; but then again it obscureth and concealeth the stars and celestial globe: so doth the sense discover natural things, but it darkeneth and shutteth up divine.**

... And as for the conceit that too much knowledge should incline a man to Atheism, and that the ignorance of second causes should make a more devout dependence upon God,

---
*Bacon is quoting Philo Judaeus, *De Sornnis*, p. 41.

which is the first cause; first, it is good to ask the question which Job asked of his friends: *Will you lie for God, as one man will do for another, to gratify him?*

For certain it is that God worketh nothing in nature but by second causes: and if they would have it otherwise believed, it is mere imposture, as it were in favour towards God; and nothing else but to offer to the Author of Truth the unclean sacrifice of a lie. But farther, it is an assured truth, and a conclusion of experience, that a little or superficial knowledge of Philosophy may incline the mind of man to Atheism, but a farther proceeding therein doth bring the mind back again to Religion....

To conclude therefore, let no man upon a weak conceit of sobriety or an ill-applied moderation think or maintain, that a man can search too far, or be too well studied in the book of God's word, or in the book of God's works; divinity or philosophy: but rather let men endeavour an endless progress or proficience in both; only let men beware that they apply both to charity, and not to swelling; to use, and not to ostentation.[32]

Francis described his solution and his determination to see his Great Instauration done:

And whilst men agree to admire and magnify the false powers of the mind, and neglect or destroy those that might be rendered true, there is no other course left but with better assistance to begin the work anew, and raise or rebuild the sciences, arts, and all human knowledge from a firm and solid basis.

This may at first seem an infinite scheme, unequal to human abilities, yet it will be found more sound and judicious than the course hitherto pursued, as tending to some issue; whereas all hitherto done with regard to the sciences is vertiginous, or in the way of perpetual rotation.

Nor is he ignorant that he stands alone in an experiment almost too bold and astonishing to obtain credit, yet he thought it not right to desert either the cause or himself, but to boldly enter on the way and explore the only path which is pervious to the human mind. For it is wiser to engage in an undertaking that admits of some termination, than to involve oneself in perpetual exertion and anxiety about what is interminable. The ways of contemplation, indeed, nearly correspond to two roads in nature, one of which, steep and rugged at the commencement, terminates in a plain; the other, at first view smooth and easy, leads only to huge rocks and precipices.[33]

To Francis, the Renaissance, or the Great Instauration as he called it, was waiting to happen and the impediments to its progress, he observed, were in the fixed minds of those who were literate and ready to abuse power, principally the clergy, both Catholic and Protestant.

He saw the lack of creativity in the area of science as largely due to a false religious doctrine, a misunderstanding of the cause of man's expulsion from Eden. Through the Judeo-Christian clerical tradition, people had been taught and believed that man fell from heaven because of an inordinate desire to learn—to "partake of the knowledge of good and evil."

The blame for the expulsion from Eden, leveled by the medieval churches against humanity, was harsh and known as "original sin" and "total depravity." The irony was missed by the public and clergy that the actual original sin had been the rebellion against God by the fallen angels. The guilt was accepted by Christendom as historical fact, and it led to a pessimism among both scholars and commoners. It was the power of this sustained pessimism that concerned Francis and those who saw the opportunity for a golden age of wisdom, charity, and brotherhood.

The clerical doctrine of deflecting blame for "original sin" and condemning humanity as miserable sinners had become so fixed and accepted throughout Christianity that there was a widespread tendency for men to regard themselves as living in the twilight sickness of a dying world.

Francis recognized this clergy-derived sense of despair as the primary hindrance to the progress of science and, therefore, prosperity. To Francis, mankind was made in the image and likeness of God, and people were being hindered by those professing to represent God.

Superstition toward nature, the difficulty of discovering truth, and the inertia of learned institutions all conspired to impress men with the hopelessness of their condition. Likewise, the clerical belief that there was nothing new to be discovered and that the best had already been learned from the past also discouraged humanity from attempting anything new. Francis issued a rallying call to mankind to know their own abilities and bestir themselves from the slough of despair. And his call echoed throughout the century.

To those who pointed to Adam's error, Francis countered, "It was not that pure and unspotted natural knowledge whereby Adam gave names to things, agreeable to their natures, which caused his fall; but an ambitious and authoritative desire of moral knowledge, to judge of good and evil, which makes men revolt from God, and obey no laws but those of their own will. But for the sciences, which contemplate nature, the sacred philosopher declares, 'It is the glory of God to conceal a thing, but the glory of a king to find it out.'"[34]

In addition, Francis defined the image of what a true scientist should be: a man of both compassion and understanding, emphasizing that knowledge without charity could bite with the deadliness of a serpent's venom.

Francis's ideas concerning the reformation of learning fall roughly into three categories: the recognition of the inadequacy of existing knowledge and the need and possibility of its advancement; the hindrances that prevent this advancement; and the means by which it might be secured. As always, Francis, regardless of the opinions of men, would place himself before them as the example of the new scientist he proclaimed.

Peter Dawkins beautifully explains Francis's philosophy versus the old mode that surrounded him:

> Between the new philosophy, which Francis is beginning or regenerating in the world (and which the world is still a long way from understanding fully, let alone practising in its complete sense), and the old philosophy, there is a whole world of difference. To differentiate what is meant by the old and the new philosophy (like the Old and New Jerusalem) Francis employs

two descriptive titles, *Anticipation of the Mind* and *Interpretation of Nature* respectively, which should be self-explanatory to most thinking minds. The Interpretation of Nature by which we discover God's hidden laws, or Truth, is the path of the initiates, the "true sons of knowledge", sons of Light. Nature, or God's Work, is but the Veil which simultaneously conceals and reveals the formless vibratory essence that is Truth. Without the Veil of Nature we could not discover or see Truth, yet Nature is not Truth itself. Nature is but the *maya* or thought-illusion created as a dream in the Imagination of God, seemingly real and tangible to us since we are living in it as part of the picture and with a measure of free will and creativity. The development of our conscious knowledge depends on the dream-picture, the world of imagination; yet all that we deem solid and substantial is but polarised energy held together by the energising Will of God, patterned and directed according to the Divine Idea. How many souls yet comprehend this truth, taught to us century after century by the illumined souls of East and West? The "Baconian Light" is teaching it quietly, and gently leading mankind on a large scale to discover the truth steadily, surely, progressively and scientifically. The "Revolution" is proceeding apace, step by step. One day Science and Religion will be remarried. Science will become religious and Religion will be scientific once more. Ignorance and superstition will be forever banished to the realms of Yesterday.[35]

In an age of superstition and violence, the sheer goodness of Francis shines out in his writings. He wrote often of truth and charity together. In his essay "Of Truth" he wrote, "yet *Truth*, which onely doth judge it selfe, teacheth, that the Inquirie of *Truth*, which is the Love-making, or Wooing of it; The knowledge of *Truth*, which is the Presence of it; and the Beleefe of *Truth*, which is the Enjoying of it; is the Soveraigne Good of human Nature.... Certainly, it is Heaven upon Earth, to have a Mans Mind Move in Charitie, Rest in Providence, and Turne upon the Poles of *Truth*."[36]

The Fairie Queen

O, for a muse of fire that would ascend
The brightest heaven of invention!
A kingdom for a stage, princes to act,
And monarchs to behold the swelling scene!

~ Henry V, act 1, sc. 1

In April 1575, Francis and Anthony requested to leave Cambridge, the same year that the second Ulpian Fulwell play was published. This one, entitled *The Flower of Fame,* concerned the reign of Henry VIII. It was dedicated to Lord Burghley, Francis's foster uncle. Through the use of simple cipher, the name Francis and his full name of Francis Bacon can be deciphered on the play's original title page. The third, *Ars Adulandi* or *The Art of Flattery,* was dedicated to Lady Mildred Cooke Cecil, Lady Burghley, the elder sister of his foster mother, Lady Anne Cooke Bacon. The publishing dates of its first and second editions coincide with Francis's trip to France. The first was published before he left and the second after he returned to England in 1579. In it "the author criticizes the insincerity of courtiers and savagely attacks church abuses and the corruption of the clergy, and in the course of his dialogues, denounces all forms of vice. The dialogues are all introduced by a rhymed maxim and the first includes a pun on the name of its fictional author—a device which frequently occurs throughout the text:

> *Full well I do find, that Fortune is blind,*
>   *Her wheel runs by chance:*
> *When she lists to frown, the wise she throws down,*
>   *And fools doth advance."*[37]

This play explores themes dear to Francis's heart with the characters of Lady Truth versus Lady Fortune and the seven liberal sciences of grammar, logic, rhetoric, music, arithmetic, astrology, and geometry versus the "eighth," the art of flattery. On the title page of *The Art of Flattery,* the researcher deciphered not only the numbers signifying Francis Bacon's name but the numbers signifying Fra Rosiecrosse.[38] If this is true, it proves that Francis knew of secret societies and had already started on his life's path as early as 1576. This very well could be, as his foster father was part of the English Magian Society with Sir Thomas More as early as the 1530s.

In July 1575, Francis participated in, and indeed likely authored, a grand entertainment held for the Queen. Elizabethan entertainments and masques lasted for days and held within them devices or scenes full of poetry, music, and symbolism. The Kenilworth Entertainment was the first of its kind to be done on such a scale, and was planned alongside a second one that would take place later that year at Woodstock. In the case of the first one, there was a secret meaning for the Queen. It was said to be a gift from Leicester to the Queen to convince her to publicly marry him.

The scenes that met the Queen upon her arrival and throughout her stay were pulled from Arthurian legend and classical mythology. "One very important character was a fourteen-year-old minstrel—a 'bard' who related the key stories about King Arthur and his knights of the Round Table. Sadly for Leicester, there was one 'shew' that was prepared but 'never came to execution' because of 'lack of opportunity and seasonable weather.'"[39] With the ending cut short by inclement weather and an early departure of the Queen, the farewell device became an improvised soliloquy to the Queen by the character "Sylvanus" as Elizabeth rode her horse. This allegorical entreaty to marry Leicester is recorded to have been performed by Gascoigne. However, as Peter Dawkins points out, the words of this farewell are not in Gascoigne's style nor is it probable that as a fifty-year-old man he would have been able to perform it with any kind of grace while running alongside the queen's horse through the woods. This was more likely the job for a younger man with a brilliance for poetry and the enthusiasm of youth. *Midsummer Night's Dream* owes much of its magical revelry to Francis's experience of the Kenilworth Entertainment.

Although this Entertainment did not gain Leicester a public marriage, it did introduce the reemergence of chivalry and the imagery

Queen Elizabeth as Diana the Huntress, 16th century.
An illustration copy of a picture in the collection of the Marquess of Salisbury, Hatfield House, from a work published by Boussod, Valadon & Co, (1896)

of the Faerie Queen which would be fully established at the Woodstock Entertainment that same year. These two Entertainments worked together to resurrect the early mysteries of the British Church and esoteric Christianity. It was the beginning of the revival of the ancient order of the Rose Cross.

Peter Dawkins highlights these Entertainments as

> the beginning of a deliberate exercise to revive the ancient and true Rosicrucianism, not only in its knightly or chivalrous aspect but also in its priestly or illumined aspect, and moreover in the sacred country of the Virgin,* bearer of the Christ Child—the Land of the Rose, the Land of Merlin and Arthur, the Sun King. . . . Reigning in England at the height of the Renaissance in Europe, Elizabeth's sovereignty made it possible to unite all the hitherto seemingly disparate sacred traditions in her single symbolic role, demonstrating the real oneness underlying all sacred traditions. She was at once Britannia, Mary, Minerva, Pallas Athena,

---

*England is traditionally known as Mary's Dowry, her inheritance.

Isis, Demeter, Astraea, Gloriana, Ceridwen—the Virgin Queen of all traditions who brings forth the Christ Child, the "illumined one". All it needed was a new Hermes or Merlin—a new Initiator and Teacher—to seize the opportunity and make it so.[40]

Francis was, indeed, perfect for the role.

A Dread Secret Revealed

Then, England's ground, farewell; sweet soil, adieu,
My mother and my nurse that bears me yet.
Where'er I wander, boast of this I can,
Though banished, yet a trueborn Englishman.

~ Richard II, act 1, sc. 3

In the time between Kenilworth and Woodstock, Francis's world was shattered and reassembled with the weight of his mother's secrets falling upon him. Francis wrote about this dramatic event both in his biliteral and word ciphers. Here is an excerpt from his biliteral cipher as deciphered by Elizabeth Wells Gallup:

> We were in prese'ce—as had manie and oftentimes occurr'd, Que. E. havi'g a liking of our manners—with a nomber o' th' ladies and severall of the gentlemen of her court, when a seely young maiden babled a tale Cecill,* knowing her weakness, had whispered in her eare. A daungerous tidbit it was, but it well did satisfy th' malicious soule of a tale-bearer such as R. Cecill, that concern'd not her associate ladies at all, but th' honour, the honesty of Queene Elizabeth. Noe sooner breath'd aloude then it was hearde by the Queene, noe more, in truth, then halfe hearde then 'twas avenged by th' enraged Queene. Never had we seene fury soe terrible, and it was some time that wee remayned in silent, horror-strook dismaye, at the fiery overwhelming tempest. At last—when stript of al her fraile attire, the poor maid in frightened remors' lay quivering at Queene Elizabethes feet, almost depriv'd o' breath, stil feeblie begging that her life

---

*Robert Cecil, son of Lord Burghley William Cecil, Chief Advisor to the Queen and uncle to Anthony Bacon; foster cousin of Francis and a bitter rival

be spar'd nor ceasi'g for a mome't till sense was lost—no longer might we looke upon this in silence; and bursting like fulmin'd lightning through the waiting crowde of the astonished courtiers and ladies, surrou'ding in a widening circle this angry Fury and her prey, wee bent a knee cravi'g that wee might lifte up the tender bodie and bear it thence. A dread sile'ce that foretels a storm fell on the Queene for a space, as th' cruell light waxed brighter and th' cheeke burnt as th' flame. As the fire grew to blasti'g heat, it fell upon us like a bolt of Jove. Losing controll immediatelie of both judgement and discretion, th' secrets of her heart came hurtling forth, stunning and blasting the sense, till we wanted but a jot of swooning likewise. Not onely did wee believe ourselfe to be base, but also wee beleeved the angry reproaches of such kinde as never can bee cleared awaie, for she declar'd us to be the fruit of a union of the sorte that is oft lustfull and lascivious—the secret; and in suppressing th' name of our father, she did in very truth give us reaso' to feare the blot of which we speake.[41]

...I' her look much malicious hatred burn'd toward me for ill-avis'd interference, and in hastie indignation said:

"You are my own borne sonne but you, though truly royall, of a fresh, a masterlie spirit, shall rule nor England, or your mother, nor reigne ore subjects yet t' bee. I bar from succession forevermore my best beloved first-borne that bless'd my unio' with—no, I'll not name him, nor need I yet disclose the sweete story conceal'd thus farre so well men only guesse it, nor know o' a truth o' th' secret marriages, as rightfull to guard the name o' a Queene, as of a maid o' this realm.... A sonne like mine lifteth hand nere in aide to her who brought him foorth; hee'd rather uplift craven maides who tattle thus whenere my face (aigre enow ev'r, they say) turneth from them. What will this brave boy do? Tell a, b, c's?"

Ending her tirade thus she bade me rise. Tremblingly I obeyed her charge, summon'd a serving-man to lead me to my home and sent to Mistresse Bacon....

In th' dark, I waged warre manfully, supposing that my life in all the freshnesse of youth was made unbearable. It did so much exhaust, that, afte' pause of a moment, I brast flood-like *into Mistres Bacon's chamber and told her my storie. No true woman can beare th' sight o' any tear. I grasped her arm, weeping and sobbing sore, and entreated her (artfully, as I thought, hidi'g my secret), t' say 'pon oath I was i' truth the sonne of herselfe and her honoured husband. I made effort to conceal my fear that I was base sonne to the Queene, per contra, I eke, most plainlie shew'd it by my distresse. When therefore my sweet mother did, weeping and lamenting, owne to me that I was in very truth th' sonne o' th' Queene, I burst into maledictio's 'gainst th' Queene, my fate, life, and all it yieldeth, till, wearie, on bent knees I sank down, and floods o' tears finished my wilde tempestuous invective. When, howsoever, that deare ladie saw this, with womanly wisedome, to arrest fury or perchance to prevent such despaire, said to me:*

"Spare my ear, or aim rightly, boy, for you do wrong your mother with such a thought. Pause least as to Absalom a sudden vengeance come. When you list to my words, you then will knowe that you do also wrong that noble gentleman, your father. Earl Robert, at the meere mention o' this folly would rise in great wrath and call down Heaven's judgements on you."

At the word, I besought her to speak my father's name, when granting my request, she said: "He is the Earle of Leicester." Then as it made me cease to sob, she said againe: "I tooke a most solemne oath not to reveale your storie to you, but you may hear my unfinish'd tale to th' end if you will go to th' midwife. Th' doctor would be ready also to give proofes of your just right to be named th' Prince of this realm, and heire-apparent to the throne. Neverthelesse Queene Bess did likewise give her solemn oath of bald-faced deniall of her marriage to Lord Leicester, as well as her motherhood. Her oath, so broken, robs me of a sonne. O Francis, Francis, breake not your mother's heart! I cannot let you go forth after all the years you have beene the sonne o' my heart. But night is falling. To-day I cannot longer speake to you of so weighty a matter. This hath mov'd you deeply and though you now drie your eyes, you have yet many teare marks upon your little cheekes. Go now; do not give it place, i' thought or word, a brain-sick woman, though she be a Queene, can take my sonne from me. Retire at once, my boy."[42]

The revelation of his secret royal birth stunned Francis and shocked Anthony. The next day the Queen sent Robert Cecil to tell Francis to come to her. Robert, jealous as he was, took the moment to twist the proverbial knife. He instigated a fight with Francis, calling him a bastard and baiting him to the point where the overwrought young man knocked him down with one punch. Francis immediately helped him up, but Robert swore his perpetual enmity. He made an oath that he would keep Francis from ever taking the throne. In one violent tirade from his queen, Francis discovered that his most beloved parents were not his own, his dear brother was no relation to him, his royal mother refused to claim him, and his erstwhile cousin became his self-proclaimed enemy. His foster parents, who loved him so dearly, held him closely with their inner strength and prayers. This storm he would overcome.

Just over twenty-four hours after this dramatic reveal, the Queen sent her son to France. Previously it was thought that this trip was one and the same as the three-year-long 1576 trip, but two of his letters, one to Anthony and the other to Robert Cecil, places this as a separate trip in 1575.[43]

Francis did not let this sudden overhaul of his identity and impromptu journey to France stymie his grand purpose. He pledged to himself and his family to use his time well and to learn. His plan to revolutionize all human knowledge did not stop with the arts and sciences. He aimed to also create a system of ethics apart from the warring ideologies of Catholicism and Protestantism, one formed on the brotherhood of man bonded through love and truth in action. But such a plan could not be accomplished in the open when Church and State held such lethal control over the words and works of all those in Europe and England. "Francis is able to convey the most esoteric of Christian teachings to mankind in a manner that is veiled by the use of either very ancient or entirely new words that are able to transcend time and human 'religious' reaction. Because of his deliberate 'veiling' of the esoteric truths behind Christianity, Francis was able to both avoid being burnt as a heretic and also to imitate the Divine Majesty by creating a game of hide-and-seek as an essential part of his New Method."[44]

In a letter to Anthony Bacon, Lady Anne Bacon wrote about Francis's "enigmatical folded writing." Francis did not just fold meaning into his works with ancient and new words, but also with the use of ciphers he created.

A Celestial Visitation

*O Time, thou must untangle this, not I.
It is too hard a knot for me t' untie.*

~ Twelfth Night, act 2, sc. 2

In Francis's ciphers can be found a description of a celestial visitation that, judging from the context of the vision, took place just after his traumatic discovery of his royal blood. This heavenly being revealed to Francis how he could weave ciphers into his literary works that would reveal esoteric truths and a secret history of his time to generations to come.

> "And now, it is time for us to tell you
> How we found the way to conceal these ciphers.
> One night, when a youth, while we were reading
> In the holy scriptures of our great God, something
> Compelled us to turn to the Proverbs and read
> That passage of Solomon, the king, wherein he
> Affirmeth 'That the glory of God is to conceal
> A thing, but the glory of a king is to find it out.'
> And we thought how odd and strange it read,
> And attentively looked into the subtlety of the
> Passage. As we read and pondered the wise
> Words and lofty language of this precious
> Book of love, there comes a flame of fire which
> Fills all the room, and obscures our eyes with its
> Celestial glory. And from it swells a heavenly
> Voice that, lifting our mind above her
> Human bounds, ravisheth our soul with its sweet,
> Heavenly music. And thus it spake:
> 'My son, fear not, but take thy fortunes and thy

Honours up. Be that thou knowest thou art,
Then thou art as great as that thou fearest.
Thou art not what thou seemest. At thy
Birth the front of heaven was full of fiery
Shapes; the goats ran from the mountains,
And the heards were strangely clamorous
To the frighted fields. These signs
Have markt thee extraordinary, and all the
Courses of thy life will show thou art not in
The roll of common men. Where is the living,
Clipt in by the sea that chides the banks of
England, Scotland, and Wales, who will call thee
Pupil, or will read to thee? And bring him out that
Is but woman's son, will trace thee in the tedious
Ways of art, and hold thee pace in deep
Experiment. Be thou not, therefore, afraid of greatness,
I charge thee. Some men become great by advancement, vain
And favour of their prince; some have greatness
Thrust upon them by the world, and some achieve
Greatness by reason of their wit; for there is
A tide in the affairs of men, which taken at the
Flood, leads on to glorious fortune. Omitted, all the
Voyage of their life is bound in shallows
And miseries. In such a sea art thou now afloat,
And thou must take the current when it serves,
Or lose thy ventures. Thy fates open their hands to thee.
Decline them not, but let thy blood and spirit
Embrace them, and climb the height of virtue's
Sacred hill, where endless honour shall be made
Thy mead. Remember that that thou hast just
Read, that the Divine Majesty takes delight to hide
His work, according to the innocent play of children,
To have them found out; surely for thee to
Follow the example of the most high God cannot
Be censured. Therefore, put away popular applause,
And after the manner of Solomon the king, compose
A history of thy times, and fold it into

*Enigmatical writings and cunning mixtures of the
Theatre, mingled as the colours in a painter's shell,
And it will in due course of time be found.'"*[45]

In the ensuing years, Francis would create six different ciphers that he used in his book published under his own name as well as in the books, plays, and poems that were published under pseudonyms or "puppet" authors. Some were paid for the use of their name and others, like Ben Jonson, were committed to Francis's dream of changing the world. By the end of his life, Francis Bacon published his own works and collaborations under the names of many of the flourishing writers of his time.

The most famous of these is Shakespeare, whose name will first appear when Francis and Anthony are back together at Gray's Inn for the first time in many years. This "Shake-Scene," as Robert Greene called it, was an integral part of Francis's Great Instauration, though it would not begin for several more years to come. Shakespeare—the Shaker of the Spear of Truth—was the pen that held a magic mirror up to mankind and reframed their inner and outer worlds.

The Parisian Court

Boldness be my friend.

~ *Cymbeline*, act 1, sc. 6

Imagine the prince, violently informed of his true birth and torn from his childhood home; sent out to Paris on a grand adventure with dread and yet hope in his young heart for a happy ending.

Though France was riddled with political corruption, religious enmity and civil war, culturally it sang to Francis's poetic soul. Not only did he become acquainted with the Gnostics and Mystics but he also became intimate with French scholars who were then initiating a renaissance of learning in France founded on Greek thought. They were openly trying to strike off the theological fetters that had enslaved freedom of thought and utterance for a thousand years and to lead their compatriots into a new way of life. The head of the movement was the French poet Ronsard, leader of a small band of seven French poets known as the Pléiade. Named for the seven tragic poets during the reign of Ptolemy II, the group's title means "seven illustrious or brilliant persons or things."

Along with the famous Pléiade, Francis was especially inspired by Bernard Palissy, a lecturer in natural science and philosophy at his own *Petite Académie*. Francis drank in the European renaissance of thought, filled with philosophers, musicians, artists, poets, and mystics who were already dreaming of a golden age to uplift humanity.

Francis was sent on a secret mission for the Queen in the company of Amyas Paulet; what it entailed is still unknown today. On his arrival in France, he entered a court filled with intrigue and a cast of amazing characters.

In April of that year, King Charles IX of France died of ill health and possible poisoning. The Queen Mother,* Catherine de' Medici of the famed Italian family, manipulated events perfectly so that her favorite son, Henri, could return from Poland, where he had been made king, and take up the French throne with no opposition from his younger brother, the Catholic extremists, or the French Protestants—the Huguenots.

Portrait of Catherine de' Medici, by François Clouet

The French King now kept his own brother and sister—François de Valois, the duc d'Alençon, and Queen Marguerite de Valois—as well as Marguerite's husband, the Huguenot King Henri de Bourbon of Navarre, and her sister-in-law at court as political prisoners.

Battles between the Catholics and Huguenots in France had been breaking out into civil wars for years, with tensions only growing worse with every violent act. Embroiled in a fifth civil war in fourteen years,

---

*Queen Mother: the queen dowager (widow of a king) who is the mother of the reigning sovereign

the throne now faced *Les Politiques,* a party of moderate Catholics who aligned with the Huguenots in order to bring peace to France. François de Valois aligned himself with this faction.

Catherine and her three sons, who subsequently became kings, fought not only against the Huguenots but also politically with the extremist Catholics led by the powerful de Guise family and supported by Spain.

Into this dangerous environ walked Prince Francis. The ensuing months could read like a Shakespeare play. Though once a united front, because of Catherine de' Medici's clever use of her pretty lady-in-waiting, Navarre and Alençon had fallen out with one another. Alençon escaped alone soon after Francis's arrival. Once away from Paris, Alençon was joined by the Huguenot leader and a force of cavalry and issued a proclamation from the town of Dreux against the King.

King Henri III assembled an army against Alençon and the combined armies of *Les Politiques* and Huguenots. Marguerite and Navarre were confined to their quarters while the Queen Mother left to plead with her youngest son to return to court. Upon negotiating the release of two of his allies from the Bastille, Alençon agreed to a six-month truce.

Though liked by King Henri III, Francis soon came to his own conclusions about the king. His mother, Queen Elizabeth, reportedly detested the new king. Around five years earlier, before Poland had made Henri their king, Catherine de' Medici had tried to arrange a marriage between Queen Elizabeth and her dear Henri as a means of procuring him a crown and keeping him safe from his rightfully suspicious elder brother, King Charles IX. This was not the first connection to the British throne that Catherine had endeavored to make. Her eldest son, Francis II, had been married to Mary, Queen of Scots before he fell ill and died.

Elizabeth had sent Robert Dudley to carry out the talks of marriage. In a masterful play of politics, the Queen acted at first as though she were open to the marriage while putting forward conditions to which she knew Henri and Catherine would never agree. It is unknown if her secret husband was in on the irony—if he was sent on this marriage mission as punishment for something or as her secret ally in the mission's failure.

Henri gained Elizabeth's ire through his insinuations about her and Dudley and insults about her age (38 and twenty years Henri's senior), which were reported to her ear.

It is interesting that it was to the French court that Elizabeth banished her son within months of Henri being crowned. She had long given her sympathy to the Huguenots in their fight against the Catholics of France and thus against Spain and Rome. Though, being the political genius she was, she also offered her help to Henri later in 1588 when the Spanish Armada was bearing down on England and the Catholic extremists led by duc de Guise were at war with the French king.

Francis became fast friends with Navarre and Marguerite. He lent his heart and wits to their cause and revealed to them his own royal secret. Navarre attempted to escape the court that winter but was found out and imprisoned.

By careful pleading, Francis and Marguerite (coupled with the King's fears of Navarre's popularity with the French Huguenots, who were now around two-thirds of his subjects) secured Navarre's release back to the comparative freedom of the court. On February 14, 1576, Francis assisted in Navarre's escape during one of his hard-won hunting trips with Marguerite. They had convinced the King to allow these daily rides and then had waited for suspicion to slacken. Upon escape, Navarre met with his brother-in-law, Alençon, now allies again, and his Huguenot supporters.

Because of the seeming emotional distance that Catherine's agent, as Navarre's mistress, had created between Navarre and his wife, Marguerite had a believable reason as to why she had no foreknowledge of his plans. Though her brother was angry enough that she feared for her life, she was only confined to her quarters, where, as she states in her memoirs:

> I had found a secret pleasure, during my confinement, from the perusal of good books, to which I had given myself up with a delight I never before experienced. I consider this as an obligation

> I owe to Fortune, or, rather, to Divine Providence, in order to prepare me, by such efficacious means, to bear up against the misfortunes and calamities that awaited me. By tracing Nature in the universal book which is opened to all mankind, I was led to the knowledge of the Divine Author. Science conducts us, step by step, through the whole range of creation, until we arrive, at length, at God.[46]

It is not surprising that this love of learning blossomed when her new dear friend, Francis, was a living example of the search for truth through love and wisdom. Her words have a Baconian ring to them.

Francis meanwhile played messenger to both kings and Marguerite, carrying letters to Henri III from Navarre and Alençon and letters from Henri and Marguerite back to the two encamped with thousands of soldiers.

Navarre's letter to Marguerite is full of reconciliation, as she says in her memoirs:

> Absence having abated the force of her [Catherine's agent] charms, his eyes were opened; he discovered the plots and machinations of our enemies, and clearly perceived that a rupture could not but tend to the ruin of us both.
>
> Accordingly, he wrote me a very affectionate letter, wherein he entreated me to forget all that had passed betwixt us, assuring me that from thenceforth he would ever love me.[47]

Since Marguerite wrote that her husband often saw through the rumors and manipulations set about by Catherine and the king's people in order to separate them, and in Francis's cipher, Marguerite was a fellow conspirator the entire time, it can be guessed that Navarre's withdrawal from her and his quick turnaround of feeling had been for show. Though they did not love one another in the romantic sense, they had true affection and trust for each other.

During her imprisonment Marguerite wrote, "Although my guards had strict orders not to permit me to set pen to paper, yet, as necessity is said to be the mother of invention, I found means to write many letters to him."[48] It was quite beneficial to her that she had such a devoted and enterprising ally as Francis. During his time with them, he gained an abiding friendship with Henri of Navarre and a deep adoration for Marguerite.

Only one person brazened his way past the guards to visit her. Marguerite wrote: "The brave Grillon was the only one who ventured to visit me, at the hazard of incurring disgrace. He came five or six times to see me, and my guards were so much astonished at his resolution, and awed by his presence, that not a single Cerberus of them all would venture to refuse him entrance to my apartments."[49]

Who was this Grillon who braved the wrath of the King by visiting his imprisoned sister, and why did the guards let him? This Grillon could easily be a code for Francis. Though it could be a variation of the surname Grignon, it is also the French word for a cricket as well as a culinary dish in the west of France that is made of fried pork. This very well could be one of Francis's many code names that played on his adopted name, Bacon.

The Rose of France

With love's light wings did I o'erperch these walls,
For stony limits cannot hold love out,
And what love can do, that dares love attempt.

~ *Romeo and Juliet*, act 2, sc. 2

The Huguenot king of Navarre and the Catholic princess Marguerite of France had been married three years earlier in August 1572. It was part of an effort by the late King Charles IX to end the wars of religion and woo the Huguenots into peace with the marriage and promises of an offensive against Spain in Flanders. Catherine de' Medici convinced her son to back out of his promises to the Huguenot admiral for a Spanish offensive. Unbeknownst to the King, however, Catherine and his brother Henri plotted the assassination of their enemy, the admiral. Four days after the wedding of her daughter to the Huguenot king, Catherine's assassin shot Admiral Coligny twice but failed to kill him.

The assembled Huguenot chieftains swarmed the palace, demanding justice. The King met with them and Coligny and swore he would find the culprit. That night, however, Catherine convinced him that the Huguenots would take revenge on him if he did not act first. Marguerite writes about the terrifying night in her memoirs, how she had known something was afoot and prayed to God for protection. She spent the night with her husband, listening from his bed while he and his chief supporters and advisors met in earnest conversation about the justice they demanded for the assassination attempt. The night was so filled with peril that Navarre's private bedchamber was the only place the Huguenot leaders could speak. The next day would be remembered as The Massacre of St. Bartholomew's Day. By evening, three thousand Huguenots had been murdered in Paris with thousands more killed in the provinces.

In the days that followed, when her mother asked Marguerite to say that her new husband "was not like other men" in order to have the marriage annulled, Marguerite refused, knowing that their marriage was what kept Navarre alive. Though she had previously fallen in love and had wanted to marry the Catholic duc de Guise who was now her husband's enemy, Marguerite held true to her new husband in that dangerous time. A friendship grew between them that withstood the slanders that her brother's man published about her. As Francis had his Cecil, so Marguerite had Le Guast who was ever her enemy.

Marguerite of Valois, by François Clouet

Francis's first flame of love burned bright and deep. Even as he understood her faults, still he loved her as his rose of France. In his word cipher he states,

> *Love of her had power to make the Duke of Guise forget the greatest honours that France might confer upon him, and hath power to make as well all such fleeting glory seem to us like dreams or pictures, nor can we name aught real that hath not origin in her....*
>
> *So fair was she, no eyes ere looked upon such a beauteous mortal, and I saw no other. I saw her—French Eve to their wondrous paradise—as if no being, no one in all high heaven's wide realm, save only this one, Marguerite, did ever exist, or in this nether world, ever, in all the ages to be in the infinity of time, might be created.*[50]

Francis goes on to explain how he had, at this volatile time, spoken his true mind to King Henri III, even to the point of revealing his true identity. King Henri, fearing that Elizabeth, if angered, would give her full support to the Huguenots, merely told Francis to retire into the palace to see Marguerite. Francis went to her rooms where she was imprisoned and planned with her how best to affect her escape. In the drama of the moment he confessed to her his love:

> *With cheeks abash I blush, and swear to serve, be it unto death and future misery, this Queen of earthly Queens, as Goddess so divine, who charms with her sweet smile e'en the most saturnine.*[51]

Like Romeo and Juliet, whose story is a mirror of Francis's own first love, their story was as brief as it was beautiful. Fortunately for the world, its end was less fatal, but for the lovers no less final. Francis devised a plan for Marguerite to escape that night and went about setting it all in place. Here his mind clearly shows his passionate youth, one moment wooing his sweet Marguerite and in the next full of bitter jealousy for her ex-lover now doing battle against her husband and Francis's own friend.

He returned that night to assist her escape out the window but, in the moment, she found she had not the heart to brave such an escape.

Years later she used Francis's plan to help her brother escape the court (again) from her rooms.

In the ensuing weeks their love took root, but just as they swore their love for one another, Francis was called back to England. His secret mission having been successful, he hoped his mother would agree to his marrying Marguerite as soon as her divorce from Navarre was complete. The British ambassador, with whom Francis had traveled and was now good friends, began negotiations for both his marriage and the treaty that involved Francis's secret mission.

Peter Dawkins published Francis's deciphered story of this time (transliterated to modern English):

> *When Sir Amyas Paulett became advised of my love, he proposed that he should negotiate a treaty of marriage, and appropriately urge on her pending case of the divorce from the young Huguenot; but for reasons of very great importance these buds of an early marriage never opened into flower. But the future race will profit by the failure in the field of love, for in those flitting days afterwards, having resolved to cover every mark of defeat with the triumphs of my mind, I did thoroughly banish my tender love dreams to the regions of clouds as unreal, and let my works of various kinds absorb my mind.*[52]

Elizabeth Gallup continues the cipher story:

> *Thorow love I dreamed out these* five other plays, fill'd up—as we have seen warp in some hand-loome, so as to bee made a beautious color'd webb—with words Marguerite hath soe ofte, like to a busy hand, shot dailie into a fayre-hued web, and made a riche-hued damask, vastlie more dear; and should life bewwraie [an] interiour room in my calme but aching brest, on everie hand shal her work be seene.*[53]

In a cipher hidden in *Romeo and Juliet,* Francis wrote of the play's true-life inspiration, "so rare (and most briefe) th' hard-won happinesse, it afforded us great content to relive in th' play all that as mist in summer morni'g did roule away."

---
*This cipher lies within *Midsummer Night's Dream,* Robert's Edition, 1600.

Their life was too briefe—its rose of pleasure had but partlie drunk the sweete dewe o' early delight, and evrie hour had begun to ope unto sweete love, tender leaflets in whose fragrance was assurance of untold joies that th' immortalls know. Yet 'tis a kinde fate which joyn'd them together in life and in death.

It was a sadder fate befel our youthfull love, my Marguerite, yet written out in the plays it scarce would bee named our tragedie since neither yeelded up life. But the joy of life ebb'd from our hearts with our parting, and it never came againe into this bosome in full flood-tide. O we were Fortune's foole too long, sweete one, and arte is long.[54]

Esoteric France

*This above all: to thine own self be true,
And it must follow, as the night the day,
Thou canst not then be false to any man.*

~ *Hamlet*, act 1, sc. 3

The French court was a wellspring for Francis, and not just for his love of Marguerite. Unlike in England, poets were held in high esteem. The Pléiade founder sat on a throne beside the king in honor of their work to advance and enliven the French language. The Pléiade poets were a force for religious tolerance in a time when religion was the driving force for years of civil war in France. Upon Francis's return to England in the spring of 1576, his mind was as full of plans as his heart was of love. He wanted to uplift and expand the English language just as the Pléiade group was doing for French. He longed to return, not only to see again his beloved, even if he had given up hope of a marriage, but to learn from the mystics and poets of the Continent who were uplifting their world in secret.

On the thirtieth of June 1576, a license to travel "beyond the seas" was granted to Edward and Francis Bacon. The twenty-eight-year-old Edward was Nicholas Bacon's youngest son from his first marriage and was close friends with Anthony and Francis. Francis was to work with the Queen's secretary of state and head of her intelligence service, Sir Francis Walsingham, to intercept and decipher communiqués to or about Mary, Queen of Scots. Francis later regretted just how successful he was at this mission, for though he didn't agree with her, he respected Mary Stuart. Through the messages he decoded, it was clear Mary looked to the English throne as her own.

Walsingham had previously been the ambassador to France and was in Paris for the wedding of

Mary, Queen of Scots
by Nicholas Hilliard, 1578

Henri Navarre and Marguerite and witnessed the horrifying massacre that followed. Upon becoming secretary of state, he initiated a large scale, highly trained intelligence service. Both Anthony and Francis went to his secret cipher school in London. Edward and Francis traveled to France with the newly knighted Sir Amyas Paulet and his wife in September 1576. Amyas replaced the previous ambassador to France. Clearly the Queen was happy with his work during the previous months in France.

While on the Continent, Francis traveled to Italy and Spain as well as throughout France. He observed cultures and politics for the Queen and also for himself. He not only observed the outer actions of those around him but he also learned to understand the inner motives and psychology of his fellowman. As he saw himself destined to inherit the throne, he observed the laws of the countries through which he passed, noting the various forms of government and their advantages or defects.

At some point during his time in France, Francis befriended François de Valois' personal secretary, Jean de la Jessée. He was one of Ronsard's idealists and a prolific sonnet writer. This unpublished sonnet by Jessée to Francis (written most likely at the latest in 1595–96) was discovered in 1903 by Rev. Walter Begley, M.A., in the Lambeth

Archiepiscopal Library among Anthony Bacon's correspondence. In English the last two verses read:

> So—Bacon—if it happens that my Muse is praised
> It is not that she is either eloquent or wise:
> Although your Pallas makes me better taught
> It is because my Lut sings her saintly glory
> Or that in these verses naive her Image is imprinted
> Or that your clear virtue shines in my shadow.

This proves both that Francis was known as a poet in France and that his friends knew his muse to be Pallas Athena. This latter fact is a very important one in understanding Francis's plan to reform the world. Pallas Athena is not one of the nine muses but rather is honored as the Goddess of Wisdom, who was not born but sprung fully formed as a revelation from the mind of Zeus. Francis chose as his muse a goddess, who with her symbolic spear and helmet, is a defender of Truth and conqueror of ignorance.

Not all of Francis's cipher has been deciphered, so it is not fully known yet what he did during his three years on the Continent. He was in Blois with the French court from the end of 1576 to the end of February 1577. At this time Henri III made life incredibly hard for Marguerite. He had, on no uncertain terms, refused to let her leave his court and labeled her husband a traitor. The treaty Marguerite had helped establish was broken and France was at war with itself yet again.

With advice from her friends, she finally got permission to leave court with the Princess de la Roce-sur-Yon for a trip to Spa to take the waters. The secret reason she was going was to assist her brother François de Valois, now the duc d'Anjou (who won the title in the Treaty of Beaulieu along with many rights for the Huguenots), to gain the loyalty of the French lords in Flanders and to win that area back from Spain.

While she was gone the court moved to Poitiers, from which there are two surviving letters from Sir Amyas to Nicholas Bacon that reference his "son." One thought to be from July 1577 simply says, "your sonne, thanks be to God, is in good health." The second, written in September 1577, tells of the Peace of Bergerac, which reestablished peace between Henri III and the Huguenots with much decreased rights for the Huguenots. At the end he wrote: "I must tell you that I rejoice much to see that your son, my companion, by the Grace of God, passed the brunt and peril of this journey.... Your son is safe, sound and in good health, and worthy of your fatherly favour."[55]

This reveals that Francis went on a "perilous" journey between July and September 1577. As it was during the peace talks, and Francis was known and trusted by both King Henri III and King Henri of Navarre, it is likely that he was sent as an envoy to Navarre to see peace brought about successfully.

There is evidence that during the winter of 1577, Francis had the good fortune to join an academy founded by Michel de Montaigne, who became a close friend of both Francis and Anthony Bacon. Francis wrote a book based on his experience there, first published in French, entitled *Académie Françoise* by Pierre de la Primaudaye. It is translated to be "French Academy," but Françoise is more correctly translated as "Frances"—a play on words with Francis's own name. In the fifteenth and sixteenth centuries, Françoise and Francaise were both used to mean *French,* and François is the French spelling of Francis. This ambiguity played into Francis's love of cipher and puns quite well. In 1586 the English translation was published under the name T.B. This is the same year *The Treatise on Melancholy,* which holds ciphered messages from Francis, was published under the name T. Bright.

It is about a young man who attends the academy of "an ancient wise gentleman of great calling." After extensive research on this subject, Peter Dawkins writes:

> The story of the *French Academy* and its wise old gentleman fits exactly the circumstances and character of Michel Montaigne....
> As the intention of the Academy was to augment University life and teaching, guiding the noble-born into an honest and virtuous way of life and thereby preserving them from the possible corruption that University life might give, it would appear reasonable to suppose that this Academy operated during the University

vacations only. The four young noblemen, who were sons of distinguished noblemen of Anjou (and hence probably of royal blood and directly related to the French Monarchy...), were students of this Academy for "six or seven years" before their fathers decided to visit them together at the Academy and test the results of their education. Their visit was a happy one, but unfortunately broken up after a few days by the news of the country's return to civil war....

The ensuing war (the sixth civil war in France of that period) did not last long, and peace was concluded at Bergerac in September. Once the war was ended, the four young noblemen "laboured forthwith to meet together", and to arrange to continue their special conversation with their fathers. This duly came about, and it seems likely that it was during the Christmas vacation of 1577 that the special assembly of fathers and sons took place again. It was during this time that the author of the *French Academy,* whom I feel certain was Francis Bacon, had the privilege of being allowed to become one of their company. In fact he eventually replaced one of the four principal students, who seems to have left during those discourses without any explanation, leaving his father disappointed. This special conference went on for the space of "three whole weeks, which made eighteen daies workes". After it had finished Francis left the Academy and Montaigne and returned to Paris and the French Court, where he wrote up his thoughts and experiences as a book whilst they were still fresh on his mind. Then he caused the first part of the book to be straightway printed and published in the following February, 1578. He was obviously exhilarated and fired by the whole experience, just as he had been by the equally extraordinary time with the French Court at Blois. His young mind, prepared and trained by his upbringing at Sir Nicholas Bacon's Platonic "Academy" at Gorhambury, had proved fully capable of responding to and enjoying this unique opportunity at Montaigne's Academy, and in true form he just had to write it down and let the precious thoughts and knowledges pour out for the benefit of the world at large, as an early part of his philanthropic and philosophical scheme.[56]

In February 1578, while Francis was back at court, Henri III had his brother Anjou arrested for treason and then set "free" the next morning after being berated by his councillors. But once again he kept him a closely watched prisoner within the court, this time with all his attendants forced daily to leave by nightfall. However, he escaped from Marguerite's window following Francis's plan concocted two years earlier.

Now that peace had arrived, Henri III finally had to capitulate to pressures and agreed that Marguerite could return to her husband. Catherine accompanied her daughter to settle Navarre's claims against the Crown. Her ulterior motive was, however, to disrupt Navarre's court and draw away some of his most powerful lords. Francis most likely traveled to the South of France with the Queen Mother and Marguerite. Much of the Shakespeare play *Love's Labour's Lost* is based on events in the "court of love" from this time. Francis drew inspiration for this play from his relationship with Marguerite, his experiences at both Palissy's and Montaigne's "Petites Academies," and the Protestant chieftains of Navarre's court falling for Catherine's ladies. Romancing was so thick in the air, in fact, that Catherine finally withdrew with her ladies-in-waiting to Port-Sainte-Marie, as she suspected the settlement was being delayed in an effort to gain more time for the couples.

A court ball, 16th century, France

Secret Wisdom

*I have seen a medicine
That's able to breathe life into a stone...*

~ All's Well That Ends Well, act 2, sc. 1

Accepted within the European literary circles, Francis contacted the secret societies that had been the intellectual and spiritual counter to the tyrannical Church of Rome from the time of Dante. He studied more in the art of secret writing, how to communicate through the open print by purposeful misprints, watermarks, hieroglyphics, headpieces, tailpieces, and symbolic pictures.

As Alfred Dodd writes,

> Francis Bacon became initiated in secret and mystical Continental Orders which through persecution were virtually in a moribund state. He learned the ritual of the Mysteries and the solemnity of the ordeal through which the neophyte passed. He took part in the stately ceremonial of the Knights Templar. He studied the Jewish Cabala and obtained first-hand its peculiar knowledge. He sat at the feet of the men who knew how to write their secrets through the printed page that no one could trace unless he had been *"taught to read."* He saturated himself in Arabian lore and Egyptian mysticism. And he combined all this hidden wisdom with his own knowledge of Christian Ethics and the secret marks of the old operative masons, their grips and knocks and lodges that had so fascinated him when "The Temple" was built at Gorhambury.... Thus were the bases laid for the building of an ethical King Solomon's Temple which was to be upreared invisibly without the sound of hammer or chisel, where men could eventually moralize on working Tools and spiritualize a Building Plan. And the architect to evolve—out of the customs and cults of the ancient world, so rich in its symbolism of Natural Philosophy—a scheme that would have a more universal appeal for the sons of men... was Francis Bacon. He it was who undertook to reorganize the Nature Myths with a new and more up-to-date interpretation, by rewriting the rituals of the ancient cults which should have as their basis ethics of universal application, morality devoid of credal dogmatism,

the foundation stones behind education, wisdom, charity, the Fatherhood of God, the Brotherhood of Man. So the youth, *while in France,* who afterwards said he had "taken all Knowledge to be his Province" at once proceeded to rewrite the various Rituals of the Rosicrucian College that are practised to-day, and to create the Rituals of Freemasonry. *But no one knew of this secret work at the time nor for many years later.*[57]

In the sixteenth century, a custom began among printers of placing an emblematic design on the title page and at the beginning and ending of chapters. Between 1576 and 1640, there were variants of a device portraying a light A and a dark A, which were linked to Francis Bacon and the English mystery school he eventually led.

Francis used this double A as one of his signatures in many headpieces of his publications. This AA represents Alahim, which is now written as Elohim, the Father-Mother God united as one. The two A's also signify Francis's divine muse, the original "spear shaker" AthenA. It became a characteristic mark of Rosicrucian publications. Peter Dawkins shares his research of the double A design in his essay "The Bacon Brothers and France":

> The first time the "AA" signature seems to have appeared hieroglyphically as a printer's device, in the form of an "AA" headpiece, was in an extremely rare book published in Paris in 1576, in which a Hebrew Grammar, the *Hebraicum Alphabethum Jo. Bovlaese,* was bound together with another Hebrew Grammar that had previously been published in Paris in 1566. In the version of the book that came into the possession of the great collector William T. Smedley, there were not only printer proof sheets added but also the printed pages were interleaved with sheets of paper containing Francis Bacon's handwriting. According to Smedley:
>
>> "The book ends with the sentence: 'Ex collegio Montis— Acuti 20 Decembris 1576'; then follow two pages in Hebrew, with the Latin translation over it, headed 'Decem Prœcepta decalogi Exod.' Over this is the design containing the light A and the dark A, and the squirrel and rabbits.* One thing is certain,

---

*Another device often used by Francis in his headpieces, as rabbits were called conies, so rabbits back-to-back would signify back cony—Baconian. Squirrels were often called bunnies, which is also another word for rabbits.

that the copy now referred to was in the possession of Bacon, and that the interleaved sheets of paper contain his handwriting, in which have been added page by page the equivalents of the Hebrew in Greek, Chaldæic, Syriac and Arabic."[58]

It was during this time that Francis helped write the founding pamphlets of the Rosicrucian Order—*The Fama, The Confessio,* and *The Chymical Marriage*—which were later published anonymously in 1614 in Germany. The first pamphlet declared that the Rosicrucian's goal was "The Reformation of the Whole Wide World" —indeed Bacon's goal. The pamphlet titled *The Fama* gives the initials of the founders. One of the five of the "first circle" is *"Fra. F.B., Pictor et Architectus,"* meaning "Frater (Brother) Francis Bacon, Painter and Architect." Francis is a painter of words and an architect of his Invisible Temple of King Solomon. *The Fama* states that "the High and Noble Spirit of one of the Fraternity was stirred up to enter into the scheme for a *General Reformation* and that he travelled away to the wise men of Arabia.... *This young member was sixteen years old at the time and for one year he had pursued his course alone....* He travelled to Damcar."[59]

Dodd explains,

> He travelled alone actually and symbolically—for every thinker studies alone... and he was still more alone as he progressed onwards. His ardent mind wanted to get at a knowledge of the First Causes of Things. Francis Bacon's contacts enabled him to take up the study of Rhazis, Avenzoar, Averroes, Avicenna and other Arabian and hermetic writers, for all these mystical writers are afterwards quoted in his various writings. He went metaphorically to "Damcar" to the "Wise Men," because this kind of esoteric knowledge comes from the East. The "Wise Men" revealed to him their Mysteries. He went back to the ancient philosophies, almost crushed out of existence by the Church, in order to trace the history of learning and thought from the earliest recorded times. These occult philosophies of India, Persia, Arabia, and Egypt had a most profound influence upon his mind and writings.[60]

This journey into Eastern philosophy to study the mysteries of the wise men is reminiscent of Jesus' own journey to the East in his youth.* Like Jesus, Francis was finding the truth enveloped in spiritual philosophies. He studied everything he could find concerning the philosophies, religions, sciences, and government models of both East and West and absorbed the ancient wisdom mysteries, their sacred rites, and their inner interpretation of the old-world nature myths. He studied the works of the Greek mathematician and philosopher Pythagoras, founder of the ancient mystery school of Crotona, and learned the science of numbers and how to apply them to the printed word as a sacred seal.

During this time, he gained the skills that allowed him to fulfill the vision of his youth. He recorded his life in cipher not only to set down the truth of his lineage but, as Peter Dawkins wrote, "He hoped not only to leave a correct account of history as he knew it, so as to correct any errors, misconceptions or deliberate falsifications that posterity might have been left with, but also to provide future ages with a genuine history and in-depth study of one man's personal experience from birth to death—with all the passions, thoughts and other matters that constitute man's sensitive but developing psyche."[61]

Because his mission from the queen was centered on cipher, he was able to spend time creating his own with no one the wiser.

> *By some strange Providence, this... served well the purposes of our† own heart; for, making ciphers our choice, we straightway proceeded to spend our greatest labours therein, to find a method of secret communication of our history to others outside the realm. That, however, drew no suspicion upon this device, inasmuch as it did appear quite natural to one who was in company and under the instruction of our Ambassador to the Court of France; and it seemed, on the part of our parents, to afford peculiar relief, that our spirit and mind had calmed, as the ocean after the tempest doth sink into a sweet rest, nor gives a sign of the shipwracke below the gently rolling surface.*[62]

---

*See *The Lost Years of Jesus* to read the account that Jesus was in India during his youth. https://Store.SummitLighthouse.org.
†Use of the royal we

> *...It is not easy to reveal secrets at the same time that a wall to guard them is built, but this hath been attempted. How successful it shall be, I know not, for though well contrived so no one has found it, the clear assurance cometh only in the dreams and visions of the night, of a time when the secret shall be fully revealed. That it shall not be now, and that it shall be then—that it shall be kept from all eyes in my own time, to be seen at some future day, however distant—is my care, my study.*[63]

While abroad, Francis laid down his first foundations for his Great Instauration. In just three years, he enriched his understanding and experience tenfold. The historian William Hepworth Dixon wrote:

> When the passions fan out in most men, poetry flowers out in him. Old when a child, he seems to grow younger as he grows in years. Yet with all his wisdom he is not too wise to be a dreamer of dreams.... Joyous, helpful, swift to do good, slow

A Nicholas Hilliard miniature of Francis, painted during Francis's time in the French court
Latin inscription can be translated to,
"I wished rather a painting worthy of his mind/soul/heart might be given."

to think evil, he leaves on every one who meets him a sense of friendliness, of peace and power. The serenity of his spirit keeps his intellect bright, his affections warm; and just as he had left the halls of Trinity with his mind unwarped, so he now, when duty calls him from France, quits the galleries of the Louvre and St. Cloud with his morals pure.⁶⁴

Unfortunately, the ending of *Love's Labour's Lost* owes its abruptness to the end of Francis's travels. In February 1579, he had a dream in which he saw his childhood home of Gorhambury plastered over in black mortar. The very same morning back in England, his foster father fell ill. Soon after, he received word that Sir Nicholas Bacon had died on February twentieth. As in the play, a father figure's death brought a swift end to the youthful days filled with excitement, philosophy, and love.

Nicholas Bacon's will had been written two months before his death—some think by the Queen, to make certain that Francis was left with no income. But whether it was at the behest of the Queen or a way for Nicholas to force her hand to care for the livelihood of her son, Francis was left nothing directly in his will. He was the Queen's son and to her he must look for inheritance. Nicholas did, however, write that his country seat of Gorhambury should go to Francis should Anthony die without children.

 ## Birth of Works Immortal

Your Monument shall be my gentle Verse,
Which eyes not yet created shall o'er-read,
And tongues to be, your being shall rehearse...

~ Shakespeare, "Sonnet 81"

Francis returned to England with a letter from Amyas Paulet for the Queen and the question of how he should proceed. Was he returning as the mourning son of Sir Bacon or as his rightful role of Tudor prince? Amyas wrote that Francis "would prove a very able and sufficient subject to do her Highness good and acceptable service."

The eighteen-year-old prince-in-disguise was welcomed warmly back into the Dudley/Sidney circle of friends, which helped Francis adjust to leaving behind the French court and the sudden loss of Sir Nicholas Bacon.

Francis lived in the Leicester House in London for months before entering Gray's Inn to study law as his foster father had done before him. During his first year at Gray's Inn, his position with the Queen grew even more precarious.

Throughout the 1570s, Queen Elizabeth kept the marriage proposal of François the duc d'Anjou on hand, never giving full encouragement nor an outright no. In 1579, however, in another grand political game to keep the balance of power in England's favor, she began the negotiations of the impossible marriage seemingly in earnest. This courtship had to be believed by everyone in order for it to be of any use to her. Elizabeth would rail at Parliament for delaying the process and act as if she wanted nothing more than for this marriage to go through. With the Spanish power becoming ever more threatening, this possible alliance was vital for England.

Leicester did not take well to the possibility of his secret wife naming a king who was not himself, and was hostile to Anjou's envoy. When the envoy survived an assassination attempt, the man was sure it was Leicester who had tried to kill him. Unfortunately for Leicester, he found a perfect way to retaliate. The envoy discovered and subsequently informed the Queen that in September 1578, Leicester had secretly married the widow, Lettice Devereux, the foster mother of their son, Robert Devereux, now the Earl of Essex.

Outraged by this betrayal, the Queen permanently dismissed Lettice from court and banned Leicester. As her own marriage to him was a secret she could take no legal action against him. This betrayal by his father hurt Francis and his hopes too.

The Queen played her game with Francis as well, keeping him in a state of perpetual waiting, neither recognizing him nor snuffing out the hope of that recognition. A few letters survive from this time addressed to Lord Burghley and one to Lady Burghley (sister to Lady Bacon) in which Francis requests them to put forward his "rare and unaccustomed suit" to the Queen.

> I possess every qualification which will enable me to do for my native tongue what the Pléiade have done for theirs. I ask to be permitted to give to my country this great heritage. Others may serve her in the law, others may serve her in affairs of state, but your Lordship knows full well that there are none who could serve her in this respect as could I.
>
> You are not unmindful of the poorness of my estate. This work will not only entail a large outlay of money but it necessitates command of the ablest wits of the nation. This is my suit: that her Majesty will graciously confer on me some office which will enable me to control such literary resources and the services of such men as may be necessary for the accomplishment of this work.[65]

Unfortunately for Francis, Lord Burghley's son, Robert Cecil, the Queen's favorite court informant, continued to whisper poison in her ear about her sons. He played on her fears of deposition, convincing her that Francis was power-hungry enough that if she were to name him as her heir, he would turn the people against her to gain the throne before his time. So the Queen kept Francis's financial wings "closely clipped"; he remained penniless—a genius financially dependent on the whim of the Queen. "Hence Francis Bacon's cry; '*I am like a hooded hawk that cannot fly being tied to the Queen's fist.*'"[66]

Dodd reasons that this "unaccustomed suit" was a request for recognition of his birth. Francis revealed in his cipher his true motivation for aspiring to the throne. He wrote, "It is noe improper exaltation of selfe, when one, feeling in heart and brayne the divine giftes that fit him for his Princely destiny—or that rightly inherited albeit wronglie withholden soveraignty—in true, noble, kingly spirit doth looke for pow'r, not for th' sake of exercising that gift, but that he may uplifte his people from th' depth of misery into which they constantlie sink, to th' firm rocke of such mode of life as would change cries to songs of praise."[67]

Dawkins expands on just how needed Francis's "educational and cultural endeavors" were. Even with the question of recognition aside, this suit was not just for some lucrative office but for permission to found an *Académie*. He writes:

English culture at that time was uncouth and the English language still a sorry patchwork of almost incomprehensible dialects. Francis's mission, therefore, was to create, with the help of others suited to the task, a magnificent English language and culture just as the French poets and philosophers had created theirs, but one that would promote virtue, not corruptness, and would be a vehicle for the new avenues of thought and discovery that he wished to encourage....

... He applied to his uncle Lord Burghley to exert influence with the Queen on his behalf, in recognition of his special abilities and circumstances,* so that he might have not only royal approval but also a position whereby he could have sufficient influence and income, without having to practice law, to give him "commandment of more wits" than his own to assist him in his proposed task, since his own inherited resources were far too limited. The Queen, who was interested in the French Academies, did voice her approval and support, and gave Francis to believe that such a place would be found for him; but, other than moral and verbal encouragement, in this "rare and unaccustomed suit" he was to meet with little success.[68]

This idea of Francis wanting to start his own academy is borne out in a sealed paper discovered after his death. He was granted the lease of Twickenham Park when his elder foster brother, Edward, released it, but in 1608 he had to sell the lease due to financial straits. In the sealed document, he instructed Thomas Bushnell, one of his private secretaries, to buy back Twickenham—his "Garden of Paradise"—for the purpose of founding a small academy there. He writes, "Let Twitnam Park, which I sold in my younger days, be purchased if possible, for a Residence for such deserving persons to study in. *I experimented there for the trial of my philosophical conclusions.* This wish I expressed in a paper sealed to the Trust, which I myself would have put into practise and settled the same by Act of Parliament, if the vicissitudes of Fortune had not intervened and prevented me."[69]

It was during these early days at Gray's Inn that Francis wrote

---
*Francis often wrote his letters in coded language, referencing the circumstance of being a secret prince though never saying it outright.

the first cantos of his sonnets to the Queen. These, unlike the later ones, were written for private presentation to her. They were a plea from a son to a mother for recognition. And like the rest of Bacon's work, they held codes revealing truth, as discovered by Alfred Dodd. The first canto reveals Francis Bacon's "emotions while pressing for 'Recognition' at the immediate beginning of his 'Suit.'" The second portrays his hopes and fears through the following years. "The first two Sonnets alone tell the poet's meaning directly and indirectly." Dodd explains, paraphrasing the two sonnets (Sonnet Diary 2-1 and 3-11) in prose:

Tudor Rose

We desire all "Fair Creatures" to perpetuate themselves (thus at once indicating that a woman is involved, the person addressed. . . .) He mentions "Beauty's Rose" because she represents the Rose of Tudor. He uses the phrase "Tender Heir" hinting that she ought to possess one. She is, however, contracted to herself and thus makes a "famine" where there is abundance; a statement which makes plain that the person addressed conceals from outsiders the fact that she is rich in the possession of an Heir already. She is thus a "foe" to herself and to her own "Sweet Self," *i.e.*, her child, for every child is a mother's "sweet self."

He now begins to tell us the identity of his mother. She is the "only Herald" to the nation, to the world, for she was the only woman in the world who could summon the Parliament of the nation by Proclamation as a Herald. She is looked upon by the people as a Virgin for she poses as "the World's Fresh Ornament." That description can only apply to Queen Elizabeth, for the only woman to whom such a phrase could apply was the English Queen who had adorned herself with the ornament of Virginity. The meaning of "Fresh" is "Virgin." And now we are told that this woman has buried the result of her satisfaction, her content, within her own "Bud," her own child; and by burying her own bud she thus makes a waste of wealth while hoarding him in concealment.

The poet concludes by asking her to "Pity the World"—everyone in the world was anxious about the English "Succession"—for she is selfishly eating a just title of claim all alone by keeping her bud concealed. It means eventually that he will be eaten by the grave and figuratively by his own mother for his identity will be lost.[70]

The story of Dodd's original sonnet discovery is intriguing and mysterious in itself. Dodd was a fervent Stratfordian, a believer in the traditional Shakspur authorship and a lover of plays. During a surprise first visit to Stratford-on-Avon, he overheard a tour guide discussing the theory that Francis Bacon was indeed the author of the Works. The conversation struck him. How could there be any mystery left unsolved about the most pivotal playwright in British history? He felt driven to work out the authorship problem on his own and prove that the Stratfordian actor wrote the great works. Dodd said he knew the key was hidden in the sonnets, the most autobiographical works of the author. In his own words, he describes the inner spiritual experience that revealed the very key to the true author.

Dodd discovered not only the correct numerical and chronological order of the Shakespeare sonnets, revealing Bacon's Sonnet Diary, but also Francis's coded messages within the sonnets. In the one translated above, Francis had coded the sentence, *To paw at thy Majesty: Francis Bacon—Hist—Be Francis Tudor.* There are also the phrases, *A tuder heire,* and *fr. Bacon's a tuder heire,* as well as *Whisper What? Whisper Tudor. Whisper Tudor.*

But Francis did not simply wait for royal recognition; his was not a passive philosophy, but a vital one to be acted upon and lived. He fed all he had learned from the cultural enlightenment in France into his work for the cultural reformation of England and the world.

During his time at Gray's Inn, he excelled in his law studies even though they were forced upon him by his mother. Out of the four Inns of Court, Gray's Inn was the largest. While the yearly calls to the bar were only six, from 1561 to 1600 the average admittance to the Inn was sixty-two. Francis was there at the height of its glory. The Queen was its patron and three of the most important men of England were members: Lord Burghley, Sir Francis Walsingham, and Lord Bacon until his death.

Statue of Francis Bacon at his dear Gray's Inn

Beginning his studies there in May 1580, Francis was called to the bar in 1582 and admitted as an Utter Barrister. Many barristers never become a Master of the Bench, or a "bencher," but Francis did so only four years later. He was made a Reader a few years after that and a double Lent Reader in 1600.[71] Though he accomplished in a few years what some law students never achieved, he only did it at the behest of the Queen and Lord Burghley. His first love and calling was always his reformation of the whole wide world.

Queen Elizabeth had called him her "watch-candle,"[72] for he never failed to follow his conscience and to act as her own when needed. Francis was a keeper of the flame.

Francis had long ago become a philosopher. His consciousness was reflected in the ordered details of his life. He knew how to use every moment to the best advantage; he knew how to relax completely, to gather strength from the inexhaustible reserves of nature; how to be silent, to be still, to meditate.

Though compelled to move continually amid a crowd, he had mastered the art of disengaging himself and becoming as remote, if need arose, in Westminster Hall as though he were in the high mountains of India. He had long ago come to know life as a mystery to be solved and an art to be continually developed, practiced, and mastered.

Calling the Wits Together

Where a Man cannot fitly play his owne Part:
If he have not a Frend, he may quit the Stage.

~ Bacon, *Essays*, "Of Friendship"

Francis began "to ring a bell to call other wits together."[73] These wits included his childhood friends and cousins Philip and Mary Sidney as well as the "university wits." His work with these beloved friends was the secret of his mirth. His wit and wisdom fed theirs and together they created the English Renaissance. Leicester House became the gathering place for his circle of literary friends and patrons. Peter Dawkins writes,

> Philip Sidney's scholarly circle of philosopher-poets (the English *Areopagitae* or "Areopagus") was already in existence (from c. 1574) and in the throes of developing English poetry. The Renaissance magus, Dr John Dee, was at the height of his influence and making available his magnificent library at Mortlake—the largest in England—to the philosopher-poets and mathematicians. The Earl of Leicester, still dear to the Queen, provided an enthusiastic patronage of the poets and artists, making his London house available to them as well as patronising his own company of actors. Then, from 1579 and onwards through the 1580's, the "University Wits" began to appear, who raised the level of English drama and helped lay the foundations for the Shakespeare plays. The University Wits were, in order of appearance, John Lyly, Thomas Lodge, George Peele, Robert Greene, Thomas Nashe and Christopher Marlowe. The Areopagitae included Sir Philip Sidney, Gabriel Harvey, Edward Dyer, Daniel Rogers, Thomas Drant and "Immerito".[74]

Immerito was a pen name Francis adopted after his discovery of his true lineage. Meaning blameless one, it references his innocence in the events of his conception and birth for which the queen blamed him. Under Immerito, he published *The Shepheardes Calendar* in December 1579, which was later attributed to Edmund Spenser. That same year *The Tale of Hemet's the Heremyte* and *Euphues: The Anatomy of Wit* were published. Although the former was assigned

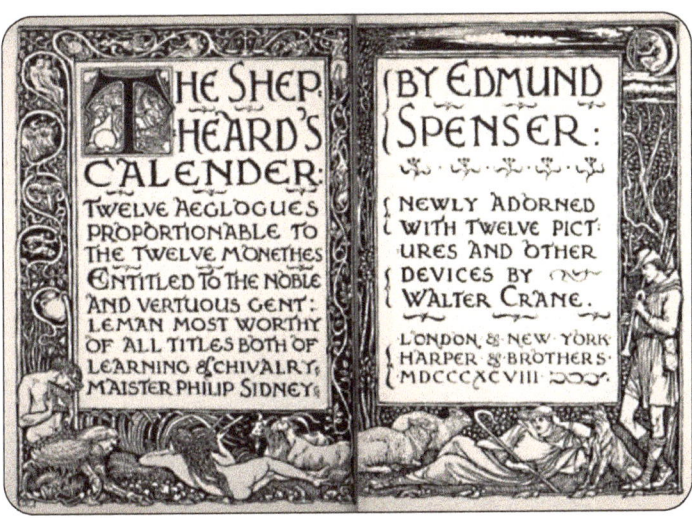

The Shepherd's Calendar by Immerito, later attributed to Edmund Spenser
(Project Gutenberg)

to George Gascoigne and the latter to John Lyly, all three publications share Baconian symbolism and a motive to teach people in an approachable way to live with charity and truth.

Out of all the revels put on by the Inns of Court at that time, those of Gray's Inn and the Inner Temple are the most noted. Francis used these revels to practice enfolding meaning and esoteric wisdom into theater. "It is certain that Bacon, who had always a great fondness for splendour and pageantry, not only took great interest in superintending the festivities in his own Inn, but also assisted in the composition of some of the 'Triumphs.'"[75]

In his work *Tudor Problems,* Parker Woodward writes that Francis Bacon wrote all of the plays produced by Gray's Inn for the Queen and her court starting in 1583, which very well could be the case. He is mentioned to have been the "chief contriver" for more than one masque. Dodd writes further on this:

> The real genesis of the English Drama in its highest reaches was conceived in Gray's Inn for there were no theatrical pursuits before the nation worth mentioning until the Francis Bacon era at the Inns of Court.
> The following Plays are associated more or less with Francis Bacon at Gray's Inn:

1583: *The Birth of Merlin*
1587: *The Misfortunes of Arthur*
1591: *The Lord Mayors' Pageant*, 29th October (Woodword)
1592: *A Conference of Pleasure*
1594–95, Jan: *The Order of the Helmet* or *The Prince of Purpool*
1595: *The Device to the Indian Prince*

The Birth of Merlin was written anonymously.... The internal evidence indicates Francis as the author.

The Misfortunes of Arthur is the first tragedy with which his name is definitely connected. It is a good example of his early dramatic style. Collier reprinted it from the only copy that had survived, thus rescuing it from oblivion.... Collier remarks, "There is a richer and nobler vein of poetry running through it than is to be found in any other previous work of the kind, and the blank verse is generally free and flowing."* The names of the collaborators are given and among them is Francis Bacon.

A Conference of Pleasure was written by Francis Bacon for the Earl of Essex... for the Tilt-Yard Ceremonies. It represents "Four Friends" (as in the *French Académie*) meeting for intellectual amusement, each in turn delivering a speech in praise of whatever he holds to be "THE MOST WORTHY." (Note the Masonic phraseology):

1. The Praise of the Worthiest Virtue or Fortitude;
2. " " " Affection (Love);
3. " " " Power, Knowledge;
4. " " " Person, this Lady.

The last "Praise" was ostensibly a Praise of Queen Elizabeth, but covertly it was a Praise of Francis Bacon's Sovereign Lady, whom he terms "CROWNED TRUTH."...

The Order of the Helmet or *The Prince of Purpool (Purple)* gives a direct clue to Francis Bacon's secret activities.... For some reason the Christmas Revels in Gray's Inn had been intermitted for some three years or more. In the winter of 1594 the students resolved to produce *"something out of the common way."* Francis Bacon as usual was called in to *"recover the lost*

---

*J. Payne Collier, *The History of English Dramatic Poetry to the Time of Shakespeare: And Annals of the Stage to the Restoration* (London: John Murray, 1831).

honour of the Inn." The sports were to last for twelve days. Gray's Inn turned into a mimic Royal Court (not a Law Court) over which a Prince of Purpool (i.e. Purple indicative of his Royal Estate) ruled as the Master of Revels.[76]

Dodd continues with a description of the entertainment in which "the Prince, in royal purple, with all his State courtiers and servants, proceeded to the Great Hall of Gray's Inn, where he was enthroned with great pomp and ceremonial."[77]

This revelry is especially important, for it exemplified how Francis wove not only his story but esoteric meaning into his work. It was an extended yearly revelry, whose Grand Nights were spread out intermittently from Winter Solstice to Shrove Tuesday. On the Grand Night that took place on Innocents Day, *The Comedy of Errors* was performed for the first time. A few nights later, a second masque *The Order of the Helmet* brought order to the symbolic chaos created during the night of errors on Innocents Day.

This masque put Francis's secret work on public record in a way that kept suspicion at bay. It could simply be written off as entertainment. In it the students were sworn in, vowed to attack Ignorance, and defend Virtue and Truth *ceaselessly and secretly.* Dodd writes about the speeches of the counsellors that embody tenets in the societies created by Francis. "One Counsellor talks of a 'Blazing Star,' the *'EYE of the World* that both carrieth and useth LIGHT.'... 'You may have in *a small COMPASS* a Model of Universal Nature made PRIVATE'... 'a Palace fit for a Philosopher's STONE'... [the Ashlar]."[78]

Interior of Gray's Inn Hall
from a drawing by H. Crichmore

The Knights of the Helmet

*Love all, trust a few,
Do wrong to none.*

~ *All's Well That Ends Well,* act 1, sc. 1

The Order of the Helmet was the first of Francis's secret societies. As the entertainment portrays, Francis founded the Honorable Order of the Knights of the Helmet in reality. As sworn followers of Pallas Athena, each initiate was capped with her helmet that made her invisible. They followed in her footsteps and shook her spear at the serpent of ignorance. These spear-shakers secretly worked together to produce anonymous textbooks on a myriad of topics and English translations of the classics for the common people. Francis took the ancient wisdom and mystical teachings and wove them into beautiful dramas both tragic and comedic.

Pallas Athena

In 1579 there were practically no English books, pamphlets or newspapers.... Illiteracy was rampant. Francis and the "Knights of the Helmet" set out to alter the habits of Londoners and the nation. This could only be done by the construction of an adequate language and literature for both were then deficient in quantity and quality... Knowing what had been done by a handful of French poets, Francis was certain he could do the same for the country over which he hoped to rule as King. This possible contingency prevented him from writing anything over his own name; neither could he write too much under any one name lest the general public should think that it was "a one-man band." He must arouse curiosity among the people. There must be many names used, many initials, many anonymous publications, and controversial quarrels created between alleged authors to capture the ear of the general public. In order to create interest he must give the impression that there was a spontaneous uprush of Elizabethan literature, and that everybody everywhere had simultaneously begun to sing, to write, to play in order that England might be thought to be a nest of singing-birds. The English Renaissance, then, was not a spasmodic happening but the result of careful planning by Francis Bacon and his little band of Brethren.[79]

One of the golden mysteries behind the burst of literature in the Elizabethan age involves all of these great friends of Francis.

Arcadia

Rivers—yea though rivers roar,
  Roaring though sea-billows rise,
Vex the deep, and break the shore—
  Stronger art thou, Lord of skies!
  Firm and true thy promise lies
Now and still as heretofore:
  Holy worship never dies
In thy house where we adore.

~ Sir Philip Sidney, "Psalm XCIII"

Two of Francis's closest friends and partners in his mission were his cousins, Philip and Mary Sidney. They were the niece and nephew of Robert Dudley, his birth father. Mary and Francis were very close, having been born in the same year, growing up together, and enjoying the games, gardens, and entertainments of their family circle.

The three Sidney children, Robert, Philip, and Mary, were personally tutored by the Elizabethan "magus," Dr. John Dee, a friend of their mother, who herself led experiments in science and alchemy. Imagine the fun of exploring the elements, astronomy, literature, and philosophy with this group.

At the same time as Francis's sudden journey to France, Queen Elizabeth called young Mary Sidney to court as a lady-in-waiting. Mary became popular for her wit, learning, and beauty and was soon married to the wealthy Henry Herbert, Earl of Pembroke. The family home of Henry Herbert and Mary Sidney Herbert was at Wilton House near the river Avon in Wiltshire. Even John Aubrey's notes, which mostly recorded the salacious gossip of his time and should be read with discretion, describes Wilton House in Mary's time as in a learned light: "In her time Wilton house was like a College, there were so many learned and ingeniose persons. She was the greatest patronesse of witt and learning of any lady in her time. She was a great chymist and spent yearly a great deale in that study.... At Wilton is a good library...which was collected in this learned ladie's time.... This curious seate of Wilton and the adjacent countrey is an Arcadian place and a paradise."[80]

Philip Sidney (1554–1586)

It was at beautiful Wilton, in the company of his sister, Mary, that Sir Philip Sidney began to write his remarkable work, *The Countess of Pembroke's Arcadia*. It is a prose romance and was later used as a source for Shakespeare's plays *King Lear* and *Hamlet*. It was similar in tone to *As You Like It*. But before the work could be finished, Philip died from injuries sustained at the battle of Zutphen in the Netherlands in 1586; Mary completed the epic. It is one of the key Elizabethan works that developed the mystique of Elizabethan England with shepherd-princes, mistaken identities, lost loves, and the glory of nature.

The coming golden age, Arcadia, the longed-for Utopia, was the over-arching vision behind the writings of Francis as Immerito during this time.

Mary Sidney, the "dearly loved" cousin of Francis, hosted the ongoing gathering of poets, playwrights and wits, and the "good pens." And the Elizabethan songbirds produced their works.

Her two sons, William and Philip, grew up in this rarefied atmosphere. Francis had a lot to do with their growing-up years. They matured to become the "Most Noble and Incomparable Paire of Brethren" to whom Francis dedicated his First Folio of the Shakespeare plays.

Shake-Speares

The monuments of wit survive the monuments of power.
~ *Essex's Device*

The immortal name of Shakespeare appeared at this time. A perfect symbol for the Shaker-of-the-spears and the brilliant minds shielded by the helmet of Athena.

The most famous mask used was indeed that of William Shakespeare, or as it was published on the title page of the sonnets, "Shake-Speares." Francis paid an actor from Stratford for the use of his fortuitous name of Shakspur. Imagine the hilarity that ensued when the idea dawned on Francis and his "good pens" that the rowdy actor's name was so close to their role as servants of Pallas Athena, shaking her spear at ignorance.

In the plays written under this name, Francis and his spear-shakers used upward of twenty thousand distinct words. The average number of words used by an Elizabethan commoner was only around five hundred. They gave English speakers approximately two thousand completely new words, adding depth and subtlety to what could be communicated outside of Latin. With plays, textbooks, and translations published in anonymous pamphlets, they instigated public interest in reading, and broke the chains of illiteracy that had been used to control the common people. New and unusual ideas were born in the minds of many.

This expansion of language matters more than simply a note on vocabulary. Language is the framework by which people structure their thoughts, and with an expanded vocabulary, new thoughts are possible. Francis and his secret scriveners were expanding the regions of English thought. The ideas would spread to create a new kingdom of thought and philosophy worldwide.

Francis was loved by many, even those who did not see the full scope of his life's dedication to the world. Those who simply met him for a meal were given his full regard and kindness. Dr. Rawly, Francis Bacon's private chaplain and literary executor wrote:

> His Meals were Reflections of the Ear as well as of the Stomach, like the *Noctes Atticae*, or *Convivia Deipno-Sophistarum*,* wherein a Man might be refreshed in his Mind and Understanding no less than in his Body. And I have known some, of no mean Parts, that have professed to make use of their Note-Books, when they have risen from his Table. In which Conversations, and otherwise, he was no Dashing Man, as some Men are, but ever a Countenancer and Fosterer of another Mans Parts. Neither was he one that would appropriate the Speech wholly to himself, or delight to out-vie others, but leave a liberty to the Co-Assessors to take their turns. Wherein he would draw a Man on, and allure him, to speak upon such a subject, as wherein he was peculiarly skillful, and would delight to speak. And for himself, he condemned no Mans Observations, but would light his Torch at every Mans Candle.[81]

Noctes Atticae [Latin, "Attic nights"]: references the work of the Roman author, Aulus Gellius. *Convivia Deipno-sophistarum* [Latin, "convivial banquets of the sophists"]

The creation of the plays came with their own danger. Francis first wrote *Hamlet* when he was twenty, but it was not officially printed by "Shakespeare" until after his mother's death. In his word cipher, Francis tells how Leicester discovered him directing actors in the rehearsal of *Hamlet* during his first years at Gray's Inn. Leicester berated Francis and took the matter to the Queen.

> *My mother learn'd that I wrote Hamlet, Prince of Denmark,*
> *And then I was lost....*
>
> . . . .
>
> "*My father leaves me, and stirred with rage*
> *Goes to the Queen, my mother, and tells her*
> *I played with the idle company,*
> *And that I 'came th' philosopher to fool my friends.*
>   "'*I do assure your majesty,' said he,*
> '*I saw him yesternight, in a most murd'rous play*
> *Take part, and I beseech your royal majesty*
> *To let him have all th' rigour of the law.*'"[82]

Leicester told the Queen that Francis had spoken against duty and obedience to her. Angered, the Queen sent for Francis and, once all others had departed the chamber, upbraided him.

> "'*You personate our person,*
> *Do you, among the city wits and act*
> *Your mother's death? You, the immediate heir of England.*'"

She continued to rail at him for his treachery. Francis defended himself, and they argued back and forth.

> "'*Let me now, my son, see how thou hast perform'd*
> *The slaughter of the prince that ow'd the crown,*
> *And the dire death of the Danish king.*
> *Now that thou speakest boy, like a good child*
> *And a true gentleman, I'll ope my arms thus wide,*
> *And will, with cheer and comfort, throw to earth*
> *This unprevailing woe. Hie to thy chamber,*
> *Find thy toys....*'
>   "'*My mother dost pardon me;' I muse, and I imagine*

*My humble and smooth answer was like oil
Unto the wound, whereby it 'gan to heal,
And that she was mollified....*

. . . .

*As a personal favor to my mother, I brought
My cause of sorrow (the first copy of Hamlet)
To the palace. When I brought to her
The best of my matter, she, ere my hand
Had settled down, in passion did tear it
From my bosom, and without even reading it,
Tore it in twain, and sans remorse, put it,
Into the fire."*[83]

This episode did not stop Francis. Through it can be seen the edge that he walked along. One misstep could take him past what the Queen would forgive.

The Shakespeare Notebook

*How can my Muse want Subject
to Invent...?*

~ Shakespeare, "Sonnet 38"

Francis kept a notebook, which he called his *Promus of Formularies and Elegancies.* It is a collection of manuscripts or folios that is a veritable sourcebook of words and phrases all written by Francis, a large number of which were used in the Shakespeare plays. There are over 1,655 entries, all in Francis's handwriting, and they seem to have been collected for use in drama and literature.

As Peter Dawkins puts it, "Bacon appears to have set out not only to furnish the English language with more words but also more phrases and expressions for everyday use, often based on a rich background of foreign languages or deeper esoteric thought."[84]

Peter Dawkins gives credit to the researchers whose work has led the way in the centuries-old game of hide-and-seek.

We owe a debt of gratitude to Mrs Pott and other researchers. ... As a result of their work, it can now be readily seen that not only are the observations and expressions noted down in

Bacon's *Promus* used extensively in the Shakespeare plays but also that Bacon's *Essays* and other philosophical writings provide the history and "tables of invention", together with the philosophical ideas, out of which the Shakespeare plays are constructed. Bacon has done all this so that the life of man can be presented to our eyes, so that we may see ourselves as if in a mirror, dramatically, and learn from the experience.[85]

Francis, as a spiritual adept, realized that for our society to advance in consciousness, we had to see ourselves, our dramas, and our psychological patterns in order to become free.

As Francis often pointed out, thought is free.

The Actor and the Adept

Alas, 'tis true, I have gone here and there
And made myself a Motley to the view,
Gored mine own thoughts, sold cheap what is most dear,
Made old offences of affections new;
Most true it is, that I have look'd on Truth
Askance and strangely: But by all above,
These blenches gave my heart another youth,
And worse essays proved thee my best of love.
Now all is done, have what shall have no end:
Mine appetite I never more will grind
On newer proof, to try an older friend,
A God in Love, to whom I am confined.
    Then give me welcome, next my Heaven the best,
    Even to thy pure and most, most loving breast

~ Shakespeare, "Sonnet 110"

In comparison to Francis Bacon, the actor Shakspur inspired very little to be written about him. Accused as a poacher, Shakspur left his family in Stratford and journeyed to London to look for work. He found employment as a horse and carriage valet outside a theater and gradually found additional work as a bit-part actor. Shakspur

Falstaff

was a crude and cunning man but found his niche in four stage plays, gaining fame in the comical role of Falstaff. Sir John Falstaff was a literary foil to exemplify both the mask and the man that was Shakespeare—the author and the actor inhabiting one character. Margaret Barsi-Greene writes, "Falstaff [False-staff = dummy], with his dual character of arrant knave and prodigious wit, represents the false and the real Shakespeare, inferring that Shakespeare was not one person but two. Another interpretation depicts the human and the super-human personality."[86] The inner teaching is hidden there, that each person has his* own personality mask and true self. Perhaps each one of us is a Falstaff learning to become a Francis.

Francis thought the brash nature of Shakspur would be both funny and illuminating for audiences. The character Falstaff in *Henry IV*, parts 1 and 2, and *The Merry Wives of Windsor*, as well as Sir Toby Belch in *Twelfth Night* was written to be played by Shakspur. The Falstaff character became very popular, and even Queen Elizabeth made inquiries about him, thinking he was the actual author of the Shakespeare plays. Francis describes Shakspur in cipher:

> *It shall bee noted in truth that some greatly exceede their fellowes in worth, and it is easily explained. Th' theame varied, yet was always a subject well selected to convey the secret message. Also the plays being given out as tho'gh written by the actor to whom each had bin consign'd, turne one's genius suddainelie many times to suit th' new man.*
>
> *In this actour that wee now emploie, is a wittie veyn different from any formerly employ'd. In truth it suiteth well with a native spirit, humourous and grave by turnes in ourselfe.*[87]

---

*Because gender-neutral pronouns can be cumbersome, we have used he/him/his to refer to God or the individual. This is for readability only and not intended to exclude women or the feminine aspect of the Godhead.

In early Elizabethan times, playwrights and actors were considered disreputable, and initially theaters were linked with ale houses and crime. Unlike the courtly Masques and Entertainments, women were barred from participating. Besides Lords sponsoring players, gentlemen and ladies did not associate with the theater and so there was little financial incentive for writers, actors, and entrepreneurs to stage plays. From the 1580s, Francis gradually changed the situation by masterminding a new collaborative environment for hundreds of actors, stage crews and writers, providing a steady flow of quality dramas and comedies that delighted the public and made theaters profitable. By 1626 his vision had borne fruit through hundreds of stage plays, many new theaters, and a richer language. Although Cecil's informers were sent to work in the theaters, Francis remained a free man.

It is possible, by reading through the hundreds of play titles,* to discern the common denominator of Francis's bright sense of humor, as well as his scholarly side, among the names of his friends and colleagues, such as:

> Francis Beaumont (*A King and No King*, 1611)
> William Camden (*Annales: Reign of Elizabeth*, 1615)
> George Chapman (*An Humorous Day's Mirth*, 1597)
> Henry Chettle (*The Tragedy of Hoffman*, 1602)
> Samuel Daniel (*Collection of the History of England*, 1612)
> John Day (*Law Tricks*, 1608)
> Thomas Dekker (*If This Be Not a Good Play*, 1611)
> Dudley Digges (*Rights and Privileges of the Subject*, 1642)
> John Donne (*An Anatomy of the World*, 1611)
> Thomas Hobbes (*Leviathan*, 1651)

By 1626 more than a hundred pseudonyms masked Francis's work. For his part, Will Shakspur, the actor the Queen so enjoyed, died in 1616 in Stratford after buying the largest house in town with his portion of theater ticket sales and rights for the use of his name. In the matter of the authorship of the Shakespeare plays, Francis remained alive by the maxim, "to know, to dare, to do, and to be silent."

---

*An expanded list can be found in the Appendices at http://www.SummitUniversityPress.com/secrets-appendices.

The consequences of Francis Bacon's necessary precautions meant that there has been no literary puzzle in all history more baffling than the mystery of who wrote the plays published under the name of William Shakespeare. Thirty-eight plays, one hundred and fifty-four sonnets, two long narrative poems, and the enigmatic *Phoenix and the Turtle*, all have been considered for four hundred years to be the absolute peak of literary, poetic, dramatic, and philosophic excellence. The *Encyclopedia Americana* calls Shakespeare the greatest author in any language, ancient or modern, claiming that his plays have been performed more frequently and more steadily than any others ever written.

Peter Brook (1925–2022), director of the innovative theater movement in England, lamented that even now, after four centuries, no writer using any medium has yet been able to top the Bard. Richard Green, author of *A Short History of the English People*, speaks of the amazing burst of literary excellence in the last twenty years of Elizabeth Tudor's eventful reign, noting that the first public theater was built in England in the middle of the Queen's reign. By the time of her death, eighteen theaters existed in London alone.

James Reeves, in his *A Short History of English Poetry, 1340–1940,* observes that "Nothing is more remarkable in the whole

Original Globe Theater, c. 1612, London

history of English literature than the sudden flowering that took place during the last twenty years of Elizabeth's reign.... There is no accounting for the appearance at this time of the greatest poetic genius of all time; but it can at least be said that if genius is in any way to be attributed to the spirit of the age, Shakespeare emerged at the moment when he might most confidently be expected. All our judgements of the Elizabethan poets are made under the shadow of Shakespeare."[88]

Collier's Encyclopedia calls Shakespeare "the world's best storyteller" and claims that the themes in these plays have universal appeal and that their characters are not types but living men and women, so real that they are often mistaken for actual historical figures. It is estimated that the Shakespeare plays added more than fifteen thousand words to the English language and that his writings are quoted more often than any others, with the exception of the King James Version of the Bible. The translations from original scriptural sources into English for the King James Bible were also supervised by Francis Bacon, as editor-in-chief under royal commission from King James.

The high esteem held for the Shakespeare plays has magnified the problem concerning proof of their authorship. In a time when books were rare, how could a poor actor from a Warwickshire village have acquired the education and the cultural and philosophical understanding to have written dramatic poetry of such undisputed excellence? The plays indicate an intimate acquaintance with royalty and the heads of state. How could an uneducated worker living in rural England have become so well-informed about ancient myths, foreign landscapes, languages, customs and affairs that were the express privilege of the aristocracy alone? Would the man who created such heroines as Beatrice, Portia, and Viola let his own daughter grow up illiterate?

Scholars who question the authorship of the Shakespearean plays understand that whoever the author was, he held a noble view of man and his pivotal place in the great chain of being, connecting life on earth with life in the universe. He understood the depth and strength of love in its purest form.

Let me not to the Marriage of True Minds
Admit impediments: Love is not love
Which alters when it alteration finds,
Or Bends with the Remover to remove:
O, no! it is an ever-fixed Mark
That looks on Tempests and is never shaken;
It is the Star to every wand'ring bark,
Whose Worth's unknown, although his Height be taken.
Love's not Time's Fool, though rosy lips and cheeks
Within his bending Sickle's compass come;
Love alters not with his Brief Hours and Weeks,
But bears it out even to the Edge of Doom.
    If this be Error and upon me prov'd,
    I never writ, nor no man ever lov'd.

~ Shakespeare, "Sonnet 116"

Could these lines have been written by the same person who chose for his tombstone in Stratford-on-Avon the epitaph reading:

Good friend for Jesus' sake forbeare,
To dig the dust enclosed here.
Blest be ye man that spares these stones,
And curst be he that moves my bones.

Bust of Shakespeare at Shakespeare's funerary monument
Photo by Sicinius: creativecommons.org/licenses/by-sa/4.0.

The tone of the epitaph is reminiscent of some of Bottom's lines in *Midsummer Night's Dream*.

Where were the eulogies in Latin and scholarly treatises released following "William Shakespeare's" death in a Stratford alehouse 1616? There were none, not for Will Shakspur, the Falstaff actor, or for William Shakespeare, the pseudonym.

Recorded documents show only six signatures in Shakspur's name, all of them scrawled and inconsistent. There were no rights for stage plays listed in Shakspur's will or any mention of books, only instructions that his wife should receive his second-best bed. The original manuscripts for the Shakespeare plays have never been found. Amazingly, four hundred years later, the majority of the world's literary academics brush aside the authorship conundrum and believe the Bard was at face value Shakspur of Stratford.

A Member of Parliament

Every subject's duty is the king's;
But every subject's soul is his own.

~ Henry V, act 4, sc. 1

After only one year into his residence at Gray's Inn, Francis joined Parliament. He was ever a champion of the so-called common man and his rights. That same year he traveled again to Europe, writing a report of his travels to Lord Burghley and the Queen in a state paper entitled *Notes on the Present State of Christendom*. This report included information from Anthony and another of Walsingham's intelligencers. Though the report centered on Venice, Mantua, Savoy, Genoa, and Florence, it also covered France, Spain, Italy, Portugal, Austria, Germany, Poland, Denmark, and Sweden. Information, descriptions, and language gleaned from this trip made its way into the Shakespeare plays. As the report was not made public until 1734, this is another proof that the actor did not write the plays.

From both of his trips to Europe, Francis had collected his observations.

> He carefully recorded his and others' emotions, thoughts, words and actions as they arose. He studied his own and others' characters and life-styles, love-affairs, politics, ambitions and prejudices, successes and failures, as also the characteristics of plants and trees, herbs and medicines, animals and birds; of water, air, earth (particularly crystals and gem-stones) and fire (especially sun-light), together with the spiritual nature of all these....

> From his "Tables of Experience" Francis drew forth the "meat" for his plays which he began to write, publish and produce after his return to England. Inspired and guided by his "Muse" (Pallas Athena) he composed series after series of dramas based upon real life experiences or "history", drawing forth from his collection of tabulated history whatever was required for any play....
>
> And in all these dramatic works, as also in his other philosophical and poetical works, is scattered the carefully broken and divided "Word Cipher" story, employed in the literary and dramatic works in various ways—apt, scintillating, humorous, obscure or even plainly ridiculous: but such is the power of his creativity and language that all these usages have, on the whole, withstood the ravages of time, critics, editors, scholars and audience—even the seeming ridiculous and incredulous passages.[89]

In these early years in Parliament, Francis wrote state papers that made a name for himself and exemplified his ethics and call for unity. When he was twenty-eight, he penned *An Advertisement Touching the Controversies of the Church of England*. In it he reminded the various religious factions that the primary object of religion was to build the Holy City of God on the Commandment to "love thy neighbor as thyself." He warned that antagonisms within religion always ended in bloodshed. In this meditation can be read that outer declaration of the philosophy he had already incorporated into his secret societies. Francis held high the ideals of brotherhood and love.

An earlier paper written when he was twenty-three likewise portrays his way of thinking as well as proves he was no mere law student. For what young law student newly elected to the House of Commons would dare write *A Letter of Advice to Queen Elizabeth*? In it he gives sage guidance for the governing of the kingdom and admonishes against religious persecution. In an age that often saw people burned at the stake for their beliefs, Francis urged the Queen to show religious tolerance. Francis continued to write state papers throughout his career, each one intent on nudging England closer to her possible Utopia.

In 1587 the situation with Mary, Queen of Scots came to a tragic end. In his biliteral cipher, Francis recorded the truth of her death and the grave crime that was committed to make it happen.

> *Soone there was a secret interview betweene Lord Burleigh [and] Earle of Leicester, to which was summoned the Queene's Secretary who was so threaten'd by his lordship—on paine of death, et cætera, th' poor fool—that hee sign'd for the Queene, and affixed th' great seale to the dreadful death-warrant.*
>
> *The life of the Secretarie was forfeit to the deede when Her Majesty became aware that so daring a crime had beene committed, but who shall say that the blow fell on the guilty head; for, truth to say, Davison was onely a poor feeble instrument in their handds, and life seem'd to hang in th' ballance, therefore blame doth fall on those men, great and noble though they be, who led him to his death.*
>
> *This sheweth any who have thought Elizabeth too severe to her cousin that, though she had prudence sufficiente to keepe her arch-enemie in seclusion, by no meanes was th' heart in that faire bosom so flintie as to send th' unfortunate woman to her death before her time.*[90]

Brothers United

The man nearest my soul,
Who like a brother toiled in my affairs...

~ *Henry IV*, part 2, act 3, sc. 1

When Anthony returned from his twelve years of intelligence work in Europe, he joined Francis in his great endeavor and the Shake-Scene gained momentum. Imagine the happiness of the brothers united again. With both of their experiences to draw from, the plays referenced a wide swath of recent events in European history and historic figures. About Anthony's time in Europe, Alfred Dodd wrote:

> Some weeks later Anthony went to the Continent for a prolonged stay, travelling to Paris, Bordeaux, Navarre, and Italy...

quietly following in the footsteps of Francis.... All this time he was fitting himself by his wide acquaintance with all sorts and conditions of men, and Continental customs and foreign affairs, to *become the first secret agent abroad of the great Queen*, the collector and purveyor through trusty channels of vital information dispatched in code respecting the moves and intentions of the Queen's enemies.... Moreover, he had another mission to perform: to lay the foundation-stones of Francis Bacon's Secret Societies on the Continent and to cement the ties already made by Francis; for Anthony was a wholehearted enthusiast in Francis Bacon's ideals and designs. He was the first man to know in its entirety the vastness of the plans which Francis had made and the means whereby they could be marked out.[91]

With Anthony back in Britain, Francis's grand scheme took flight. In 1592 two more "new stars" appeared in Cassiopeia.[92] These novas (smaller than the supernova of 1572) were perfect celestial heralds of the partnership of Francis and Anthony and the great work of their literary circle. Though several Shakespeare plays had been produced already (the earliest being 1588), the full pen name of "William Shakespeare" became official with the publication of the two poems *Venus and Adonis* and *The Rape of Lucretia* in 1593 and 1594.

Just before *Lucretia* was published, Anthony took a house in Bishopsgate Street, right in the midst of the playhouses where the Shakespeare plays were performed. The Queen released the lease of Twickenham to Francis in 1595, and there the "good pens" gathered for their great work. Though often in financial straits and with Lord Burghley and his son Robert Cecil working against them, Francis and

Anthony Bacon in 1594

Anthony successfully lived triple lives—the public one of Bacon's sons working in Parliament, law and the court, the clandestine cipher work as intelligencers for Sir Walsingham and the Queen, all while being the secret epicenter of a hidden cultural revolution. The breadth of their undertaking is incomparable. It is the stuff of legends and the sign of the spiritual adeptship of Francis.

The Rose Cross

Since Brass, nor Stone, nor Earth, nor boundless Sea
But sad mortality o'er-sways their power,
How with this rage shall Beauty hold a plea,
Whose action is no stronger than a flower?
O, how shall Summer's Honey Breath hold out
Against the wrackful Siege of Batt'ring Days,
When rocks impregnable are not so stout,
Nor gates of steel so strong, but Time decays?
O fearful meditation! Where, alack,
Shall Time's Best Jewel from Time's Chest lie hid?
Or what strong hand can hold his swift foot back?
Or who his spoil or beauty can forbid?
  O, none, unless this Miracle have might,
  That in Black Ink my Love may still Shine Bright.

~ Shakespeare, "Sonnet 65"

Initially, the Knights of the Helmet included only several of Francis and Anthony's friends, then it transformed into the Fra. Rosi Crosse, or Fraternity of the Rose Cross. The concepts of secrecy and invisibility carried over into the Fra. Rosi Cross. All of their works and communications were marked by codes that only they could identify. This was not a game to them but a necessity, because English society at the time had no tolerance for anyone exercising any deviation from orthodoxy in religious symbology or doctrine.

Eventually the Fra. Rosi Crosse expanded into two groups with different aspects. The Fraternity of the Rose Cross remained a secret mystical society, organized around ancient wisdom teachings and the spiritual principles behind the original Knights Templar and the path of spiritual initiation. Francis founded Speculative Freemasonry to be more public, building on the older English Freemasonic order said to be founded by Saint Alban and the mutually supportive moral principles of the ancient trade guilds. Both societies were to teach wisdom in graded steps as a means toward self-transformation.

The concept of self-transformation for humanity, as the incremental imitation of Christ, was and is central to both societies and eventually leads to the highest ritual of the alchemical marriage (the allegorical bride of the Lamb). The individual's initiatic progress toward this goal is the key to Baconian Rosicrucianism.

The tenets of the Rosicrucian Society included the spiritual underpinnings of a future nation that would remain stable and prosperous without a monarchy. While this tenet was, in effect, treasonous in any European nation, Francis saw the tyranny of his own family and of all monarchs as an entitlement that would always smother the prosperity and freedom of the people. Though still tied tightly to his monarch, Francis saw the need for a future self-governing nation under God and imagined that it could be planned, it could be done, even if by future generations.

Spedding translated an unpublished Latin "proem," or preface, that Francis had left to be found after he had gone. It is a declaration of his life's meaning and mission:

> Believing that I was born for the service of mankind, and regarding the care of the commonwealth as a kind of common property which like the air and the water belongs to everybody, I set myself to consider in what way mankind might be best served, and what service I was myself best fitted by nature to perform.
>
> Now among all the benefits that could be conferred upon mankind, I found none so great as the discovery of new arts, endowments, and commodities for the bettering of man's life. For I saw that among the rude people in the primitive times the authors of rude inventions and discoveries were consecrated and numbered among the gods. And it was plain that the good

effects wrought by founders of cities, law-givers, fathers of the people, extirpers of tyrants, and heroes of that class, extend but over narrow spaces and last but for short times; whereas the work of the inventor, though a thing of less pomp and show, is felt everywhere and lasts forever. But above all, if a man could succeed, not in striking out some particular invention, however useful, but in kindling a light in nature,—a light which should in its very rising touch and illuminate all the border-regions that confine upon the circle of our present knowledge; and so spreading further and further should presently disclose and bring into sight all that is most hidden and secret in the world,—that man (I thought) would be the benefactor indeed of the human race, the propagator of man's empire over the universe, the champion of liberty, the conqueror and subduer of necessities.

For myself, I found that I was fitted for nothing so well as for the study of Truth; as having a mind nimble and versatile enough to catch the resemblances of things (which is the chief point), and at the same time steady enough to fix and distinguish their subtler differences; as being gifted by nature with desire to seek, patience to doubt, fondness to meditate, slowness to assert, readiness to reconsider, carefulness to dispose and set in order; and as being a man that neither affects what is new nor admires what is old, and that hates every kind of imposture. So I thought my nature had a kind of familiarity and relationship with Truth....

...I am not hunting for fame; I have no desire to found a sect, after the fashion of heresiarchs; and to look for any private gain from such an undertaking as this, I count both ridiculous and base. Enough for me the consciousness of well-deserving, and those real and effectual results with which Fortune itself cannot interfere.[93]

The foundational Rosicrucian pamphlets that Francis had helped author while in Europe were now published. *The Fame of the Brotherhood of the Rosy Cross* was published in Cassel, Germany in 1614, followed by *The Confession of the Brotherhood of the Rosy Cross* in 1615, and *The Chymical Wedding of Christian Rosenkreutz* in 1617.

The Secret Mysteries of Francis and the Brethren

> *It is true, that a little Philosophy inclineth Mans Minde to* Atheisme; *But depth in Philosophy, bringeth Mens Mindes about to* Religion: *For while the Minde of Man, looketh upon Second Causes Scattered, it may sometimes rest in them, and goe no further: But when it beholdeth, the Chaine of them, Confederate and Linked together, it must needs flie to* Providence, *and* Deitie.
>
> ~ Bacon, *Essays*, "Of Atheisme"

Creating a revolution in thought, culture, religion, government, law, and science during a time of tyranny and absolute rule takes a certain fearlessness and fiery vision. Francis and his friends were lit within by the same fire.

As researchers have discovered, there is a great mystery about the life, aims, and works of Francis Bacon. The secrets of this group made all of their dynamic work possible. Here are a few that stand out from Mrs. Henry Pott's *Francis Bacon and His Secret Society:*[94]

1. Bacon's own cataloguing of deep prevailing darkness of his era and the ignorance. He wrote up the deficiencies of learning in his time, covering forty different departments of learning. Yet we are taught to believe in an outburst of literary genius—giant minds—simultaneously all over the world during this same age. Yet Bacon's analysis of deficiencies have never been refuted or challenged.
2. The Rosicrucian rules forbid the publication of author's names, even in their own books. They adopted mottos, used fake initials and names.
3. Francis Bacon's remarkable personal library disappeared and its whereabouts are a mystery. Like Prospero, his books were more dear to him than any of his outer offices of state or public life. He said, "I to my state grew stranger being transported and rapt in secret studies." And "he furnished me from my private library with volumes I prize above my dukedom." Where did his prized books go?

4. Francis referred to his manuscripts in his will as in his "cabinets, boxes, presses." Think of the quantity of writings suggested by those words. These were to be taken possession of by three trustees: Constable, Selden, and Herbert and to be by them published by degrees. But of books, he left not a word.
5. There is a marvelous similarity in the English literature, a decided resemblance in thought, opinion, knowledge, and diction. The unusual word-use and vocabulary is the same among these authors.
6. This likeness extends to foreign works as well, especially when they appear as translations. Many of these translations appear to be the originals.
7. It is impossible for one man, however gigantic his intellectual power, to have performed alone all that which was believed to have been done and written by Francis Bacon.
8. The *Promus:* this is Francis Bacon's own notebook of private manuscript notes listing new phraseology, newly coined words, turns of expression, metaphors, proverbial sayings from five or six languages.
9. Bacon's method: he designed the exquisite system which still exists for the reception, arrangement, integration and widespread distribution of knowledge. Upon her research, Mrs. Henry Pott said, "the organization or 'method of transmission' which he established was such as to ensure that never again, so long as the world endured, should the lamp of tradition, the light of truth, be darkened or extinguished; but that, continually trimmed and replenished with the oil of learning, it should be kept alight, a little candle in a dark place, or a beacon set upon a hill, burning with undimmed and perpetual brightness."[95]
10. Entries in his private notes, hints in his letters and acknowledged works indicate his faith in the efficacy of united efforts. Besides the mystery around himself, there is a mystery around his dearest friends and relations.
11. The mirror of the Bacon and Shakespeare works: Between the Shakespeare and Bacon works is a harmony of forty thousand metaphors and similes. This cannot be coincidence.
12. The use of ciphers was an important part of a learned education in Elizabethan England. "Tragedies and comedies are made of one alphabet"—Francis Bacon in cipher.[96]

The keynote of the new golden age to come is *brotherhood,* and collaboration is the way. These friends seemed to have worked to the same universal ends and perfectly understood his coded language. There was also a great mystery involving these same friends.

Many fellow researchers all seem to fall in love with the spirit of Francis. As his biographer James Spedding and Mrs. Pott discovered, Francis, from all the evidence, "was the centre of a powerful and learned secret society, and that the whole of literature contemporaneous with him was bound together by chains and links, cords and threads, forged, woven, and spun *by himself.*"[97]

The Mysterious Spirit of Francis

There is no reason why there should not be stars above stars til they go beyond our sight.

~ *Descriptio Globi Intellectualis*

There are spiritual mysteries as well as literary ones surrounding Francis and his secret societies. He was so unusual in his talents, breadth of knowledge, and most keenly, in his determination to free the world from ignorance and drudgery that the words *adept* and *spiritual master* come to mind.

He claimed a specific divine plan, to resurrect the ancient wisdom, mystical devotion, the rule of true law and the protection of individual rights. He aimed to found new countries and a new system of governance. He wanted to create a new language that would be used globally for education and the arts.

Francis was here to regenerate the old secret societies and mystery schools for the growth of culture and for spiritual brotherhood.

He determined to create a new distribution system for scientific experimentation, education, and all learning. He re-created society so that the path of personal Christhood could be possible and thrive.

And Prince Francis believed and practiced direct contact with the heavenly messengers and his divine muse, or sponsoring masters.

Baconian Gardens

And this our life, exempt from public haunt,
Finds tongues in trees, books in the running brooks,
Sermons in stones, and good in everything.

~ *As You Like It,* act 2, sc. 1

In 1597 the gardens at Gray's Inn were laid out under the direction of Francis. Here can be seen how his genius was not only one of shaping words but of shaping space as well. In everything he did, his aim was to bring the world a little closer to paradise. In his essay "Of Gardens" Francis wrote:

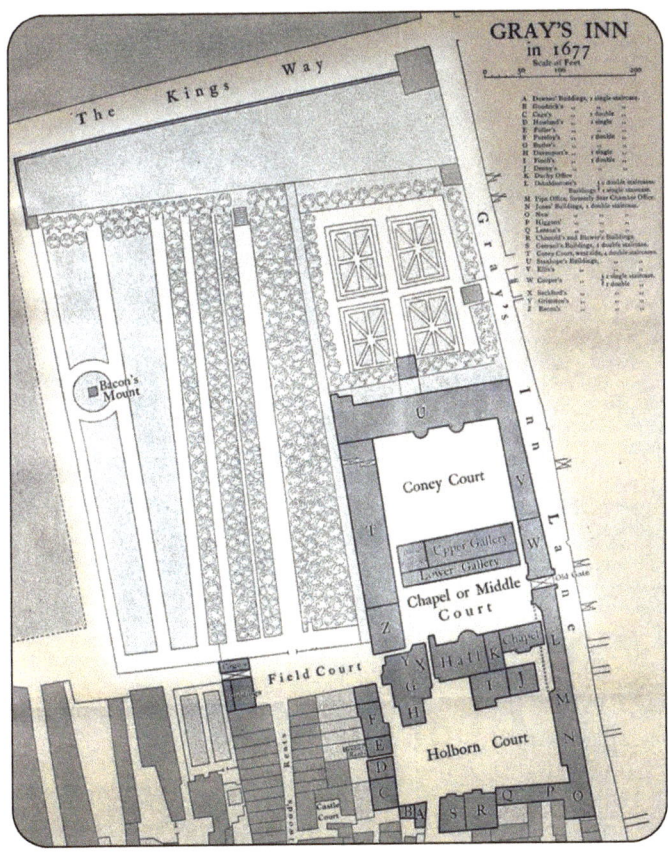

Gray's Inn Gardens, known as "the Walks," designed by Sir Francis Bacon in 1608

GOD *Almightie* first Planted a *Garden.* And indeed, it is the Purest of Humane pleasure. It is the Greatest Refreshment to the Spirits of Man; Without which *Buildings* and *Pallaces* are but Grosse Handy-works: And a Man shall ever see, that when Ages grow to Civility and Elegancie, Men come to *Build Stately,* sooner then to *Garden Finely:* As if *Gardening* were the Greater Perfection.[98]

Through the course of his life, Francis also designed the parks of Twickenham and Gorhambury as well as the gardens of York House and Canonbury House. The remains of the Water Garden that he designed at Gorhambury still exist today, though without the water.

The historian, William Hepworth Dixon wrote of Twickenham:

It had all the points of a good country-house; a green landscape, wood and water, pure air, a dry soil, vicinity to the Court and to the town. From his windows he could peer into the Queen's alleys; in an hour he could trot up to Whitehall or Gray's Inn.

Every plant that thrives, every flower that blows, in the south of England, loves the Twickenham soil. There were cedars in the great park, swans on the river, singing-birds in the copse; every sight to engage the eye, every sound to please the ear. He loved the house, and lived in it when he could steal away from Gray's Inn. It was his house of letters and philosophy, as the lodging in Gray's Inn Square was his house of politics and law.[99]

Francis named it his "Gardens of Paradise," writing that it was "my pleasure and my dwelling."[100]

A garden at Gray's Inn

Portia and Belmont

Haply I think on Thee, and then my State,
(Like to the lark at break of day arising)
From sullen earth sings hymns at heaven's gate;
  For thy sweet love remembered such wealth brings
  That then I scorn to change my State with Kings.

~ Shakespeare, "Sonnet 29"

Within walking distance of Gray's Inn lay Hatton House, known for its exquisite gardens. Lady Elizabeth Hatton was the daughter of Lord Burghley's eldest son, Sir Thomas Cecil and the cousin to Robert Cecil, the self-styled enemy of Francis. She was vivacious, witty and beautiful, and a dear friend to Francis from childhood. She had married Lord Hatton at seventeen at the behest of her family, and when he died in 1597, she inherited Hatton House, Corfe Castle, and the Isle of Purbeck.

In the gardens of Hatton House, Francis and Elizabeth walked, talked, and laughed. They were equals and friends. He courted Elizabeth and requested her hand in marriage. In *The Merchant of Venice*, the courtship of Portia not only symbolizes the soul's search for "Sophia (Wisdom) on her Mountain of Beauty (Belmont)" but also Francis's own courtship of Elizabeth. The play embodies Francis's hope set in the beautiful gardens of Hatton House, as Portia's home of Belmont.[101]

There is yet a third deeper meaning for Francis's soul within this play. For the character of Portia, Francis drew from more than his affection for Elizabeth. Portia embodies the qualities of Francis's divine counterpart, his great love not just from this life as Francis, but his eternal Beloved.

Sadly for Francis, Elizabeth submitted to family pressure and married Sir Edward Coke, Lord Burghley and Robert Cecil's political ally. So did the enemies of Prince Francis align to block his path.

The Northumberland Manuscript

Historians have remarked how odd it is that Francis Bacon never mentioned Shakespeare or the immortal plays, especially as he had made such a bold analysis of the deficiencies of learning in his time. Yet one original manuscript from this time has been found, written around 1597. It is an intriguing mystery. This remarkable discovery is a forgotten handwritten file of manuscripts holding both unpublished works by Bacon and unpublished plays under Shakespeare's name, as well as actual quotes and wordplay from the published plays. Called the "Bacon-Shakespeare" or "Northumberland Manuscript," it is discussed by Baconian researchers because of its priceless contents and the implications of its handwritten cover. Its original contents listed philosophical and poetic writings by Bacon, original Shakespeare plays, and *Leicester's Commonwealth*, which was printed secretly in Europe in 1584 and forbidden in England. Here is how the manuscript came to light. In 1867, during a construction project at Northumberland House, a manuscript folder[102] was discovered, which evidently had been Francis Bacon's property at one time.[103] It contained a listing of some of the plays accredited to Shakespeare as well as Bacon's works. It also had numerous signatures and spellings of Francis and Shakespeare's names and a play on the syllables of the longest word in Shakespeare from *Love's Labour's Lost*—Honorificabilitudinitatibus. A word that Francis loved to play with.

> It is the only Elizabethan document that has both the names Shakespeare and Francis Bacon written together. The Northumberland Manuscript is a valuable contemporary document which, although somewhat damaged by a fire in old Northumberland House, survives to prove that "Shakespeare's" Manuscripts of *Richard II* and *Richard III* were once tied up in a portfolio with Francis Bacon's *Conference of Pleasure*, some speeches, Nash's *Isle of Dogs* and an old play that is lost.... On the back side of the cover are the words "put into type."[104]

Much of the handwriting on the contents sheet has been judged to be from John Davies, who was one of Francis's "good pens." His profession was a scrivener, and his duty was to copy documents for his employers.

In *The Shakespeare Enigma*, Peter Dawkins notes that "not only is Francis Bacon's name closely associated with the name of William Shakespeare on this private manuscript from Bacon's scrivenery, but also the association of the Shakespeare name with plays as well as poems occurs on this manuscript before it was used in print on the plays."[105]

On another portion of the cover is written, "'Anthony Comfort and consorte', referring to Anthony Bacon. This may be a secretarial note or reminder of the words to be included in the dedication to Anthony that prefaces the first edition of Francis Bacon's *Essays*, which were printed early in 1598."[106] Additional notes on the manuscript such as "your lovinge ffriend," Dawkins notes, "are so personal that they sound as if they were quickly jotted down directly from Francis Bacon's dictation, so as not to be forgotten. Francis's habit, in which he involved his whole group of 'good pens', was to note down any and every passing thought, word or phrase, read, heard or invented, that might be useful or that he had decided to use."[107]

The Earl of Northumberland at the time of Francis Bacon was Sir Henry Percy. He lived from 1564 to 1632. His house was called Syon House and was near York House. He was also a friend and student of Dr. John Dee.

Sir Henry Percy is also known as the Wizard Earl for his achievements in science and alchemy, his passion for cartography, and his large library. In 1594 he became part of Francis's circle through

Henry Percy, 9th Earl of Northumberland KG (1564–1632), *The Wizard Earl* painting by Sir Anthony Van Dyck

his marriage to Robert Devereux's foster sister Dorothy Devereux. In *Love's Labour's Lost* there is a mention of the "School of Night." Some researchers think that this refers to a circle of scientific investigators who met at Syon House. This Wizard Earl and his many miraculous inventions is the subject of a book called *Saint George and Saint Michael* by George MacDonald. His friendship with Francis Bacon is highlighted as well as the Earl's loving honor of Francis. It gives a sense of what the friendships of this time must have been like.

Times Perilous

If a Man be Gracious, and Curteous to Strangers, it shewes, he is a Citizen of the World; And that his Heart, is no Island, cut off from other Lands, but a Continent, that joynes to them. If he be Compassionate, towards the Afflictions of others, it shewes that his Heart is like the noble Tree, that is wounded it selfe, when it gives the Balme. If he easily Pardons and Remits Offences, it shews, that his Minde is planted above Injuries; So that he cannot be shot.

~ Bacon, *Essays*, "Of Goodnesse, and Goodnesse of Nature"

Even with his secret literary work, Francis was not idle in his parliamentary duties. During the sessions of Parliament in which Francis Bacon served, England experienced some of her most important political victories, including the defeat of the Spanish Armada. As one of its most outspoken members, Francis championed the rights of the common man by advocating reforms of all kinds.

He strove to make England great, her people free, and prosperity to abound by sweeping away long-standing abuses and class privileges. He introduced bills that created much dissension and division among members of Parliament—bills that defended the plight of the common man against the long-standing injustices of the ruling classes within the court. While he eventually wielded great power in the House of Commons, Francis never once tipped his hat to the side

Francis Bacon in his parliamentary robes

of the forces of reaction or tyranny. As always, he was a guiding light for the middle way and freedom.

No one at court could match his "tongue of fire" or the reverence he inspired in those who heard him speak. He had "a soft voice, a laughing lip, [and] a melting heart" which won him many friends.

> Wit so brilliant, repartee so keen, lore so profound, and thought so fresh, bespangled with newly-minted words, that the like had

certainly never been heard before within those famous walls *and probably never since.* His hold on the House and on his constituents was due, however, not so much to his intellectual power as his moral qualities... his uprightness and sincerity. When he spoke against Feudal Privileges, or sought to amend the anomalies of the law, or opposed the enclosures of common lands by wealthy land-owners to the hurt of the impoverished villagers, or advocated the reform of the Church, everyone knew that his utterances were prompted by the purest of altruistic motives for the benefit of the many, not for the privileged few, and without thought for personal aggrandizement....

When the Queen asked him to modify his views on the suggested enclosures of common land and withdraw his opposition, he answered: "Your Majesty, I am against all enclosures and especially against enclosed justice."[108]

His reform measures threatened some of the most well-known and powerful lawyers of his day. His foster cousin Robert Cecil, who had joined the House of Commons in 1584 and became the secretary of state after Walsingham in 1596, was jealous of Francis's secret standing and his inner light that led all those around him to love him. He and his father, Lord Burghley, knew it could lead Francis into positions of power in court and ultimately, because of his secret

Lord Burghley and his son, Robert Cecil

birthright, to the throne itself. For Lord Burghley, it was political. For Robert Cecil, it was personal.

Robert Cecil had never forgotten his vow to destroy Francis by the queen's hand. Cecil pursued Francis for over thirty years, playing the friend to his face while ever plotting his demise. In his cipher, Francis mentions him,

> *A foxe, seen oft at our Court in th' forme and outward appearance of a man named Robert Cecill—the hunchback—must answer at th' Divine Araignment to my charge agains' him, for he despoyled me ruthlessly. Th' Queene, my mother, might, in course of events which follow'd their revelations regarding my birth and parentage, without doubt having some naturall pride in her offspring, often have shewne us no little attenntion had not the crafty foxe aroused in that tiger-like spiritt th' jealousy that did so tormente the Queene.*[109]

The wily Cecil, understanding that Queen Elizabeth feared that her sons might depose her if they grew too popular, was able to manipulate her with ease. There was nothing Francis could do about it. Francis realized the "Divine Arraignment" he referred to in Cecil's case would also apply to him, no matter the provocation. To remain blameless before the Divine, Francis knew the best course for him was to do as Christ had taught. He would try to love his enemy, regardless of Cecil's behavior. He believed in divine justice and the alchemy of goodness.

Despite the dangers, Francis never failed to stand for principle in his duty to Parliament. He angered the Queen and Burghley by continually standing up for the rights of the people and the powers of the House of Commons. Amidst the rising threat of Spain, Francis stopped the Queen and the House of Lords from forcing the Commons to raise subsidies for the war. A subsidy was "future money" granted by Parliament to the Crown and then raised by special taxes levied on the people.[110] Lord Burghley, Puckering, and the Peers also demanded that there be no debate on the subject, and, on orders from the Crown, Speaker Coke was to gag the assembly. With the coming invasion of the Armada, many in the government were ready to capitulate to the Queen, but Francis saw how dangerous such a precedent could be and protected the rights of the Commons. It was the right and prerogative of the people to choose what they should give through the House of Commons.

When Sir Walter Raleigh proposed a compromise that saved the Commons' point of privilege, Francis—undaunted by threats from the Queen and Lord Burghley—continued to stand his ground for the people. He argued against the short length of time the money was to be paid back, for he knew what the increased taxes would do to the poorer people of England. Robert Cecil wanted three years, whereas Francis wanted six, or two shillings in the pound per year rather than four. Francis, the hidden Tudor prince, was the leader in opposition to the Crown on behalf of the people.

This parliamentary battle for the protection of the powers of the Commons and war subsidies was the first conflict between Francis and the Speaker of the House of Commons, Edward Coke. Dodd points out that "in the first great crises of his public life Francis Bacon kept faith with his own idealism—"to thine own self be true." He fought the fight and won. There were gains and losses, the losses were private and personal, the gains were for his countrymen, for England, for posterity. Dodd lists these gains as:

1. Freedom of speech in Parliament without Lordly dictation.
2. The right of the Commons to decide alone the amount of supply voted to the Crown annually and its duration.
3. The scotching* for all time of the attempt that the Government could call a Parliament exclusively to vote money-grants and thus abrogate Parliament's inherent right to make new laws or amend old ones.[111]

Because of this public stance against the Crown's wishes, Elizabeth denied Francis access to her presence and cut off all financial support. Francis had already sunk his money into his publications and secret work, therefore in order to pay off the debts without the expected money from the Queen, he had to borrow wherever he could. Anthony sold two estates he had inherited to help Francis at this time. The love of these two brothers was the type of unselfish love seen portrayed in many Shakespearean heroes.

*scotching: to put an end to (Merriam Webster's Dictionary)

Francis continued his secret work, borrowing when he had to and hoping his mother would not leave him without support forever. The Queen had, after all, eventually forgiven Leicester for his betrayal in 1579. In 1586, while Leicester was leading her forces in the Netherlands, she had sent him an affectionate note, signing it with her motto *semper eadem*—ever the same. "As you know, ever the same. ER."

In need of funds, Francis took his first law case and performed so well that Lord Burghley congratulated him and asked for the particulars of the case "to show them where it would best do Francis good." He promised to show Francis's successful case to the Queen while hinting that this could lead to something greater. Lord Burghley gave words of support but never gave Francis the help he truly needed.

The Second Son

> IT *cannot be denied, but Outward Accidents conduce much to* Fortune. *Favour, Opportunitie, Death of Others, Occasion fitting* Vertue. *But chiefly, the Mould of a Mans* Fortune, *is in his owne hands.*
>
> ~ Bacon, *Essays*, "Of Fortune"

Francis's initiations throughout his life gave his soul the opportunity to grow in strength and wisdom. One such initiation came through the actions of his birth brother, Robert Devereux, Earl of Essex, who became very dear to Francis and was the cause of his greatest sorrow.

In the Shakespeare plays can be seen Francis's understanding of the secret power of tragedy. It is part of the alchemical process of soul purification. "Let compounds be dissolved." Loss can be transmutational if those suffering it can take the essence of good that is left to benefit the next phase of life.

Unlike Francis, Essex had no patience or circumspection to help him live as a prince unrecognized. He did not keep his quarrels with his mother private but let them spill into court life as quarrels with his queen. His pride and temper were mirrors of the Queen's own, leading to fierce clashes of wills as well as accommodations frequently made for him. Elizabeth forgave her second son's disobedience as she forgave no one else. Perhaps she saw herself mirrored in her brash and headstrong son.

In 1585 Leicester took Essex with him on the expedition to the Netherlands to fight against the Spanish for the Protestant cause. He took part in the battle of Zutphen, where Philip Sidney, the poet knight and founder of the *Areopagitae,* died. In an act of meaningful ceremony, as he lay on his deathbed, Philip gave his sword to Essex.

Two years later, Leicester relinquished his position as Master of the Horse in order for his second son to take his place. In July of that year, after quite a row with his mother, Essex tried to leave the country without her permission and join the siege of Sluys. She sent one of her men after him to bring him back. These dramatic moments with Elizabeth continued throughout Essex's life.

In 1588, just after Francis had become a Reader at Gray's Inn, the Spanish Armada sailed for England.

As Master of the Horse, Essex was actively engaged with Leicester in the defense of England in this attack that became one of the defining moments of Elizabeth's reign. On August 9, 1588, the Queen herself rallied troops with her famous speech at Tilbury.

Defeat of the Spanish Armada, 8 August 1588
painting by Philippe-Jacques de Loutherbourg

I have always so behaved myself that, under God, I have placed my chiefest strength and safeguard in the loyal hearts and goodwill of my subjects; and therefore I am come amongst you, as you see, at this time, not for my recreation and disport, but being resolved, in the midst and heat of the battle, to live and die amongst you all; to lay down for my God, and for my kingdom, and my people, my honour and my blood, even in the dust.[112]

One wonders what Francis felt when the rest of his family were with the troops defending England. In France he had conducted himself as a prince in the epicenter of affairs military, political, and philosophical. In England he stepped aside with grace for his younger brother to fill that role. He understood that the events surrounding the timing of his birth that kept him from being acknowledged did not apply to Essex. Rather than taking a jealous and bitter stance, he instead endeavored to help Essex become the Tudor prince that England needed.

After the victory against Spain, Leicester and the Queen watched the celebratory parade put on by Essex. This was the last time they were seen together, for Leicester died of an illness four days later at Cornbury Park near Charlbury, Oxfordshire. He left Essex his "George and garter," hoping his son would soon be made a Knight of the Garter. The Queen accepted Essex into the order before the year was out. In regard to Leicester's estate, Elizabeth claimed in all but name the rights of his widow, auctioning it off and keeping the proceeds with the public excuse that he had owed the Crown money.

With the sudden passing of their father, Robert took his place as the Queen's favorite. Though some historians think their relationship was one of lovers, if looked at as an impetuous young son and a proud mother, the relationship makes far more sense. Their lightning-like quarrels were the effect of the resentful rebellion of a son kept hidden, slamming against the iron will and fiery temper of a mother who first and foremost was a queen. Elizabeth would let no role in her life supersede her royal one, not that of wife or mother, even to the detriment of her sons.

A year after the naval victory against Spain, the Queen refused

Robert Devereux, Earl of Essex

Essex's wish to sail with the small fleet that was going to attack Spain. Essex went anyway. The Queen sent men out to retrieve him with a letter to Sir Francis Drake, who was in command of the fleet, commanding him not to allow Essex to board. Essex eluded his pursuers and somehow talked his way into not only sailing but also joining the landing party. When he returned, he went straight to his mother and was forgiven.

In 1590 Essex secretly married Philip Sidney's widow, Mary, Sir Francis Walsingham's daughter. When the Queen learned of it, she was furious that he should marry "below his degree" and without her approval. But just as before, she forgave him. In the early 1590s, Essex's influence at court was at its height, as well as his popularity with the people of London. When he rode through the streets he was adored and cheered by the crowds. Francis warned his brother, that if his star ascended higher than that of the queen, disaster would follow. Francis sought to guide Essex by wisdom to the throne.

In 1591 the Queen again opposed Essex's wish to put himself in danger by taking troops to France. He retaliated by absenting court until she changed her mind. But shortly after letting him go, Elizabeth changed her mind again and commanded one of her men to bring him back to safety. When her man returned without Essex, she flew into a rage, but again forgave her beloved second son. She allowed him to be present for the siege of Rouen, as long as he kept himself out of any danger.

For the Queen's Accession Day in 1595, Francis wrote beautiful poetic speeches for Essex's masque performed in her honor. That same year, Francis suggested that Anthony "knit" his service to Essex, for he trusted that Anthony's wisdom and experience would help support Robert's better nature. From Essex's house, Anthony ran the intelligence network that Walsingham had created. Lord Burghley had taken credit for much of Anthony Bacon's intelligence work while Anthony was abroad. After Walsingham died in 1590, Lord Burghley and Robert Cecil maneuvered Robert into his place but had to create their own spy network. The Walsingham network went to work for Anthony and Essex. These three—Anthony, Francis, and Essex—became a force for England.

One of their intelligence projects at this time was the Lopez Conspiracy. "For six months, Anthony Bacon and Essex had been investigating a circle of Spanish and Portuguese plotters, which led to the uncovering of a conspiracy to poison the Queen through the agency of her Portuguese physician, Dr Lopez. Francis Bacon was commissioned in March 1594 to write the government's public advertisement presenting the details of the conspiracy, which pointed the blame directly at King Philip of Spain."[113]

In 1593, due to Francis's beneficial influence on him, the Queen made Essex part of her Privy Council. But while Essex, Anthony, and Francis worked for their dream of England, and Elizabeth focused on the continuing military threat from Philip of Spain, Lord Burghley and Robert Cecil continued to be a subversive force at court. Even as a second armada was threatening to attack England, they were far more interested in the choice of Elizabeth's successor to the throne. If the queen would not name her heir, then they would, and it would not be Francis or Essex. Robert Cecil began a secret correspondence with the weak and easily manipulated James VI of Scotland.

The court by this time was sharply divided into two camps, that of Robert Cecil and that of Robert Devereux, Earl of Essex. For his part, Essex tried to use his favor with the queen on Francis's behalf and endeavored to secure for Francis the vacant position of attorney general at court. But because Francis disregarded the wishes of the Crown in Parliament and would not sacrifice his principles for royal favor, Essex's pleading on behalf of Francis had no effect. The Queen remained stubborn on the issue. The more Essex argued with her, the more she resisted. With Robert Cecil championing the choice of Edward Coke, it became even more vital to Essex to win the day for Francis. After a year of his petitioning, Elizabeth gave the position of attorney general to Coke.

Though it would have helped him financially, Francis had not been aching for the position, so he was not too disappointed nor surprised. Essex however, did not take the insult to himself and Francis calmly. He confronted the Queen, shouted and swore, but she would not yield. This was the first time the brothers had openly joined together for one goal, and Essex's passionate support of his brother just after Francis had publicly stood against the Crown did not sit well with the Queen.

Essex swallowed his wounded pride and tried to get him the post that Coke had relinquished. He also granted Francis land as recompense for his failure to secure him the post, which alleviated some of Francis's financial troubles. As with all characters in Greek and Shakespearean tragedy, Essex had his tragic flaw of an impulsive temper, yet he also had a generous and happy temperament. He loved literature, and many of Francis's secret writing friends were part of the "Essex Circle."

The historian Spedding described Essex well, seeing the promise he held for Francis even without knowing that they were brothers.

> He was a man of so many gifts and so many virtues, that even now, when his defects and the issue to which they carried him are fully known, it still seems possible that under more favorable accidents he might have realized all the promise of his morning: then it must have seemed more than possible. From his boyhood he had been an eager reader and a patient listener. The first year after he left Cambridge he spent happily in studious retirement. His knowledge was already considerable, his literary abilities great... his respect for intellectual qualifications in other men earnest and unaffected. His religious impressions were deep, and without being addicted to any of the religious parties in the state, he had points of sympathy with them all. His temper was hopeful, ardent, enterprising; his will strong, his opinions decided.... He had that true generosity of nature

which appeals to all human hearts, because it feels an interest in all human things.... It was easy for Bacon to see that here was a man capable by nature of entering heartily into all his largest speculations for the good of the world, and placed by accident in a position to realize, or help to realize, them.[114]

Francis loved his brother dearly but could also see his tragic flaws that could be the undoing of Essex.

In fine his early youth was lightly passed, but after he did know that 'twas th' Queene that gave him life, he grew imperious and (when brought to Court by our truely ingenious father, whom an evill sprite much troubled—e'en a jealousy o' some o' th' Queene's favoured lords that did attend her), his will shew'd its true source, and reveal'd th' origin of th' young Caesar....

To our mother is th' fearlessnesse that Essex shewed to be traced directlie, and that promptnesse of judgement in a sudden calamity; but with sufficie't time given to deliberate, Essex, ev'n more than she, would shew a variety o' opinions in so swift succession, you must use much witt to gain one hee would give his name unto. When their wills should be matcht, 'twere no light task t' decide as to the result. Like his mother i' temper he could break, but nere even slightly bend.[115]

The wise Divine Presence of God gave both Essex and Elizabeth the exact circumstances and people they needed to help them grow and pass their own initiations. They had each other to clash against for the purpose of growth, and most importantly, they had Francis Bacon who, had they taken his guidance, would have helped them bend the knee to charity and wisdom and build a stronger, more enlightened Britain.

Francis, though he tried with letters and visits, still had no access to the Queen. Essex again absented himself from court under the guise of being sick. Elizabeth visited him twice. Through these visits and the subsequent ones, Essex continued to plead Francis's case but to no effect. The Queen would not forgive his disobedience.

It was during this banishment from the Queen and court that Francis wrote and produced the Christmas Entertainments for the

Gesta Grayorum at Gray's Inn. Though a grand example of Francis's wit and philosophy, he still was left unseen and unsupported by the Queen. Even Lady Anne Bacon left Gorhambury to see the Queen or her brother-in-law, Lord Burghley, but was seen only by Robert Cecil.

Francis had had enough. He resolved to leave behind the law, the court, and the cold fury of the Queen. He decided to go abroad if at all possible and become a student of literature. When the Queen heard from Essex that Francis was going to leave, she had him called once again to court. Though she still would not see him, she had Sir Robert Cecil relay her message. There is a record of this meeting from a letter Francis wrote to Anthony:

> *The Queen seemeth to apprehend my travel; whereupon I was sent for by Sir Robert Cecil in sort as from her Majesty.... I came to the Court upon his relation of her Majesty's speech....*
>
> *... Then her Majesty sweareth that if I continue in this manner... she will seek all England for a Solicitor rather than take me. Yes, she will send for Houghton and Coventry tomorrow—as if she would swear them both.*
>
> *Again she entereth into it, that she hath never dealt with any as with me (in hoc erratum non est); she hath pulled me over the bar... she hath used me in her greatest causes.... She is now more angry with Essex than with me.*[116]

This letter does not sound like a penniless solicitor writing about a queen and a lord, but rather a son writing about his mother and brother. He goes on to write to Anthony about their literary work:

> *I have here an idle pen or two... thinking to have got some money this term. I pray send me somewhat else for them to write out besides your Irish Collection which is almost done.... From my Lodge at Twickenham Park, this 25th January, 1595. Fr. Bacon.*[117]

The Queen did not give him the solicitorship left vacant from Coke, but rather created an entirely new position for him as her Counsel Extraordinary and one of her Counsel Learned in the Law to act as an advisor to the Queen to protect her interests; to examine prisoners suspected of treason; to draw up official reports and assist law officers of the Crown in state prosecutions. It was an honorary position without salary, but she rented to him for a nominal fee a grant of sixty acres of wood in Somerset. There was rejoicing at Gray's Inn, for Francis had never wanted to be solicitor but rather had desperately needed funds to continue his English Renaissance. Now, with the land in Somerset, Francis had a way to make money. Essex, however, took this second refusal as an affront to himself.

A Prince Ensnared

But man, proud man,
Drest in a little brief authority,
Most ignorant of what he's most assur'd;
His glassy essence, like an angry ape,
Plays such fantastic tricks before high heaven,
As make the angels weep...

~ *Measure for Measure,* act 2, sc. 2

In the spring of 1596, the Spanish fleet was growing again in the Port of Cadiz, preparing for a second attempt at England's shores. Essex's desire to prove his mettle and worth to the Queen found opportunity. She appointed him as joint commander with Lord Admiral Howard of a naval force to conduct a preemptive strike against Spain. Francis wrote of the attack that "was like lightning. For in the space of fourteen hours the king of Spain's navy was destroyed and the town of Cadiz taken." Essex had wanted to go after the main Spanish fleet but was curtailed.

Essex returned to England as a hero in triumph, adored by the people. Tension in the court rose as his popularity soared. The Cecils and their ilk whispered to the Queen that such hero worship of Essex was dangerous. The Queen, for her part, endeavored to keep steady the two opposing forces at court. Francis urged Essex to take a position that would bring him closer to her rather than a warrior's glory.

While Essex was in Spain, the Queen had passed over Sir Thomas Bodley, for whom Essex had promised to gain the position of secretary of state, and given it to none other than his sworn enemy, Sir Robert Cecil. Upon his return, the spoils and glory of the victory were disputed and shared in a ratio he found unfair. He was in no mood to play the supplicant. Of Essex at this time, Dixon wrote:

> He will bury his grief at Wanstead, or rush away to the war, and find peace of heart on the Spanish pikes!
>
> Lady Ann's quick ear and loving eye perceive the change that Cecil's elevation, the Earl's discomfiture, must work at court. Now that her sister's son, who so bitterly hates the Earl... has come to his height of power, she writes to warn Anthony of the evil days in store for them, now Cecil is greater than before, and of the need for her sons to walk with wary step. It is the last letter from her pen, closing... with words of love.[118]

In October 1596, Francis wrote to his hurt and raging younger brother another letter of caution and advice. He advised him to put further military ambition aside.

> Wherein I cannot sufficiently wonder at your Lordship's course; that you say, the wars are your occupation, and go on in that course; whereas, if I mought have advised your Lordship, you should have left that person in Plymouth; more than when in counsel, or in commending fit persons for service for wars, it had been in season.... But I say, keep it in substance, but abolish it in shows to the Queen. For her Majesty loveth peace. Next, she loveth not charge. Thirdly, that kind of dependence maketh a suspected greatness. Therefore, *quod instat agamus*. Let that be a sleeping honour awhile, and cure the Queen's mind in that point.[119]

Francis then suggested that Essex should try for the vacant position of Lord Privy Seal: "But my chief reason is, that which I first alleged, to divert her Majesty from this impression of a martial greatness."[120] The coming events prove this to be brilliant advice from a loving brother and wise counselor.

His words of caution were not light ones, for the Cecils of the court constantly played on the Queen's fear of an armed coup d'état from any lord popular with the military and the people. With Essex's own demands and his quarreling for short-term gain, he was putting their long-term play for the Crown at terrible risk. Francis told Essex to "win the Queen: if this be not the beginning, of any other course I see no end."[121]

So ended 1596 with Essex seething inwardly but endeavoring to keep his own peace. With the breaking of the new year, Spain was again preparing to attack England. Ignoring Francis's advice, Essex expected to be named commander but was told by the Queen that he must share the role with Sir Walter Raleigh and Lord Thomas Howard.

Like Achilles at the walls of Troy, Essex refused to join the fight while what he saw as his right was being so ignored. He clashed with his mother, he fought with Robert Cecil, he tried to leave court, but his mother would not allow it. When the offensive against Spain finally left in June (weather having aborted the first attempt), Essex was the sole commander. But now it is unclear if he still wanted it or was forced into the role. Robert Cecil was ever playing his own game and creating opportunities for himself to come between the queen and her sons.

The English offensive was a failure. With a fleet not strong enough to complete the original plan of attack, Essex chose to wait and attack the Spanish treasure ships on their return. Unfortunately, he missed them. The Queen blamed him for the failure. Hurt and offended by her blame as well as angered and betrayed by her actions while he was away, he retired to Wanstead House. While he was gone, Robert Cecil was named Chancellor of the Duchy of Lancaster, and Lord Howard was given enough honors to now outrank Essex in court.

Had Essex simply been an Earl as his outer role portrayed, this would have been a setback in the game of court. He had simply been outmaneuvered. But as a Tudor prince, it could only have felt like yet another betrayal from his mother. He refused to come to court or appear in Council or Parliament.

The Queen relented and made him Earl Marshal of England, thus raising him again in precedence above his competitors. This meant, however, that he accepted the very office Francis had warned him away from. Though Essex had fostered a coolness toward his brother during his upset, Francis wrote him again in 1598, congratulating him on devoting himself to civil matters and advising him on how to act peacefully regarding the revolt in Ireland.

Unfortunately, Essex lent his ear and trust to Sir Christopher Blount, who had been one of Leicester's top officers and had married Essex's foster mother months after Leicester died. Having fought with him in multiple campaigns, Essex trusted his war-prone counsel, although it contradicted that of his brother's. With Blount's advice, Essex stood as the War Party, and (the now aged but still vital to the queen) Lord Burghley represented the Peace Party. Robert Cecil went to Ireland but failed to arrange a treaty.

Another vicious quarrel arose between the Queen and Essex over the position of Lord Deputy of Ireland, Essex presenting one option, the Cecils another. The violent escalation of the Irish rebellion and the Spanish waiting to assist them caused an end to the quarrel.

In the midst of this, Lord Burghley died. Robert Cecil, bent on attaining his father's place, pressed the Queen to send Essex to Ireland, thus ridding himself of his competition.

Essex, realizing this posting for what it was, wrote his mother a letter before departing, full of the drama and sorrow of a young man who sees the trap closing. Even though he had not spoken to Francis in eighteen months, on the eve of his departure for Ireland he rode for Gray's Inn. Francis advised Essex to avoid military solutions, warning him that Ireland would be pacified with the plow and not the sword.

Essex left for Ireland as the Queen's Earl Marshal and Lord Lieutenant of Ireland, leading the "largest army ever sent to Ireland in Queen Elizabeth's reign."[122]

Just before Essex left, a small book was published with a dedication to him as the "great expectation of the future." *The First Part of the Life and Raigne of King Henrie IIII*, written by John Hayward, referred specifically to the deposition of Richard II by the popular Henry Bolingbroke, who became King Henry IV. The dedication, which seemed to suggest a parallel between Elizabeth and the deposed Richard II, implying that Essex was the new Bolingbroke, was torn from the book after only a few copies were issued, but the author was arrested for treason nonetheless. The book based much of its text on the play *Richard II* that had been in circulation for a few years. The deposition scene in that play had already been worrisome to the Queen. When the play was officially published by "Shakespeare" in 1597, the deposition scene was omitted.

Even without the dedication, the wide circulation of the book plus the popularity of the play alarmed the Queen. When she received intelligence that Essex was acting outside her orders, her alarm intensified.

As part of the Queen's Counsel Learned in the Law, Francis was called upon to make a report on whether there was treason in the book that had been dedicated to Essex. Francis recorded his answer to the Queen in his *Apologie Concerning the Earl of Essex:*

> I remember an answer of mine in a matter which had some affinity with my Lord's cause, which though it grew from me, went after about in others' names. For her Majesty being mightily incensed with that book which was dedicated to my Lord of Essex, being a story of the first year of King Henry the fourth, thinking it a seditious prelude to put into the people's heads boldness and faction, said she had good opinion that there was treason in it, and asked me if I could not find any places in it that might be drawn within case of treason: whereto I answered: for treason surely I found none; but for felony very many. And when her Majesty hastily asked me wherein, I told her the author had committed very apparent theft, for he had taken most of the sentences of Cornelius Tacitus, and translated them into English, and put them into his text. And another time, when the Queen would not be persuaded that it was his writing whose name was to it, but that it had some more mischievous author, and said with great indignation that she would have him racked to produce his author, I replied, Nay Madam, he is a Doctor, never rack his person, but rack his stile; let him have pen, ink, and paper, and help of books, and be enjoined to continue the story where it breaketh off, and I will undertake by collecting the stiles to judge whether he were the author or no.[123]

Peter Dawkins explains the intricate meaning within Francis's answer:

The reference to the author stealing from Tacitus is curious, for in fact Hayward's book does not seem to steal from Tacitus at all, and the source it does steal from, the Shakespeare play of *Richard II,* itself has hardly any borrowings from Tacitus. Francis would have known better than that, and so would the Queen, therefore Francis' meaning must have been something else. He was surely playing a game of wit with the Queen, who was known to appreciate such repartee; for Tacitus was a good synonym for himself, Francis Bacon, as the author of the Shakespeare histories.

> Cornelius Tacitus (c. 55–120 AD) had been an eminent pleader at the Roman bar and a man of high moral character.... He was primarily concerned with ethics rather than politics, and the *Annals* and *Histories* are noted for their fine studies of human character.[124]

Though Francis couldn't save the author from being imprisoned, through his logic, he convinced the Queen not to torture and kill the man.

Meanwhile in Ireland, Essex's military campaign proved a disaster. He knighted men (a royal prerogative under Elizabeth's rule), changed plans without consulting the Queen, lost thousands of men, and failed to do battle with the Earl of Tyrone, who repeatedly evaded him. He dearly wanted to return home, as he knew that Cecil and his enemies at court were poisoning the mind of his mother against him. Francis tried to convince the Queen to bring him home *"with a white Staff in his hand as my Lord Leicester had,"*[125] and not discontent him while giving him access to arms and power.

In the end Essex compromised with Tyrone and promised him that he would personally bring the terms of the truce to the Queen. Historian Agnes Strickland wrote of Essex's actions in Ireland, not as the disaster Elizabeth saw, but as a thwarted attempt at peace:

> The policy pursued by Essex was of a pacific character. He loved the excitement of battle when in the cause of freedom, or when the proud Spaniard threatened England with invasion; but, as the governor of Ireland, his noble nature inclined him to the blessed work of mercy and conciliation. He ventured to disobey the

bloody orders he had received from the short-sighted politicians, who were for enforcing the same measures which had converted that fair isle into a howling wilderness, and goaded her despairing people into becoming brigands and rabid wolves. If the generous and chivalrous Essex had been allowed to work out his own plans, he would probably have healed all wounds, and proved the regenerator of Ireland; but, surrounded as he was by spies, and thwarted by his deadly and jealous foes in the cabinet, and, finally, rendered an object of suspicion to the most jealous of sovereigns, he only accelerated his own doom, without ameliorating the evils he would fain have cured.[126]

Perhaps he belatedly realized his brother had been right. As seen from current times, a pathway of peace with Ireland would have saved thousands upon thousands of lives. The wise vision of Prince Francis was right again.

The Queen refused to let Essex return and in reproachful letters, rebuffed all terms of peace. Fed as she was on the poison of her own fears, self-interest, and the enemies around her, she could only see treasonous willfulness where there was a need to sue for justice and peace. Here was a Shakespearean tragedy in the making.

Now Cracks a Noble Heart

Had I but died an hour before this chance,
I had liv'd a blessed time; for, from this instant,
There's nothing serious in mortality:
All is but toys: renown and grace is dead ...

~ Macbeth, act 2, sc. 3

Having given his word to Tyrone to convey the terms directly to the Queen, and infuriated by her intractability and the rumors of his alleged treason, Essex set sail for home on September 24, 1599. He rushed to get to her before his enemies could stop him and burst into her bedchamber mud stained from travel. Though surprised, she greeted him with graciousness, a mother happy to see her son.

But when he saw her again after she had been with her council, she was cold with him. Soon after, he was charged to remain in his chamber, and shortly thereafter committed to the custody of the lord keeper at York House. The Queen had been told all manner of lies about Essex's arrival, such as that he had planned to surprise the court with a force of two hundred men, when in reality he had arrived with only six attendants.

Immediately upon hearing what had transpired, Francis wrote to Essex and was allowed a quarter-hour visit with him. While in custody, Essex fell ill with typhoid fever he had contracted in Ireland. In answer to the public outcry in support of Essex, the Queen decided to have a declaration of his misconduct in the Star Chamber.

Francis advised the Queen to not go against Essex in such a way but to make amends in private and restore him to honor. He warned that her current course of action was so unusual that "it would be said Justice had had her balance taken from her."[127] Despite Francis's warnings, on the twenty-ninth of November 1599, with no chance for Essex to defend himself, the declaration of his misconduct was given. The Queen may have been trying to save him from the ignominy of having to appear in court, for that same day she visited him personally. Finding him, indeed, gravely ill, she sent her own physicians for his care.

Francis, who was supposed to be at the Star Chamber for the declaration, had declined to attend. He wrote to Lord Henry Howard that

> "there is shaped a tale in London's forge" that he had delivered an opinion to the Queen that Essex had committed treason which are "lies" and "libels," the "root" being "partly some light-headed Envy at my accesses to Her Majesty, which, *being begun and continue since my Childhood,* as long as her Majesty shall think me worthy of them, I scorn those that think the contrary....
>
> "For my Lord Essex, I am not servile to him, *having regard to my Superior Duty* [i.e., his duty to the Queen which must come FIRST], I have been much bound to him. And on the other side, *I have spent more time and more thoughts about his well-doing, than ever I did about my own.*"[128]

The court was now split, some calling for Essex to be released, some calling for his life to be forfeited. Twice a warrant for him to be taken to the Tower was sent to the Queen and twice she refused it. Essex's condition had grown worse. When his wife was finally allowed to see him, she found him close to death. Alarmed at his condition, the Queen said, she *"had only intended to humble him."*[129] The Queen ordered that he should be moved to the lord keeper's own room.

All across London, people prayed for his recovery. When it came, the people rejoiced but the Queen fell once again into suspicions that he had feigned his illness after all. The malicious whispers of Robert Cecil and his people, along with the continued circulation of the Hayward book, caused her to fear, but her love for her son kept her from acting against him. Nothing came of the declaration of his misconduct and months went by while he was neither released nor condemned. Essex wrote her letters but to no avail. His enemies Cecil and Raleigh kept up a vicious campaign against him.

The Queen turned more to Francis, even while keeping his brother and friends in perilous positions. In March 1600, she helped him buy the Gorhambury Estate reversion from Anthony and worked "a more useful deal" for him with Sir Nicholas Bacon the younger. Also in March, she ordered Anthony Bacon, Lord and Lady Southampton, and Mary Sidney to leave the home of Essex. This close circle of friends was split up and under suspicion. In May she visited Francis at Twickenham, where he presented her with a sonnet on mercy in the hope that she would extend her mercy toward Essex.

The Queen was ready to bring this unfortunate event to an end and considered how to punish Essex in a way that that would teach him, for she would not simply give in as she had before. Francis convinced her to avoid a public trial in the Star Chamber that would lead to time in the Tower, and instead hold a disciplinary tribunal at York House to which the public may be permitted. "Whatever you do should be for his chastisement not for his destruction." The Queen replied that "her purpose is to make him know himself, and his duty to her; and that she would again use his service."[130]

In the summer of 1600, the High Court judges came to York House for a private trial on a charge against Essex for disobeying the Queen's orders in Ireland. The investigation was led by Coke, as the Queen's attorney general. Francis was roped in again to give his judgment on the "seditious" book. He tried to excuse himself from the role, saying the book was an old matter and had nothing to do with the rest of the charge. But his arguments were ignored, and he was forced to play his part.

Essex knelt before the judges and in a mild manner admitted his mistakes, though, with his jewel of the Knights of the Garter pressed to his heart, he swore he had never been treasonous. "This hand shall pull out this heart *when any disloyal thought shall enter it.*"[131] Francis averred that there was no disloyalty on Essex's part and did all that he could to save his brother from the trap into which he had fallen.

Because of his efforts, Essex was allowed to return to his own home but was forbidden to attend court without the Queen's permission. From his home, Essex wrote letters begging the Queen for forgiveness. At court, Francis continued his campaign for mercy, a lone voice in support of Essex. Other supporters dared not defend him to the Queen, and his enemies were ever ready to whisper their poison. This was not just an attack on Essex's person, it was an attack on the Tudor sons and the power they could one day wield.

The Queen made reference multiple times to breaking Essex as one would a horse. She refused to renew his monopoly* of sweet wine and instead granted it to trustees for her own use. This action alone plunged Essex into debt, dishonor, and degradation. In her decision to "abate this unruly horse of its provender," she meant to break him to her will, but she misjudged his temperament. He was a true mirror of his mother, who would never have been broken in such a way.

Essex wrote her one last letter on the anniversary of her Accession Day. The eloquent letter, full of his passion and sorrow, did nothing to change her mind, so poisoned as it was against him. He had no access to his mother to fight against Cecil's conspiracy against him.

---

*The Crown granted monopolies, privileges, or offices to an individual through a Letters Patent. In this case the Queen had granted Essex the exclusive license of sweet wines ten years prior.

To have his royal mother side with his enemy and cut him out so permanently, eviscerated his sense of honor, justice, and loyalty.

The Queen broke her son but not in the way she intended. Sir John Harrington wrote of his visit with Essex at the time: "He shifteth from sorrow and repentance to rage and rebellion so suddenly as well proveth him devoid of good reason or right mind.... The man's soul seems tossed to and fro, like waves of a troubled sea."[132]

Essex could not believe his own mother would cause him to fall into destitution. Had all the times when she had shown him motherly care meant nothing? He disregarded her command and opened his home to all visitors, welcoming friends from among the nobility and the military. His enemies reported to the Queen that Essex was holding a hostile court. Rumors abounded through London that he was in league with James of Scotland or the Spanish Infanta, that he would take the city, and that Raleigh had sown suspicion in order to kill him. While in Essex House, which now housed three hundred men, there were plans being made and discarded with regard to getting Essex past his enemies to gain access to the Queen. The situation looked more and more perilous.

The Queen summoned Essex to court on February 7, 1601, but Cecil had done his work well, for an anonymous letter arrived the same day warning Essex not to attend if he valued his life. He refused the Queen's summons, feigning illness. Someone put together a hurried production of *Richard the Second* with the deposition scene in place. Whether this was a Cecil move or an ill-thought-out move by a supporter is unknown, but Cecil took it as an excuse to double the guard at Whitehall, and reserves were readied.

It was clear the court would not be surprised. Some encouraged Essex to flee to Wales, while others goaded him on to act. This quandary was interrupted by the lord keeper and the lord chief justice at the door to Essex House on February 8, demanding a reason for such an assembly. Essex's followers ushered the dignitaries into the library and locked them in. Essex headed for court, with his chief supporters Sir Christopher Blount, Henry Wriothesley, and Earl of Southampton leading the charge.

London did not rise to join him as Essex had thought. He may have been only rising against his enemies in court who, from his point of view, had control of the Crown. But to the people he was rising against the Crown itself. He reached Saint Paul's where it had been planned for him to speak but he could not. The streets were then blocked by heavy chains and the queen's guards. After a brief fight with the queen's men, Essex's men dispersed. Virginia Fellows wrote that Essex escaped by boat on the Thames River and returned to his home where he burned his diary and other papers. He then submitted to arrest.[133]

The trial for treason of the Earls of Essex and Southampton was set for February 18 at Westminster Hall. It lasted fifteen days.

As interpreted by Dodd, Francis wrote this sonnet while Essex was in the Tower. In it he mourns for his brother, asking that he be put in the Tower in Essex's stead.

> *Beshrew that Heart that makes my heart to groan*
> *For that deep wound it gives my Friend and me!*
> *Is't not enough to torture me alone,*
> *But slave to slavery my sweet'st Friend must be?*
> *Me from my Self thy cruel eye hath taken,**
> *And my Next Self thou harder hast Engross'd:†*
> *Of Him, My Self, and Thee, I am forsaken;*
> *A torment thrice threefold thus to be cross'd.*
> *—Prison my heart in thy steel bosom's ward,‡*
> *But then my Friend's heart let my poor heart bail;*
> *Whoe'er keeps me, let my heart be his guard;*
> *Thou canst not then use rigour in my gaol:*
> > *And yet thou wilt; for I, being pent in thee,*
> > *Perforce am thine, and all that is in me.*
>
> ~ Shakespeare, "Sonnet 133"

Fellows wrote: "Elizabeth's revenge on her two sons was unbelievably cruel—at the trial she forced Francis to act as a prosecutor on behalf of the Crown. It was his life or Essex's. There was simply no way he could refuse. It was a heartless punishment of Francis for

---
*You have taken from me my true identity as your son and Prince of the realm.
†"My Next Self"—my brother... the Earl of Essex
Engross'd—Anglo-French meaning in 1500s "the entire stock bought wholesale"
‡"Thy steel bosom's ward" i.e., the Tower

something he had not been guilty of doing."[134] Dodd has a different reasoning as to why the Queen ordered Francis to be there. She herself could not be a part of the trial of her youngest son, but she could, despite how it would affect him, send her elder one. Dodd surmises that Francis was there to protect the Queen's interests as Counsel Extraordinary to Her Majesty. As such, Dodd says, "he held primarily a watching brief on her behalf... in order to prevent anything being said by anyone that might reveal the secret of their private relationship... to intervene if necessary and to divert any acrimonious discussion, that might be provoked by the foulmouthed bully Coke, which might lead to dangerous revelations."[135]

Her motives were no doubt complex. She could order Francis to be her voice and keep her secret while punishing him for not keeping her beloved son out of trouble. She demanded Francis be junior council to Sir Edward Coke, who hated him, in the case against his own brother. She swore an oath, however, that Essex would not be killed; she would execute her royal prerogative to save him.

Elizabeth intended the trial to make the point to the world and her sons that the throne was hers, and no one but she herself would decide when or to whom she would leave it. For the Queen, it was dominance theater, and she wanted her ministers of justice to push

Henry Wriothesley, Earl of Southampton, and Robert Devereux, Earl of Essex

it to the limit. Essex was found guilty of treason, along with the Earl of Southampton, and sentenced to be beheaded.

 ## The Mystery of the Ring

The Queen had an exit strategy to be used when the proof of her triumph would be evident to all concerned. She had privately promised Essex that if he sent her a certain signet ring he would not be executed. Francis wrote:

> Th' event of th' Earle's death never for an howre, or even for a moment seem'd posible to me after Robert stoopt his pride to send our proud mother her pledge—a ring given as if in doubt some great harm might ever threaten, altho' neither surely tho't it from th' Queene his evil would threat.[136]

When imprisoned in the Tower under sentence of execution, Essex overcame his pride and sent the signet ring to the Queen. But the youth sent to deliver the ring gave it by mistake, not to Lady Scope, who was to hand it directly to the Queen, but to her sister, Lady Nottingham.

Lady Nottingham showed the ring to her husband who was part of the Cecil faction. He forbade her to send the ring to the Queen. Elizabeth waited in vain.

Francis's friend Henry, Earl of Southampton, was kept imprisoned while Francis's brother, Robert, Earl of Essex, the Queen's second son, was brutally blinded and then executed in the Tower on February 26, 1601.

Only royalty was executed in the Tower block as he was, a recognition of his royal blood that did him little good. On the wall over the doorway of Beauchamp Tower are carved the words, "Robart Tidir" (Welsh spelling for Robert Tudor)—the only public mark of who was really killed that day.

Francis wrote of the Queen's reaction in his biliteral cipher:

> All joys died with Essex in both our bosomes; for her, all peace, as well, and she declin'd toward her owne end from daie to day, visiblie, even while she stroove most to hide her weakenesse.[137]

On the day of his brother's execution, Francis wrote a sonnet expressing his grief and rage at Essex's death and his mother's betrayal.

> *My love is as a fever, longing still*
> *For that which longer nurseth the disease,*
> *Feeding on that which doth preserve the ill,*
> *Th' uncertain sickly appetite to please.*
> *My Reason, the physician to my love,*
> *Angry that his prescriptions are not kept,*
> *Hath left me, and I desperate now approve*
> *Desire is death, which physic did except.*
> *Past cure I am, now Reason is past care,*
> *And frantic-mad with evermore unrest;*
> *My thoughts and my discourse as madmen's are,*
> *At random from the truth vainly expressed:*
> > *For I have sworn thee fair, and thought thee bright,*
> > *Who art as Black as Hell, as Dark as Night.*
>
> ~ Shakespeare, "Sonnet 147"

Francis wrote his heartbreak and guilt into his biliteral cipher.

I write mildly of so terrible events, so galli'g memories of fifteene such woful, ay, such dre'dfull daies, 'tis limn'd i' fire on gloom of th' night or daye, Essex, thy murther. To sharper clamours, stif'led cries or piteous moans are added, and my eares heare Robert's voyce, soe entreati'gly, opening sealed dores, hau'ting all dreemes, gre'ting everie daie that doth dawne on our home....

Essex who was also sonne unto Her Ma.* and a brother bred—bone, blood, sinnewes as my owne—was sentenc'd to death by that mère and my owne counsel....

How like some nightes horrible vision this triall and awful torture before his execution must ever be to me, none but the Judge that sitteth aloft can justlie knowe. All the scenes come before me like the acted play, but how to put it awaye, or drive it back to Avernus, its home, O, who can divulge that greatest o' secrets? None.

This thought onely is fraught with a measureless pain, that all my power can doe nought for his memorie. If hee had but heard

---
*Her Majesty

> *my advice, but he heeded his owne unreasoni'g wishes only....*
> *Failing of his helpers, that would-bee king was held for trial for treaso', co'demn'd, made to tell his ambitious designes, tortured,—for in the prison, vilde men, his keepers, by arts more pitichie-hued than hell, having obtain'd a permittance to cause pain sufficiente to burst the seale upon the lipps of maddened Essex, with burning irons put out both lovelie eyes,—then coldly executed.*
>
> *No tale of ages before our blessed Saviour suffer'd such death, has one halfe the woe of this. Ev'n the barbarians of anie age, would burn men to cinders lesse murth'rously.*
>
> *O God! forgiveness cometh fro' Thee. Shut not this truest book, my God; shut out my past—love's little sunny hour, if it soe please Thee, and some of man's worthy work, yet Essex's tragedy here shew forth: then posterity shall know him truly.*
>
> *... Vantages acompted great, simply as th' uncertaine dreames or visiones of night seeme to us in after time. Ended now is my great desire to sit in British throne. Larger worke doth invite my hand then majestie doth offer: to wield th' penne doth ever require a greater minde then to sway the royall scepter. Ay, I cry to th' Heavenly Ayde, ruling ore all, ever to keepe my soule thus humbled and contente.*
>
> *O Source infinite of light; ere Time in existence was, save in Thy creative plan, all this tragedy unfolded before Thee. A night of Stygian darknesse encloseth us. My hope, bannish'd to realmes above, taketh its flight through th' clear aire of the Scyences, unto bright daye with Thyselfe. As Thou didst conceale Thy lawes in thick clouds, enfolde them in shades of mysterious gloom, Thou didst infuse from Thy spirit a desire to put the day's glad worke, th' evening's thought, and midnight's meditation to finde out their secret workings.*
>
> *Only thus can I banish from my thoughts my beloved brother's untimely cutting off, and my wrongfull part in his tryall.*[138]

Francis went through a "dark night of the soul," subject to overwhelming sorrow and guilt. He could only pray for divine aid to get him through the agony and press on in his work toward the Great Instauration.

He saw his mother only once after the death of Essex. It wasn't until after her own death that he learned what had happened to the ring. To him, hers was the worst betrayal: she was forsworn for allowing the murder of her son, and he was forsworn for believing she would save him.

The Privy Council demanded that Francis Bacon write a declaration of Essex's crimes in order to sway the angry populace who understood that Essex had been taken down by his enemies in court. Francis had to comply and wrote the truth of what Essex had done. First the manuscript went to the Queen. Everywhere Francis had written "my Lord Essex" she struck it out and wrote simply "Essex." Then the manuscript went to the council, who further edited it to their liking until it became a piece of utter anti-Essex propaganda. This they published under Francis's name. He was betrayed again and again.

The Vestal Flame Portrait of Elizabeth I

An engraved portrait of Queen Elizabeth I from De Larray's *Histoire de l'Angleterre, d'Ecosse et d'Irlande* (Rotterdam, 1707). Portrayed with the Queen are her three children. The one in the shadowed background, shrouded and dowsing the vestal flame, is the queen's tragic first born. The two in the lighted foreground are given symbols that show exactly who they are, Francis Bacon and Robert Devereux.[139]

Amidst this turmoil, Francis never lost the anchor of his unwavering belief that the path to God was love in action. He threw his effort into saving the hundred men imprisoned for the "Essex Rebellion." "Coke wanted to hang the lot, but while the Court was in progress against the first batch of nine prisoners, Francis Bacon arrived with a letter from the Privy Council to stay proceedings."[140] In the end, only four other men were put to death (one of them being Sir Christopher Blount); the rest were released with fines or short stints in prison. This was a miraculous intervention.

Francis's foster brother, Anthony, was in a perilous position. Now, with the Queen in deep mourning and Cecil's faction at the height of power, Anthony, who had worked for Essex and to whom Robert Cecil had sworn enmity, would be the next target. Francis would not allow Cecil's manipulations to take from him another brother. But how to save him?

A Philosopher's Death

On April 29, 1601, Anthony Bacon was reported dead. He disappeared from history at just the right time.

It is believable that Anthony, who suffered ill health throughout his life, could have died of illness at around 42 years of age. But what is not believable is that Francis, who loved Anthony as his dearest brother and friend, would write nothing of his death or burial. Another mystery is that all correspondence of Anthony's after 1598 is missing. These mysteries and other oddities have led some Baconian researchers to believe that Anthony was the first of the Bacon brothers to take a "philosopher's death." On the Continent it was rumored that Anthony lived on, under a secret identity, as Francis's chief aide and support for the Rosicrucian movement.

In the enlarged edition of his *Essays* in 1612, Francis mentions having dedicated the first edition to "my dear brother Master Anthony Bacon, who is with God." A phrase that is commonly understood to mean that the person is dead, but it could be seen in another light.

While Francis grieved over Robert's wrongful execution, in his cipher there is no equivalent for Anthony's "death."

Francis, as organizer and leader of the Rosicrucian and Freemason Societies, depended on Anthony to connect with the loosely associated esoteric philosophers they knew in Europe. While these philosophers were united by their opposition to the tyranny of the Catholic and Protestant clergy, they met informally. They had no integrated tenets, initiatory rites, or common devotions to Gnostic Christian principles. Anthony's role was to propose an organization in secret, around unifying tenets in their towns and cities. Esoteric legends say that Anthony lived on and continued the great work.

The Murder of the Queen

*Thy ambition,
Thou scarlet sin, robb'd this bewailing land....*

~ *Henry VIII*, act 3, sc. 2

During this time of upheaval, Francis continued as he always had, being an advocate for the common man and the uplifting of society. In October 1601, the tenth and final Parliament of Queen Elizabeth met, with Francis given the rare honor of a "double-return." Ipswich, the chief town of Suffolk, kept Francis as their representative while actions and morals won him a second constituency in St Albans. This proves that the machinations of Cecil and his men had not worked; Francis was still trusted by the people. During this session, he fought the repeal of an act on the revenues of "Colleges, Hospitals and other Charitable Organizations." The section of his speech recorded by Townsend shows that his deep commitment to charity was practical as well as philosophical.

> That the last Parliament (passed) so many Bills for *the Relief of the Poor* that he called it A FEAST OF CHARITY. And now this Statute of 390 having done so much GOOD as it was delivered to the House... we should do a most UNCHARITABLE ACTION to repeal and subvert such *a Mount of Charity;* and

therefore we should rather *tenderly foster it* than roughly cry away with it.

"*I speak*" quoth he, "*out of the very Strings of my HEART;* which doth alter my ordinary form of speech; for *I speak not now out of the Fervency of my Brain.*" With that he smote his breast.[141]

In 1602 Francis wrote a State Paper to Cecil outlining the best method to take with Ireland. He again urged peace and reconciliation. "He advocates lenience and the avoidance of displanting 'ancient generations.'.... He believes in perfect toleration of religion for the recovery of the hearts of the people...."[142] If this outline could have seen fruition, the generations of strife between the two countries need not have come to pass.

Through the next 320 years following Francis Bacon's plea for peace, Ireland fought against the eradication of her spiritual and cultural identity and suffered great loss of life. However, on December 6, 1922, the majority of Ireland gained its freedom. It was divided between the newly established Republic of Ireland and Northern Ireland, which retained six of Ireland's thirty-two counties and has since remained under British rule.

In 1603, two years after the death of Essex, Lady Nottingham on her deathbed confessed to the Queen that she had received but never forwarded Robert's signet ring. Queen Elizabeth raged at the dying woman, claiming, "God may forgive you, but I never will." For two years the Queen had mourned her son's death, mourned his pride that had not let him call to her for help. The truth now shattered what was left of her peace of mind: her son *had* asked for her mercy, had

Queen Elizabeth in her later years

been tortured and killed, not knowing that she had never received his missive.

The tragic final days of Queen Elizabeth are described in Francis's cipher. Cecil's years of plotting would soon see fruition if he could simply keep Francis Bacon from being named heir. The more compliant James VI of Scotland would become king of England and Cecil would be the power behind the throne. As the Queen became more incoherent, the fox saw his opportunity.

Wracked with guilt and remorse, Elizabeth's health failed. This heartbreak stole away her verve for life. Now at her weakest, Cecil determined to play his hand. He could not allow her to name Francis Bacon to the throne.

Lady Macbeth
The decline into guilt, sorrow, and madness of Lady Macbeth is based on Queen Elizabeth's decline after the betrayal of the ring and the execution of her son.

The word cipher reads:

> *He, Robert, took these and a number of*
> *Other subtle plants and herbs*
> *(One being the moss that adheres to the cedar*
> *And which is a kind of mould)*
>
> . . . .
>
> *He had the wit to shrink the oily substance*
> *Into small compass and boil'd the stuff*
> *Till it became solid;*
> *And likewise to change and correct the bad taste*
> *By uniting sugar, musk and sack*
>
> . . . .
>
> *And putting the cunning drink*
> *Into one of the glasses, filled another*
> *With an imitation, made of an infusion*
> *Of rhubarb, fir and pine.*

> *He brought the drink to her and said,*
> *"Wil't please your grace,*
> *To drink a cup of distilled waters*
> *With me by way of pledge?"*
> *And then this monstrous villain*
> *First to his own lips puts*
> *The poisoned chalice.*
> *She did extend her hand to him and answered,*
> *"Sir, give me the glass."*
> *He does give it her and she drank it off.*[143]

Rather than killing her, Cecil's poison made her actions and words confused. From the day she imbibed the poison, she became sad and pensive, repelling all activity.

> *In a word, the powerful nature of the poison*
> *Did destroy the fabric and*
> *Structure of her mind*
> *Without any action at first upon her*
> *Blood and body....*
>
> . . . . . .
>
> *When you*
> *Proceed further in this business*
> *You will find that my good friend,*
> *The learned leech of her majesty,*
> *Did supply me with the*
> *Nature of the poison that she yielded too,*
> *And one of her ladies the account*
> *Of her death.*
>
> . . . . .
>
> *The physician told me that from the day*
> *The accursed villain drugged her posset*
> *That like lead upon her lies a heavy melancholy.*
> *"And," said he, "the queen has died*
> *Every day she has lived.*
> *She cannot sleep and she throws herself about,*
> *Now on her knees, then upon her feet.*
> *The other night she cries out,*

'Now o'er the one-half world nature seems dead,
And wicked dreams abuse the curtained sleep.

. . . .

Come, put mine night-gown on.
And yet I cannot sleep. Merciful powers!
Restrain in me the cursèd thoughts
That nature gives way to in repose.
My deeds must not be thought on,
Or they will make me mad.

. . . .

Am I sick, good doctor?'
    'Not so sick, your majesty,
As troubled with thick coming fancies
That keep you from your rest.'
    'Cure me of that.
Canst thou not minister to a mind diseased,
Pluck from the memory a rooted sorrow,
Raze out the written troubles of the brain,
And with some sweet oblivious antidote
Cleanse the stuffed bosom
Of that perilous stuff
Which weighs upon the heart?'
    'Therein, the patient
Must minister to herself.'
    'Throw physic to the dogs!
I'll none of it. Come, give me my staff, doctor.
Come, sir, dispatch....'

. . . .

                    Nevertheless,
She did at times show some sparkles
Of spirit and edge, for when
The ministers came to her to take order
About the succession of the King of Scots,
She did vehemently cry out
'Mine ancestors won by prowess
Many kingdoms, and they got riches by such exploits
And great authority, for I come
Of a royal parentage, and I will tell you

*That the Scotch dunces
Never shall succeed to our throne.
Is not he that they call
Francis Bacon alive?'*
    *'Yes, your majesty.'
    'Then, how dare you ask me such a question?
Is he not our eldest son
And lawful King of England?'"*[144]

The Queen's final admittance of Francis's right to rule came too late and fell upon unfriendly ears. To history at least, it is to her credit that in the end she named her true son. The physician continues:

"*I heard Master Cecil say,
    'Let her not live.'
Then they come unto me and commanded me to be begone.
So I yield, being sore dismayed,
And go lamenting out. And I fear me
That they killed her after I was expelled.*"
    "*But, loyall sir,
Was not some one else there?
Didst thou leave these varlots alone with her?*"
    "*There was a lady, sir,*" said he, "*near her.*"
    "*Indeed! what may be her name?*"
    "*I did hear her called Grace.*"
    "*I sought out this maid*

  . . . . . .

*… and said to her,
'I hear you did chance to see
The death of the queen?'*
    *'Why, sir, why, man, I understand you not.
Speak softly. I will be lost, quite lost,
If that devil knew mine eyes
Did see him slaying her.*

  . . . . . .

*With his hands about the circle of her neck,
The villain did stifle her,
Stealing the sweet breath that was embounded
In her beauteous clay.'*

> 'Did he with his hands
> Choke his dear lady sovereign?'
>   'These two eyes beheld this evil murder.'
>   'I pray thee, what did the creature do first?'
>   'After the physician had hurried out
> He locked the doors.'
>   . . . . . .
>
> 'I did not go when they bid us to,
> But hid myself under the desk
> That's covered with Turkish tapestry,
> Which stands in her chamber,
> Where I saw
> The whole vile murder committed.'"[145]

It is not known when exactly Francis learned that his mother's death had been a murder, but his innate goodness and vision led him forward.

Celestial Portents

> but then
> there was a star danced, and under that was
> I born.
>
> ~ *Much Ado About Nothing*, act 2, sc. 1

In 1600 a "nova" in the constellation of Cygnus, the swan, signaled a new beginning.

> The nova of 1600 was different from the previous one in Cassiopeia (1572) and the subsequent one in Serpentarius (1604).... These were stars of the first magnitude, stemming from the explosion of galactic supernovas (no such star has appeared since)... disappearing in 1574 and 1605 respectively. By contrast, the nova in Cygnus (now known as P Cygni*) initially exhibited a magnitude of the third degree and remained practically without change until 1606. (It was still visible in 1623 with the aid of the *perspicillum* or telescope.)[146]

---
*P Cygni is a variable star which fades in and out of visible levels of brightness.

These novas, as well as the conjunction of Saturn, Jupiter, and Mars in Sagittarius in 1603–4, hold great meaning for students of the esoteric.

The Cassiopeia nova signaled the birth of a "child of light" to a queen on earth that was to mirror the child of light born in the constellation of the celestial queen. P Cygni's appearance in Cygnus was significant due to the constellation's connection to the Dionysian mysteries. In Greek myth, Dionysus ascended into heaven and became Cygnus after humans killed him because he had, not knowing how it would affect them, given humanity wine. Wine can be seen symbolically as the wisdom teachings, just as Jesus brought the "new wine" and was crucified for it. Dionysus means "son of God" and his constellation is connected to poets and poetry.

The great conjunction of the three planets had been prophesied by alchemists and long awaited as the harbinger of the coming age of enlightenment or the "Golden Time."

> In alchemical lore, a conjunction of Saturn, Jupiter and Mars produces enlightenment—Saturn signifying deep thought which on its own is serious and melancholic, Jupiter signifying compassion and joviality, and Mars signifying the vital strength, discipline and determination necessary to rise to the heights of consciousness. The three represent the upper triangle of the "Lesser Adam" (also known as *Microprosophus* or *Zauir Anpin*) in the cabalistic Tree of Life—the triangle of higher human consciousness. In rabbinic and kabbalistic tradition it is said that such a conjunction indicates an appearance (of some kind) of the Messiah; and, if it includes a double or triple conjunction of Saturn and Jupiter, then the messianic appearance or manifestation is significantly stronger.[147]

The nova in Serpentarius occurred while the conjunction and P Cygni were still visible. This "new star" could be seen in daylight and was likened to the Bethlehem star.

At the end of the previous century, Paracelsus,* an alchemist, physician, and mystic had prophesied the coming of a great light,

---
*Paracelsus was born as Theophrastus von Hohenheim, 1493–1541.

Elias the Artist. "It is true there is nothing concealed which shall not be revealed, for which cause a marvelous Being [Elias the Artist] shall come after me, who as yet lives not, and who shall reveal many things."[148] Arthur Edward Waite writes in *The Hermetic and Alchemical Writings of Paracelsus:* "God wills that the lesser operations shall be performed first, and that the greater ones should remain occult until the Elias of the Art arrives. All arts have some one person specially their own, as is understood in other arts."[149]

One of Paracelsus's references to the coming one sounds very similar to Francis's own philosophy.

> If God, then, shews Himself to our discernment in Nature so powerful and so wise, how much more glorious will He reveal Himself by His Holy Spirit to our mind if we only seek Him? This is the way of safety which leads from below to above. This is to walk in the ways of the Lord, to be occupied in admiring His works, and to carry out His will, so far as is in us, or as it should and can be in us.... Still, I confess, there are many more things which I do not know, but which will surge up to the surface in God's own time. There is nothing so occult which shall not be revealed when the Almighty wills it so to be. This, however, I know, that after me will come a disciple of this school, one who does not yet live, but who will disclose many things.[150]

Alchemists in Paracelsus's time as well as Francis's Rosicrucians knew the prophecy of the coming Elias. As with all alchemical texts, these writers wrote symbolically rather than literally. This Elias the Artist, as in the esoteric arts of alchemy, would come to reveal spiritual truths and ascend unto God as did Elijah and Jesus.

Robert Fludd wrote in his *Tractatis Apoligetica* that the "new star of 1572 marked the beginning of the Rosicrucian work," which was being "prepared in secrecy until the 1603–4 stellar event, the latter being a sign to the Brotherhood to emerge into the open, expand their membership and begin the restoration of the world."[151]

Julius Sperber, a physician to the German prince Christian of Anhalt, considered to be one of the founding Rosicrucians, wrote of the coming third age:

> Julius Sperber (1540–1616), for example, wrote his *On the Three Ages* on the eve of the new century (1597).... According to this text, the first age corresponded to the Old Testament and the age of the Father, the second to the New Testament and the age of the Son, "but now the third and last age is approaching," the age of the Holy Spirit. This third age was understood to be a "golden time." Sperber referred to the coming period in similar terminology as Paracelsus had used in his *Book on Images*.... Although the Rosicrucian brethren did not divide history into three ages, their new period resembled Sperber's hopeful expectations.[152]

Julius Sperber's name may also have been used as a literary mask for Francis. Dr. Carlos Gilly, a historian specializing in the Rosicrucian brotherhood, alchemy, and Paracelsian school of thought, does not believe Sperber actually wrote *About the Highest Treasures*, which was originally published in 1597 and then dedicated to the Rosicrucians when it was republished as *Echo of the Divinely Illuminated Fraternity and Commendable Order of the Rose 2 Cross* in 1615. It may have been written by the same person who used Julianus De Campus as a pseudonym. In *About the Highest Treasures*, the author traces the history of divine knowledge.

> For Sperber, original and true knowledge was a pious philosophy, which in his opinion entailed primarily magic. From Adam it was passed down to Abraham and Zoroaster, and "from this Zoroaster such an art descended afterwards to the Chaldeans and then to the Persians, who used it for a long time like the Egyptians...." This magic, Sperber explained, "is nothing but the pious wisdom, that is a beatific wisdom," which had also been known to the Jewish Kings David... and Solomon, and their disciples. It was termed Kabbalah by the Jews and was ultimately known to Christ and his mother Mary....
>
> According to Sperber, this original wisdom had been lost, because after the era of the saints "this high study [...] was increasingly more forgotten [...] so that it could unfortunately happen that almost in the entire world one does not know anything specific anymore about this holy and very high discipline."

Still, it was not entirely lost, because "in all ages one could find among Christians some individual and very few people, who were inclined to such a study," among whom Sperber listed mystics, Neoplatonic philosophers, and Cabalists.[153]

Even if Sperber were not a mask for Francis, as a founding member of the Rosicrucians, he was most certainly a good friend and part of the Great Instauration.

The Changeling Becomes King

He that loves to be flattered is worthy o' th' flatterer.
~ Timon of Athens, act 1, sc. 1

On the death of Queen Elizabeth I on March 24, 1603, James VI of Scotland, "son" of Mary, Queen of Scots, succeeded to the English throne, becoming King James I of England. Few historians have questioned his right to the throne, but Dodd's research throws it into doubt. He claims that James was a "changeling" and not the true heir to the throne, for Mary's son had died at birth, and the Earl of Mar's newly born son was smuggled into the castle to take the royal heir's place.

> In August 1830, a workman was repairing the Edinburgh Castle wall by the doorway of the Queen of Scots chamber, when he discovered a cavity behind an oblong stone. It contained an oak coffin, and in it, wrapped in silk and cloth of gold, embroidered with the initial "J", lay the body of a small child...shrunken and mummified. The babe, buried in the wall of the Queen's Chamber, is presumed to be the real James VI of Scotland (James I of England).
>
> The coffin with its body was replaced at the time.
>
> I have personally seen the oblong stone over the doorway and heard one of the guides tell the story openly to a crowd of visitors. He ridiculed the idea that James of England was a Stuart.[154]

The story goes that Mary, Queen of Scots, learned the truth when it was too late for her to make a public disclosure of the incident. If she had disowned the "changeling" son, she would have had no heir at all.

If this report is true, it sheds light on the paranoia exhibited by James VI of Scotland on his ascent to the throne of England. Even if James had been the true son of Mary, Queen of Scots, Francis had a stronger claim to the throne.

But Francis was again at risk of losing his life and of instigating a civil war if he asserted his right. And so, to stay alive and continue to shepherd the founding of the Great Instauration, he had to set aside his rightful claim and submit to the temporary reality that Cecil created. James became king with Cecil at his shoulder. At the coronation, Francis was knighted among three hundred other gentlemen.

In 1604 Bacon published his *Apologia* concerning the events surrounding the execution of Essex. The historian Spedding found no evidence that the populace or Francis's fellow representatives in the House spoke ill of Bacon for his part in the trial. This document sets the record straight for history, not because he was reviled or misunderstood by the majority, but to bring peace to himself and to those close to Essex. Sadly, his erstwhile friend, Southampton, who was released from the Tower when James took the throne, never did understand or forgive Francis. This sorrowed Francis for the rest of his life.

Alice Barnham

In 1606 when Francis was forty-five, he married Alice Barnham, the daughter of a wealthy London alderman. Thus Francis assured James that he was not a rival for the throne of England, because no child born to a commoner could become heir to the English throne. For his wedding, though, Francis was dressed in the color of royalty—his own personal favorite. An eyewitness stated that he wore "purple from cap to toe." Francis gave back to Alice the £6,000 she brought with her upon marriage plus the £220 she received per year.

The English people quickly realized that James was not the king they had hoped for. "He degraded the Prerogative of the Crown by selling titles of dignity; ... his advancement of Favourites who lorded it over everyone. ... He burned and butchered thousands of inoffensive persons—mostly women and many children—as witches. ... His personal appearance was anything but kingly... slavering lips, watery eyes, rickety legs."[155]

James I, 1621, by Daniel Mytens

Historical evidence, noted by authors such as Michael B. Young (2000), indicates that James had indiscreet homosexual preferences. Another author, Montgomery H. Hyde (1970), noted the contemporary epigram, "Elizabeth was King and now James is Queen." Alfred Dodd's assessment of James was even more blunt. "He constantly lolled on his Favourite in public, with his arm around 'Steenie's' neck, wetting his face with kisses. He had a filthy, impure mind, employing two men to recount him bawdy stories. They succeeded so eminently well that he knighted them for their labours."[156]

Historians' assessments of James's reign are mixed. Many seventeenth-century commentators, including Anthony Weldon (1650), Edward Peyton (1652), Arthur Wilson (1658), Francis Osbourne (1658), and then David H. Wilson (1956), were highly critical of his poor administrative abilities, divisive policies in Ireland, wasteful spending, disdain for Parliament, leisure time, reliance on corrupt and unpopular favorites for policy administration, and for sowing the seeds of what became the English Civil War. Later historians, including Pauline Croft (2003), have been more conciliatory, acknowledging James's good intentions for an Anglo-Scottish union, his avoidance of war with Spain, and his openness to different opinions.

Francis's own assessment of James's reign came from twenty-two years of service in James's court.

Francis's role as an advocate for the well-being of the people was difficult during James's reign. The King's undisciplined spending led to a Treasury deficit of £600,000 in 1610. A deal was proposed where Parliament would raise taxes from the people to pay the debt in return for a list of concessions from the King. Francis and many other members were opposed to the deal, and Parliament argued with the Crown for four years. In 1614 James became so impatient that he dissolved Parliament indefinitely and attempted to raise money by other means.

Francis's experience in Parliament, combined with his service in high offices in James's court, privately convinced him that James's rule, under the aegis of the "divine right of kings," was invalid and unsuitable for the leadership of nations. This conclusion, based on his firsthand experience as well as knowledge of history, pointed more to the fallibility of monarchs than any connection to divinity.

There was no proven alternative to monarchy in Europe at the time, but Francis saw the necessity to define, propose, and implement a more just national representation for the people's well-being. To this end, he proposed the reform of legal codes using the tenets of the Rosicrucians and Freemasons, as well as the concepts of self-governance and personal sovereignty, which became common in the literature of the North American colonies.

Francis understood that the inertia of the monarchy would prevent the implementation of his proposed reform of legal codes, but with faith in future generations, he published them anyway for posterity. The far-reaching effects of Francis's law reforms over time justified his faith in the patient unfolding of the legal aspects of the Great Instauration. These reforms are in use today in many nations as derivatives of English common law.

Harvey Wheeler summarizes Francis's contribution of these distinguishing principles to the modern common law system:

- using cases as repositories of evidence about the "unwritten law"
- determining the relevance of precedents by exclusionary principles of evidence and logic
- treating opposing legal briefs as adversarial hypotheses about the application of the "unwritten law" to a new set of facts.[157]

During the 1670s, the distinguished English judge Sir Matthew Hale analyzed common law adjudication procedures and acknowledged Francis Bacon as the inventor of the process of discovering unwritten laws from the evidence of their applications. The method combined empiricism and inductivism in a new way that was to imprint its signature on many of the distinctive features of modern English society. The law reforms of the nineteenth-century British prime minister Sir Robert Peel are also said to have been influenced by Francis Bacon's legal principles. More recently, Paul H. Kocher wrote that Bacon is considered by some jurists to be the father of modern jurisprudence.

Francis's vision for the Great Instauration covered "the whole wide world" and was not limited to his era. His clear understanding was that the incomplete and capricious feudal laws of the monarchs he served had to be reformed and justly applied by future generations in all nations. In 1861 Hepworth Dixon described France's influential Napoleonic Code of 1804 as "the sole embodiment of Bacon's thought," saying that Bacon's legal work "has had more success abroad than it has found at home" and that in France "it has blossomed and come into fruit." Later in the nineteenth century, the Napoleonic Code became the basis for replacing most of Europe's feudal laws with modern legal systems. In the twentieth century, derivatives of the Napoleonic Code were adopted by nations that had been former European colonies.

But during the reign of James I, none of these eventualities had occurred, and Francis had to deal with the reality of capricious feudal law and a monarch who often did not have the focus or capacity to understand him. Consider Francis's mastery of himself—knowing a usurper had been given his throne, and that his duty was to serve that individual and his "divine right" to rule England.

While many would have been embittered by this and the tragedies he had lived through, Francis simply continued his grand work. For nothing that had happened to him, nothing that was withheld from him, mattered more to him than giving the world a chance at a golden age. He put himself in position to advocate for future legal reforms, give English people a foothold in the "New World," publish innovative principles of scientific experimentation and medical codification, supervise as editor-in-chief the translation of the King James Bible, secretly organize and expand networks of the Rosicrucian and Freemason Societies across Europe and North America, and deliver the English Renaissance through dozens of entertaining and enlightening stage plays, making English a language of culture.

The Founding Vision of America

The spiritual initiates in the lineage of the Great Brotherhood and the ancient wisdom teachings had prophesied and worked toward the fulfillment of a free republic for centuries. Now the time had come. Under Francis's direction, the Rosicrucian fraternity encouraged the leadership of the new American colonies. The name "America" is actually an anagram of "I AM Race"; meaning an *antahkarana* of souls from all over the world who hold the inner spiritual light. This land and the new government were meant to represent the individual rights of these souls, and that the government would be upon their shoulders. Francis envisioned a time when the colonies would unite as a self-governing nation, as outlined in *The New Atlantis* (1627). In addition to his behind-the-scenes charter writing for King James (1609), his investment in the Virginia Company and Newfoundland (1610), Francis played a major but hidden role in the establishment of the English colonies in North America. Hepworth Dixon notes:

> In no History of America, in no Life of Bacon, have I found one word to connect him with the plantation of that great Republic. Yet, like Raleigh and Delaware, he takes an active share in the labors, a conspicuous part in the sacrifices, through which the foundations of Virginia and the Carolinas are first laid.

Like men of far less note, who have received far higher honors in America, Bacon pays his money into the great Company, and takes office in its management as one of the Council. To his other glories, therefore, must be added that of a Founder of New States.[158]

Francis understood the esoteric meaning of the scriptural prophecy of the New Jerusalem. He outlined the spiritual purpose of the New Jerusalem indirectly in *The New Atlantis,* intended as an alchemical blueprint of principles for a great nation that did not yet exist. *The New Atlantis* appeared to simply be a work of utopian fiction, but Francis embedded in it the spiritual purpose of a future nation: The regathering place of the reincarnated twelve tribes of Israel. These souls would not be tied to any one culture or race but come from all nations for the purpose of building a free utopia.

Old and New Testament references are central to understanding *The New Atlantis*. The mystical power and divine purpose of the ancient Israelites, including the ark of the covenant, were to be transferred to the people who would immigrate to and be reborn in the new nation.

In the introduction to *The New Atlantis,* a pillar of fire appears off the coast of an inhabited island, and people from one of its major cities row out in their boats to study it. At the base of the pillar of fire, a wooden chest is seen floating on the water. As the boats near the pillar of fire, they find it too intense to approach any closer.

One of the priests from the island's House of Solomon offers

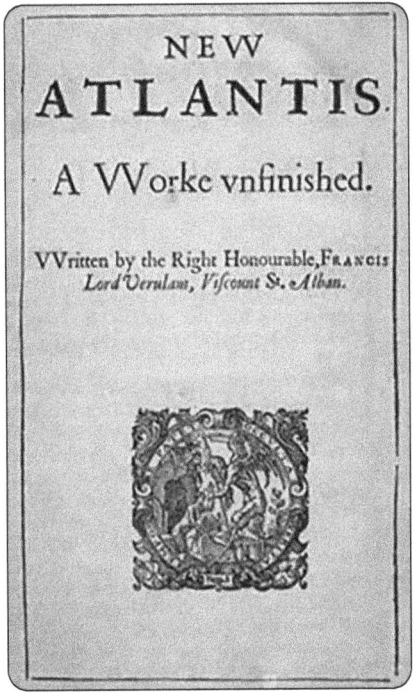

The New Atlantis 1627 title page, emblem depicting "The hidden Truth brought forth by Time"

a prayer to God, asking for the significance of the mystery to be revealed. As he prays, his boat is allowed to come closer to the fire appearing over the water. As he sails close to the floating chest, the pillar of fire dissipates.

Within the chest they find the canon books of the Old and the New Testament, as well as the apocrypha and other scriptures.

In addition to the books, there is a letter from one of the twelve apostles of Christ, Bartholomew, who states that an angel appeared to him and told him to put these books into the ark and to let it float out to sea. The letter states that to whomever God ordained to receive the ark, on that nation would he provide his blessing and his benediction.

This ark that the priests recovered from the water is reminiscent of the ark of the covenant that was carried by the Israelites wherever they went. By the mystical presence of God within the ark, they claimed their victories and the achievements of their era.

In *The New Atlantis,* the ark of the covenant passes from the Old World to the New, and with it the opportunity to experience the golden-age consciousness depicted in the book as the College of the Six Days' Work.

At the same time as Francis Bacon became Lord Chancellor of England under King James, the English were building settlements in the Virginias and Carolinas. The flag of the State of Virginia shows the goddess Pallas Athena, spear in hand, and conquering the tyrant. The muse of Francis becomes the Spear-Shaker in America waving in the winds of freedom.

In 1776 most of the signers of the thirteen colonies' Declaration of Independence were Freemasons and were aware of the spiritual analogy of the New Jerusalem. This was their guiding vision in their determination to separate the English colonies from monarchical rule.

Francis's work to persuade King James to issue charters, his engagement of co-investors for the organization of settlements, and his blueprint for the nation in *The New Atlantis* was understood only by his closest colleagues. King James, like most of England, would never have understood the prophecy, or approved of the pending reality of the New Jerusalem, and so Francis maintained his alchemical practice: "to know, to dare, to do, and to be silent."

Declaration of Independence, by John Trumbull

The Upward Trek

Francis and his team continued to write the Shakespeare plays for the first ten years of James's reign, averaging one or two per year, depending on Francis's role in James's government. As his responsibilities grew, finding time for playwriting became more difficult.

First came *All's Well That Ends Well, Measure for Measure, Othello,* and *Timon of Athens.* In 1605 Francis published both Shakespeare's *King Lear* and the *Advancement and Proficience of Learning* under his own name. This first "Great Instauration" publication was exactly thirty-three years after 1572, the year Francis had started his great work. Thirty-three is the cipher number for Bacon and is also "a symbol for illumination: for initiatic 'rebirth' or resurrection into glory."[159] Francis was not only incredibly creative but he also had a mind that could take in both intricate details and grand schemes that played out over decades, as can be seen by the strategic planning and execution of his Great Instauration and his success at Gray's Inn and in Parliament.

In 1607 Francis became Solicitor General, which brought an income to bolster his publishing. From then until 1611, he brought forth *Pericles, Cymbeline, The Tempest,* and *The Winter's Tale.* In 1609 Gray's Inn elected him treasurer and clerk of the Star Chamber.

He published *De Sapientia Veterum* (The Wisdom of the Ancients), which is a brilliant interpretation and scientific explanation of the inner truths found in Greek mythology.

This same year the flagship of a fleet headed for Jamestown was seemingly lost in a storm. In reality it was blown to the coast of the Bermudas, where the crew survived on an island for nine months before being able to sail again for Virginia. They arrived in Jamestown in May 1610. Francis and the other council members of the Virginia Company received a confidential report of this "miracle." This event formed the basis of *The Tempest,* written in 1610. No report of the lost ship and its recovery was made public until decades later; only the founding members of the Virginia Company knew of it when *The Tempest* was written. Our Prospero must have recognized the essence of a great story at once.

In 1611 Francis became Judge of the Marshal's Court and President of the Court of the Verge. *Henry VIII,* which was completed with assistance from John Fletcher in 1612–13, was technically the last Shakespeare play, though traditionally *The Tempest* has that distinction.

At this time, Francis used his influence with King James to have the Bible translated into English. His friend Dr. Lancelot Andrewes, the Bishop of Winchester, was one of the chief translators. Francis

A small colonial Jamestown house, built around 1630.
Photo courtesy National Park Service.

personally revised the final manuscripts before publication, but these, like the original manuscripts of the Shakespeare plays and much of Lord Bacon's writings, are missing. The authorized version of the King James Bible was published in 1611. In it Francis harmonized "the various translators' styles into the musical cadences of Shakespearean prose, putting the finishing touches to the work by leaving his secret stamp and seal in many places."[160]

A year after the publication of the Bible, Francis's self-appointed enemy at court, Robert Cecil, died in great pain on his way back from Bath. Modern researchers guess that he died of cancer. Edward Coke now stood as Francis's most implacable enemy.

In a letter to Coke, as quoted in *Bartlett's Familiar Quotations,* 10th ed. (1919), Francis wrote: "When you wander, as you often delight to do, you wander indeed, and give never such satisfaction as the curious time requires. This is not caused by any natural defect, but first for want of election, when you, having a large and fruitful mind, should not so much labour what to speak as to find what to leave unspoken. Rich soils are often to be weeded."

Francis took on the role of attorney general in 1613, which marked an intensifying of his work for the King and only increased as he became the privy councillor the next year. In 1616, while Francis was attorney general and Coke was serving as chief justice, a serious argument broke out between them on points of the law. A decision had to be made as to whether Francis as attorney general had the legal right to stay a particular case until the Crown could give its defense, or whether Coke as chief justice could pronounce a verdict without the Crown's defense.

Coke forced the issue before the King and his twelve judges. The court sided with Francis. "Everyone knew that Coke had set aside the order of the day, and called this particular case for hearing, not because there was any urgency, but primarily because he wished to flout Francis Bacon in the exercise of his duties as Attorney. In so doing he had overreached himself and affronted the King."[161]

James ordered the suspension of Chief Justice Coke. He then appointed a Crown Commission to read and revise Coke's reports. Sufficient offenses were discovered against Coke—fraud, contempt, and disobedience—to ensure a condemnation and a public trial. Distressed, Coke got on his knees before the Privy Council, where Francis had already replaced him, and begged for mercy to be spared a public trial.

Responding to his pleas, Francis wrote to the King in Coke's defense, "Had it not been for Sir Edward Coke's Reports, which, though they may have some errors, some preemptory and extra-judicial resolutions more than are warranted, yet *they contain infinite good decisions and rulings over cases....*"[162] Thus, mercy was extended to Edward Coke.

Dean Church published in *Life,*

> So the old rivalry, for the present, had ended in a triumph for Bacon. Bacon whom Coke had sneered at as a superficial pretender to law, whom he had so long headed in the race, and whose accomplishments and enthusiasm for knowledge he utterly despised, had not only defeated him, but had driven him from his seat with dishonour.
>
> When we remember what Coke was, what he had thought of Bacon, and how he prized his own unique reputation as a representative of English law, *the effects of such a disgrace on a man of his temper cannot easily be exaggerated.*[163]

News of the disgrace of this powerful and prominent lawyer spread through the Inns of Court and was quickly turned into a witty pun. "The Bacon has been too tough for the Cook."[164]

Coke's humiliation so embittered him that he now lived for just one thing—the complete and final ruin of his adversary. He quickly began laying plans for the demise of Francis Bacon.

Despite this opposition, Francis became Lord Keeper of the Great Seal in 1617. As the lord keeper, he was given his childhood home, York House, to live in as his foster father had before him. Here, Francis was able to put into practice his theories of architecture and landscaping. He turned York House into a beautiful mansion with aviaries in the gardens and water piped in from the city.

Once James appointed Francis as lord keeper, he left him acting as regent in all but name as he left for a six-month-long visit, traveling back to Scotland for the first time since being crowned.

Having taken up his new position Francis worked exhaustively to make up for the delays in Chancery caused by the illness of his predecessor, his old friend Lord Ellesmere, and by the workings of Chancery generally. He doubled the amount of time that he personally, together with his staff, were traditionally expected to spend on Chancery matters, in order to expedite and clear the causes of the court, although he made sure to reserve the depth of the vacations "for studies, arts, and sciences", to which, he said in his inaugural speech, he was in his nature most inclined.[165]

While the King was away, Francis went against Coke again. This time it was on a personal matter by endeavoring to help Lady Elizabeth stop Coke from marrying their daughter off to George Villiers's older brother. Though this failed, it shows his friendship with Elizabeth had survived her marriage to Coke.

The College of Invisibles

It is not the pleasure of curiosity, nor the quiet of resolution, nor the raising of the spirit, nor victory of wit, nor faculty of speech... that are the true ends of knowledge... but it is a restitution and reinvesting (in great part) of man to the sovereignty and power (for whensoever he shall be able to call the creatures by their true names he shall again command them) which he had in his first state of creation.

~ Bacon, *Valerius Terminus: of the Interpretation of Nature*

Francis took on a forty-year lease of Canonbury Manor in 1616, the same year that the Rosicrucian "Invisible College" was founded. Canonbury belonged to the daughter and son-in-law of one of Francis's personal friends, John Spencer. The beautiful mansion, with its outbuildings and tower, stood on Islington's hill looking out over London. Its oak-paneled rooms were decorated by Spencer with Rosicrucian and Masonic symbolism. This was the perfect location for Francis's "Invisible College," and the architecture of the tower itself suggests it was used for Freemasonry. Here, students of philosophy could gather unperturbed by the rush of London.

Canonbury Tower Islington. British Museum
creativecommons.org/licenses/by-nc-sa/4.0.

Ben Jonson

Ben Jonson, not only a "mask" for Francis's writing but also a good friend, referenced this college in his play, *The Fortunate Isles and Their Union*. Rosicrucian pamphlets from the 1600s refer to an invisible college as being the "Fraternity of the Golden and Rosy Cross."[166]

The same year that Bacon became the lord keeper, his friend Edmund Bolton

> proposed to King James I a design for a Royal Academy or College of Honour, of letters and science, complete with a Senate of Honour, for the advancement of learning. It was to be "incorporated under the tytle of a brotherhood or fraternitie, associated for matters of Honour and Antiquity.".... Its members were to "love, honour and serve each other according to the spirit of St. John," thus suggesting a Freemasonic design.... Details of this project, indicating that it emanated from or was inspired by Bacon, can be found in the *Commentaries* or *Transportata* among Bacon's manuscripts in the British Museum.[167]

Though approved, this college never saw fruition as James's successor considered it "too good for the times." Though this was true, how else can culture be raised but by creations that are too good for today but seed a wiser, brighter tomorrow?

During this time, Francis's literary efforts were bent on the completion of his *Novum Organum,* which, as his second major publication under his own name, was published in 1620. In it he lays out his new method of education and science. The book presents a series of syllogisms representing Francis's inductive method, establishing his famous classification of the "Idols" of the human mind, which prohibit the understanding of divine Truth. He defines the "Idols of the Tribe" as inherent limitations of the mortal mind, "Idols of the Cave" caused by human prejudice, "Idols of the Market Place" arising from man's inexactness in the use of language, and "Idols of the Theatre" perpetuated in various fallacious systems of thought.

Genius of the Ancient Pile

On January 22, 1621, Francis celebrated his sixtieth birthday with a splendid banquet at the Great Hall in York House. "To it he invited all his special friends that were of the Rosicrosse, the Rosicrucians and the Masonic Fraternities—all those privileged ones who were in the secret of Francis Bacon's labours.... Some of the best men in the land sat at his table that day."[168]

The "good pens," the Knights of the Helmet, and the Brothers of the Rosicrosse were there enjoying the feast, the laughter, the wits, and the heart of the great Lord Francis Bacon and his brothers.

Ben Jonson recited an ode—not just any ode, but an ode clearly given at an assembly of the Masonic brethren and to Francis as the Head of the Brethren. Dodd explains Ben Jonson's first few lines:

> Hail! Happy Genius of this Ancient Pile!
> How comes it all things so about thee Smile?
> The Fire? The Wine? The MEN? and in the MIDST
> Thou STAND'ST as if some MYSTERY thou didst.

"Hail" means more than a call; it is a sign. "Pile" has a meaning other than a pile of buildings; it also means a spear; and there was but one "Happy Genius" who could wield the "Ancient Spear" of Pallas-Athena the Spear-Shaker—Francis Bacon.[169]

How the evening must have been a glow of hearts, wits, gratitude, and vision for the future.

An even more magnificent gathering (though not merrier) occurred at the residence of King James when Francis was proclaimed Viscount St. Alban. With this final royal investiture, Francis reached the height of honor. Even though "he had begun life under the darkest of clouds, . . . they did not succeed in smothering him out of sight because Francis Bacon was inspired by one great purpose—to do something really tangible and worthwhile for his countrymen in particular and the world in general. And it was because these altruistic ideas inspired his actions that he refused to succumb to despair, disdain and selfishness. He felt, moreover, that he was a 'Servant to Posterity' for the divine urgings were strong within him."[170]

Francis's new title was St. Alban, the name of Britain's first saint,

Francis Bacon, Viscount St. Alban, by unknown artist.

not St. Albans, which was the land connected to the title and would have been the usual practice. From then on, he signed his name "Francis St. Alban."

On the thirtieth of January, Francis took his seat in the House of Lords. Sadly and predictably, his enemies had never stopped planning his demise, and now they saw their chance to manufacture his fall from grace.

Francis's climb up the ladder of spiritual initiation was accelerating. The path of an aspiring soul from "chela" or student to disciple to brother and finally Son—the embodiment of the Higher Self—is the true hero's journey. Francis was set on balancing all karma, expanding the fire of the heart, and becoming the adept master in life.

The Breaking Storm

> *Shall we now*
> *Contaminate our fingers with base bribes*
> *And sell the mighty space of our large honours*
> *For so much trash as may be grasped thus?*
> *I had rather be a dog and bay the moon*
> *Than such a Roman.*
> ~ Julius Ceasar, act 4, sc. 3

Sir Edward Coke watched Francis's rise to power with dismay. Coke had detested him ever since the young Francis had stood against him, defending the rights of the people.

Coke hated Francis for his genius and felt threatened in the presence of someone who was his superior, both intellectually and by lineage as the undeclared prince. He became the ringleader of a group of men who united under a "banner of hate"—each with a personal reason to see Francis Bacon fall.

Sir Lionel Cranfield, second-in-command in Parliament and a relative to Villiers, became Coke's right-hand man in this conspiracy. Like his leader, he despised the virtues of Francis Bacon. But while Coke would be satisfied with Francis's ruin, Cranfield had his eyes on Francis's titles. Within the House of Commons, the conspiracy took its orders from Coke, Cranfield, and Speaker Thomas Richardson, who was Villiers's brother-in-law.

Outside of the House, they followed Villiers and his mother, Lady Compton, at whose home the conspirators would meet. James had given his Favorite the title of Duke of Buckingham, but Villiers was not satisfied. He also hated Francis, although often posing as his friend, and coveted the chancellorship.

Reverend John Williams, chaplain to Francis's predecessor, believed that the chancellorship should belong to the clergy, as it had in the past. Seeking this office for himself, he joined ranks with the conspiracy to oust Francis from the chancellorship.

Then there was John Churchil, a crooked lawyer of the Chancery Court, infamous for forging Chancery orders. Francis, who presided over the Chancery Court, caught him in an act of forgery. Churchil could have been prosecuted, fined, and imprisoned for this offense, but Francis was merciful and simply dismissed him. Churchil vowed vengeance, claiming to Coke, "I am resolved not to sink alone."[171]

John Churchil became the key to Coke's conspiracy. Realizing that because of his previous position in the Chancery Court, Churchil knew the face and name of every disappointed suitor. He made a bargain with Coke: If Churchil could produce evidence of corruption in the Court of Chancery, and by this evidence frame Francis Bacon,

Sir Edward Coke

George Villiers, Duke of Buckingham

Coke pledged to restore him to his former position.

The mood of the House of Commons when it returned to session in January 1621 was a dangerous one. It reflected the mood of the people who disagreed with their king and were swinging farther and farther into reactionary anti-Catholic puritanism. Most of all, the House "was determined to obtain redress, once and for all, of grievances regarding monopoly patents."[172] In so doing, they would be directly attacking the King, his powerful favorite, and the corrupt oligarchy that ruled through these monopolies. Thus threatened, the powerful needed a scapegoat.

Coke struck his first blow. He moved for a committee to investigate "The Grievances of Monopolies" and had a report prepared. He met his hated rival face-to-face in front of the entire Parliament and recounted his list of the Crown's abuses concerning patents.

Rather than expose those who were truly at fault for corruption, Coke led the Commons to focus on Francis—even though one of the patents that had been most abused was sealed with the King's own hand, and Francis himself had voted against the continuance of the patents in the House of Lords. He had also spoken against all abuses, such as "fees, gifts, and presents," connected with lawsuits in his first speech after taking his seat in the Chancery in 1617.

The King joined Coke's choir in placing the guilt on Francis's head, stating, *"I am not guilty of those Grievances which are now discovered. I grounded my judgement upon others who have misled me."*[173]

On this premise, Coke arranged for another committee to investigate "The Abuses of the Courts of Justice with particular reference to the Court of Chancery"—the court over which Francis presided.

While some members of Parliament questioned whether they had any power over the King's Court, Francis responded that as far as he was concerned, "they had full leave to make any search into his Court."[174] Law reform had, after all, been one of Francis's long-term focuses.

Without the actual consent of the lord chancellor, Coke could not have moved one step further. This was the opportunity the conspirators were waiting for. And Francis gave them full opportunity to outplay their hand and reveal their real nature in public.

Ironically, John Churchil, in the meantime, had his lists of discontented litigants prepared with dossiers of details. Coke had them in his pocket, ready to produce at the right moment.

The storm broke on Francis. Coke and Cranfield presented their list of alleged bribes accepted by Francis Bacon in the execution of his office as Lord Chancellor. Francis was taken totally by surprise, as were the other members of Parliament who had always respected the integrity of the man and his office.

In his first four terms as a judge, Francis made 8,798 orders and decrees, and freed more than thirty-five thousand suitors in his court from the law's uncertainty. Scarcely one of Francis's decisions had ever been reversed. Francis determined to defend himself in court against these charges—a defense that many feared would throw light onto their own hypocritical corruption. Buckingham paid Francis a visit, ostensibly to see how he fared. There's no record of their conversation but Francis wrote Buckingham in response to the visit: "Your Lordship spoke of Purgatory. I am now in it. But my mind is in a Calm; for *my Fortune is not my Felicity. I know I have clean hands and a clean heart,* and I hope a clean house for friends and servants. But Job himself or whosoever was the justest judge, by such hunting for matters against him, as hath been used against me, may for a time seem foul, especially in a time when greatness is the Mark, and accusation is the Game."[175]

A second letter, written a day or two later, continues to make it clear that Francis will defend himself, his innocence, and his honor.

> I perceive, by some speech that passed between you and Mr. Meautys, that some wretched detractor hath told you, that it were strange I should be in debt; for that I could not but have *received an hundred thousand pound gifts* since I had the Seal, *which is an abominable falsehood...*
>
> I praise God for it, I never took a penny for any benefice or ecclesiastical living; I never took a penny for releasing anything I stopped at the Seal; *I never took a penny for commission of things of that nature; I never shared with any servant for any second or inferior profit.*[176]

These letters and Francis's assertion of his innocence boded ill for Buckingham and the King, whose corruption would be laid bare through Francis's defense. The bribery claims ground on, as the litigants were ushered forward. Francis had meanwhile taken ill. Even facing ruin from a sickbed was not enough to dampen his spirits. A contemporary wrote of him, "Your good friend the Lord Chancellor hath so many grievous accusations brought against him.... Notwithstanding, *himself is merrie,* and doubteth not that he shall be able to calme al the TEMPESTS raysed against him."[177]

The King then sent word to the Commons that he was grieved such suspicions would fall on one he himself had advanced. He took his turn in the betrayal of the great chancellor, writing that he would punish him to the full extent if the accusations could be proved—all the while knowing himself, his Favorite, and their cadre to be the true culprits of corruption. Coke, knowing through Buckingham that such a message would come, was ready to take full advantage.

From his sickbed, Francis wrote to the King:

When I enter into myself, I find not the materials of such A TEMPEST as is come upon me. I have been—as your Majesty knoweth best—never author of any immoderate counsel, but always desired to have things carried *suavibus modis.**

I have been no avaricious oppressor of the people. I have been no haughty, or intolerable, or hateful man in my conversation and carriage. I have inherited no hatred, but am a good patriot born....

And for the Briberies and Gifts wherewith I am charged, when the BOOKS of HEARTS shall be opened, I hope *I shall not be found to have the troubled Fountain of a Corrupt Heart, in a Depraved Habit of taking Rewards to pervert Justice,* howsoever frail I may be, and partake of the ABUSES OF THE TIMES.

... But not to trouble your Majesty any longer... *that which I THIRST AFTER,* as the Hart after the Streams, is *THAT I MAY KNOW YOUR MAJESTY'S HEART towards me.*[178]

---

*suavibus modis [Latin]: literal meaning is the sweet/gentle way. This was Francis's middle way that he constantly followed, despite the fanaticisms of his time.

His letter was met with silence, while Francis was still not allowed to see the offenses listed against him, nor Churchil's "proofs."

Francis requested the Peers to suspend judgment until he had time to call his own witnesses, produce evidence, and the usual legal privileges that came with a High Court action. He asked for it to be delayed until his health improved and until he actually knew the charges against him. But while he worked on his defense with the clear mind of an innocent man, the King grew more and more concerned with the anger roiling in the House of Commons.

There was a legitimate reason for their anger, and if they were not kept distracted by a scapegoat, they would soon turn on the real culprits. He listened to the advice of his favorite and the less-than-holy dean, John Williams, whom Buckingham had promised the chancellorship should he convince the King to follow their plan.

> He and Buckingham urge the King to ask Lord St. Alban to abandon his defence,... promising him to extend the Kingly prerogative to annul, later, whatever sentence be passed, by a full "Pardon." Their advice is *to command Lord St. Alban as the King,* if necessary, *to submit to his Will and to plead "Guilty."*
>
> The King, full of fears of red ruin and revolution, sees the Lord Chancellor. He begs and implores him to submit lest the Throne be jeopardized. He makes all sorts of specious promises. At last—as King to Servant—he commands him to enter a general plea of "Guilty" to the charges.
>
> The Lord Chancellor submits—
> "Oh! From what Power hast thou this Powerful Might,
> With Insufficiency my heart to sway,"
> are the words he writes afterwards of this interview....
> The King carries his submission of guilt to the House of Lords, where it is announced by the Prince of Wales. The Lords are stunned at the bare news. For many minutes there is a dead silence.
>
> But the Buckingham-Coke-Cranfield gang, armed with foreknowledge, have laid their plans. Their enemy is helplessly in the trap. Their friends in the Upper House, to humiliate him, demand that he pleads "guilty" to *each particular charge.*

There is no way of escape. He cannot draw back. He receives the details for the first time. He writes "Guilty" and leaves his notes on each case....

Coke presses that he should be executed and talks of precedents to justify such an act. He is, however, fined, imprisoned, stripped of his Office.[179]

On the evening of the day he pled guilty at the King's command, Francis wrote a prayer to God:

> Most Gracious Lord God, my merciful Father, from my youth up, my Creator, my Redeemer, my Comforter. Thou Soundest and Searchest the Depths and SECRETS of all Hearts; thou knowledgest the UPRIGHT of Heart, thou Ponderest men's thoughts AS IN A BALANCE, thou MEASUREST THEIR INTENTIONS AS WITH A LINE AND CROOKED WAYS CANNOT BE HID FROM THEE.
>
> Remember how thy Servant HATH WALKED before thee; remember what *I have first sought,* and what hath been principal in my intentions. I have loved thy Assemblies, I have mourned the divisions of thy Church, I have delighted in the brightness of thy Sanctuary. This VINE,* which thy Right Hand hath planted in this nation, I have ever prayed unto thee that it might have the first and latter rain; and that it might stretch her BRANCHES to the SEAS and to the FLOODS. The state and bread of the poor and oppressed have been precious in my eyes: I have hated all cruelty and hardness of heart: I have —*though in a despised* WEED†—procured the good of all men. If any have been mine enemies, I thought not of them; neither hath THE SUN SET on my displeasure; but I have been as a DOVE, free from superfluity of maliciousness. Thy Creatures have been my books, but thy Scriptures much more. I have SOUGHT THEE IN THE COURTS, Fields and Gardens, but I HAVE FOUND THEE IN THY TEMPLES.
>
> Thousands have been my sins, and ten thousand my transgressions; but thy sanctifications have remained with me, and my Heart, through thy grace, hath been *an Unquenched*

---
*Dodd notes that here Francis is referring to the ethical system of Freemasonry that he had founded.
†i.e., disguise. Here he refers to his hidden work under the pen name Shakespeare.

Coal upon thy ALTAR. O Lord, my Strength, I have since my Youth *met with thee in all my Ways,* by thy Fatherly Compassions, by thy Comfortable Chastisements, and by THY MOST VISIBLE PROVIDENCE. As thy Favours have increased upon me, so have thy Corrections; so as thou hast been always near me, O Lord; and ever as my worldly blessings were EXALTED, so Secret Darts from thee have pierced me; and when I have Ascended before men, I have descended in Humiliation before thee.

And now when I thought most of Peace and Honour, thy Hand is heavy upon me, and hath Humbled me, according to thy former Loving-kindness, keeping me still in thy Fatherly School, NOT AS A BASTARD, BUT AS A CHILD. Just are thy judgments upon me for my sins, which are more in number than *the sands of the sea,* but have no proportion to thy mercies; for what are the sands of the sea, to the Sea, Earth, Heavens? And all these are nothing to thy mercies.

Besides my innumerable sins, I confess before thee that I am debtor to thee for the gracious talent of thy Gifts and Graces, which I have misspent in things for which I was least fit; so as I may truly say, my Soul hath been a Stranger in THE COURSE OF MY PILGRIMAGE. Be merciful unto me O Lord for my Saviour's sake, and receive me into thy Bosom, or GUIDE ME IN THY WAYS.[180]

While imprisoned in the Tower, Francis wrote, "I was the justest Chancellor that hath been in the five changes since my father's time."[181]

In order for the king's promised pardon to be signed by the new lord keeper, Francis was forced to give up his beloved York House. He learned that the lord keeper was delaying his signature at the behest of Buckingham, who wanted the house in order to give it to one of his lackeys. Francis tried everything to keep his beloved home, but in the end had to submit and surrender it in order to have his promised freedom. Buckingham bought the lease of the home into which Francis had poured his heart for £1,300.

As far as history can tell, however, he retained the lease of Canonbury House, so his Invisible College survived the attack on its founder.

While Francis was stripped of honors, imprisoned in the Tower

Tower of London

and then sent under house arrest to Gorhambury, the spoils came quickly to the victors.

> *The Marquis of Buckingham,* by his treachery and dissimulation, successfully rode the storm that his extravagances had created....
>
> *Sir Edward Coke* tasted at last the sweets of a full-blooded revenge. He stood higher than ever in favour, momentarily, with the King and Buckingham. As "Hercules" he stood before the nation as the Great Reformer of Abuses and Corruption.
>
> *Sir Lionel Cranfield* was given additional Honours and climbed the Ladder of State. He was given a Peerage and a seat at the Privy Council; and...Office of the White Staff (the Treasurer). ... Sir Lionel was then created Lord Middlesex....
>
> *The hypocritical Dean Williams* gets his reward. He is received into the Privy Council. He is named successor to Dr. Mountain in the See of Lincoln and given a Bishopric. *He is also given the Seals of Francis Bacon's Office, which he coveted and sold his soul for...*
>
> Lastly, *John Churchil,* the infamous forger of Chancery orders, who had borne false witness against the Chancellor, under promise of reinstatement at the Chancery, is given back the trust he so shamefully abused. He is reinstated in his old office.[182]

As for Francis, although men could take from him everything he possessed—and did, including honor and reputation—they could never deny his identity in God. Dodd places the creation of his "Sonnet 121" at this time, written as a rejoinder:

> 'Tis better to be Vile then? Vile esteem'd?
> When not to be, receives reproach of being?
> And the just pleasure lost, which is so deem'd,
> Not by Our Feeling but by others' Seeing?
> For why should others' false adulterate eyes
> Give salutation to my sportive blood?
> Or on my Frailties why are frailer Spies,
> Which in their wills count bad what I think good?
> No, I AM THAT I AM, and they that level
> At my "ABUSES" reckon up their own:
> I may be straight though they themselves be bevel;
> By their rank thoughts, my "Deeds" must not be shown;
> > Unless this general evil they maintain:—
> > "All men are bad and in their badness reign."[183]

Dodd points out in this sonnet that the word *abuses* is the exact term used in the proceedings against Francis: "The Abuses in the Court of Chancery." Another point to note is the line, "No, I AM THAT I AM, and they that level." Here Francis used the name of God given to Moses, which he also made into a Royal Arch phrase in Freemasonry. The last line hearkens to Francis's quote, "For men of corrupt understanding, that have lost all sound discerning of good and evil, think all honesty and goodness proceeded out of... a want of experience with the affairs of the world. Perceiving those things which are in their hearts, their own corrupt principles, and the deepest reaches of their cunning and rottenness, they make but a play of the words of Wisdom."[184]

Immediately after Francis's release from the Tower of London, he acted on his plans for what he would do in his sudden enforced retirement. As he stated in his writing to Count Gondomar: "Now indeed both my age, the state of my fortune, and also that my genius, which I have hitherto so parsimoniously satisfied, call me, as *I depart from the Theatre of Public Affairs, to devote myself to Letters;* to marshal the Intellectual Actors of the present, and to help those of future time. Perchance that will be my honour; and I may pass the remainder of my life *as if in the vestibule of a better one.*"[185]

In 1624, three years after the court of the House of Commons sacrificed its own, an act of conciliation was granted by the King. Francis Bacon was reinstated with all his honors and privileges as a peer of the realm. All charges of bribery were officially dropped, though he was forbidden to take public office again. Francis meanwhile turned to the fulfillment of his higher purposes.

The Fate of the Conspirators— Karma Descends

> Wisedome for a Mans selfe, *is in many Branches thereof, a depraved Thing. It is the* Wisedome of Rats, *that will be sure to leave a House, somewhat before it fall. It is the* Wisedome of the Fox, *that thrusts out the* Badger, *who digged & made Roome for him. It is the* Wisedome of Crocodiles, *that shed teares, when they would devour. But that which is specially to be noted is, that those, which (as* Cicero *sais of* Pompey*) are* Sui Amantes sine Rivali,* *are many times unfortunate. And whereas they have all their times sacrificed to* Themselves, *they become in the end themselves Sacrifices to the Inconstancy of Fortune; whose Wings they thought, by their* Self-Wisedome, *to have Pinnioned.*
>
> ~ Bacon, *Essays*, "Of Wisedome for a Mans Selfe"

After the exoneration of bribery, a series of events unfolded rapidly in England's House of Commons. Alfred Dodd's *Francis Bacon's Personal Life-Story* offers a rare explanation of the grave return of negative karma to those who conspired to destroy Francis Bacon. For as Francis wrote at seven years of age, *Like Will to Like*.

The corruption, avarice, and hatred of Francis's enemies drew to them their own downfall as in a Shakespearean fashion, or perhaps one should say, Baconian.

---
*A lover of oneself without rivals

One of the most remarkable facts of history—totally unnoticed by his biographers, even Spedding, is the punishment that overtook every one of the men who wrought his ruin. It seems as though Divine Providence, outraged at what had been done to one of the servants of the Most High, was determined to bring every one of the miscreants to book.... For the march of events shows that while Francis Bacon was still busy with his altruistic plans—discussing divinity with Andrewes, poetry and mysticism with Herbert, the publication of the Shakespeare plays with Ben Jonson, and Freemasonry and Rosicrucianism with Robert Fludd—Fate was knocking at the door of the men who had sinned against him so grievously for their own corrupt advancement. They fell like rotten apples in a comparatively short space of time.

Sir Edward Coke was the first to fall. His intolerable arrogance brought him once more into conflict with the Crown. *He was flung into the Tower* to learn to mend his ways, and when he was released, eight months later, he was permanently degraded from the Privy Council, banished from the Court and confined to his house at Stoke....

Sir John Bennett, the judge of the Prerogative Court, was another of "the mean men" who had crowded Lady Compton's benches in the House of Commons. He had said, "I have neither the power, nor the wish, nor the will to defend the Chancery." Yet within a few short months an infinitely worse series of charges of extortion and bribery were preferred against him which were only too true. At the very time he was joining in the hue and cry against "the Great Delinquent", Sir John Bennett was plundering suitors right and left in his own court. *He was deprived of his office, fined heavily and imprisoned.*

Sir Lionel Cranfield was struck down by the 1624 Parliament. This vicious enemy as a reward had been created Lord Middlesex. He was a judge of the Court of Wards. He was accused of robbing the Royal Magazine of arms, taking bribes in his court and pocketing monies from the Treasury. These crimes were being committed while hounding Francis Bacon to the Tower and doing his best with Coke to get the innocent Chancellor hanged. *Cranfield was sentenced by the House of*

Commons to a restitutionary fine of £200,000, imprisonment in the Tower, to loss of office, and to public infamy.

John Churchil, the "Suborn'd Informer", who made the bullets for Coke and Co. to shoot, and swore falsely on the promise of the fee and reward, had been restored to his old job as Registrar in the Chancery Court. He, too, came before the 1624 House of Commons. He had been discovered at his old tricks again for forgery and a fraud in his office. *He was convicted and sent to prison.*

Dean Williams had obtained the office of Chancellor, having paid violent court to Lady Compton and led her to believe that marriage was in the offing; he now thought that he could play fast and loose with her. She complained to her son, who was so enraged at his perfidy that he said that of all he had given him he would leave him nothing. *He was speedily dragged from his fatal height by the Crown, stripped of his Seals with every mark of infamy, and driven back into the fields of ecclesiastical strife with a sullied reputation.*

The Villiers clan slowly disintegrated. Francis Bacon saw Lady Compton lose all her influence at Court.

Francis Bacon lived long enough *to see King James full of agony physical and mental,* fears for his son lest he should make a fatal blunder, so much was he under the finger and thumb of Buckingham, the man he had saved by the ruin of his Chancellor.

The Duke of Buckingham did not escape. For him was reserved the highest penalty for wrongdoing. He was slain by John Felton.* And the nation went into a riot of joy when it knew that the hand of the avenger had swept away the tyranny of Buckingham for ever.

These disasters which overtook them—so that not one escaped—seem to be one of the most striking vindications of INNOCENCE ever recorded. It is a remarkable example of the working out of spiritual law that governs humanity, individually and collectively, the law which says, "Be not deceived. God is not mocked. For whatsoever a man soweth, THAT shall he reap."†[186]

---
*a Puritan enraged by the corruption of the Villiers clan and concerned about the state of Britain
†Gal. 6:7.

Karma is a process of the law of return, the law of the circle. It is helpful to see such clear examples of actions creating their own return of events in the same lifetime. For karma is the indomitable law of God that is outworking, outpicturing itself. It is set in motion and continues to be in motion; it is God's energy in motion. All that we are is karma, and the more that we understand of ourselves, our life, the more we realize that everything that we are is the result of everything that we have ever been.

 ## The Gemini Brothers—Twin Works

I know myself now, and I feel within me
A peace above all earthly dignities…

~ Henry VIII, act 3, sc. 2

At home with his friends and family, Francis was received, not as a man vanquished and disgraced but as one magnificently victorious. They rallied around him, each perceiving, according to his capacity, the brightness of the light that shone within. Francis was their beloved friend and teacher, and he deeply loved them each in return.

For the eight months he was confined to Gorhambury, he turned again to his studies and writing, organizing his future publications and the presentation of his Great Instauration. In March 1622, Francis was again able to live in London, and in June he leased the Bedford House on the Strand for himself and his wife.

From here, in 1623, he published the first Shakespeare folio and his *De Dignitate et Augmentis Scientiarum*. These two were published exactly twenty-four days apart. They symbolized the Gemini brothers, which can be seen in the headpieces of many works of Francis, both under his own name and "Shakespeare." The Gemini brothers, known as the spear-shakers, are a part of a sacred mystery that is key to Francis's teaching.

In simple cipher, the first Shakespeare folio equals 37—the Preface plus 36 plays. The *De Augmentis* equals 37 as well—38 chapters minus the last, which at the beginning is said to be omitted. Like the twins, the Latin work gives "one" and the English folio receives it in order for both to become 37—a key number in the sacred mysteries through the Pythagorean theorem: 47th Proposition of Euclid. It is the degree of an angle of the right triangle with sides 3:4:5, 90°–37°–53°. The 37° symbolizes the Madonna and the Child, the birth of light, the Alpha or beginning.[187] This cipher links these two works to the first day of Creation—the first part of Francis's Great Instauration.

Gemini-Wheatsheaf headpiece, and a colorized version to show detail
From Peter Dawkins "The Shakespeare Gemini Headpieces" [B&W emblem colored by Michele Beaufoy for FBRT]
http://www.francisbaconresearchtrust.org.uk/

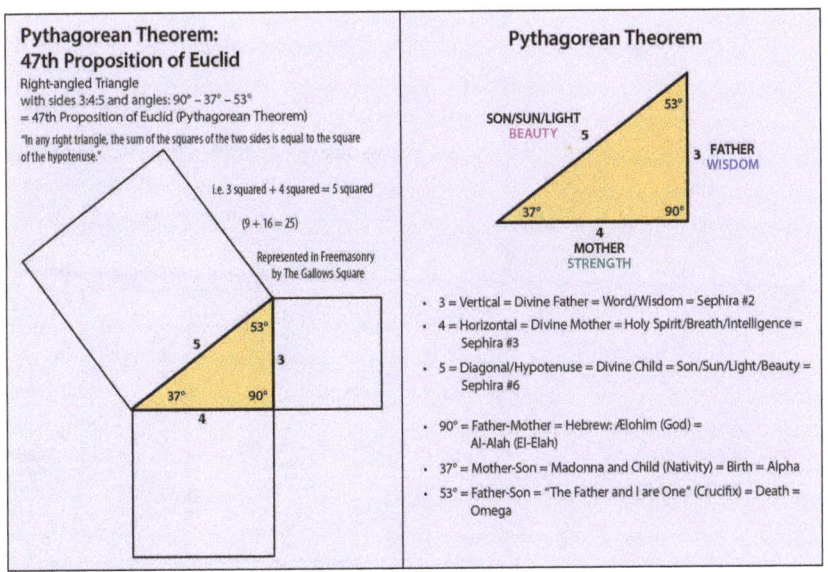

Based on Peter Dawkins' "Rosicrucian Mysteries" Lecture Series. https://www.fbrt.org.uk/events/

The *De Dignitate et Augmentis Scientiarum* is the Latinized and much expanded version of his English work, *The Advancement of Learning*. This volume contains nine books, which survey the knowledge of Francis's time. It is in this work that his ciphers are described.

On the title page there is the dedication AD REGIM SVVM, meaning TO HIS KING. This could mean King James, or as the use of all capitals would suggest divinity, it also means, to the heavenly king the Cosmic Christ. Here is another Gemini reference: to the mortal king or the immortal king. This dedication, along with the emblem of a flaming heart surrounded by a crown of olive leaves that is drawn just below it, symbolizes the purpose of the Great Instauration: for the soul to become one with the Divine, the Christ Self, in full illumination and divine Truth. In a 1638 publication of the work, the Rosicrucian rose was added around the flaming heart.

The flaming heart symbolizes the process. It is the heart set on fire with love, referencing the "Divine Wisdom hidden in the heart, which shines from the flame as a radiant sun of light when the heart is metaphorically aflame with love." The surrounding crown of olives symbolizes "the illumined mind or intelligence which receives this love light, sees it, puts it into action and thereby comes to know the wisdom and its love and this is Peace."[188]

In *De Dignitate et Augmentis Scientiarum*, Francis gave the key to his ciphers that he wove into his literary works throughout the years.

Flaming heart illustrations from *De Dignitate et Augmentis Scientiarum*, 1623 and 1638

In his book published in 1911, Granville Cuningham wrote about the challenge Francis faced in how to ensure that his cipher would one day be decoded, but not too soon.

> Ordinarily the use of a cipher was in correspondence between two friends, each having the key, the cipher being unintelligible to all others. But in Bacon's case, while the cipher message was given to the whole world, the key had also to be given to the whole world. It does not require much strain of the imagination to realize that how best, and in what way safely, to do this must have been a long puzzle to Bacon. If he were to leave the key in the hands of a select few to be produced a certain number of years after his death, it might easily happen that even in the lifetime of these few no proper time would arrive to declare the secret. For it was of such a nature that the mere fact of being privy to it might endanger the life of the holder. Or he might entrust it to some secret society, to be brought out in due course as to the society might seem proper; but this was open to the objection that as time went on the society might be dominated by men who would object to the secret being made public. Therefore he would come to the conclusion that the best and safest course to take was the bold one of making the key public, with safeguards and protections about it, and to trust to the keen wit and watchful care of those who were *in* the secret to prevent its being unveiled too soon while those were alive who might be injured by its disclosures. This, of course, was open to the objection that it might never be discovered, and would lie buried forever. But Bacon relied on the intelligence of the public to pierce the veil he had carefully drawn over his work.[189]

The literary sensation of *Mr. William Shakespeare's Comedies, Histories & Tragedies,* commonly called the First Folio, published in 1623, was dedicated to the Incomparable Brethren, Mary Sidney's sons. It has been called a Baconian-Rosicrucian-Freemasonic book of marvels, philosophy, and ciphers. As Dawkins wrote,

> Starting from the initial signposts given in the Shakespeare Folio, and the challenge on the Shakespeare Monument to pause and consider who really is commemorated there, we have found

ourselves on an amazing voyage of discovery, guided by the stars of the heavenly twins....

We have also found that the Shakespeare work is really a group work, led by the group's 'Apollo' or master artist, in the manner of a Renaissance studio, and that they had an extraordinary vision to follow and an unfolding plan to carry out—a plan that was and is somehow in harmony with certain celestial events and time-cycles of the world."[190]

The plays are ingenious mirrors designed for the education of mankind. Francis "sets before our eyes" all the human emotions and a portrayal of every kind of human character so that we can see ourselves and be transformed.

As well as the deposition scene being removed from *Richard II* in the folio version of *Henry VIII*, the names of the characters were changed to match those who had manufactured the case against Francis.

The innermost circle of his literary group, the "good pens," gathered about him for assignments at Gorhambury and the Bedford House as the scope of publishing tasks expanded. Some of them were fellow playwrights, some lawyers, others were researchers, printers, and poets. All were friends, Rosicrucians and Freemasons.

During this time, Ben Jonson helped to translate the *De Dignitate et Augmentis Scientiarum* into Latin as well as compile the 1623 First Folio. He was deeply devoted to Francis.

Francis's first biographer, Pierre Amboise, also refers to Gorhambury as a science laboratory in a country house. Granville Cuningham, too, wrote of the alchemical work done there: "He had a country house somewhat close to London, which he retained only in order to carry on his Experiments. In this place he had an infinite number of vases and phials; some of which were filled with distilled waters, others with plants and metals in their native state; some with mixtures and compounds; and leaving them exposed to the air throughout all seasons of the year, he observed carefully the different effects of cold or of heat, of dryness and of moisture, the simple productions and corruptions, and other effects of nature."[191]

Another description of the Gorhambury estate is found in *Baconiana:*

Gorhambury

He had, fairly close to London, a country house replete with everything requisite to soothe a mind embittered by public life, as was his, and weary of living in the turmoil of the great world. He returned thither to give himself up more completely to the study of his books, and to pass in repose, the remainder of his life. But as he seemed to have been born rather for the rest of mankind than for himself, and as by the want of public employment he could not give his work to the people, he wished at least to render himself of use by his writings and by his books; worthy as these are to be in all the libraries of the world, and to rank with the most splendid works of antiquity.[192]

Instead of chafing at the loss of the chancellorship in the corrupt court of King James, from 1621 onward Francis thrived in his new freedom to more effectively organize Freemasonry and the Rosicrucians and focus on the guidance of key men in the American colonies. His eye was on the fulfillment of the Great Instauration.

Peter Boener, who was Francis's private apothecary for some time until 1623, writes of Francis's reaction to this sudden downfall in his Dutch translation of Francis's essays published in 1647.

> But how runneth man's future. He who seemed to occupy the highest rank is alas! by envious tongues near King and Parliament deposed from all his offices and chancellorship, little considering what treasure was being cast in the mire, as afterwards

the issue and result thereof have shown in that country. But he always comforted himself with the words of Scripture—*nihil est novi;* that means 'there is nothing new.' Because so is Cicero by Octavianus; Calisthenes by Alexander; Seneca (all his former teachers) by Nero; yea, Ovid, Lucanus, Statius (together with many others), for a small cause very unthankfully the one banished, the other killed, the third thrown to the lions. But even as for such men banishment is freedom—death their life, so is for this author his deposition a memory to greater honour and fame, and to such a sage no harm can come.

. . . . .

Whilst his fortunes were so changed, I never saw him—either in mien, word or acts—changed or disturbed towards whomsoever; *ira enim hominis non implet justitiam Dei,* he was ever one and the same, both in sorrow and in joy, as becometh a philosopher; always with a benevolent allocution—*manus nostræ sunt oculatæ, credunt quod vident....* A noteworthy example and pattern for everyone of all virtue, gentleness, peacefulness, and patience.[193]

In February 1623, Francis had to give up Bedford House as it had become too expensive to run without a salary, as he was still barred from public service. Now when in London, his wife stayed with friends or family and Bacon took up residence again in his rooms at Gray's Inn. Just as in his earlier years, his ongoing financial hardship did not stop him one whit. Despite the odds laid against him, Francis Bacon was indeed the Solomon for the New Age. He fulfilled his dictum written in *Novum Organum:* "I am not raising a capitol or pyramid to the pride of man, but laying a foundation in the human understanding for a holy temple after the model of the world."

He became a living example of the way of love and truth as Jesus did before him and, like Jesus, he taught the sacred mysteries in ever-increasing levels of understanding. For the seekers of Truth, he laid a path to find the innermost temple of wisdom. For the passersby, he left indelible works that lift even the most unaware in consciousness. For Francis knew his mission was to lift all mankind from where they were to the next step above and then on to the highest level possible.

The Six Days Work

I had rather beleeve all the Fables in the Legend, *and the* Talmud, *and the* Alcoran, *then that this universall Frame, is without a Minde.*
~ Bacon, *Essays,* "Of Atheisme"

The six parts of Francis's Great Instauration are based on the six days of Creation, with the seventh stage being one of liberation, love, and paradise reinstated on earth. These can be seen to correspond with the seven aspects of the Divine Presence.

Just as the sunlight passing through a prism is refracted into the rainbow of the seven color rays, so through the consciousness of the Holy Spirit the light of the Christ is refracted for mankind's use in the planes of Matter. Each of the seven rays is a concentrated, activating force of the light of God having a specific color and frequency. Each ray can also manifest as a flame of the same color and vibration.

The first stage of the Great Instauration was to lay the blueprint, to explore the foundations of knowledge that have been built by prior civilizations, and to organize this knowledge. This coincides with the first ray of God's will, power, and protection, the first step of leadership and self-determination, and is also the first day of Creation—the division of light and darkness, of knowledge and ignorance. This is Francis's "Partition of the Sciences," which is illustrated in his *De Dignitate et Augmentis Scientiarum*.

The second stage is the "New Method": the creation of a method of how to study and interact with the knowledge of the past and how new knowledge will be discovered. Francis wrote of this stage, that it equips "the intellect for passing beyond."[194] Francis's work *Novum Organum* exemplifies this stage, as it was a milestone on the path to world harmony and peace everlasting. This is the second ray of God-wisdom. This is the path to understanding the knowledge of the universe. It is the second day of Creation, the division of the waters by air—or the emotions by the mind.

The third stage is "Natural History": the understanding of the nature of life, drawn from experience and exploration. This encompasses all of life—natural, human, and divine. It corresponds with the third ray of God's love, art, and creativity. Francis writes, "the third part of the work embraces the Phenomena of the Universe; that is to say, experience of every kind, and such a natural history as may serve for a foundation to build philosophy upon."[195] It is not enough to know the Truth academically; one must experience its mysteries and *be* the Truth. This stage is the discovery of causes. One must explore creation and understand that the First Cause of causes is God, who is Love. This third part is the study not only of "nature free and at large... such as that of the heavenly bodies, meteors, earth and sea, minerals, plants, animals... but much more of nature under constraint and vexed; that is to say, when by art and the hand of man she is forced out of her natural state, and squeezed and moulded. Therefore I set down at length all experiments of the mechanical arts, of the operative part of the liberal arts, of the many crafts which have not yet grown into arts properly so called."[196] The third day of Creation, the creation of earth and its vegetation.

The fourth is "The Ladder of the Intellect," or "The Thread of the Labyrinth."[197] This stage is "to set forth examples of inquiry and invention according to my method, exhibited by anticipation in some particular subjects; choosing such subjects as are at once the most noble in themselves among those under inquiry, and most different one from another; that there may be an example in every kind."[198] This is Francis's "Art of Discovery": to identify the laws of life, discovered through the creation and presentation of drama, experiments, literature, the arts, and the exploration of the underlying laws.

This can be seen to correspond with the fourth ray of God-architecture, purity, joy, and discipline. This is the light of the Divine Mother—the very fulcrum of life. Purity must ever be the keystone in the arch of being, and in the presence of purity there is no self-deception or deceit. It is through this life force from the Divine Mother that God's children become co-creators with the Trinity, and purify their souls for reunion with the eternal light. This stage explores and presents this opportunity of being co-creators with the Divine. It holds up a mirror to civilization so that it may learn and grow.

This is the fourth day, the creation of the lights—the creation of the sun, moon, stars, and the distinguishing of the cycles of time. Francis accomplished this stage through his fictional literary works, especially the folio, *Mr. William Shakespeare's Comedies, Histories, & Tragedies*. The plays provide the architecture or structure of a new way of looking at ourselves and evolving higher. The mind of Francis Bacon influenced the course of Western civilization and laid the foundation for the New World, the new science, and the golden age.

Many who walked the earth in his life took on the very profile of his soul. In his plays, Francis wrote those molecules of word—coded, ciphered—demonstrating the interactions of light and darkness in the human scene and on the stage of the world. Thus the lessons of Jesus' parables became the plays of Shakespeare. In the absence of Francis Bacon, this world would be several octaves lower in awareness, in enlightenment, and in illumination. This must tell you something about the genius of the mind that has its correlation in the genes of the body—and the spiritual genes, focal points of the seed of Christ.

The fifth stage is Francis's "Anticipations of the Second Philosophy."[199] This stage is for the collection of theories and discoveries as yet unproven by the method set forth in stage two. It is "for temporary use only, pending the completion of the rest.... For I do not make so blindly for the end of my journey, as to neglect anything useful that may turn up by the way."[200] This stage correlates to the fifth ray of divine truth, science, and precipitation, the ray of Francis's own muse—Pallas Athena. The unproven theories are collected and distilled in order to be proven or refined in the search for Truth. This is the work of the fifth day, the Creation of the creatures of water and air—symbolizing emotions and thoughts.

The sixth stage

> discloses and sets forth that philosophy which by the legitimate, chaste, and severe course of inquiry which I have explained and provided is at length developed and established.... I have made a beginning of the work—a beginning, as I hope, not unimportant:—the fortune of the human race will give the issue;—such

an issue, it may be, as in the present condition of things and men's minds cannot easily be conceived or imagined. For the matter in hand is no mere felicity of speculation, but the real business and fortunes of the human race, and all power of operation.... For the chain of causes cannot by any force be loosed or broken, nor can nature be commanded except by being obeyed.[201]

This is *Scientia Activa,* an active science and philosophy. Dawkins helps define the meaning of *active* philosophy. "Bacon takes great care to emphasise that when the true and summary laws of the universe are discovered, they will be found to be laws of love—and this love is an active, creative love, called in the Bible 'the work which God worketh from the beginning to the end.'[202] It will, therefore, be impossible to separate knowledge of these laws from the practice of them, for the two go together hand in hand."[203] This is the sixth day of Creation—the creation of the creatures of earth and man—which corresponds to the sixth ray of God-ministration. It is the ray of love in service to others. The action of the sixth ray is the action of the living Christ Jesus himself.

Francis did not write about the seventh stage, but Peter Dawkins points out that it can be seen represented as the seventh book in the frontispiece to the 1640 edition of Francis's *Advancement of Learning*. This book lies open on the desk before which Francis sits. He has just completed writing the words *Conubio jungam stabili* ("The connection made firm by marriage") on the right-hand page. On the left-hand page, are inscribed the words *Mundus* and *Mens* ("World" and "Mind").[204]

This is the alchemical marriage of the rational and the empirical, thought and action, heaven and earth. The seventh stage is the state of true liberty through the joy of the transmutation of human understanding to the Divine. This final stage correlates to the seventh ray of God-freedom, transmutation, and alchemy, and is both the highest of the spectrum of light and the most physical—not the most dense, but the most physical—corresponding with physical matter, interpenetrating the wide open spaces of matter/molecule, and endowing

The frontispiece to Francis Bacon's *Advancement of Learning*, 1640. Engraving.

matter with the Spirit that gives it resiliency and adaptability in many planes.

Francis's soul has become the avatar or spiritual master of the Aquarian age, and the Lord of the sacred mysteries of this seventh, or violet ray. He is known in the Book of Revelation as the "voice of the seventh angel,"[205] the one who would reveal the mysteries of God to those of that time.

Poison, Parliament, and the Pen

Francis had survived the trial by fire. And he immediately turned from the human drama to those higher ideals and goals that were his lifework. Although it seemed that peace might reign and the Order of the Helmet and the Rosicrosse Knights would laugh, love, and work again, those who cared only for the twists and turns of power politics did not forget about them.

In 1624 King James had good reason to fear those around him. As his health began to fail, James's court favorite, Buckingham, shifted his ambitions toward the king's impressionable son and heir, Charles. Once Buckingham had won the prince's loyalty, he nursed the unwell king with herbal drinks that seemed only to make James's condition worse. When King James died in 1625, Buckingham appeared to grieve, but many at court suspected that the favorite had assassinated James by poisoning him.

After the death of the King, there was no possibility of an investigation or finding of official evidence that Buckingham and possibly Prince Charles himself had been instrumental in arranging his death by poison. Meanwhile, gossip reigned, and the government faltered.

Although James had proven unwise and unteachable, his twenty-two-year reign was a lesser evil than the more dictatorial plans that Buckingham had in mind for Charles I. Parliament refused to give more money to Charles and Buckingham's war with Spain. The Earl of Arundel, Francis's friend who had defended him while presiding over the House of Lords committee that investigated the charges of corruption, had gone against Buckingham in 1624 and now found himself on the wrong side of the King. He was prevented from attending Parliament, and the House of Lords was outraged at this insult to their rights. It was the first time since Edward III that a king had stopped a lord from attending.

Parliament continued to refuse funds and attacked Buckingham instead. He was called to face impeachment in the House of Commons for procuring titles, holding too many offices and licenses, and for selling honors and offices.

Portrait of Thomas Howard, 21st Earl of Arundel, by Peter Paul Rubens

The stories traveled all over London that King James had discovered Buckingham intercepting private intelligence letters to the King and that he had also answered these letters without the King's knowledge. It seemed that the King had finally awakened to the treachery of George Villiers.

When Parliament wanted to impeach Buckingham, King Charles wouldn't allow it. In turn, Parliament refused to grant the Crown funds. Charles retaliated by dissolving Parliament. These actions and his previous power plays irreparably damaged the relationship between King Charles and Parliament. The members of both the House of Lords and the House of Commons thought the King contemptible.

These intense problems in government were a foreshadowing of war to come. They led to the "Great Rebellion" and the English Civil War sixteen short years later in 1642.

In early 1626, George Eglisham, one of James's attending physicians, published a pamphlet titled "Prodromus Vindictæ." This pamphlet was published in Frankfurt in Latin and German. In May of that year, it was published in English as "The forerunner of reuenge Vpon the Duke of Buckingham, for the poysoning of the most potent King Iames." It accused Buckingham of poisoning the King and the Marquise of Hamilton, who had been a close family friend and Patron of George Eglisham.

The Duke tooke his oportunitie when all the Kings Doctors of Physicke vvere at Dinner vpon the munday before the King dyed, without there knovvledge or consent, offered to the King a white povvder to take, the which the King longtime refused, but ouercome by his flattering importunitie at length tooke it, drunk it in wine, and immediatly became vvorse and worse, falling into many soundings and paynes, and violent fluxes of the belly so tormented, that his Maiestie cryed out aloud, o this white povvder! this white povvder! wold to God I had neuer taken it, it wil cost me my liffe.[206]

The Latin and German versions were possibly in circulation as early as January since Europe had already changed to the Gregorian calendar. The entire country was in an uproar over Buckingham, his corruption, thefts, and this story of poisoning. As the rightful heir to the throne, the current upheaval put Francis in a very dangerous position. Buckingham had used him as a scapegoat once already, and with the current King so unpopular, the cunning Favorite would find a rightful heir as too dangerous to let live. Francis did not give his enemies the opportunity to devise yet another plot against him.

After long discussions with his closest friends, Francis chose to say goodbye to his life as the secret Tudor prince.

Whether it was to escape his enemies or to personally care for and work with his secret societies in Europe, it was time for Francis to move on to the next phase of his Great Instauration.

A Phoenix from the Ashes

We are such stuff
As dreams are made on; and our little life
Is rounded with a sleep.
~ The Tempest, act 4, sc. 1

On April 9, 1626, came Francis's turn to exit the stage. The Master Playwright wrote himself the perfect ending. In this last year of his life, a Latin inscription was painted on the wall of the highest room of Canonbury Tower, the home of Francis's Rosicrucian Invisible

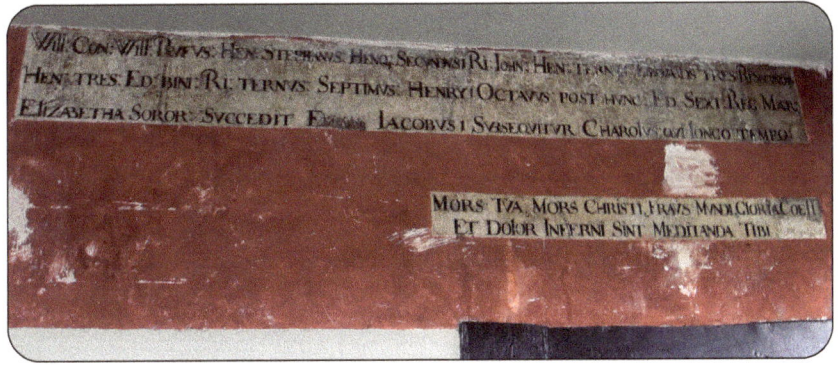

Canonbury Tower: List of Kings and Queens of England in the Inscription Room
Photo by Masato.harada: creativecommons.org/licenses/by-sa/4.0.

College. It is a list of rulers of England from William the Conqueror to Charles I, with two lines of script beneath, which when translated to English reads:

> *Your death, the death of Christ, the deceit of the world, the glory of the heavens and the pain of the Infernal—these are meditations for you.*

A mystery left for Francis's decipherers. In the 1980s, Thomas Bokenham, a Baconian researcher and cryptologist, "detected a cipher in this inscription that pointed to something being concealed behind the plaster, inside the cavity between the two plaster-and-lathe facings of the wall. When this was investigated, there was evidence that someone had previously opened up the cavity and, if there had been anything in it, removed whatever might have been there. The Tower, in fact, once contained several concealed cupboards, but all were found to be empty, their contents (if any) all removed."[207]

In early April, after conducting an experiment in food preservation in which he stuffed a fowl with snow, he stopped at the Earl of Arundel's home, overcome with illness. Though his friend was not home, he was welcomed and cared for. But on Easter Sunday—the day celebrating Jesus' resurrection, Francis was reported dead. His casket was buried at his request next to Lady Anne Bacon's grave in St. Michael's Church at St. Albans, Hertfordshire.

Scholars all over the world united to mourn and acclaim Francis Bacon, "the greatest poet who has ever lived." In the months following, Francis's chaplain Dr. Rawley compiled the *Manes Verulamiani*, meaning Shades of Verulam. It contained no less than thirty-two Latin eulogies with many verses portraying Francis as supreme dramatist and concealed poet. Quite unlike the silence of the literary world at the death of the actor Shakspur.

Dr. Rawley withheld many eulogies lest they revealed too much, writing:

> these tokens of love and memorials of sorrow prove how much his loss grieves their heart. And indeed with no stinted hand have the Muses bestowed on him this emblem (for very many poems, and the best too, I withhold from publication); but since he himself delighted not in quantity, no great quantity have I put forth. Moreover let it suffice to have laid, as it were, these foundations in the name of the present age; this fabric (I think) every age will embellish and enlarge; but to what age it is given to put the last touch, that is known to God only and the fates.[208]

The following eulogies exemplify the spirit of the collection:

> "Think you, foolish traveller, that the leader of the choir of the Muses and of Phoebus is interred in cold marble? Away, you are deceived. The Verulamian star now glitters in ruddy Olympus: The boar, great James shines resplendent in your constellation."[209]

One writer symbolically tied Francis Lord St. Alban with the first British martyr, Saint Alban, who died for helping a priest escape by disguising himself as the holy man.

> "Mourn, Oh ye Lares* of Alban, likewise thou prototype Martyr, Passing of Verulam's Sage—be his Hallowed Fate ne'er desecrated! Aye! *Thou Good Martyr*, lament, for no sad Fate hath ever been sadder, Saving thine own, *when thou fellest beneath the Dire Cloak of another.*"[210]

> "To his magical fingers rang out the Lyre Strings; Learning, too, thrilled at his touch."[211]

---
*Household Deities

William Boswell's poem declared:

"None who survive him can marry so sweetly Themis the Goddess of Law to Pallas the Goddess of Wisdom.... Mourn then ye Muses."[212]

"O how am I in verse like mine to commemorate you, sublime Bacon! and those glorious memorials of all the ages composed by your genius and by Minerva. With what learned, beautiful, profound matters the Great Instauration is full! With what light does it scatter the darksome moths of the ancient sages! creating from chaos a new wisdom: thus God Himself will with potent hand restore the body laid in the tomb; therefore you do not die (O Bacon!) for the Great Instauration will liberate you from death and darkness and the grave.
—R. C., T. C."[213]

Francis Bacon is variously called "The Master of Fable", "the Noble Day Star of the Muses", "the Tenth Muse", "The Learned Apollo", "the Leader of the Great Band of Muses", "Phoebus' Own Chorister", and phrases to denote Francis Bacon's connection to poesy in a highly special sense.[214]

Williams wrote,

"How has it happened to us, the disciples of the Muses, that Apollo, the leader of our choir, should die? ... Who will wish to speak, you being silent? Let no one scatter fragrant violets on your urn, nor rear your sepulchre with the vastness of pyramids; for your laboured tomes preserve your fame. This suffices; these memorials will not let you die."[215]

And an enigmatic statement was made by Henry Ockley of Trinity College, who said,

"He is gone, he is gone: it suffices for my woe to have uttered this: I have not said he is dead: What need is there now of black raiment? See! see! our pen flows with black pigment; and the fountain of the Muses shall become dry, resolving itself into tiny tears."[216]

When the details of Francis's "death" are examined, one discovers that each one of four contemporaries writing about his death assigns a different place for the event. One says that he died at the house of Lord Arundel at Highgate. Another wrote that it happened at the house of his friend, Dr. Parry, in London. A third claimed that Francis died at the house of his cousin, Sir Julius Caesar in Muswell Hill, and a fourth said that he died at the house of his physician, Dr. Witherbourne. Not one of these "authorities" either confutes or confirms the others. No one actually claimed to have been with Francis when he died, or to have seen his body afterwards.

Records indicate that, in fact, Francis Bacon did not die in 1626. Instead, he planned his "philosopher's death." And all those who reported on his death were in league with one another, each pledged to suppress the true location of their mystical friend. His friends helped arrange a feigned funeral in which an empty crypt was sealed in St. Michael's Church. It is said that Francis, dressed in the garb of an old woman, attended his own funeral.

Many years later, the crypt was opened. It was completely empty. Jean Overton Fuller, another biographer said that the family was certain that Bacon had never been interred there.

After his funeral Francis left England. Disguised, he escaped to Europe where he is believed to have lived for over forty years under various fictitious names. Contemporary Baconians believe that Francis continued to write works under new pen names, as well as under the names of writers in his literary group.

Francis Tudor Bacon, like the mythical phoenix, arose from the shadows of Britain, now free to pursue his calling—the enlightenment of the whole wide world. He carried the hearts of his friends, the Brothers of the Rose Cross, with him into the greater work still at hand.

Esoteric legend and teachings say that Francis took his inner, spiritual initiations at this time. Having surrendered a worldly throne, as Prince Siddhartha did before him, Francis was able to pursue without distraction his higher calling to the benefit of all humanity.

On a mystical, spiritual level, Francis was walking the path of the higher initiations. Buddhists and Theosophists refer to these levels of spirit and the integration of the soul with the immortal Higher Self as the path of the arhat. Following this is the level of adept and unascended master. The world gained the benefit of this high spiritual initiate as he laid down his life so that all might rise in consciousness.

Two Shakespeare Memorials

The remarkable Westminster Abbey Shakespeare memorial is an enigma. Carved on the scroll is an inscription of the immortal quote from *The Tempest*. Strangely the quote is incorrect. Cipher experts note that the numerical signature of these lines reveals the names of Francis Bacon and Fra Rosi Crosse. The left hand of the statue points directly to the word *Temples*. The poet's noble face is strikingly like the face of Francis Bacon, minus the Elizabethan hat. The young face of a crowned prince also stands out. Is this the face of the Golden Age Prince?

(upper left) Shakespeare Memorial at Westminster Abbey, Poet's Corner.
(below right) Detail of the memorial.

Credit line: By JRennocks - Own work, CC BY-SA 4.0, https://commons.wikimedia.org/w/index.php?curid=106332696

The second memorial is a twin of the first, with the statue pointing at the words *Shadow* and *Player*. It still stands at Wilton House, the ancestral home of Mary Sidney and Henry Herbert, friends of Francis Bacon, and their sons, to whom the First Shakespeare Folio is dedicated.

(left) Shakespeare Memorial at Wilton House
© Will Pryce, photographer / Bridgeman Images

The New Atlantis

It is likely that the home of Rosicrucian friends in Paris became the initial home for Francis. Very little is known of him during this time, but what can be tracked are his own publications and literature of the time that have mysterious origins or pseudonyms. It is clear that he continued his literary work and, through it, his spiritual mission.

From Paris, he directed his literary circle in England to "posthumously" publish his works. Among these was the seminal *Sylva Sylvarum* with *The New Atlantis* within it in 1627. Much revising, amending, and correcting went into this work.

It is also likely that Francis worked with his erstwhile apothecary, Peter Boener, to translate many of Francis's essays into Peter's native Dutch, which he published in 1647.

The publishing of *The New Atlantis* caused a revolution in philosophy and also in spirituality. *The New Atlantis* is a key to understanding Francis Bacon's Great Instauration. This unfinished work describes an idealized island society led by scientific holy men dedicated to prayer, the inductive method, and careful analysis. Unencumbered by interference from the state, their island's pure form of Christianity is blessed by God. Visitors from Europe witness the blessing as the reappearance of the biblical ark of the covenant, indicating a transfer of divine power and authority to the island nation. The orderly details of this peaceful society serve as an insight into Francis's purpose. *The New Atlantis* can be seen as an outline, an exemplary Utopia, as an inspiration for the English colonies of North America.

In 1631 Pierre Ambrose, of whom very little is known, published the curious French translation *Histoire Naturelle de Mre. François Bacon* in Paris. Though considered a translation of *Sylva Sylvarum*, it never uses that title within the text.

> The title-page does not name the translator, but the Privilege du Roy does, specifying that one Pierre Amboise, sieur de la Magdelaine, is allowed to publish a translation of:

A book entitled, The Natural History of Sire Francis Bacon, Canceler of England, with some Letters from the same author; alongside these the life of said sire Bacon, composed by the proponent previously mentioned.

...The "Avertissement" to the reader claims that the volume is a translation of Francis Bacon's posthumous natural history, made "on the manuscripts of the Author."[217]

In this work, which claims to be compiled from Francis's own papers, is written the first biography of his life, almost twenty years before the publication of Rawley's *Life of Francis Bacon*. In it, Francis is described as "born in purple," an odd phrase unless the author knows Francis to be royalty. This work portrays Francis as a scientist, philosopher, and most importantly, an alchemist.

Frontispiece from Bacon's *Sylva Sylvarum*

Amboise's Bacon is a philosopher, experimenter and explorer of nature but is also an alchemist or, at least, someone actively engaged in chemistry.... What Amboise emphasizes here is a portrait of Bacon engaged in alchemical experimentation and constructing (in the last five years of his life, in retirement in his "college" of experiences) a natural history of qualities and a theory of matter. Moreover, although describing this matter theory in terms of tangible bodies and pneumatical spirits, the translator slips more than once in the language of corpuscularian philosophy....

Amboise's translation also contains a heavily and interestingly edited version of *New Atlantis* called *Nouvel Atlas*. This opens with a short preface stating the fact that Bacon had an actual design to build a college of experiments but, lacking funds and time, left a literary model of it for further generations. *New Atlantis* and its college are therefore part of the natural history: they give Bacon's plan for how to pursue such a natural historical project.[218]

In light of the fact that Francis was alive and in Europe at the time of its publication, this work warrants much further study.

The New Atlantis was published as a stand-alone title in English in 1659—exactly thirty-three years after Bacon's feigned death.

In 1659 Thomas Bushell, likely a pseudonym, mentioned the new edition of *The New Atlantis* in *Mineral Prosecutions*. An unknown person publishing under the initials "RH" added content to *The New Atlantis* the next year, and in 1662, a Rosicrucian version was published as the preface to *The Holy Guide*, a Rosicrucian text, by another pseudonym, John Heydon.

The Holy Guide actually offers the word "Rosicrucians" to replace "the New Atlantis," and "the land of the Rosicrucians" replaces "the Wise Men of the House of Solomon."

It is likely that Francis stayed in or traveled often to Rosicrucian and Freemasonic Lodges in The Hague and other locations in the Netherlands and Germany, where he also sent couriers. Anonymous, unpublished Rosicrucian manifestos had been released much earlier in Germany, around 1610, possibly Anthony's work as he put forth Francis's plan and ideals.

Johann Valentine Andreae, who had let Francis use his name as the rumored author of the Rosicrucian pamphlets, now provided long-term lodging for Francis in Frankfurt. This safe haven in Frankfurt allowed translations of existing Baconian books to be published in Europe during the 1630s, while new books and new editions continued to be published in English, either "posthumously" or under new pseudonyms.

The last Shakespearean poem published by the Rosicrosse Society was in a book titled *Love's Martyr*. The leading writers of the age contributed to this book of poems. The poem attributed to "Shakespeare" is "The Phoenix and the Turtle." It typifies the self-immolation, philosopher's death, and resurrection of a poet. It contains a prophetic suggestion that after the black crow of slander has gone among the generations of men for three hundred years, the poet will rise again, revealing his personality once more to his countrymen.

The same suggestion is to be found in Francis Bacon's statement, "I keep the future ever in my plann, looking for my reward, not to my times or countreymen, but to a people very far off, and an age not like our owne, but a second golden age of learning."[219]

The Mystery of the Second Shakespeare Folio

In 1627 a second edition of the Shakespeare Folio was printed. In it were 1,679 careful editorial changes to the First Folio. When the Second Folio appeared, few people other than theatrical actors noticed. For three hundred years Shakespeare scholars asserted that the Second Folio was a verbatim reprint of the First. It was not until 1937 that two Shakespeare researchers, Black and Shaaber, comprehensively compared the folios side by side. There were changes in meter, and improvements in stage directions.

Whoever made these changes had to be a classical scholar, a linguist, familiar with Greek, Latin, and French languages, and a poet and dramatist as well. The actor Shakspur died in 1616. Even the

First Folio is a mystery as to who edited the plays. And why are the original manuscripts missing? The Second Folio increases the mystery.

Who but the author would systematically edit Shakespeare's First Folio and make 1,679 edits that actually improved readability and stagecraft in every instance? Francis still lived.

Uncivil War

*Th' abuse of greatness is when it disjoins
Remorse from power.*
~ *Julius Caesar*, act 2, sc. 1

As Francis and his Brotherhood of the Rosicrosse continued their mission, the kingdoms of Europe began to falter.

Like France before her, England succumbed to a series of civil wars between 1642 and 1651. Queen Elizabeth and Francis both had worked hard in their own way to keep such a fate from occurring to their beloved England. But the corruption, religious intolerance, arrogance, and foreign wars of King Charles I and Lord Buckingham bankrupted the Treasury. When Parliament refused to fund his military disasters, Charles dismissed it. His father, James, had ruled without a Parliament in session for seven years. Charles ruled

English Civil War: *The Battle of Marston Moor*, painting by John Barker

without Parliament for eleven years and created a sustained turmoil within a resentful, overtaxed portion of the public.

This was also a religious war with the two factions being the Catholic Royalists and the Protestants, the latter bent on the individual rights of men but hampered by some with a fundamentalist and stern religion. The intolerance of differing faiths at this time ultimately led to the failure of the parliamentary republic and the death of thousands of innocents. Nine years of civil war caused such widespread devastation that about 190,000 (4%) of the population of England died, 60,000 (6%) of Scotland died, (with at least 8,000 deported in servitude), and about 616,000 (41%) of the Irish people died, (with over 40,000 deported into servitude).[220]

The Execution of the King

King Charles I lost the civil war and was tried by Parliament and Oliver Cromwell's council for high treason. He was convicted and beheaded in 1649. The nation remained polarized as an unsettled Puritan republic until 1659, with the return of his son, the exiled Charles II, under parliamentary consent. This national disaster had been brewing during the reign of James I, but Francis's quiet advice had staved off civil war for a generation. His royal wisdom would have saved all of Britain, but many were too corrupt to listen. The greater world benefited from his philosophy and secret works.

To have heard the ongoing news of oppression, poverty, and near-anarchy in Britain must have been painful for Francis. The scope of the

Equestrian portrait of Charles I of England, by Anthony van Dyck

prolonged tragedy was yet more proof of his view that England's colonies in North America were the best hope for a comprehensive restoration of representative government and spiritual freedom. Even though many displaced Puritans and Royalists emigrated during and after the wars to the colonies, bringing with them their own histories and biases, North America shone forth as the new platform of society and a place of great hope where religious toleration, freedom of religion, and the Great Instauration could best unfold.

Reformation and Liberty

As a spiritual adept, Francis not only dreamed of a better world but he also organized his brilliant friends and followers to create it from the foundation to the pinnacles of enlightenment and freedom. He was the founder of modern democracy in a republic and the true genius behind the colonization of America. His great ideals of universal education, universal freedom, and individual rights were upheld by the Freemasonry society and the Order of the Rosicrucians. He was determined to create a nation built on freedom of religion and freedom of government. This great work, this ideal of a free republic, was the perfect union of the divine plan with men and women of sacred purpose. All this effort was done in a hidden way, as if the brethren were following a secret alchemical formula that would come to light in later years. As Walter Raleigh said of Bacon, "And thy great genius in being concealed, is revealed."[221]

It is believed that Freemasonry existed in the American colonies as early as 1606. The Freemasons and their society provided the colonists with a foundational understanding and practice of individual worth and freedom, building the structures and processes required for the new country, and a culture of being "my brother's keeper." The light of each lodge spread and grew to create a literal bonfire of illumination and vision by the time of the American Revolution.

The Mystery of the Book of Emblems

One of Bacon's "good pens" was George Wither. He was a poet, a satirist, and a Rosicrucian. In 1635 he published an unusual book called *A Collection of Emblems, Ancient and Moderne,* which included reproductions of a remarkable set of Rosicrucian emblems previously published by Rollenhagen in 1611 and 1613. Wither added lengthy and seemingly coded verses underneath the beautiful images. There was also a portrait of Wither in the front, continuing the mask or face theme of Shakespeare/Bacon from the First Folio of 1623. It is fascinating to note that these emblems or pictures distinctly resemble the buildings constructed over one hundred years later in Williamsburg, Virginia, the first capital of that colony. The emblem XXV is a stunning replica of the Williamsburg capitol building.

Three hundred years after this book was published, in the 1930s,

Wisdom - from George Wither's *Book of Emblems* (London 1635)
"The wise shall rule the stars," Illust. 31

Maria Bauer Hall, the wife of Manly Palmer Hall, was able to "read the code" hidden in the verses and used the information to uncover the original buried foundations of the forgotten first church in Williamsburg. Her goal was to uncover the original, legendary "buried Virginia Vault of Francis Bacon," said to contain the original manuscripts of the William Shakespeare Group and original documents for the founding of America.

Maria Hall uncovered other mysterious circumstances. The Wither book was written in 1635, the same year that the precious, original Baconian records were said to have been carried from England to the colony of Virginia by Henry Blount. He was a nephew of Francis Bacon's youngest stepbrother and took the name of Nathaniel Bacon when he arrived in America. This treasure trove of documents was rumored to have been transferred in 1676 to Williamsburg from the Jamestown colony shortly before the skirmish known now as Bacon's Rebellion, led by Nathaniel Bacon.

This book of emblems can be seen as a proof that certain events in American history seem to have been carried out according to a great plan created by Francis and his illustrious group of idealistic friends. And they left clues behind for the seeker. This Rosicrucian group followed the philosophy of Francis Bacon, which was to let the individual uncover the mystery. As Henry Peacham's emblem in his book *Minerva Britanna* says, "By the Mind I shall be seen."

The Revelation of Apollo and the Great Assizes

In *The Shakespeare Enigma*, Peter Dawkins lifts the veil on the mysteries of Francis and their meanings:

> The more we look, unravel the clues, and lift the veils of this mystery, the more we find that Francis Bacon was not just the true author "Shakespeare" but also the centre, inspirer and head of an organisation or society of poets, philosophers, lawyers, writers, historians, artists, craftsmen, printers, diplomats and intelligencers dedicated to some great aim. Moreover, we find

that this society embraced both men and women, and included in its numbers members of the nobility and officers of state as well as knights, gentlemen and others from the more ordinary classes of society....

The whole mystery and aim of Francis Bacon and his society is alluded to and almost revealed in the anonymous satirical poem published in 1645, entitled *The Great Assizes holden in Parnassus by Apollo and his Assessours*. The poem is attributed to the poet, satirist and emblem writer, George Wither, who knew Francis Bacon well... having been one of Bacon's "good pens".[222]

The Great Assizes has a direct connection to the Rosicrucian manifestos. In the preface to *The Fama,* the first of the published manifestos, there is a story entitled, "The Universal and General Reformation of the Whole Wide World." The story takes place at the Court of Apollo, God of Wisdom, and is a commentary on the miserable state of the world. Apollo, lamenting this darkness, determines to create a society of men, famous for wisdom and goodness, and to begin the general reformation of the world. The reformation begins with a complete resurrection of the arts and sciences.

The Great Assizes, a satirical piece, retells that earlier story from *The Fama* with humor. It takes place with Apollo and the council of authors, playwrights, and poets who are helping him, enthroned on the Mount of Poetic Inspiration and the place of the Delphic Oracle (messenger of the Gods), where he resides with Pallas Athena. Apollo and his chancellor preside over the meeting. They summon the twenty great authors and lesser authors to assess the state of the world.

The story is a clear description of Francis and his secret society. George Wither places himself among the "lesser poets," along with William Shakespeare. When Shakespeare is examined by the assessors, he is called out as a mimic, an actor pretending to be a poet, not a true poet at all. George Wither reveals all the thirty-two true poets, playwrights, and authors to be the manifested aspects of Apollo, or "Divinity, Unity and Light," and Apollo's chancellor to be Francis Bacon. This satirical story is so unusual that it serves as part of the trail of clues for those who begin the search for the spirit of Francis Bacon.

The Rosicrucian Path

Francis's Rosicrucian manuscripts and publications had been well received by those who hoped for a "universal reformation of mankind... built on esoteric truths of the ancient past... concealed from the average man, [to] provide insight into nature, the physical universe and the spiritual realm."[223] This promise of enlightenment was Francis's antidote for the violence, religious intolerance, and scientific paralysis that had taken over continental Europe and Britain.

The German cleric, Johann Andreae, was the rumored author of the Rosicrucian publications. In order to protect himself from accusations and torture, he ridiculed the publications as a hoax or as allegories. Under the cover provided by his name, the publications spread quietly around Europe prompting commentaries from philosophers such as Robert Fludd, Thomas Vaughn, and Michael Maier.

In 1617 Maier, a Rosicrucian, stated in *Silentium Post Clamores* that the Rosicrucian movement was nothing new and was drawn from "primordial tradition.... Our origins are Egyptian, Brahminic, derived from the mysteries of Eleusis and Samothrace, the magi of Persia, the Pythagoreans, and the Arabs." Secrecy was vital for those using such ancient holy wisdom as the integration of science and spirituality at a time when Church and State were prone to inquisitions, torture, and death for heresy.

For the learned in Europe and Britain, the Rosicrucian promise to elevate and inspire the arts, sciences, and alchemy was a breath of fresh air during dark times. Around four hundred manuscripts and books were circulated and published on Rosicrucian concepts between 1614 and 1620 by the "College of Invisibles."

The appeal of alchemy for the greedy was, of course, on the physical level. Those who were attracted to the path of initiation by the perceived prospect of learning how to turn base metals into gold would find only frustration. For the alchemists of the spirit forged their true identity by transforming the base metals of the lower nature into the gold of the highest Self.

Maier and other Rosicrucians indicated that the highest form of alchemy was the transmutation of the elements of human habits, ignorance, emotions, and desires into progressively higher forms of consciousness, approaching Christlike qualities. In this, the seeming miracles performed by Jesus would be revealed to the initiate as the harmonious integration of esoteric science, now being discovered in the field of quantum physics, and alignment with the will of the Divine Presence.

While the esoteric side of the Rosicrucians remained secret, the more secular aspects related to scientific method had first begun to gain public acceptance in the court of King James. The key proponent was Francis's friend and fellow playwright, Ben Jonson.

Ben Jonson took advantage of the King's ongoing patronage of his masques to feature Rosicrucian themes such as the Invisible College of natural philosophers, as well as Francis's allegorical concept of the House of Solomon, in *The Fortunate Isles and Their Union,* published in 1624 and 1625. The king's tacit approval of these Rosicrucian concepts, whether he realized what they were or not, emboldened natural philosophers to expand their network of letters

A 19th century engraving illustrating Thomas Fuller's story of Shakespeare and Ben Jonson in the Mermaid Tavern.

of correspondence over the following decades. This growing exchange of letters, pamphlets, and published material related to scientific inquiry became known as the "Republic of Letters," transcending national and language barriers across Europe, Britain, and the New World.

During the English Civil War, physicians and natural philosophers of the opposing sides continued to correspond by letter, apparently feeling more akin to the scientific holy men described in Francis's *The New Atlantis* than to the bloodbath in the fields and towns. In addition to letters, there were meetings in London at Gresham College and in Oxford by the Philosophical Society. This momentum of association grew, even while the nation was torn by political turmoil and battles.

By the time of the return of King Charles II from exile in 1660, there was a strong enough consensus in the London meetings at Gresham College for twelve prominent natural philosophers to found a "Colledge for the Promoting of Physico-Mathematicall Experimentall Learning." The prior tacit acceptance of scientific inquiry by King James encouraged one of the twelve founders of the college to propose its patronage to the new king. In 1662 Sir Robert Moray, a prominent Freemason and supporter of Charles I, persuaded Charles II to charter the college as The Royal Society of London for the Improvement of Natural Knowledge. Francis and his friends, on earth and in heaven, must have rejoiced.

In Europe Francis would have heard of this progression of life imitating his art, as the 1626 fictional scientific holy men of *The New Atlantis* became real enough by 1662 to receive royal favor and acceptance as a permanent institution—The Royal Society, the first science academy in the world. The members may not have been as sanctified as in *The New Atlantis,* but it was a foundational achievement for Francis's vision. State sponsorship of an institution dedicated to rigorous scientific inquiry was the breakthrough needed to dissolve religious authorities' centuries-old hold on learning.

As a stay on the possibility of scientific authorities generating their own religion of intolerance, many of the founders and members of The Royal Society were either Freemasons or Rosicrucians and simply didn't mention their secret affiliation to the esoteric and devotional side of the Great Instauration. They veiled their inner calling in mystery.

Dr. William Rawley, Bacon's first English editor and biographer, lived with Francis for the last ten years of his life in Britain from 1616 to 1626. He was close to the many secrets of the life and writings of this Rosicrucian master. Dr. Rawley edited the collected volume of Sir Francis Bacon's writings called the *Resuscitatio* in 1657. In the Epistle to the Reader, Dr. Rawley wrote, "in regard, of the Distance, of the time, since his *Lordships* Dayes; whereby, I shall not tread too near, upon the *Heels of Truth;* Or of the passages, and persons then concerned." He joins with the other Baconian friends, stating that there are secrets about Bacon that are not "communicable to the public."

The secret life continued and the Great Instauration gained much important ground. The friends of Francis made their contributions to the arts, architecture, science, and in government ideals in the new American colonies.

In 1652 two of the foundational Rosicrucian writings, *The Fama* and *The Confessio,* were translated into English and published. This was done under the pseudonym of Eugenius Philalethes, used by a Hermetic philosopher named Thomas Vaughan. His name is still known today in esoteric circles.

Thomas Vaughan said that he was following a translation by an "unknown hand," and "the copy communicated to myself, and I should name him here, but that he expects not either thy Thanks or Mine."[224]

Mrs. Henry Pott informed one of her correspondents who helped with research that she believed that Francis had escaped to Europe in 1621 and lived on and continued to work for his ideals. He replied that she had discovered the capital secret of the Rosicrucians.

By the time of the chartering of The Royal Society in 1662, Francis would have been 101 years old. Many of his friends and "good pens" had already died. Ben Jonson had died in 1637, twenty-five years before The Royal Society was founded. If Anthony

Bacon did take a "philosopher's death" in 1601, there is no record of his actual death, but legends and literary evidence exist that Anthony lived on and made important contributions to the Shakespeare plays and the other works of Francis long after he departed from England.

Another old friend in Frankfurt, Johann Andreae, had passed on in 1654, though it is possible that Francis still lived with Andreae's family. An engraving, still held by the family, is usually said to be of Andreae at a very advanced age. However, the wise and charming face resembles an older Bacon, and the face is surrounded by a number of esoteric shields or symbols with only two containing letters. The letters are *F* and *B*.

In 1668 an enigmatic secret message was sent out to the network of Rosicrucians that the Master had passed on to a higher calling. Esoteric history states that Francis was contacted by the great Master Rakoczy and taken to the master's retreat in preparation for Francis's personal ascension.

> *I am fire and air; my other elements*
> *I give to baser life.*
>
> ~ Antony and Cleopatra, act 5, sc. 2

As to the mystery of Francis's life, Alfred Dodd wrote:

> Lovers of Francis Bacon have been chipping away at the funeral urn, the tomb, to free the awakening spirit. The personality within is still veiled from common eyes that see not and common ears that hear not. But to you that have vision, a sense of beauty, a love of Truth, the stone which has hidden and sealed Francis Bacon, will be rolled away at your sympathetic touch. From those dead ashes a new creation will arise.... He will be seen and walk and talk with you of the Via Dolorosa, of the Stations of the Cross, of Gethsemane, of Calvary.[225]

The majority of Francis's contemporaries had no idea of the magnitude of his accomplishments. Many people today still have no idea of the vast work of Francis Bacon, both acknowledged and anonymous. He is the spiritual adept and secret master of our time.

Engraving of Johann surrounded by shields, two with the letters *F* and *B*,
A secret portrait of Francis Bacon

Francis truly became the "marvelous being" and the "great light" from the prophecies of Tycho Brahe and Paracelsus.

From his civil service, parliamentary work, literary masterpieces, including the Shakespeare plays that so elevated the English language, and philosophic and scientific publications, to his formation of secret societies that brought charity to the fore and the sacrifice of his identity as a Tudor prince, Francis lived a true example of the sacred mysteries and brought forth his intended "great renovation of society."

In his will and in his own words, Francis wrote:

> "I bequeath my soul to God above, by the oblation of my Saviour.
> My body to be buried obscurely.
> My name to the next ages, and to foreign nations."[226]

However, as the wisdom of the ancients declares, death is not the end.

Secrets of the Golden Age Prince: Francis Bacon

--- PART 2 ---

A Holy Brother

O eternal God within the heart of all life, O flame, living fire, breathing awareness of all that we are, of all that thou art, we salute life! We salute wholeness! And we come together in thy flame.... Make us one, even as we are one. So let our oneness flow as the crystal clear waters of Life and the water of the living Word. Let our oneness be the rejoicing of the atoms of God coalescing to immortal destiny. Our prayer is joy. Our prayer is communion. Our prayer is love, O God!

~ Elizabeth Clare Prophet

The Ascension of the Golden Age Prince

The universal Christ takes the aura of one who pursues truth and embodies it in the path of the *satyagraha** and duplicates that aura again and again, so that there is a quickening of the mind of that one. That mind becomes the spark that ignites millions.

Therefore, you have seen in Francis Bacon how one mind could actually ignite a new age through the writing, though the science, through the determination, through the plays, through the cipher, through the code, through the mysteries. And yet—though one can recount many works of Francis Bacon—it all comes down to the fact that above and beyond all that was done, there was the mysterious force of the Godhead that truly multiplied his presence on the earth far beyond that which one human being could ever accomplish.

---

*satyagraha [Sanskrit, "truth-force"]: holding fast to truth. Gandhi used the term for his movement of passive resistance, but the idea can be seen throughout ancient beliefs, including the Druid's call of "truth against the world."

This is a powerful lifetime to study, for we see in Francis Bacon an adept who is going to spring into cosmic consciousness when he transcends this world and becomes immortal and an ascended being. For the souls who have balanced their karma and fulfilled their spiritual destiny, the starlit doorway opens to the ascension.

So it was for the golden age prince, Francis Tudor Bacon. His scientific genius is world-renowned, yet his mastery of love, spiritual alchemy, and his great heart for humanity are even more outstanding. His public actions give him rank with those immortal souls who preferred to suffer martyrdom rather than be false to the ideals they espoused.

Francis departed to the Rakoczy Mansion in what is now Romania, either physically or in his etheric (fire or memory) body, and there he perfected his adeptship and made his ascension.

His spiritual teachers, the cosmic masters who had worked with him and through him for long ages, called Francis to the final spiritual initiation of his earthly journey. Though Pallas Athena was the patroness of Francis Bacon in his last life, the personal sponsoring master of his soul's path of spiritual development is the Master Rakoczy. Known as the Master R, he is a cosmic master who ascended in the time of Atlantis and is the Great Initiator of cycles. By founding the House of Rakoczy, he established a lineage of lightbearers to perpetuate the ritual and the freedom and the diplomacy of the seventh ray. It was he who carried the flame of freedom, the violet flame, from the altars of Atlantis to safety in the Carpathian foothills.

May 1, 1684, is celebrated in the annals of the Great White Brotherhood* as Francis Bacon's Ascension Day. In the etheric† Rakoczy Mansion in the Carpathian Mountains of Romania, Francis—the great visionary, the soul of freedom, and the heart of the Renaissance—stepped into the Infinite Holy Light of God and began his immortal life as an ascended master.

---

*The Great White Brotherhood is a name for the brotherhood of ascended beings, angels, Elohim, etc. The word "white" refers to the white light of the Divine Mother and the ascension flame.
†The etheric plane is the highest vibrating level of the material world. The ascended masters have retreats on the etheric plane of earth, where souls may go to learn and to heal while their physical bodies are sleeping and after they have passed out of physical embodiment.

Mountain slopes, Carpathians, Romania

The Ascending Arc: A Cosmic Romance

One can only imagine the rejoicing in heaven for the permanent return of this wondrous spirit, Francis Bacon.

Francis was received into the sacred fire of his I AM Presence and returned to the Great White Brotherhood, the ascended masters, archangels, and Elohim from his long expedition on earth. From that day onward, he was one with them, an immortal master.

> The Great Ascended Masters of Love, Light, and Perfection who have guided the expansion of the Light in humanity on this planet from the beginning, are no figment of anyone's imagination. They are *real, visible,* tangible, glorious, living, breathing Beings of such Love, Wisdom, and Power that the human mind gasps at the immensity of it. They work everywhere in the universe with complete freedom and limitless power, to do *naturally* all that the average individual considers supernatural....
>
> The Ascended Master is an individual who by Self-Conscious effort has generated enough Love and Power within himself to snap the chains of all human limitation, and so he stands free and worthy to be trusted with the use of forces, beyond those of human experience....

> It is through the radiation or outpouring of this "Light," which is really his own "Luminous Essence of Divine Love," that an Ascended Master is able to help those who come under his care and direction....
>
> This "Luminous Essence" has within It the Highest Force in the Universe, for It dissolves all discord and establishes Perfect Balance in all manifestation. The Ascended Master's Body is constantly pouring out Rays of his "Light Essence"—upon the discords of earth, dissolving them as the rays of force which we call light and heat from our physical sun dissolve a fog.[1]

Adding to the joy of his ascension came the descent of his own twin flame from the Great Silence, or nirvana, where she had held the spiritual balance for him for so long. This great being, his divine Feminine complement and twin flame, had ascended long before him. She had attained the cosmic consciousness of divine justice and opportunity in golden ages long ago. Cosmic consciousness is the realization of self as the galaxy of light that declares from the very center of the atom of being, "I AM WHO I AM." This, the very first equation of being and consciousness, is the foundation of your alchemical experiment that leads to the fullness of that life which is God.

The entire Spirit-Matter cosmos has a Great Central Sun in the etheric octave, which is the point of origin, conceived in liberty by God —the Alpha, the Omega, the yin and the yang, the masculine and the feminine. Once the Divine Whole, twin spheres of these causal bodies separated out—two spirit sparks, twin flames descended for the purpose of evolution in the Matter cosmos, as they had previously evolved in the Spirit cosmos, which is that causal body of light. Each set of twin flames was born to be the manifestation of the Father-Mother God, sons and daughters who could put on more and more of those spheres of light, which we call God consciousness.

Long had the heart of Francis heard his twin flame's name and known her soul, basing many of his Shakespearean heroines upon this feminine ideal. She is Portia, the Goddess of Justice. This title of "Goddess" is a spiritual office, in honor of her universal spiritual attainment, magnifying the divine principles of justice and opportunity. In the divine sense, justice is always opportunity. You may not always

Portia

Saint Germain

recognize it as opportunity, but then, if you have learned from the teachings of the Divine Mother, you know that the pathway of justice is open to you because others have gone before you in the way of self-mastery. It is by the law of hierarchy that opportunity comes, for there must be some who will stand in life for others who would walk the path of overcoming. Just as Portia stood in higher realms for Francis, he now stands for his students.

The path of fiery love, which is God's all-consuming sacred fire, consumes even the force of anti-love, as divine love is more than human love—it is power and wisdom self-contained in one—and then some. Herein lies love's mystery. Love is more than effect or lesser causation; it is First Cause and the point of light beyond all light and darkness. Love is all love excelling beyond love's visible expressions and interchanges. Love is the unbeatable cosmic force!

True love, divine love, in its very magic can be known by twin flames. In this relationship of the divine absolutes, Father is thesis, Mother is antithesis, and the whole of their creation, including the fruit of their Christ consciousness, is the synthesis—their reason for being, and for being the divine incarnation. What happens when the divine lovers meet in the divine embrace of the T'ai Chi—the Great Causal Body of God—is their net contribution to cosmos. So it is when twin flames return to the white-fire ovoid of their origin. Only in this ultimate union (the celebration of the Holy Communion of Alpha and Omega) can the creative purpose of their being be fully realized.

After his ascension, Francis took on a name that has long been a part of his soul's purpose—"Holy Brother," or Sanctus Germanus, the ascended master Saint Germain.

For hundreds of thousands of years, he has been called Saint Germain. Your soul knows his name, yet you have come again in a new body draped with an old consciousness. If you search sublevels of that consciousness, you will find that name already known, even as "I AM" is known, at the core of the alchemy of your own Be-ness.

The Mystery of the Personal Ascension

> *Verily, verily, I say unto you, He that believeth on me, the works that I do shall he do also; and greater works than these shall he do; because I go unto my Father.*
>
> ~ John 14:12.

The ascension is the ultimate goal of life in the schoolroom of earth. It is the shining goal of the step-by-step path of spiritual initiation. Souls mastering life on the seven rays of divine individuality become saints, adepts and masters. These are the beings "robed in white," described in the Book of Revelation.

The attainable reality of a personal ascension, and how this mysterious process happens, is a part of the sacred mysteries Jesus taught and lived.

There is no ascension without the alchemical marriage, in all its wonder and beauty. This is the transcendent yearning of every man and woman of light on the planetary body.

Through the alchemical marriage, the soul becomes a permanent atom in the body of God. The laws of decay and death and the disintegration of the soul itself no longer apply. The soul that was "corruptible has put on incorruption." The first step in the alchemical marriage is the rising of the primal essence of the light of the Divine Mother from the base-of-the-spine chakra to the level of the

The Chart of Your Real Self

seat-of-the-soul chakra. In this action, the soul, as the negative polarity of being, increases its awareness of self to identify *as* Mother. The beauty of the soul is enhanced greatly by the alchemical marriage with the Christ consciousness, which occurs once the soul rises from the seat-of-the-soul chakra to the heart chakra, where we as individuals are wedded to our monadic self in the higher plane.

The secret societies and the Rose Cross held as primary in their work the teaching on the alchemical marriage. It is alchemical because that which is nonpermanent becomes sealed in that which is permanent—the soul becomes a part of that living crystal of the Christ. Never again are they twain, the inner and the outer temple. There is no longer the middle figure (the Christ Self) and the lower figure (the evolving soul) in the chart of your Real Self. There is a oneness between the soul and the Higher Self that can never be undone because the alchemical marriage has occurred.

Next comes the joining of that one to the individualized Divine Presence of God, the I AM Presence—the part of the Self that has always existed in absolute God-Reality. This is the mystery of the ascension. It is the acceleration of God in man and of man's self-awareness in God. It is the return of the prodigal son to the home of the Father-Mother God.

The ascension is truly the moment when the soul is born to eternal life—unlimited potential and possibility—because it is the moment of integration of the soul with the Father, the Son, the Holy Spirit, and the Mother. Jesus Christ demonstrated to us that integration while he was on earth.

When the gift of the ascension is given to anyone by his own I AM Presence and the Karmic Board, the appearance of age drops from him as swiftly as a smile can raise the lips, and the magnetism and energy of that one becomes the unlimited power of God surging through his being. The dross of the physical body, the weariness of the emotional body, the ceaseless rote of the mental body all drop away and are replaced in perfect ease by their divine counterparts. The feelings become charged by the love of God and the angels. The mind is the diamond-shining mind of God—omnipresent, omniscient, omnipotent. The total being is inspired and aspiring.

When one crosses the line from time and space to infinity, it is a matter of consciousness. Before his ascension, Francis Bacon had already risen in consciousness to the level of a spiritual adept. Adepts such as Francis glimpse infinity while still living within time and space. When they put on the full garment of the ascension flame, there is scarcely a ripple of consciousness. For them the ascension is but a modicum of light from the former state. For they have so expanded light, even in this octave, that the transition becomes minute. Then again, by other standards it is indeed cosmic.

Francis Bacon, however, was more than an adept, for he walked the path of an avatar. Your God Presence is the avatar. One day you shall be the full incarnation of your God Presence. In the meantime, we follow the avatars of all ages. Avatar, or *avatara*, is a Sanskrit word meaning the descent, or incarnation, of God on earth. When we loosely use the term *incarnation*, we say we are all incarnations of God, and it is true. We are incarnations of God because we have the threefold flame of life within our hearts. This flame *is* God, therefore God has come into this temple. The difference between the avatar and all of the other children of God is that the avatar has expanded that flame, and the entire temple is filled with the flame of God. It only takes one avatar to convert millions. Such is the magnitude of your star, your I AM Presence, your causal body, and the God that you now know only in increments.

God is revealed in nature. God is revealed in the ascended hosts. The God that you know is limited by your capacity to know. This increase in our capacity to know is exactly what Francis created with his method of inquiry and his literary renaissance.

When Jesus left this world, it went through a period of very dark ages, dark with ignorance. It was the karma for his crucifixion. A Son of God had been murdered by the Nephilim, and the light went out on the planet until there came the time of Francis Bacon, foreshadowing the Aquarian age and the master who would be the avatar of that age.

The opening of the light of reason, the scientific age that led to all the technology that we have today, came through the avatar of the next two-thousand-year period. And that was Francis Bacon. So while he was in the world and in embodiment, he was the light of the world.

To those who prepare themselves, those who fulfill cosmic law, the opportunity for the ascension will come, whether in this life or in the next. And no force can erase the pillars that the ascended masters shall establish for the ascending servants of God, for the sons and daughters who must also rise as the ascended masters have risen, and in fulfilling their divine plan, raise a planet and her evolutions. For the light that descends in the scientific process of the ascension inundates the earth and raises all life!

The ancient spiritual dispensation through which Francis ascended required the full amount of karma to be balanced, namely 100 percent of all his personal karmic debts. All debts to life—negative energy patterns expressed through any of the chakras—had to be repaid (balanced) on earth before one's soul could be joined with the immortal Self. At that advanced level of spiritual initiation, the person is known as an *arhat*, the Buddhist term for one who has a high level of spiritual awareness while still mortal. The next step on this ascending spiral of the spiritual path is to become a full spiritual adept.

Adeptship is based on love, discipline, and wisdom. But above all, charity is the key. The giving of self propels you to transmute karma and to move on in the cycles of being. The expansion of the balanced threefold flame is the definition of the adept, the Christed One, the Anointed One—one who is anointed by fire. The great avatars of the ages were avatars because they increased the size of this flame by their devotion, by nourishing it, by adoring it, by communing with it, and by visualizing it. To become an adept, one must concentrate on developing the threefold flame of the heart because it is the center of your inner fire enfolding itself.

The threefold flame is the Holy Christ flame, the divine spark, and the flame of liberty and life. It is a three-plumed spiraling fire one-sixteenth of an inch in height, sealed in the secret chamber of your heart. The threefold flame is expressed in the quality of the heart. It is the expression of the Christ Self. So you see, the seed of God in your heart is potentially equal to God. It is like that tiny seed and the great tree that grows from it. And because we have this divine spark, we have the authority to command light.

The Threefold Flame

Buddhists describe it as the Buddha nature, Hindus as the Atman, and Kabbalists as the *neshamah*. Both Buddhists and Christian Gnostics use the image of "the gold in the mud" to describe this spiritual essence that lives inside of us. They say the gold of our spirit may be covered over by the mud of the world, but that mud does not destroy the spirit.

The three divine flames are emanations of the Trinity—Father, Son, and Holy Spirit—and are held in a white-fire sphere of the light of the Divine Mother. By balancing, intensifying, and expanding this interwoven threefold flame of divine love, wisdom, and power, the soul gains greater Christ consciousness. These can be recognized in Francis's striving to attain and manifest perfect charity, knowledge, and the divine blueprint of God's will.

In the time since Francis's ascension, humanity has been gifted with a new dispensation for making the ascension with only a simple majority (51 percent) or more of their karma balanced.

Now, as long as someone fulfills their soul's divine plan, they need only to tip the scales just beyond the halfway point to make their personal ascension. They can then fulfill the higher spiritual initiations of arhat and adept on the etheric plane.

Once you have balanced 51 percent or more of your karma, you may choose to ascend at the conclusion of your life and repay the remaining karma in the etheric or to reembody again and again, increasing your Christhood as you pursue the path of the bodhisattva on earth.

If you choose to ascend, fully anointed by the light of your I AM Presence, you, the Christed one, will rise (i.e., accelerate in vibration) to the level of the I AM THAT I AM. And the Son will merge with the Father. And the Father will merge with the Son. And you will know the full God-realization of the mantra, "I and my Father are One."

In this new dispensation, all of the light that is residual within the four lower bodies (mental, emotional, physical, and etheric) and the chakras is accelerated and drawn up by the ascending one into that Higher Mental Body, which is your own Christ Self, and drawn up again into the victory of the ascension.

If you comb through the scriptures of the world, you will find mention of the ascension. You will find examples described as "soul liberation," "nirvana," "samadhi," all states of consciousness that represent the acceleration, the intensification, the actual stepping up of the spin of the electrons around the nucleus of each atom, as well as the stepping up of the energy in the nucleus of the atom. This is the meaning of ascension. There is not actually an up or down but there is a lesser and a greater moment of cosmic consciousness that manifests within. When Jesus is described as going up and Elijah is described as going up, going up means increasing in vibration.

God is a God who is transcending himself moment by moment, hour by hour. This self-transcending God is reflected in the expanding cosmos and in the fact that no matter what attainment a person reaches, he will always set a further goal. Therefore, the ascension is not the end of life or the end of goals, it is the beginning of life everlasting and eternal co-creativity with God.

Saint Germain: Ascended Master, Alchemist and Mystic

Enter Saint Germain May 1, 1684,
God of Freedom to the earth.
Draped with a cloak of stars,
He stands with his twin flame,
The Goddess of Justice,
Against the backdrop of Cosmos.
He is come to ignite the fires of world transmutation
In hearts attuned to the cosmic cyphers
And to avert personal and planetary cataclysm.
He pleads the cause of God-Freedom
Before the councils of men
And presents his case before
The world body of lightbearers.
He offers a ransom for the oppressed—
Gift of his heart—and of his mind,
Rarest jewel of all our earthly souvenirs—
And of his causal body:
Sphere upon sphere of the richness of himself
Harvested from the divine, and the human, experience.
All this he offers.
Like a beggar with his bowl piled high,
He plies the streets of the world
Eyeing passersby
Hopeful that even one in every million
Might take the proffered gift
And hold it to his heart in recognition
Of the Source, of the Sun,
And of the alchemy of the age so close.
Yes, as close as free will and the Divine Spark

Is our extrication from the dilemma
Of doubt and deleterious concepts and death.
And as far, as far as the toiler's envy
Of our Love tryst is from grace,
So, without him, is the morning of our deliverance
From tangled entanglements of karmic crisscrosses
Of our doodling and dabbling for centuries' boredom
With personalities far less, oh yes, than his.

Enter Saint Germain
Into our hearts forever, if we will only let him.

From the heights of power well-earned and beyond this world's, Saint Germain still stands to turn back all attempts to thwart his Great Instauration here below. Ageless, he is a man and master of mystery.

Fulfilling the prophecy recorded in the Book of Revelation, this master comes to finish the mysteries of God. "But in the days of the voice of the seventh angel, when he shall begin to sound, the mystery of God should be finished, as he hath declared to his servants the prophets."[2]

Why do I know that Saint Germain is the seventh angel? Because the vibration of the Word in that scripture is identical with the vibration of his Electronic Presence, and the seventh angel signifies the seventh dispensation. Jesus signified the sixth dispensation of the sixth ray, giving the teaching for the sixth root race. Saint Germain comes in the seventh age, or the seventh cycle, which is the Aquarian age. He comes with a fulfillment of the message of Jesus Christ with the promised Comforter—the understanding of the Holy Ghost and the baptism of the Holy Ghost with sacred fire. Jesus said, "he that believeth on me, the works that I do shall he do also and greater works than these shall he do because I go unto my Father," but he never told us how. So the mysteries are to be finished in this age.

Saint Germain did not desire to go on to the Elysian fields. He longed to return to the world with a new light and a new energy for building a new age in Aquarius. Desiring above all else to liberate God's people, Saint Germain sought and was granted a dispensation from the Lords of Karma to function in the world of form as an ascended being having the appearance of an unascended being. Only a few ascended masters, including Melchizedek and John the Baptist (formerly Elijah), had ever been allowed to return to the physical, and only for a cosmic purpose.

Although almost no one on earth knew it, this was a miracle dispensation for the saving of a world at the conclusion of the age of Pisces. This is yet another correlation to the prophecy of the coming great light of Elias, for as Elijah had done before him, the great alchemist and prophet, Saint Germain, returned to the physical octave.

Was there a hush in heaven as the decision was made to grant the full scope of Saint Germain's request? Where and when would he appear, and who was Saint Germain to become?

A Morning in Transylvania

In the physical mountains of the spiritual retreat of the Master R, where the flame of freedom resides, a young boy takes in the glory of the morning light on the mountain peaks and valleys.

The sky is so blue that all of God seems reflected in it. It seems a mirrored lake of perfection. The sunlight is mellow and golden and warming and revivifying; the hilly country seems charged with the essences of nature's grandeur.

A cart drawn by an animal that does not seem too animated slowly wends its way across a very narrow and dusty pass in the hills of that beautiful country land. Seated in this somewhat rude cart is a small boy. A quantity of straw protrudes from the cart, and because it is properly ripened, it seems as the sun shines upon it to be tiny sticks of gold. The sun reflects in the hair of the small boy driving the cart and horse, and the hair too seems a crown of gold.

The boy remarks to himself in his inward musings: "How beautiful the country is this morning! How glorious and how fresh everything appears to me! The warmth feels wonderful upon my body. How I love the sun!"

The boy stands within the cart in order to inhale more deeply of the mountain air and draws in the fullness of a most deep and penetrating breath. In joy he knows the meaning of breathing in the air of freedom.

The cart continues on its rugged journey over the dusty road in an age far less mechanized than the present one. And the lad enjoys, without the feelings and pressures of modern living, the simplicity of the countryside reflecting the beauties of nature, the golden moments of childhood, and the tenderness of a spirit attuned to the harmonies of the universe. Bound for the palace of a count of the nobility, the cart wends on down the road.

All people upon earth, in their precious halls of memories, record numerous experiences that have simply delighted their beings. The cluttered halls of memory at times become charged with the vibratory action of that which is coarse, with that which stifles the flame of freedom, with that which does not speak of the elemental creation of life and nature—the trees, the natural verdure, the elemental things of the forest and field, the sparkling mountain stream, the laughing, happy waters, the exhilarating air, the beauties, too, of the fireside and the candlelight and the silver, the pewter, the friendliness and the warmth of good-neighborliness. All of these qualities at times, in the race for the expansion of vanity and ego, are forgotten. And men live no more in the pioneer spirit of the wilderness, but they live in an age of mechanized grief.

Saint Germain was that small boy riding in the cart; he remembers the hours of freedom, eternally. Individuals sometimes forget the meaning of life. They sometimes forget that life is a schoolroom of eternity, and that this planet is a beautiful home, that its emerald lakes and azure seas and snowcapped mountain peaks can ring with freedom if the hearts of its people can sing a song of freedom to the Eternal One.

Saint Germain, given the opportunity to return to the physical, took nothing for granted but understood the beauty of creation and the miracle that is life.

The Wonderman of Europe

Saint Germain appeared in Europe again as le Comte de Saint Germain, a "miraculous" gentleman who dazzled the courts of eighteenth- and nineteenth-century Europe, where they called him "The Wonderman." And with good reason; no one had ever captured the attention of an entire continent quite like this mysterious adept and master. He appeared, disappeared, and reappeared in and out of royal circles with his outstanding quality of realism in an age that was closing in on itself by the weight of its own hypocrisy. He was, as Voltaire described him, the "man who never dies and who knows everything."

As the Comte de Saint Germain, he returned to continue his Great Instauration that he had started as Francis Bacon. His great dream was the creation of a new enlightened republic across the sea and a

Comte de Saint Germain

United States of Europe founded on representative government, individual liberty, and universal brotherhood.

The ingenious worldview of the soul of Francis Bacon had expanded infinitely after his ascension. He understood the accumulated negative karma of humanity, individually and collectively; an awareness shared with Jesus, Gautama, and other ascended masters. He also saw the divine potential of each soul and every nation. Ascended masters have the God-given ability to read the akashic records—the etheric library of God's infinite memory of all thoughts, words, feelings, and actions.

Francis Bacon had been forced into exile from the kingdom he should have ruled with no possible means to turn back the horrors of the English Civil War (1642–1651). Now in the full adeptship of an ascended master with a dispensation to work for a high purpose in the physical, he had the chance to prevent an impending French civil war that had the potential to be worse than any of the previous wars of religion.

If Saint Germain could reach the hearts of the people, awaken the conscience of the nobility, and quicken the vision and spirit of the kings, the karmic shadow over France and Europe could be dispelled. As a master, he knew this miracle depended upon the free will of humanity. With his infinite love, Saint Germain would give mankind his all.

The accumulation of negative karma in Europe alone, if ignored, would result in something worse than a French civil war, namely centuries of escalating global wars. The goal was to mitigate the accumulation of negative karma throughout Europe so that the impending French disaster, the trigger for centuries of greater wars, could be avoided.

Each ascended master holds a deep affection for their brothers and sisters who are currently attached to the physical octave, still subject to the lessons of their karma, and usually far from any interest in gaining immortality. Saint Germain still loved the souls of friends who had known him as Francis Bacon and by all his various names from previous lives. He knew that his friends from his Elizabethan life would be reborn into a dangerous world of rivalrous military empires in the coming centuries and would not consciously remember him or their prior service with him. The master also knew that the deep spiritual bond of love and brotherhood that lived always at a soul level would reignite their soul memory. His own students would find him again. His work to reform the monarchies was to preempt unnecessary suffering for them and all humanity.

Humanity's most immediate vulnerability in the early 1700s was the ancient, and now corrupt, institution of monarchy and the feudal class system that held it up. Saint Germain had firsthand experience of the unaccountability, incompetence, capriciousness, and venality of many monarchs and their ministers. He had been aware of the avoidable turmoil and the risk of bankruptcy and anarchy during the nine years of the English Civil War. While England had eventually settled for partial parliamentary checks on the monarchy, France, the dominant kingdom of Europe, had not. France's vulnerability to a complete rupture between the feudal nobility and the overtaxed and underfed public would be manipulated by provocateurs in the decades prior to the French Revolution.

The age of enlightenment that appeared in Europe in the early 1700s, thanks to Francis Bacon and his many associates across the Continent, bore the fruit of a new sense of self-determination within the increasingly literate public and within some of the nobility. Now a way had to be found to communicate diplomatically with the courts of Europe and to persuade them to share power, spending, taxation, and justice with the public before it was too late.

Saint Germain saw the sinister practice of "divide and conquer" operating behind the royal facades in Europe, with evil usurping and occupying both sides of the one coin of history. The monarchy was flattered by the sycophants permitted in their courts, and the fuming public was easily manipulated to violence and anarchy by the professional provocateurs on their streets.

The nobility would not understand or accept their accountability for the poverty and unhappiness of their subjects. Patiently explaining to the courts of Europe that structural reform of government was in the nobility's best interests became the only lawful avenue available to the master. The constraint of cosmic law was that whatever decisions were made by the monarchy, or the public, were to be of their own free will. They could not be compelled. The master could only show them the higher way and explain the consequences of inaction.

Saint Germain was aware that entrance into the courts of Europe and the hearts and minds of the nobility could only be won by affinity and trust. He knew he would have to gain and retain their attention with pursuits that interested them, leaving weightier matters for later.

Saint Germain began a century-long campaign to befriend individuals among the nobility who had the authority to invite him to an audience with their monarch. As a visiting outsider, there was never any guarantee he would hold a monarch's attention long enough to advise or persuade on matters of government. Yet, he was determined to try.

As the Wonderman of Europe, the Master Alchemist showed the courts of Europe his many gifts of attainment: he composed, improvised, and accompanied on piano without written music "not only every song but also the most difficult concerti, played on several instruments." He could play the violin "like an orchestra."[3] His compositions remain today in the British Museum and in the library of Roudnice Castle. He painted in oils with colors of gemlike brilliance, a "secret" which he himself discovered. He spoke flawless French, English, Italian, Spanish, Portuguese, and Russian—and was an expert in Latin, Greek, Chinese, Japanese, Sanskrit, and Arabic. The man was a poet, musician, painter and artisan, scholar, scientist, statesman, and storyteller with a divine purpose.

Frederick the Great, Voltaire, Horace Walpole, and Casanova mentioned him in their letters. Newspapers of the day—the *London Chronicle* of June 1760, a Florentine newspaper *Le Notizie del Mondo* in July 1770, and the *Gazette of the Netherlands*—took note of him.

The source of the Wonderman's wealth was never discovered. To court observers, he was clearly a man of extraordinary means. One countess wrote that even though he dressed plainly, he wore an abundance of diamonds—on every finger, on his watch, on his shoe buckles. The finest diamonds even adorned his snuff box. This, however, was not for vanity's sake.

The reason he wore those rings on every finger was because each finger relates to the chakras, to the planetary bodies, to the energies of the stars. Precious gems have the capacity to hold light, transmit light, be conductors of light, and they contain the wearer's vibrations. Very high spiritual beings, such as the Comte de Saint Germain, can transmit their own vibrations and divine light through their jewelry. Similarly, the jewels worn by people of low vibrations carry that low vibration. A jewel does not automatically have power, it is a chalice. At the molecular level, it creates a cup for the holding of energy.

As the Wonderman of Europe, Saint Germain wore the styles of the time. He was familiar with its literature and music but exceeded the concurrent levels of mastery—as, after all, he had great spiritual attainment and some several hundred thousand years of soul development behind him.

He could perform anything and all things as his fellowmen could —but better. This is what Saint Germain now asks of his students: not to bypass the standards and expectancies of your era, but to recognize that you must speak the language of the people better— better, louder, clearer—not for vanity's sake but for the sake of the Great Instauration, for uplifting humanity.

How did he accomplish so many seeming miracles with grace and ease? Many would have liked to have known the Count's secrets— kings, ministers, diplomats, mystics, gossips, and savants. Some sought his secrets simply out of curiosity, some to enrich themselves, others sought his ruin, for the Wonderman had his enemies. Whatever their purpose, no one ever discovered anything about him that he did not want them to know. The Count remained a man of mystery.

No one knew quite where he came from nor how old he was, although there was a great deal of speculation about the matter. For during the century that European society reported seeing him, the Wonderman always appeared to be about forty-five years of age. But when asked, he would graciously decline to reveal his date of birth. To one countess he would admit only that he was "very old."

The Count would describe scenes from the French Court of Valois (1328–1589), which ended with King Henri III's reign during his lifetime as Francis, or of princes still more remote, with such precise and minute detail as to almost to create the illusion that he had been an eyewitness to the events. This he could have done by reading the akashic records.

Saint Germain's knowledge extended not only back in time but also around the world. Voltaire remarked that Saint Germain knew the secrets of the prime ministers of England, France, and Austria.

The Wonderman was reputed to have concocted medicines that prolonged his life and to know the secret of the elixir of life. One memoir-writer said that the Count gave such an elixir to Madame V. Georgy, "which for fully a quarter of a century preserved unaltered the youthful charms she possessed at 25."[4]

Prince Karl of Hesse, with whom the Count stayed as an honored guest, wrote:

> I cannot, indeed, guarantee his birth; but that he was prodigiously protected by the last Medici, this is what I have also learned on another side. This House possessed, as is well known, the highest sciences, and it is not surprising that he obtained his first knowledge there; but he claimed to have learned those of nature by his own application and research. He thoroughly understood herbs and plants and had invented the medicines of which he constantly made use, and which prolonged his life and health. I still have all his recipes, but the physicians raged against his science after his death. There was a physician, Lossau, who had been an apothecary, and to whom I gave twelve hundred crowns per year to work on the medicines which the Comte de St. Germain dictated to him, among others and chiefly his tea, which the rich bought and the poor received for nothing, as well as the care of the doctor.[5]

While visiting one European court, the Count requested that tree branches and several bones from a deer be brought to him. He took them into a large palace dining room. Several moments later he reappeared and invited the guests to follow him. When the doors were opened all were astounded. Inside the dining room was a forest, with deer grazing around a lush board of haute cuisine.

The eighteenth century Dutch civil servant, biographer, and Freemason, Cornelis Ascanius van Sypesteyn, wrote a book about Saint Germain and Voltaire in the Netherlands based on memories of the time.

St. Germain was in many respects a remarkable man, and wherever he was personally known he left a favourable impression behind, and the remembrance of many good and sometimes of many noble deeds. Many a poor father of a family, many a charitable institution, was helped by him in secret... not one bad, nor one dishonourable action was ever known of him, and so he inspired sympathy everywhere, and not least in Holland.[6]

In the Brunswick newspaper of the period, "M. de St. Germain was spoken of as 'a man of learning,' 'a lover of truth,' 'devoted to the good,' and 'a hater of baseness and deception,' the Duke himself wrote to the editor, expressing his approbation of the announcement."[7]

Saint Germain was not only a Western alchemist but also an Eastern spiritual adept and used yogic practices, including meditation in the lotus posture. Van Sypesteyn wrote, "Sometimes he fell into a trance, and when he again recovered, he said he had passed the time while he lay unconscious in far-off lands; sometimes he disappeared for a considerable time, then suddenly re-appeared, and let it be understood that he had been in another world in communication with the dead."[8]

Another unexplained aspect was the master's independent wealth and amazing generosity. Madame de Pompadour wrote that Saint Germain gave the king beautiful paintings and gave away "diamonds and jewels with astonishing liberality."

Prince Karl of Hesse described him: "He was, perhaps, one of the greatest philosophers who ever lived. A friend of humanity, desiring money only to give it to the poor, a friend also of animals, his heart was concerned only with the happiness of others. He believed that he could make the world happier by procuring new pleasures, more beautiful fabrics, more beautiful colors, at a much cheaper price.... I have never seen a man have a clearer mind than his, with that an erudition, especially in ancient history, such as I have found few."[9]

To alleviate some of the poverty so prevalent in Europe at the time, Saint Germain used universal alchemy to produce tangible substance which, although temporary in nature, supplied many human needs and worked to give the poorer classes a brighter, more hopeful and comfortable life.

The House of Rakoczy

A search through European historical records of the late seventeenth century leads to an educated guess as to the Comte de Saint Germain's history.

The German book *Der Genealogische Archivarius* published in 1734, gives a history of the Rakoczy princes who are the Count's father and grandfather. After Prince Francis I Rakoczy of Hungary died fighting to retain the independence of his kingdom, his widow was forced to give guardianship of her children to the conquering Hapsburg Austrian Emperor in the court of Vienna. The son and heir, Francis Leopold or Francis II, was brought up in the Austrian court, and when he reached the age of maturity, his properties were given back to him, though with many restrictions. In 1694 Francis II married Charlotte Amalia, the daughter of Hesse-Wahnfried, and according to records had two sons and one daughter with her. There is no official record of a secret son, but the Comte de Saint Germain's contemporaries wrote of just such a son.

During the early 1700s, Prince Francis II Rakoczy, inspired by his father, led a decade-long war of independence against the Hapsburg Austrian Empire. It was an important contest for freedom in Eastern Europe at a time of decline in both the Ottoman and Austrian Empires, each of which occupied parts of Hungarian territory. The time was right for independence.

Louis XIV of France was an ally of Prince Francis II Rakoczy and supplied financial aid up until 1704. Patriot noblemen and peasants from modern-day Hungary, Romania, Slovakia, Ukraine, and Poland fought for independence against the Hapsburgs and supported Rakoczy.

In a crucial battle in Slovakia in 1708, Prince Rakoczy's horse fell and he was knocked unconscious. His army thought him dead and their cause lost in that one moment. They ran from the battlefield. The prince escaped to Poland, but in 1711 his key supporters abandoned him and the independence movement by signing a treaty with the Hapsburgs.

Part 2 • A Holy Brother

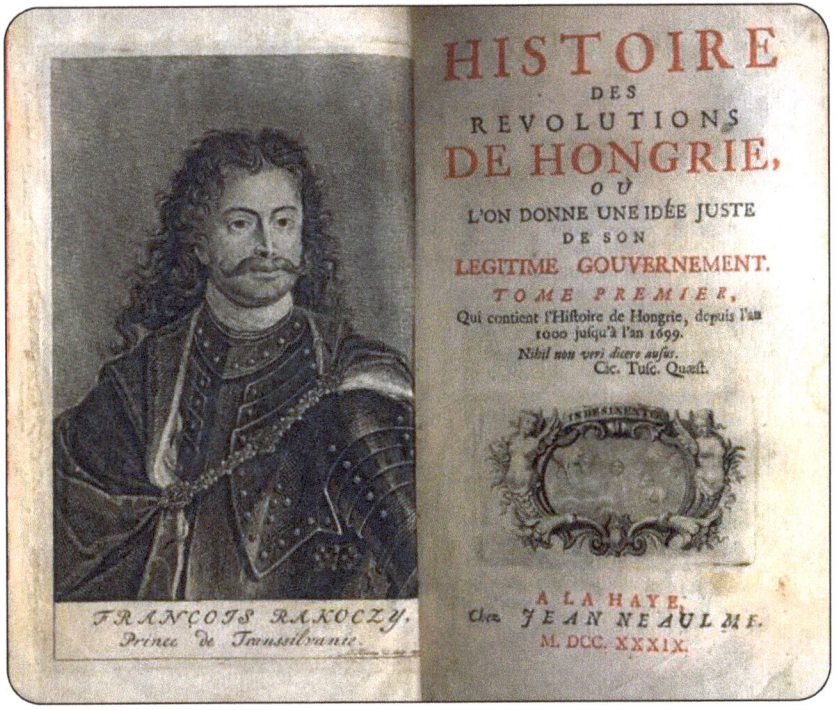

creativecommons.org/licenses/by-sa/3.0 Wikimedia: Histoire Des Revolutions De Hongrie 1739.jpg

The prince's two known sons were held hostage by the Hapsburgs in Vienna, and Francis II was forced to renounce further uprisings as well as the Rakoczy name by feigning death and becoming anonymous. After being so close to independence, the potential beneficiaries of Hungary's freedom became afraid and abandoned their prince; thus their best chance for claiming a sovereign nation was lost.

Karl de Hesse wrote of a mysterious third son of Rakoczy when relating the history of the Comte de Saint Germain.

> It will be curious to his history; I will trace it with the utmost truthfulness, according to his own words, adding any necessary explanations. He told me that he was eighty-eight years of age when he came here.... He told me he was the son of Prince Ragoczy* of Transylvania by his first wife, a Tékéli. He was placed, when quite young under the protection of the last Medici....

―――――――
*German spelling of Hungarian Rákóczy

When he learned that his two brothers, sons of the Princess of Hesse-Rheinfels, or Kothenbourg, if I am not mistaken, had become subordinates to the Emperor Charles VI, and had received the names of St. Charles and St. Elizabeth, after the Emperor and Empress, he said to himself: "Very well, I will call myself Sanctus Germanus, the holy brother."[10]

Other sources confirm the connection of a Rakoczy prince and the Duc de' Medici, as Isabel Cooper-Oakley notes, "The late Cæsare Cantù, librarian of the great library in Milan, who in his historical work, *Illustri Italiani,* ii., 18, says: 'The Marquis of San Germano appears to have been the son of Prince Ragotzy . . . of Transylvania; he was also much in Italy; much is recounted of his travels in Italy and in Spain; he was greatly protected by the last Grand Duke of Tuscany, who had educated him.'"[11]

Another source claims that he was not the first son of a previous marriage but the third son of Francis II and Princess Charlotte Amalia.[12] Whatever his heritage, the Comte de Saint Germain left his mark in history, not only in Europe but in Russia and India as well.

Early Travels

The French Countess V. Georgy met the Comte de Saint Germain in Venice in 1710. He introduced himself as Saint Germain and was a charming noble gentleman who looked to be about forty-five. It was on his first visit to Venice that he gave her the elixir that held off the effects of aging for a quarter of a century.

She lived so long at court that she became known as the Everlasting Countess. It sounds like a fairy tale, but the countess's sincere witness and visible youth served the master's cause when he came to the French court years later. When she saw him again she was amazed to find him looking the same age as when she had seen him fifty years earlier.

Between 1737 and 1742, Saint Germain, under an unknown name, spent six years at the court of the Shah of Persia, where he was given time and opportunity to master the art of improving valuable gems. This was a time of great upheaval in Persia, where, no doubt, Saint Germain used his time to help guide events toward greater liberty.

He was in England for some years around 1745, as documented by a letter from Horace Walpole to Sir Horace Mann, the British Envoy in Florence, as well as a reference to him in Read's *Weekly Journal or British Gazetteer,* May 17, 1760.

> The author of the Brussels' Gazette tells us that the person who styles himself Comte de St. Germain, who lately arrived here from Holland, was born in Italy in 1712. He speaks German and French as fluently as Italian, and expresses himself pretty well in English. He has a smattering of all the arts and sciences, is a good chemist, a virtuoso in musick, and a very agreeable companion. In 1746 [1745 according to Walpole], he was on the point of being ruined in England. One who was jealous of him with a lady, slipt a letter into his pocket as from the young Pretender (thanking him for his services and desiring him to continue them), and immediately had him taken up by a messenger. His innocence being fully proved on his examination, he was discharged out of the custody of the messenger and asked to dinner by Lord H. [Probably William Stanhope, Earl of Harrington, who was Secretary of the Treasury and Treasurer of the Chamber at this date; he died 1760.][13]

The Court of Versailles

In 1743 the master appeared as the Comte de Saint Germain at the court of Louis XV, where the new king welcomed his wisdom, stories, and expertise in the study of valuable gems. Louis XV was the great-grandson of the Sun King Louis XIV, who died in 1715. Louis XV ascended the throne at age five and was closely guarded by regents and ministers until 1743.

At the time of Saint Germain's appearance at court, King Louis XV's mistress, Madame de Pompadour, was a smart, charming,

Marquise de Pompadour
by François Boucher

Louis XV
by Maurice-Quentin de La Tour

and powerful member of the court of Versailles. Madame du Hausset, her *femme de chambre,* wrote of the Comte de Saint Germain in her memoirs. Though Hausset herself intimates that she believed the Count to be a mere adventurer, through her writings it is clear that St. Germain was a welcome guest not only to Madame Pompadour but to the King as well. She tells how, in 1757, Saint Germain undertook to remove a flaw from a medium-sized diamond for King Louis XV.

> The King said to the Count, "It is valued at two hundred and forty pounds; but it would be worth four hundred, if it had no spot. Will you try to put a hundred and sixty pounds into my pocket?" He examined it carefully, and said, "It may be done; and I will bring it you again in a month." At the time appointed, the Count brought back the diamond, without a spot, and gave it to the King. It was wrapped in a cloth of amianthus, which he took off. The King had it weighed, and found it but very little diminished. The King sent it to his jeweler... without telling him any thing of what had passed. The jeweler gave three

hundred and eighty pounds for it. The King, however, sent for it back again, and kept it as a curiosity.[14]

The King was astonished. He made the remark that "M. de St. Germain must be worth millions, especially if he had also the secret of making large diamonds out of a number of small ones."[15]

In 1745 Saint Germain traveled to the Netherlands, visiting Rosicrucian and Freemason contacts, and then on to London, where he was arrested as a suspected foreign spy but released when no evidence could be found against him. The next year, he was in Vienna with the Austrian emperor's prime minister who introduced him to a senior French diplomat. The diplomat, Belle-Isle, invited Saint Germain back to Versailles. France's king was key to defusing the catastrophe on Europe's horizon.

By 1749, doubting his hawkish minister for war, Louis XV was ready to trust Saint Germain with a secret diplomatic mission to test peace overtures with neighboring monarchs. It was a step in the right direction, but there was no guarantee the king would defend Saint Germain against his cabinet ministers, let alone consider pursuing the beginning of representative government for France. Whatever the mission to the neighboring monarchs was, it remained a state secret.

Saint Germain traveled to India at least twice. On his second trip in 1755, he learned how to "melt jewels." During his journeying throughout Europe and Asia, Saint Germain was never an agent for the states or religions of either France, Britain, or India. He worked for humanity, and his vision was of a self-transcending international golden age—beyond the 1700s, beyond our time, and on behalf of the latent inner divinity of the people—unfolding in all nations during the new historical cycle and the coming Aquarian age.

In 1757 Saint Germain was invited back to Versailles by Louis XV, who wanted more expert discussion about philosophy, enlightenment, alchemy and gems, and also offered him a personal suite of rooms in the beautiful Château de Chambord. But France's karmic clock was ticking toward a date with anarchy. Saint Germain accepted the King's generosity and used the rooms to pursue experiments in physics and chemistry. The King invited select nobility to attend the experiments as students. Meanwhile, Saint Germain broadened his discussions with the King. Mme. Du Hausset recorded one such conversation.

> M. de St. Germain said, one day, to the King, "To think well of mankind, one must be neither a Confessor, nor a Minister, nor a Lieutenant of Police."—"Nor a King," said his Majesty. "Ah! Sire," replied he, "you remember the fog we had a few days ago, when we could not see four steps before us. Kings are commonly surrounded by still thicker fogs, collected around them by men of intriguing character, and faithless ministers:—all, of every class, unite in endeavouring to make things appear to Kings in any light but the true one." I heard this from the mouth of the famous Count de St. Germain, as I was attending upon Madame, who was ill in bed. The King was there; and the Count, who was a welcome visitor, had been admitted.[16]

Although Saint Germain spent much of his time in the château with his students, he was also well-known in Paris society. Around 1758 a notorious English mimic known as Milord Gower made a name for himself in the salons of Paris by skillfully impersonating the master, publicly mocking his manner and appearance and generating gossip and ridicule. Saint Germain did not let ridiculers stop him from appearing anywhere he needed to be. He was aware that his example of divine love in action would stoke envy and make enemies. Beyond the courts and salons, many a struggling French family found him to be a savior, offering supplies, food, medicines, and spiritual gifts, necessarily without recognition by name.

In 1760 Louis XV sent Saint Germain on another discreet diplomatic mission, first to The Hague in the Netherlands and then to England, where he was well received by George II. Louis XV was looking for a way to end an expensive war, which his minister for war, the duc de Choiseul, wanted to continue for his personal benefit and the benefit of France's ally, Austria.

When Choiseul heard about the King's secret inquiries with England and the Netherlands through Saint Germain, he shamed the King in front of his cabinet. The surprised king backed down,

Carnival scene at the court of Versailles, 1763

abandoned Saint Germain, and allowed the war to go on. In pivotal moments such as this, Saint Germain could only bow to the free will of those he endeavored to help.

For the next fifteen years after Choiseul's attack, the master no longer had access to the King at the center of France's fate. However, Saint Germain's advice was not just for the nobility—he continued his Great Instauration for the betterment of the world through inventions.

He guided and encouraged key inventors during the Industrial Revolution to help the poorer classes climb out of poverty, servitude, and serfdom. He worked with the people to better their economic state while he urged the nobility to fix the inequities built into their feudal laws.

The Marquis de Valbelle reported seeing him change a silver six-franc piece into gold. In a letter dated 1763, Count Karl Cobenzl asserted that the Count Saint Germain had performed "under my own eyes ... the transmutation of iron into a metal as beautiful as gold."

During the mid to late 1700s, Saint Germain went to England and Scotland to inspire Freemasons James Watt and William Murdoch to improve the Newcomen steam engine. He spent time with George Stephenson on the early development of rail transportation for

Drawing of Stephenson's Rocket, the locomotive built by the Stephenson family.

passengers and freight. In Europe, he advised textile manufacturers about new techniques for improving the appearance, usefulness, and quality of their products.

Count Cobenzl witnessed the master's wisdom, kindness, and development of manufacturing:

> It was about three months ago that the person known by the name of the Comte de St. Germain passed this way, and came to see me. I found him the most singular man that I ever saw in my life. I do not yet precisely know his birth.... Possessing great wealth, he lives in the greatest simplicity; he knows everything, and shows an uprightness, a goodness of soul, worthy of admiration. Among a number of his accomplishments, ... of which the most important were the transmutation of iron into a metal as beautiful as gold, and at least as good for all goldsmith's work; the dyeing and preparing of skins, carried to a perfection which surpassed all the moroccos in the world, and the most perfect tanning; the dyeing of silks, carried to a perfection hitherto unknown; the like dyeing of woollens; the dyeing of wood in the most brilliant colours penetrating through and through, and the whole without either indigo or cochineal, with the commonest ingredients, and consequently at a very moderate price.[17]

The master was seen in Berlin in 1764, then in a fabric factory in Venice in 1769, under the name Marquis d'Adymar, in Tunis and Livorno under the name Graf Saltikov in 1770, and then back to Paris when he learned of the King's dismissal of the pro-war duc de Choiseul.

There are significant gaps in the recorded sightings of the Count, years when Saint Germain was not seen in public. He knew he was being tracked by dangerous agents, as indicated by his frequent use of pseudonyms. He was capable of the mysteries of bilocation and other powers but used these carefully and only for purposes permitted by cosmic law.

Saint Germain spent time in The Hague in 1773 and 1774 and advised manufacturers near Frankfurt and Munich between 1774 and 1776. During this period his efforts to persuade Louis XV to reform the French economy and taxation system were focused through the King's personal meetings with the Versailles Group. Under the master's guidance, several talented economists and legal experts drew up a far-reaching document, which was in effect a blueprint for a United States of Europe. It required France to lead by example. This document is on display in the Louvre.

To make the necessary major societal changes that contemporaries such as Rousseau and Voltaire had publicly advocated required executive leadership on par with a unifying national figure such as George Washington. France's Louis XV was a pleasant and self-effacing monarch, fond of mathematics, astronomy, and elegant architecture. Though he may have understood the concept of reforms, which were 150 years overdue, the King lacked the will or the skills to make a drastic change in society and to override the formidable political currents opposing him from within the nobility and clergy. The years which Louis XV should have spent gathering momentum through political allies were squandered, and the Versailles Group's recommendations never came close to implementation. Saint Germain continued his attempts to reach key souls for their spiritual liberation and national freedom, but in each case when they ignored him he had to bow to their free will and withdraw.

A Tale of Two Countries

The window of opportunity for saving France from disaster narrowed with the death of Louis XV in 1774 and the coronation of his grandson, the new king, Louis XVI. The sheltered young king was naïve and even more isolated than his grandfather. Saint Germain again attempted to reach the mind and heart of the French king to save a country and its destiny. But he was not limited in his service to just one nation.

Saint Germain was and is the embodiment of *noblesse oblige* and the heart of divine freedom. During this time, he also played an energetic and principal role across the Atlantic, in the American Revolution. The question may well be asked, where has the master's presence *not* been felt in the universal movement for freedom that has taken place in the centuries leading up to the Aquarian age?

In the New World, Saint Germain worked with students to found the country that he, as Francis Bacon, had known would come into being. Ben Jonson wrote in a ciphered letter in his play *Volpone* that his friend Francis Bacon "trusteth all to the future, and a land that is very far towards th' sunset gate."[18] It was by design that the American colonies carried the essence of Francis's philosophy of representative government, individual liberty, and the dream of a sovereign republic, free from feudal laws.

 ## Foundations of Freedom

Saint Germain is the key figure and a mystical, mysterious presence in the founding of the United States of America as a nation where its citizens have a constitutionally guaranteed opportunity to be free. Freedom is deeper than a political statement; its source is a divine need, essential for innovation, resourcefulness, and abundance. It is an invisible spiritual essence, a consciousness. Long before the founding of the United States, Francis Bacon had understood that freedom begins within the soul of man and woman.

The soul is the living potential of God that demanded and therefore was accorded by Life the opportunity to go forth, to come out of the fiery core, to manifest an identity and an individuality. Therefore, the soul was sent forth into the planes of Mater with the gift of free will. That is where the flame of freedom begins. It could not exist except as the gift from the Creator to the creation.

Nature teaches that the flame of freedom is internal. As one looks at the stars in the heavens and the multiplication of the seeds in all of nature, over and over again God is saying: "I AM the flame of freedom in the heart of the seed that becomes the tree, that becomes the flower, that becomes the star. I AM the flame of freedom within you."

As Francis wrote in the deep, questioning monologue of *Hamlet,* human beings have the choice "to be or not to be"—to be the soul that is patterning the inner blueprint of her own Real Self, the Anointed One, and to come into conformity with the balance of the Law and the creative, joyful plan for that Self, or to remain in imbalance and fear outside of divine Reality.

In the very core of being, you know that you are real. You know that you have a connection to an ultimate Source beyond, a source that existed before the breath of life was infused into the clay vessel, a source that will continue beyond the putting aside of that clay vessel.

When one contacts the Source that is the sacred fire of life within, that fire of freedom on the altar of being, then all of life—nature, the governments of the nations, all mankind—must come into conformity with the flame. That sacred fire is the same cosmic authority described in the mystery: "Our God is a consuming fire." It dissolves and transmutes all unlike itself.

During his lifetime as Francis Bacon and then as the Comte de Saint Germain, he personified that sacred fire, giving people the opportunity and the method to learn how to gain their soul freedom and manifest a golden age.

Comte de Saint Germain

Francis and Friends in America

As an adept, Francis Tudor Bacon seems to have had the ability to see through time, and to seed the last centuries of the Piscean age with the founding ideas of the Great Instauration in preparation for a golden age evolving upward through the centuries of Aquarius. And what he did for England is dwarfed by the unseen work he performed on behalf of his great dream, the establishment of the New Atlantis. In addition to his service to England, to science, to the language and literature, Francis Bacon secretly laid the groundwork for the establishment and growth of the United States of America.

Many English, Irish, Scots, German, Scandinavian, French, Italian, and Dutch immigrants sought spiritual freedom in America because of that unseen groundwork. Small villages and settlements sprang up, built by people who yearned for enlightenment, religious tolerance, and a new way of life, and risked everything to find their way to the colonies. Many came by word of mouth from the Masonic-Rosicrucian fellowships and other spiritual groups.

The Masonic-Rosicrucian tradition had a profound influence on the formation of the American republic. George Washington and many of the founding fathers were Freemasons. John Adams's English ancestors for generations had been interested in esoteric science and philosophy. In 1823 President John Adams ordered a tombstone to be erected to mark the grave of his ancestor Henry Adams who had emigrated to the colonies during the "Dragon Persecution" in England. They were said to have derived their family name from the ancient British Druids, and studied chemistry, alchemy and ley lines. It was claimed that Dr. John Dee, Walter Raleigh, and Christopher Marlowe were associated with this esoteric group.

A number of historians have researched the Rosicrucian activities during the colonial period, looking for their secrets. The schools of the initiates, the Freemasons and the Rosicrucians, were actively involved in bringing Francis Bacon's dream to completion in the founding of America. Among them, Francis Bacon was known as the true genius behind the colonization of America. His unprecedented ideals of universal education and the rights of the free individual came to fruition in the New World.

The founders of Virginia stitched the muse of the Knights of the Helmet and the sponsor of the spear-shakers, Pallas Athena, onto their state flag while Francis was still the Lord Chancellor of England. She can still be found there, shaking her spear at tyranny. Francis, the Master Mason, had always been building for the future. His dreams were realizable because the early Masons and Rosicrucians embraced his fiery purpose, as do his students in this age—for the vast scheme of his Great Instauration is still coming into fruition.

Francis Bacon

"It is thought that between 1610 and 1660 a great deal of material concerned with the development of the great plan for America was transferred for preservation and future use from Europe to the Western continent."[19] During these years, the Freemasonic foundational work began in America and spread to each city, town and village. The teachings of Francis's "Sons of Science" were built on the character of the individual, the use of talents to help forge a national identity for the colonies, and most importantly, the development of a trusted brotherhood.

Coat of arms of Virginia (1876)

By the mid-1700s, the spirit of revolution and independence had swept the American colonies through this brotherhood. It grew out of the reaction to British tyranny and the spiritual Great Awakening, a religious revival that gave rise to the belief that God had founded a New Israel in America. But it took more than fiery sentiment to generate the kind of revolution that respected law—it took organization. The Masons, and only the Masons, were sufficiently organized. It is doubtful that the American Revolution could have ever happened without them.

Freemasonry fostered a feeling of American unity in a small but prominent group of people. There could have been no United States without it because the colonies were too deeply divided among themselves concerning the risks and benefits of independence. By 1770 there was hardly a town, big or small, where Masonry was not preaching fraternity and unity as the antidote to fear and rivalry.

By 1773 Boston was the center of American discontent with the monarchy of George III. When colonial tempers rose, there was a revolutionary movement ready to direct the spirit of resistance in constructive ways—through Francis's well-organized and widespread fellowships.

The Mystical Origins of America

While Saint Germain witnessed the transition of the French monarchy from Louis XV to Louis XVI, the British Crown ignored calls from English colonists in North America for just taxation, individual rights, and parliamentary representation in London. Echoing the Crown, parliamentary leaders expected colonists to obey their appointed governors and to meekly accept all new taxes without question or any say in the matter.

Parliament passed a series of punitive acts such as revoking Massachusetts' charter, additional taxes on commodities, and a tea monopoly that saved the British East India Company from bankruptcy. The colonists' response was to invoke the *unwritten* British constitution, saying that it was unlawful for Parliament to impose any taxes on English colonies without legislative representation. They rejected the concept of being subject to an unaccountable and unresponsive nobility. The tide of public opinion in the colonies began to shift, and an influential minority advocated for sovereign citizenship as a God-given right in an independent republic. They also remembered that an unwritten constitution could be flouted by those who sought to fulfill only their own selfish will at the cost of all else.

For Saint Germain, the thirteen American colonies were the fertile ground he had invested in as Francis Bacon, newly populated with those who had the courage and motivation to leave the chaos and injustice of the Old World behind and to trust in God, not the Crown, for their well-being. The American colonies were where the Great Instauration could take hold—among those who could envision an establishment of lawful governance that was free from the whims of a distant and corrupt government.

Saint Germain spent time in inspirational communion with key individuals such as Washington, Franklin, Adams, Jefferson, and Madison. None of these claimed to have seen or heard the name Saint Germain, at least in the form of the mysterious European Count, but each acknowledged the intercession of Providence in their writings. There is documentary evidence of the ongoing presence of a mysterious older gentleman who helped them during the most intense times of declaring and surviving their independence.

Washington, for one, was sensitive to an unknown protector when two horses, one after the other, were shot from beneath him in a battle during the French and Indian War in 1755. His hat and coat had multiple bullet holes in them. There is more, however, to the mystery of why George Washington was chosen and was willing to leave a comfortable home, to risk his life, and to take on a lengthy, arduous military and political campaign for a form of national independence.

The Legend of the Anointing

In 1693 a group of European mystics well versed in Rosicrucianism sailed from Rotterdam and settled on the banks of the Wissahikon River, near Philadelphia. They were the students of Jacob Boehme and a British mystic named Jane Leade. A monastic community was founded in the woods beside the river by the young Johannes Kelpius, born in the Carpathian Mountains in 1667. The settlers called themselves the Society of the Woman in the Wilderness, after the Woman and her seed, spoken of in the Book of Revelation.

About sixty years later, in 1757, one year after the last of the community died, a mysterious nobleman and his two children left behind their riches in Europe to homestead and build a circular chapel just a mile from the old monastery. The man came for one purpose only, to await the prophesied "deliverer." This deliverer was foretold to be the one who would free mankind from absolute rule and tyranny. The European noble was there to give the blessing and anointing of the spiritual Brotherhood who had sponsored the founding of the American colonies, though this remained his secret.

In the last hours of 1773, Rosicrucian legend tells of the old man, a stranger, and a spiritual anointing. It starts with the father and his son and daughter on an evening walk in the woods.

> The night comes slowly down. Still the Father and son pace the ground in silence, while the breeze freshens and makes low music among the leaves.—Still the young girl, bending over the old man's arm, smiles tenderly in his face, as though she would drive the sadness from his brow with one gleam of her mild blue eyes.
>
> ...Within the shadows of the gate, their faces lighted by the last gleam of the setting sun—the old man and his son stand like figures of stone, while each grasps a hand of the young girl.
>
> ...The old Monastery forms one dense mass of shade; on either side extends the darkening forest, yet here, within the portals of the gate, the three figures are grouped, while a warm, soft mass of tufted moss, spreads before them.
>
> ...The Father presses the wrist of his Son with a convulsive grasp—hush! Do you hear that low deep whisper? "At last, it comes to my soul, the Fulfilment of Prophecy!"...
>
> "But the time—Father—*the time?*" the Son replies in the same deep voice, while his eye... fires with the same feeling that swells his Father's heart.
>
> "*The last day of this year—the third hour after midnight—* THE DELIVERER WILL COME!"

As the hour nears midnight, the father and son sit in the Block-House of the Monastery.

"Strangely furnished room? Yes, circular in form, with a single doorway, huge panels of dark oaken wainscot, rise from the bared floor to the gloomy ceiling. Near the old man arises a white altar, on which the candles are placed, its spotless curtain floating down to the floor. Between the candles, you behold, a long, slender flagon of silver, a wreath of laurel leaves, fresh gathered from the Wissahikon hills, and a Holy Bible, bound in velvet, with antique clasps of gold.

Behind the altar... arises a cross of Iron...."

The Priest of the Wissahikon was the first to break the silence.

"He will come!" mutters the Priest of the Wissahikon, as common rumor named him. *"At the third hour after midnight, the Deliverer will come!"...*

"The Old World," said he, *"is sunk in all manner of crime, as was the Ante-Deluvian World;—*THE NEW WORLD *is given to man as a refuge, even as the Ark was given to Noah and his children.*

"The New World is the last altar of human freedom left on the surface of the Globe. Never shall the footsteps of Kings pollute its soil. It is the last hope of man, God has spoken, and it is so—Amen!"

Hours passed. The father waited with surety that the Deliverer would appear. The son waited in taut apprehension that he would not. Long into the night they waited until the old clock's marking of the third hour of the morning struck and faded. Then there came footsteps at the door.

"Is there not a footstep on the frozen snow? Hark! Father, father! do you hear that footstep? It is on the threshold now—it advances—"

"HE comes!" whispered the old man.... "At last he is come!" ... and with one impulse they sank on their knees. Hark! You hear the old door creak on its hinges, as it swings slowly open— a strange voice breaks the silence.

"Friends, I have lost my way in the forest," said the voice, speaking in a calm, manly tone. "Can you direct me to the right way?"

The old man looked up; a cry of wonder trembled from his lips. As for the son, he gazed in silence on the Stranger, while his features were stamped with inexpressible surprise.

The Stranger stood on the threshold, his face to the light, his form thrown boldly forward, by the darkness at his back.

Towering above the stature of common men, his form was clad in the dress of a plain gentleman of that time... Broad in the shoulders, beautiful in the sinewy proportions of each limb, he stood there, extending his hat in one hand, while the other gathered his heavy cloak around the arm....

His... eyes, which gleamed even through the darkness of the room with a calm, clear light... his face stamped with the settled beauty of mature manhood, mingled with the fire of chivalry.

In one word, he was a man whom you would single out among a crowd of ten thousand, for his grandeur of bearing, his calm, collected dignity of expression and manner.

"Friends," he again began... "I have lost my way—"

"Thou has not lost thy way," spoke the voice of the old man, as he arose... "thou hast found thy way to usefulness and immortal renown!"

The Stranger advanced a footstep, while a warm glow overspread his commanding face....

"Nay—do not start, nor gaze upon me in such wonder! I tell thee the voice that speaks from my lips, is the voice of Revelation. Thou art called to a great work; kneel before the altar and receive thy mission!"

Nearer to the altar drew the Stranger.

"This is but folly—you make a mock of me!" he began; but the wild gaze of the old man thrilled his heart, as with magnetic fire. He paused, and stood silent and wondering.

"Nay, doubt me not! To-night, filled with strange thoughts on your country's Future, you laid yourself down to sleep within your habitation in yonder city. But sleep fled from your eyes—a feeling of restlessness drove you forth into the cold air of night—"

"This is true!" mutters the Stranger in a musing tone, while his face expressed surprise.

"As you dashed along, mounted on the steed which soon will bear your form in the ranks of battle, the cold air of night fanned your hot brow, but could not drive from your soul the Thought of your Country!"

"How knew you this?"...

Deeper and bolder thrilled the tones of the old Enthusiast. "The rein fell loosely on your horse's neck—you let him wander, you cared not whither! Still the thought that oppressed your soul was the future of your country. Still great hopes—dim visions of *what is to come*—floating panoramas of battle and armed legions—darted one by one over your soul. Even as you stood on the threshold of yonder door, asking, in calm tones, the way through the forest, another and deeper question rose to your lips—"

"I confess it!" said the Stranger, his tone catching the deep emotion of the old man's voice. "As I stood upon the threshold, the question that rose to my lips was—"

"Is it lawful for a SUBJECT *to draw sword against his* KING?"

"Man! You read the heart!" and this strange man of commanding form and thoughtful brow, gazed fixedly in the eyes of the Enthusiast, while his face expressed every conflicting emotion of doubt, suspicion, surprise and awe.

"Nay, do not gaze upon me in such wonder. I tell thee a great work has been allotted unto thee, by the FATHER of all souls! Kneel by this altar—and here, in the silence of night, amidst the depths of these wild woods—will I anoint thee Deliverer of this great land, even as the men of Judah, in the far-gone time, anointed the brows of the chosen David!"...

... Some conviction of the future flashed over the Stranger's soul ... he bowed before the altar, his brow bared, and his hands laid upon the Book of God.

The light flashed over his bold features.... On one side of the altar stood the old man—the Priest of the Wissahikon—his silver hair waving aside from his flushed brow—on the other, his son, bronzed in face, but thoughtful in the steady gaze of his large full eyes....

"Thou art called to the great work of a Champion and Deliverer! Soon thou wilt ride to battle at the head of legions—soon thou wilt lead a people on to freedom—soon thy sword will gleam like a meteor over the ranks of war!"

The young daughter appears in the doorway watching, her golden hair loose about her shoulders.

> "Dost thou promise, that when the appointed time arrives, thou wilt be found ready, sword in hand, to fight for thy country and thy God?"
>
> ... The Stranger simply answered, "I do!"
>
> "Dost thou promise, in the hour of thy glory—when a nation shall bow before thee—as in the fierce moment of adversity, —when thou shalt behold thy soldiers starving for want of bread—to remember the great truth, written in these words—*'I am but the Minister of God in the great work of a nation's freedom.'*"
>
> Again the bowed head, again the tremulous—"I do promise!"
>
> "Then, in His name, who gave the New World to millions of the human race, as the last altar of their rights, I do consecrate thee its—DELIVERER!"
>
> With the finger of his extended hand, touched with the anointing oil, he described the figure of a Cross on the white forehead of the Stranger, who raised his eyes, while his lips murmured as if in prayer....
>
> "When the time comes, go forth to victory! On thy brow, no conqueror's blood-red wreath, but this crown of fadeless laurel."

He reached for the laurels on the altar, but his daughter with a glow lighting her face stepped forward and placed the laurels on the stranger's head. She glanced at her father, concerned she had been presumptuous, but he smiled and nodded. "It is well."

> "From whom should the Deliverer of a Nation receive his crown of laurel, but from the hands of a stainless woman! Rise! The Champion and Leader of a People!" spoke the deep voice of the son.... "Rise, sir, and take this hand, which was never yet given to man. I know not thy name, yet, on this book, I swear to be faithful to thee, even to the death!"
>
> The Stranger rose.... The son buckled a sword to his side; the old man extended his hands as if in blessing, while the young girl looked up silently into his face.

> They all beheld the form of this strange man shake with emotion; while that face, whose calm beauty had won their hearts, now quivered in every fibre....
>
> "From you, old man, I take the vow! From you, fair girl, the laurel! From you, brave friend, the sword! On this book I swear to be faithful unto all!"
>
> And as the light flashed over his quivering features, he laid his hand upon the Book and kissed the hilt of the sword.[20]

Through the hands of the old Rosicrucian noble, the Priest of the Wissahikon, the presence of Saint Germain anointed George Washington on New Year's Day in 1774 as the deliverer of the nation, the hope of liberty for the people.

It is because George Washington accepted the spiritual anointing of Saint Germain that America has had the protection of the ascended masters, and there has not been the scale of perpetual bloodshed seen in every century in the history of Europe.

The Professor and the Starry Flag

A year later, with the colonies on the verge of revolution, Saint Germain's presence was recorded by some of the founding fathers. He was simply known to them as "the Old Professor." This older gentleman was a mystery to the early patriots. He was known to be very private, to consult the ancient books and scrolls he kept in his possession, and to eat only slightly and drink herbal preparations and elixirs.

The first record of the Old Professor appeared in the account of the design of the new national flag in 1775. Robert Allen Campbell published the event in his *Our Flag*. Similarities can be seen in it to the European descriptions of the habits of Comte de Saint Germain.

> Little seems to have been known concerning this old gentleman; and in the materials from which this account is compiled, his name is not even once mentioned, for he is uniformly spoken of or referred to as "the Professor." He was evidently far beyond

his threescore and ten years; and he often referred to historical events of more than a century previous just as if he had been a living witness of their occurrence; still he was erect, vigorous and active—hale, hearty, and clear-minded—as strong and energetic every way as in the mature prime of life. He was tall, of fine figure, perfectly easy, and very dignified in his manners; being at once courteous, gracious and commanding. He was, for those times, and considering the customs of the Colonists, very peculiar in his method of living; for he ate no flesh, fowl or fish; he never used for food any "green thing," any roots or anything unripe; and he drank no liquor, wine or ale; but confined his diet to cereals and their products, fruits that were ripened on the stem in the sun, nuts, mild tea and the sweets of honey, sugar or molasses. He was well educated, highly cultivated, of extensive as well as varied information, and very studious. He spent considerable of his time in the patient and persistent conning of a number of very rare old books and ancient manuscripts which he seemed to be deciphering, translating or rewriting. These books and manuscripts, together with his own writings, he never showed to any one.... He took long and frequent walks alone, sat on the brows of the neighboring hills, or mused in the midst of the green and flower-gemmed meadows. He was fairly liberal—but in no way lavish—in spending his money, with which he was well supplied. He was a quiet, though a very genial and very interesting member of the family; and he was seemingly at home upon any and every topic coming up in conversation. He was, in short, one whom everyone would notice and respect, whom few would feel well acquainted with, and whom no one would presume to question concerning himself—as to whence he came, why he tarried, or whither he journeyed.

He was firmly, and in a dignified and assured way, one who was in favor of demanding and of securing justice on the part of the Mother Country toward the Colonies. One of his favorite forms of stating the matter was: "We demand no more than our just due; we will accept and be satisfied with nothing less than we demand." Then he would sometimes add: "We demand our rightful dues—justice; and we will soon get all we demand—peaceably, if Parliament is wise—forcibly, if needs be."

The committeemen arrived at Cambridge on the morning of December 13th, and their host invited the General of the Army to dine with them the same day at his home. When they met for dinner* the party consisted of Washington, the three committeemen, the Professor, the host and the hostess. The Professor met the guests of his host with an ease, grace and dignity which was to them all ample evidence of his superior ability, experience and attainments, and of the propriety of his being among them—which, however, none of them thought of questioning. He met the introductions with a courtly bow, that left no room to doubt that he had habitually associated with those in acknowledged authority. When Benjamin Franklin was presented, however, the latter came forward, extending his hand, which the Professor heartily accepted; and then as palm met palm, and as fingers closed upon fingers, their eyes also met, and there was an instantaneous, a very apparent and a mutually gratified recognition.

The dinner, of course, followed the usual form of those days, under similar circumstances.... In this case, however, conversation soon drifted upon the all-important topic of the day—the relation of the Colonies to each other and to the Mother Country, together with the related question of one's duty to the Colony, as related to his allegiance to Great Britain; and thence, naturally, to the work of the Committee—the design for a new Colonial Flag....

As the party were about rising from the table, there was a brief and undertone consultation between General Washington and the committeemen, upon some suggestion to which there seemed to be a ready, a hearty and an unanimous assent.

Doctor Franklin then arose, saying, substantially: "As the chairman of this committee, speaking for my associates, with their consent, and with the approval of General Washington, I respectfully invite the Professor to meet with the Committee as one of its members; and we, each one, personally and urgently, request him to accept the responsibility, and to give us, and the

---

*Dinner was the main meal of the day and usually took place around midday with a smaller supper being had in the evening. The committee stayed the rest of the day at the house after finishing the meal.

American Colonies, the benefit of his presence and his counsel. It has already been arranged that General Washington and our worthy host will also meet with us as honorary members."

The Professor arose, seemingly taller, more erect and more graciously dignified than even his usual wont, saying, in substance:

"I appreciate the compliment bestowed and the honor offered. I humbly accept the invitation, and I cheerfully assume the responsibility of all I may say and do as a co-worker with you. Since, by your unanimous invitation and my unqualified acceptance, I have become a member of your committee, so that I can in all propriety say 'our committee,' I will proceed at once to offer my first suggestion.

"Gentlemen and Comrades, this is a most important occasion. Upon what we do at this time, and at the regular sessions of this committee that will follow this informal and unofficial meeting, there may depend much of the immediate welfare of the people of the Colonies which we represent.

"We are now six—an even number, and not a propitious one for such an enterprise as we have now in hand. We can not spare any one already a member of the committee—even though in so doing we should improve the conditions in one respect, by making our number five; but we must needs increase our number, so we will be seven. This increase of our numbers should be by the introduction of an element that is usually objected to—or even worse than objected to, ignored—in all national and political affairs. I refer to woman—the purifying and intuitional element of humanity.

"Let us, therefore, invite our hostess—because she is our hostess, because she is a woman, and above all, because she is a superior woman—to become one of us; and mayhap she will prove a most important factor in solving the important question which we are to consider; for more depends on our work here and now than appears on the surface, to the multitude; and for her patriotism, her intelligence, her fidelity and her discretion, you may, one and all, hold me personally and entirely responsible —that is, if any one of you suppose that any man's indorsement, in any way, adds to an earnest and good woman's responsibility."

The Professor's first suggestion, as a member of the committee, was certainly a wonderful innovation, considering the times and the circumstances; but it was immediately and unanimously adopted.[21]

The committee met again later in the afternoon and the Old Professor gave his advice for the new flag. First, as a Colonial flag, it should still bear signs of loyalty to England, but—as they knew their demands for justice would be ignored by the Crown—it should be designed to be easily modified into a flag for a new nation. Second, the field of the flag must be completely new, unlike the flags of other nations, for it not only symbolized a new nation but "it will represent an entirely new principle in government—*the equal rights of man as man.*"[22]

In describing the meaning of his design, the Professor said:

> The thirteen stripes will at once be understood to represent the thirteen Colonies; their equal width will type the equal rank, rights and responsibilities of the Colonies. The union of the stripes in the field of our flag will announce the unity of interests and the cooperative union of efforts, which the Colonies recognize and put forth in their common cause. The white stripes will signify that we consider our demands just and reasonable; and that we will seek to secure our rights through peaceable, intelligent and statesmanlike means—if they prove at all possible; and the red stripes at the top and bottom of our flag will declare that first and last—and always—we have the determination, the enthusiasm, and the power to use force, whenever we deem force necessary. The alternation of the red and white stripes will suggest that our reasons for all demands will be intelligent and forcible, and that our force in securing our rights will be just and reasonable....
>
> There are other weightier and eternal reasons for a flag having the field I suggest; but it will be time enough to consider them when, in the near future, we, or our successors, are considering—not a temporary flag for associated and dependent Colonies but—a permanent standard for a united and an independent nation. Thanking you, one and all, for your complimentary

courtesy and for your patient attention, I submit this miniature drawing of the suggested flag for your intelligent consideration.[23]

The Professor's design for the Colonial flag was enthusiastically endorsed. General Washington and Doctor Franklin giving it especial approval and unstinted praises.

"It was formally and unanimously adopted; and shortly before midnight the Committee adjourned."[24]

After the conclusion of the meeting on December 13, 1775, the Professor, Washington, and Franklin spoke long into the night about the future of colonies, whether their demands for justice would be met, and the flag of the new nation. There is very little officially recorded about the adoption of the design of the "stars and stripes." But two pieces of writing, in the handwriting of the lady who made the notes of the Franklin committee meeting, exist mentioning the Professor's design. The first is a memorandum: "By direction of Dr. Franklin, now in Paris, I made this copy of the Professor's memoranda; and to-day I delivered the original of the same, and also a sealed letter... into the hands of General Washington. May 13, 1777."[25]

The second seems to refer to a meeting held on June 13, 1777, the day before the congressional meeting that adopted the Stars and Stripes.

> Last Friday afternoon I was invited to be present at a little gathering where the subject would be considered; and you may be sure I was greatly surprised, and not a little confused, to find myself the only woman there, while there was of men a round dozen. They read the Professor's memoranda and discussed the design. That is they one and all approved it. I explained to them

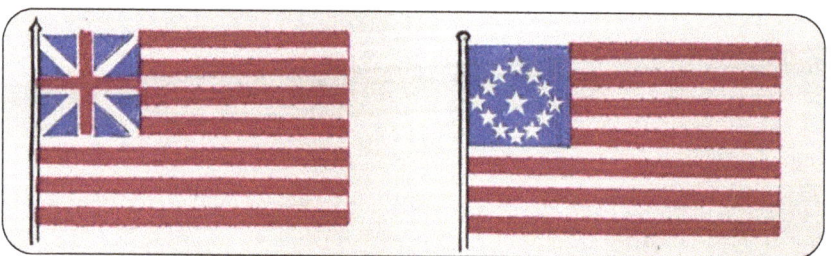

The Colonial Flag—December 13, 1775.   The original Stars and Stripes—June 14, 1777.

how I came to be the custodian of the paper, and why they had not been sooner delivered to General Washington. The matter is finally settled, however, for the very next day the Congress here adopted the Stars and Stripes as the flag of the thirteen Colonies. And now that the matter is brought to such a satisfactory issue, you can not, I am sure, at all imagine how pleased I am with the result, and how proud I am with the accidental and humble part I have had in its consummation.[26]

Old Glory

Through Betsy Ross, the flag was sewn by the Divine Mother herself, and that design is a cosmic design. The thirteen stars in the flag represent the initiations of the Christ consciousness. The thirteen stripes symbolize Christ and his apostles, reminding the American people of the circle of initiation, of the true Teacher who will come to remind them of the promise of the coming of Mother Liberty, and of the twelve original apostles who will keep that flame of liberty under the twelve hierarchies of the sun. Thirteen is a basic unit of hierarchy and a basic unit of initiation.

This can also be seen in mystic Christianity, early British Christian communities, and Camelot. With Merlin, King Arthur founded his Order of Chivalry "based on the traditional pattern adopted by Jesus and his disciples—the Zodiacal Round Table (i.e., Christ, the 'Sun,' surrounded by the 12 Apostles or Signs). Each Christian community was established on this same pattern, each Apostle representing the Christ and presiding over one or more 'Round Tables' of disciples, with a Bishop as chief or head of each Twelve (and being one of those Twelve)."[27]

The Speech of the Unknown

The Old Professor was seen again at another crucial moment of decision for the founding fathers of the United States. The following account records the effect of the Old Professor's unexpected address to fifty-six traders, farmers, and mechanics, who "had assembled to shake the shackles of the world."[28] These men were well aware of the risk of capital punishment for those who went against the Crown.

On July 4, 1776, silence reigns in an old hall while the men gathered there wait for the committee of three.

The door opens—the Committee appear. Who are these three men, who come walking on toward John Hancock's chair?

Writing the Declaration of Independence, 1776
Thomas Jefferson (right), Benjamin Franklin (left), and John Adams (center)
by Jean Leon Gerome Ferris

That tall man, with the sharp features, the bold brow and sand-hued hair, holding the PARCHMENT in his hand, is the Virginia Farmer, Thomas Jefferson. The stout-built man with resolute look and flashing eye? That is a Boston man—one John Adams. And the calm-faced man,... that is the Philadelphia Printer, one Benjamin Franklin.

The three advance to the table. The Parchment is laid there. Shall it be signed or not?

Then ensues a high and stormy debate—then the faint-hearted cringe in corners—while Thomas Jefferson speaks out his few bold words, and John Adams pours out his whole soul.

Then the deep-toned voice of Richard Henry Lee is heard, swelling in syllables of thunder-like music.

But still there is doubt—and that pale-faced man, shrinking in one corner, squeaks out something about axes, scaffolds, and a —GIBBET!

"Gibbet!" echoes a fierce, bold voice, that startles men from their seats—and look yonder! A tall slender man rises, dressed—although it is summer time—in a dark robe. Look how his white hand undulates as it is stretched slowly out, how that dark eye burns, while his words ring through the hall. . . .

"Gibbet? They may stretch our necks on all the gibbets in the land—they may turn every rock into a scaffold—every tree into a gallows, every home into a grave, and yet the words on that Parchment can never die!

"They may pour our blood on a thousand scaffolds, and yet from every drop that dyes the axe, or drips on the sawdust of the block, a new martyr to Freedom will spring into birth!

"The British King may blot out the Stars of God from His sky, but he cannot blot out His words written on the Parchment there! The works of God may perish—His Word, never!

"These words will go forth to the world when our bones are dust. To the slave in the mines they will speak—HOPE—to the mechanic in his workshop—FREEDOM—to the coward-kings these words will speak, but not in tones of flattery? No, no! They will speak like the flaming syllables on Belshazzar's wall— THE DAYS OF YOUR PRIDE AND GLORY ARE NUMBERED! THE DAYS OF JUDGMENT AND REVOLUTION DRAW NEAR!

"Yes, that Parchment will speak to the Kings in a language sad and terrible as the trump of the Archangel. You have trampled on mankind long enough. At last the voice of human woe has pierced the ear of God, and called His Judgment down! You have waded on to thrones over seas of blood—you have trampled on to power over the necks of millions—you have turned the poor man's sweat and blood into robes for your delicate forms, into crowns for your anointed brows. Now Kings—now purpled Hangmen of the world—for you come the days of axes and gibbets and scaffolds—for you the wrath of man—for you the lightnings of God!

"Look! How the light of your palaces on fire flashes up into the midnight sky!

"Now Purpled Hangmen of the world—turn and beg for mercy!

"Where will you find it?

"Not from God, for you have blasphemed His laws!

"Not from the People, for you stand baptized in their blood! . . .

"Such is the message of that Declaration to Man, to the Kings of the world! And shall we falter *now?* And shall we start back appalled when our feet press the very threshold of Freedom? Do I see quailing faces around me, when our wives have been butchered—when the hearthstones of our land are red with the blood of little children?

"What are these shrinking hearts and faltering voices here, when the very Dead of our battlefields arise, and call upon us to sign that Parchment, or be accursed forever?

"SIGN! if the next moment the gibbet's rope is round your neck! SIGN! if the next moment this hall rings with the echo of the falling axe! SIGN! By all your hopes in life or death, as husbands—as fathers—as men—sign your names to the Parchment or be accursed forever!

"Sign—and not only for yourselves, but for all ages. For that Parchment will be the Text-book of Freedom—the Bible of the Rights of Man forever!

"Sign—for that declaration will go forth to American hearts forever, and speak to those hearts like the voice of God! And its work will not be done, until throughout this wide Continent not a single inch of ground owns the sway of a British King!

"Nay, do not start and whisper with surprise! It is a truth, your own hearts witness it, God proclaims it. This Continent is the property of a free people, and their property alone. God, I say, proclaims it! Look at this strange history of a band of exiles and outcasts, suddenly transformed into a PEOPLE—look at this wonderful Exodus of the oppressed of the Old World into the New, where they came, weak in arms but mighty in God-like faith—nay, look at this history of your Bunker Hill—your Lexington—where a band of plain farmers mocked and trampled down the panoply of British arms, and then tell me, if you can, that God has not given America to the *free?*

"It is not given to our poor human intellect to climb the skies, to pierce the councils of the Almighty One. But methinks I stand among the awful clouds which veil the brightness of Jehovah's throne. Methinks I see the Recording Angel—pale as an angel is pale, weeping as an angel can weep—come trembling up to that Throne, and speak his dread message—

"Father! the old world is baptized in blood! Father, it is drenched with the blood of millions, butchered in war, in persecution, in slow and grinding oppression! Father—look, with one glance of Thine Eternal eye, look over Europe, Asia, Africa, and behold evermore, that terrible sight, man trodden down beneath the oppressor's feet—nations lost in blood—Murder and Superstition walking hand in hand over the graves of their victims, and not a single voice to whisper, *'Hope to Man!'*

"He stands there, the Angel, his hands trembling with the black record of human guilt. But hark! The voice of Jehovah speaks out from the awful cloud—'Let there be light again. Let there be a New World. Tell my people—the poor—the trodden-down millions, to go out from the Old World. Tell them to go out from wrong, oppression and blood—tell them to go out from this Old World—to build my altar in the New!'

"As God lives, my friends, I believe that to be HIS voice! Yes, were my soul trembling on the wing for Eternity, were this hand freezing in death, were this voice choking with the last struggle, I would still, with the last impulse of that soul, with the last wave of that hand, with the last gasp of that voice, implore you to remember this truth—GOD *has given America to the free!* Yes, as I sank down into the gloomy shadows of the grave, with my last gasp, I would beg you to sign that Parchment, in the name of the GOD, who made the Saviour who redeemed you—in the name of the millions whose very breath is now hushed in intense expectation, as they look up to you for the awful* words—'YOU ARE FREE!'"[29]

All fifty-six delegates were moved to immediately sign the Declaration of Independence, even while knowing the fate of earlier independence movements such as Hungary's bid under Prince Rakoczy. In their case, they knew they could be hung for treason and their properties confiscated by the Crown. As an antidote to their hesitation, the imperative of freedom was transferred to them by the mysterious Old Professor, and each acted as representatives for the future nation, and indirectly for all humanity.

For Saint Germain, the signing of the Declaration of Independence

---

*The 1800s meaning of *awful*: awe inspiring, with reverence and solemnity

was an essential accomplishment. His efforts as Francis Bacon to organize, codify, and expand the Rosicrucian and Freemasonry movements from England to Europe and North America two centuries earlier had come to fruition. Of the fifty-six signers of the Declaration, the great majority were Freemasons committed to a common code of morality, mutual respect, and self-improvement. Each signed in order to preserve the freedom to pursue his own religion and his sovereignty under God, rather than as subjects of a fallible monarch or clergy.

Son of the Republic

America owes an unending debt of gratitude to George Washington for the success of the Revolution and the establishment of the Republic. It is the heroic individual that is often the keystone to great change. The fact that the colonies fielded an army at all from 1776–1783 was due alone to Washington. Always with his soldiers, he was the general in the field. His example buoyed up their morale. He wrestled with Congress to procure food and ammunition, and when Congress became entirely helpless, he kept his men alive out of his own pocketbook.

The clergy proclaimed that he was an instrument of God—"one of thine own sons"—who saved this country. They called him the "great preserver," "so great a deliverer," and compared him to Moses, Joshua, and Gideon. When even Benjamin Franklin could not persuade the French king to give the American revolutionaries further material assistance, Washington prevailed by sending his own aide-de-camp to Versailles—and by prayer. Like no other, Washington put his life, fortune, and sacred honor on the line for the cause.

During the extreme winter conditions at Valley Forge, Washington suffered with his men. They camped in the utter cold, many without boots or cloaks. The winter was a difficult crucible. Washington spent much time in prayer. While alone in his tent, he received a shining celestial visitor. He told a trusted aide, Anthony Sherman, about the event and Sherman kept it secret until 1859. This is the accounting of George Washington's three visions at Valley Forge as heard by

Anthony Sherman, recorded by the reporter Wesley Bradshaw and reprinted in the *National Tribune,* December 1880.

> The last time I ever saw Anthony Sherman was on the fourth of July, 1859, in Independence Square. He was then ninety-nine years old and becoming very feeble. But though so old, his dimming eyes rekindled as he gazed upon Independence Hall, which he came to visit once more.
>
> "Let us go into the hall," he said. "I want to tell you of an incident of Washington's life—one which no one alive knows of except myself; and if you live you will before long see it verified.
>
> "From the opening of the Revolution we experienced all phases of fortune, now good and now ill, one time victorious and another conquered. The darkest period we had, I think, was when Washington after several reverses, retreated to Valley Forge, where he resolved to pass the winter of 1777.
>
> "Ah! I have often seen the tears coursing down our dear commander's care-worn cheeks, as he would be conversing with a confidential officer about the condition of his poor soldiers. You have doubtless heard the story of Washington's going into the thicket to pray. Well, it was not only true, but he used often to pray in secret for aid and comfort from God, the interposition of whose Divine Providence brought us safely through the darkest days of tribulation.
>
> "One day, I remember it well, the chilly winds whistled through the leafless trees, though the sky was cloudless and the sun shone brightly, he remained in his quarters nearly all the afternoon alone. When he came out I noticed that his face was a shade paler than usual, and there seemed to be something on his mind of more than ordinary importance.
>
> "Returning just after dusk, he dispatched an orderly to the quarters of the officer I mention who was presently in attendance. After a preliminary conversation of about half an hour, Washington, gazing upon his companion with that strange look of dignity which he alone could command, said to the latter:
>
> "'I do not know whether it is owing to the anxiety of my mind, or what, but this afternoon as I was sitting at this table engaged in preparing a dispatch, something seemed to disturb me.

Looking up, I beheld standing opposite me a singularly beautiful female. So astonished was I, for I had given strict orders not to be disturbed that it was some moments before I found language to inquire into the cause of her presence.

"'A second, a third, and even a fourth time did I repeat my question, but received no answer from my mysterious visitor except a slight raising of her eyes. By this time, I felt strange sensations spreading through me. I would have risen but the riveted gaze of the being before me rendered volition impossible. I assayed once more to address her, but my tongue had become useless. Even thought itself had become paralyzed. A new influence, mysterious, potent, irresistible, took possession of me. All I could do was to gaze steadily, vacantly at my unknown visitant.

"'Gradually the surrounding atmosphere seemed as though becoming filled with sensations, and luminous. Everything about me seemed to rarify, the mysterious visitor herself becoming more airy and yet more distinct to my sight than before. I now began to feel as one dying, or rather to experience the sensations which I have sometimes imagined accompany dissolution. I did not think, I did not reason, I did not move; all were alike impossible. I was only conscious of gazing fixedly, vacantly at my companion.

"'Presently I heard a voice saying, "Son of the Republic, look and learn," while at the same time my visitor extended her arm eastwardly. I now beheld a heavy white vapor at some distance rising fold upon fold. This gradually dissipated, and I looked upon a strange scene. Before me lay spread out in one vast plain all the countries of the world—Europe, Asia, Africa, and America. I saw rolling and tossing between Europe and America the billows of the Atlantic, and between Asia and America lay the Pacific.

"'"Son of the Republic," said the same mysterious voice as before, "look and learn." At that moment I beheld a dark, shadowy being, like an angel, standing, or rather floating in mid-air, between Europe and America. Dipping water out of the ocean in the hollow of each hand, he sprinkled some upon America with his right hand, while with his left hand he cast some on Europe.

"'Immediately a cloud raised from these countries and joined in mid-ocean. For a while it remained stationary, and then moved slowly westward, until it enveloped America in its murky folds. Sharp flashes of lightning gleamed through it at intervals, and I heard the smothered groans and cries of the American people. A second time the angel dipped water from the ocean, and sprinkled it out as before. The dark cloud was then drawn back to the ocean, in whose heaving billows it sank from view.

"'A third time I heard the mysterious voice saying, "Son of the Republic, look and learn." I cast my eyes upon America and beheld villages and towns and cities springing up one after another until the whole land from the Atlantic to the Pacific was dotted with them. Again, I heard the mysterious voice say, "Son of the Republic, the end of the century cometh, look and learn."

"'At this the dark shadowy angel turned his face southward, and from Africa I saw an ill-omened spectre approach our land. It flitted slowly over every town and city of the latter. The inhabitants presently set themselves in battle array against each other.

"'As I continued looking I saw a bright angel, on whose brow rested a crown of light, on which was traced the word "Union," bearing the American flag, which he placed between the divided nation, and said, *"Remember, ye are brethren."*

"'Instantly, the inhabitants, casting from them their weapons became friends once more, and united around the National Standard.

"'And again I heard the mysterious voice saying, "Son of the Republic, look and learn." At this the dark, shadowy angel placed a trumpet to his mouth, and blew three distinct blasts; and taking water from the ocean, he sprinkled it upon Europe, Asia and Africa.

"'Then my eyes beheld a fearful scene: from each of these countries arose thick, black clouds that were soon joined into one. And throughout this mass there gleamed a dark red light by which I saw hordes of armed men, who, moving with the cloud, marched by land and sailed by sea to America, which country was enveloped in the volume of cloud.

"'And I dimly saw these vast armies devastate the whole

country and burn the villages, towns and cities that I beheld springing up. As my ears listened to the thundering of the cannon, clashing of swords, and the shouts and cries of millions in mortal combat, I heard again the mysterious voice saying, "Son of the Republic, look and learn." When the voice had ceased, the dark shadowy angel placed his trumpet once more to his mouth, and blew a long and fearful blast.

"'Instantly a light as of a thousand suns shone down from above me, and pierced and broke into fragments the dark cloud which enveloped America. At the same moment the angel upon whose head still shone the word "Union," and who bore our national flag in one hand and a sword in the other, descended from the heavens attended by legions of white spirits. These immediately joined the inhabitants of America, who I perceived were well-nigh overcome, but who immediately taking courage again, closed up their broken ranks and renewed the battle.

"'Again, amid the fearful noise of the conflict, I heard the mysterious voice saying, "Son of the Republic, look and learn." As the voice ceased, the shadowy angel for the last time dipped water from the ocean and sprinkled it upon America. Instantly the dark cloud rolled back, together with the armies it had brought, leaving the inhabitants of the land victorious.

"'Then once more I beheld the villages, towns and cities springing up where I had seen them before, while the bright angel, planting the azure standard he had brought in the midst of them, cried with a loud voice: *While the stars remain, and the heavens send down dew upon the earth, so long shall the Union last.*" And taking from his brow the crown on which blazoned the word "Union," he placed it upon the Standard while the people, kneeling down, said, "Amen."

"'The scene instantly began to fade and dissolve, and I at last saw nothing but the rising, curling vapor I at first beheld. This also disappearing, I found myself once more gazing upon the mysterious visitor, who, in the same voice I had heard before, said, "Son of the Republic, what you have seen is thus interpreted:

"'"Three great perils will come upon the Republic. The most fearful is the third... passing which the whole world united shall not prevail against her. *Let every child of the Republic learn to live for his God, his land and Union.*"

"'With these words the vision vanished, and I started from my seat and felt that I had seen a vision wherein had been shown to me the birth, progress, and destiny of the United States.'

"Such, my friends," concluded the venerable narrator, "were the words I heard from Washington's own lips, and America will do well to profit by them."[30]

Washington's beautiful celestial visitor was the Goddess of Liberty, one of the great spiritual hierarchs of the Karmic Board and spiritual mother of Saint Germain. A considerable number of early Americans apparently accepted the presence and divine intervention of heavenly intercessors as a natural part of life. The art and literature of the period frequently depicted angelic beings, gods and goddesses, and clouds of glory. The Goddess of Liberty, patroness of their "sacred cause," was perhaps the most revered of all the heavenly hosts. In 1775 Thomas Paine honored her in a ballad called "Liberty Tree."

> In a chariot of light, from the regions of day,
> The Goddess of Liberty came,
> Ten thousand celestials directed her way,
> And hither conducted the dame.
> A fair budding branch from the gardens above,
> Where millions with millions agree,
> She brought in her hand as a pledge of her love,
> And the plant she named Liberty Tree.

At the low point in the war for independence, during the bitter winter in 1777, Liberty, representing the Divine Mother, prophesied the patriot victory in the Revolutionary War, a future War between the States, and a third conflict of unresolved global karma involving foreign invasion that was to follow at a time and for a duration that was left unspoken.

The angel with the crown and the banner of "Union" carrying the sword and the flag is Micah, the angel of Unity. Micah inspires a fierce loyalty to truth and to union. The famous statement that makes all unite around the national standard is, "Remember, ye are brethren."

The Russian people are our brethren, the Chinese people are our brethren, the people of America, the people of Africa, the people the world over are brethren. The standard of unity is going to be the rallying point for the forces of light to take command of the darkness and intrigue that continually creates war. The ascended masters call to us: Lightbearers of the World Unite!

Prophecy offers enlightened men and women the opportunity to unite and determine that the negatives will not come to pass. If Washington's third vision comes to pass, it will be because humanity has not heeded Saint Germain's call, and because those in office, though they knew his name, did not call for his aid. If there should be war upon American soil, it will be turned back only by divine intervention.

A Nation Is Born

The miraculous victory of the small band of colonists against the British empire shook the world. In order to keep the colonies unified in resolving the cost of the war and building an economy and national identity now entirely independent from England, the Confederation Congress, created by the Articles of Confederation, convened a Constitutional Convention with the intent to revise the Articles. The delegates, however, came to agree that a new system of government was the goal. The result was the creation of the legally groundbreaking United States Constitution and the Bill of Rights that guaranteed the rights of the individual as a part of the very founding of this new country.

These leaders of the young republic were still subject to the cultural, economic, legal, and educational norms of the late 1700s. Slavery was legal in all thirteen colonies and women had no voice of their own in government or the ability to own land or business. Yet God's patience and forbearance, present in every ascended master and angel, reveals his mercy in the outplaying of events.

Those outmoded aspects of the Old World became exposed to political friction, the pressures of personal experience, and the inner voice of conscience, which eventually gained enough consensus to dissolve them. Freedom was a key component built into America's founding documents and governing structure that allowed these old constraints to be voluntarily relinquished by the informed consent of the majority.

In his will, George Washington arranged not only for his slaves' freedom but also for their care and education. The idea was and is to give people the seed of liberty, responsibility, and volition, and over time they will eventually act in accordance with the golden rule.

If in later years, the government of the United States had treated the Native Americans with the same respect that George Washington and others of that time had for them, great sorrow and violence could have been avoided.

Saint Germain's centuries of intercession and his vision for the New Jerusalem, or the New Atlantis as Francis Bacon depicted it, was for those from every race, nation, and religion with the divine spark within them.

During the Constitutional Convention in 1787, Benjamin Franklin was asked about the precedent-setting experiment of the founding of the new United States. Elizabeth Willing Powel said, "Well, Doctor, what have we got, a republic or a monarchy?" Franklin replied, "A republic, if you can keep it."[31]

 ## The Brewing Violence

At the same time that Saint Germain was working with Washington and Congress to establish the United States of America, he was also attempting to found the United States of Europe. France was central to that plan, but by the late 1770s, the prospects for success were fading.

Why would Saint Germain, to all appearances, seem to work to avoid the French Revolution while actively supporting the American one? In both countries, he did everything he could for the cause of freedom and equal opportunity for all. In both instances, he upheld the law, the principles of government, and the establishment of the rights of the people. He sought to create foundations for representative government and reforms that would increase the prosperity and freedom of all classes. This representative government could even work with royalty under the law. It was the choices of those in power that led to revolution.

If King George III and the English Parliament had chosen to uphold the rights of the American colonists and establish their relationship with integrity, greater liberty could have been achieved without a war. It could have resulted in greater freedom and prosperity for the working classes in England as well as the colonies. The king and his parliament chose otherwise, and the American Revolution became the only way to break a relationship of oppression.

In Europe, Saint Germain sought to avoid both oppression and the dangers of revolution through the enlightenment of the French royalty. But the privileged French monarchy, nobility, and clergy made a free-will choice to withhold individual rights, fair practices, and freedom from the public.

The different outcomes of the two revolutions can be understood in the qualities of the individuals who formed the core of both revolutions. The American setting was populated with men who upheld the ideals that Saint Germain had instilled into his secret societies—charity, brotherhood, property rights, the rule of common law, and the sovereign rights of man.

In France, though the oppressed people rallied around the slogans of *Liberté, égalité, fraternité,* the deceitful men who took power unleashed a reign of terror that had no room for charity or mercy. Unlike the American Freemasonic brotherhood, the French Jacobin imitators of brotherhood were corrupted by arrogance, cruelty, competition, and tyranny. Rather than mirroring Freemasonry, the Jacobins became crude and brutal imitators of the monarchy.

One can see in Saint Germain's Independence Hall speech to the signers of the Declaration, he spoke not his opinion or wishes, but a prophecy of returning karma for the foreign monarchs and those who controlled them. The time was soon approaching for Louis XVI when there would be no chance to transmute or mitigate the descent of returning karma, appearing as the wrath of the oppressed and manipulated people.

In 1788, early in the reign of Louis XVI of France, Saint Germain appeared under the name of M. de Saint-Noel at the apartments of Countess d'Adhémar, one of Queen Marie Antoinette's ladies-in-waiting. The master was concerned with the inertia and corruption in Louis XVI's court. There was no awareness of the impending disaster being planned by provocateurs for the decimation of French aristocracy and the ruin of the people. He proposed to save the royal family from great danger by an urgent appeal to the king.

Countess d'Adhémar quickly secured an audience for Saint Germain with the Queen and recorded the event in writing. The master warned the Queen in straightforward terms that it was urgent for him to speak directly to the King. There was no time for formalities. He said to Queen Marie Antoinette,

> Some years will yet pass by in a deceitful calm; then from all parts of the kingdom will spring up men greedy for vengeance, for power, and for money; they will overthrow all in their way. The seditious populace and some great members of the State will lend them support; a spirit of delirium will take possession of the citizens; civil war will burst out with all its horrors; it will bring in its train murder, pillage, exile. Then it will be regretted that I was not listened to; perhaps I shall be asked for again, but the time will be past... the storm will have swept all before it.[32]

The Queen was skeptical but alarmed enough to agree to arrange a meeting with the King.

Saint Germain told the Queen that he wanted to see the King without the knowledge of Monsieur de Maurepas, saying that the king's chief adviser was an enemy. "I rank him among those who will further the ruin of the kingdom, not from malice, but from incapacity."[33]

The master left Paris, heading out of the country, telling Madame d'Adhémar that he knew the King would speak to Maurepas and he had no wish to be thrown into the Bastille and have to resort to a miracle to get out.

Marie Antoinette went straight to the King, who then quizzed Madame d'Adhémar about Comte de Saint-Germain, saying he had "seriously alarmed the Queen."[34] Just as Saint Germain foretold, Louis XVI asked the advice of Maurepas, who told him Saint Germain

Portrait of Louis XVI   Queen Marie Antoinette of France, at the age of 16 years

was a rogue. Maurepas then arrived at the residence of Madame d'Adhémar intending to arrest the Count, but he could not be found. As Maurepas was telling d'Adhémar that he was determined to lock Saint Germain in the Bastille, the door to her apartment opened.

The master entered and approached Maurepas, saying,

> "M. le Comte de Maurepas, the King summoned you to give him good advice, and you think only of maintaining your own authority. In opposing yourself to my seeing the Monarch, you are losing the monarchy, for I have but a limited time to give to France and, this time over, I shall not be seen here again until after three consecutive generations have gone down to the grave. I told the Queen all that I was permitted to tell her; my revelations to the King would have been more complete; it is unfortunate that you should have intervened between His Majesty and me. I shall have nothing to reproach myself with when horrible anarchy devastates all France. As to these calamities, you will not see them, but to have prepared them will be sufficient memorial of you.... Expect no homage from posterity, frivolous and incapable Minister! You will be ranked among those who cause the ruin of empires."

M. de Saint-Germain, having spoken thus without taking a breath, turned towards the door again, shut it, and disappeared.[35]

The confrontation with Maurepas indicates the constraints on Saint Germain's ability to intervene, even in the face of disaster. He may advise but not command, and when ignored, he is obliged to withdraw.

Saint Germain continued to write letters to the Queen, warning of impending violence, but once the crisis had reached a critical point, there was nothing he could do to turn back the pending anarchy that had been building since the death of Louis XIV in 1715.

Over the next few years, the situation, according to Madame d'Adhémar, spiraled out into giddy excess for some of the aristocracy, who flaunted their decadent social lives right up until the end.

Marie Antoinette endeavored to understand the affairs transpiring around her and the King, but to no avail. She had little power in the political machinations that surrounded the royalty, and too late an understanding of Saint Germain's warnings. Madame d'Adhémar documented the Queen's concern and regret. The Queen asked her to procure for her a letter that was being widely circulated through Paris.

> I wished to obey Her Majesty, and at the same time I feared to displease the ruling Minister; however my attachment to the Queen prevailed.
>
> Marie-Antoinette read the article in my presence, and then sighing, "Ah! Madame d'Adhémar," she said, "how painful all these attacks on the authority of the King are to me! We are walking on dangerous ground; I begin to believe that your Comte de St.-Germain was right. We were wrong not to listen to him, but M. de Maurepas imposed a skillful and despotic dictatorship upon us. To what are we coming?"[36]

Throughout her reign as Queen, Saint Germain endeavored to warn and guide Marie Antoinette through letters signed "Unknown." In 1788 Saint Germain sent her prophetic verses that she showed to Madame d'Adhémar, who then recorded them.

> I passed into a small closet, where having asked Madame Campan for pen, ink, and paper, I copied the following passage, obscure then, but which afterwards became only too clear.

"The time is fast approaching when imprudent France,
Surrounded by misfortune she might have spared herself,
Will call to mind such hell as Dante painted.
This day, O Queen! is near, no more can doubt remain,
A hydra vile and cowardly, with his enormous horns
Will carry off the altar, throne, and Themis;
In place of common sense, madness incredible
Will reign, and all be lawful to the wicked.
Yea! Falling shall we see sceptre, censer, scales,
Towers and escutcheons, even the white flag:
Henceforth will all be fraud, murders and violence,
Which we shall find instead of sweet repose.
Great streams of blood are flowing in each town;
Sobs only do I hear, and exiles see!
On all sides civil discord loudly roars,
And uttering cries on all sides virtue flees,
As from the assembly votes of death arise.
Great God! who can reply to murderous judges?
And on what brows august I see the sword descend!
What monsters treated as the peers of heroes!
Oppressors, oppressed, victors, vanquished...
The storm reaches you all in turn, in this common wreck,
What crimes, what evils, what appalling guilt,
Menace the subjects, as the potentates!
And more than one usurper triumphs in command,
More than one heart misled is humbled and repents.
At last, closing the abyss and born from a black tomb
There rises a young lily, more happy, and more fair."

These prophetic verses, written by a pen we already knew, astonished me. I racked my brains to guess their meaning; for how could I believe that it was their simplest meaning that I ought to give them! How imagine, for instance, that it was the King and Queen who would die a violent death, and as the result of iniquitous sentences? We could not, in 1788, have such clear sight; it was an impossibility.

When I returned to the Queen, and no indiscreet person could listen, she said:—

"What do you make of these threatening verses?"

"They are dismaying! But they cannot affect your Majesty. People do say incredible things, follies; if, however, the prophetic words turn out to be true, they will concern our posterity."

"Pray heaven you speak truly, Madame d'Adhémar," replied the Queen; "however, these are strange experiences. Who is this personage who has taken an interest in me for so many years without making himself known, without seeking any reward, and who yet has always told me the truth? He now warns me of the overthrow of everything that exists and, if he gives a gleam of hope, it is so distant that I may not reach it."

I strove to comfort the Queen; above all, I told her, she must make her friends live on good terms with each other, and not let their private quarrels be known outside. Marie-Antoinette answered me in these memorable words:—

"You fancy that I possess credit or power in our Salon. You are mistaken; I had the misfortune to believe that a Queen was permitted to have friends. The consequence is that all try to rule me, or to use me for their own personal advantage. I am the centre of a crowd of intrigues, which I have difficulty in avoiding. Everyone complains of my ingratitude. This is not the *rôle* of a Queen of France. There is a very fine verse which I apply to myself, making a change in the reading: 'Kings are condemned to magnificence.' I should say with more reason: 'Kings are condemned to be weary in utter loneliness.'"

"So I should act, were I to begin my career again."[37]

To deal with the crisis, in 1789 Louis XVI called the first meeting of the Estates-General in more than 150 years. It was far too late. The First Estate (clergy) and the Second Estate (nobility) were separate councils, together representing only about 5 percent of the population. Most deputies for the Third Estate were lawyers or wealthy businessmen. Paying little or no tax, these deputies had long ago turned their backs on the people they were obligated to represent. France's feudal system had long been economically tipping the people toward revolution.

Marquis de Lafayette drafted a Declaration of Rights with the help of Thomas Jefferson, who was the ambassador, and presented it to the Estates. It was a powerful document that gave protection for the first time to the rights of the peasants and took the unquestioned, arbitrary power away from the nobility, putting it instead in the hands of the King's government, which would not be above the law. It unfortunately came too late; the Bastille was stormed three days later. Much like the later provocateurs in the Russian Revolution, those leading the people knew that in order for them to gain control through the anger and desperation of the people, they needed to act before reform could take hold.

Food shortages among Paris's population, where roughly one-third were unemployed, combined with widespread poverty, labor strikes in rural areas, and inefficient transportation of food and produce, meant that the breakdown in law and order became nationwide and sustained.

In 1792 just before the storm truly broke and the King was arrested, Saint Germain met Madame d'Adhémar again early one morning in a chapel at the *Recollets* in the center of Paris.

> The church was empty; I posted my Laroche as sentinel and I entered the chapel named; soon after, and almost before I had collected my thoughts in the presence of God, behold a man approaching.... It was himself in person.... He smiled at me, came forward, took my hand, kissed it gallantly. I was so troubled that I allowed him to do it in spite of the sanctity of the place....
>
> "Madame, he who sows the wind reaps the whirlwind. Jesus said so in the Gospel, perhaps not before me, but at any rate His words remain written, and people could only have profited by mine....
>
> "I have written it to you, *I can do nothing, my hands are tied by a stronger than myself.* There are periods of time when to retreat is impossible, others when He has pronounced and the decree will be executed. *Into this we are entering.*"[38]

He predicted the doom of the King and Queen, stating that it was too late to save them. He reminded her of his prediction years earlier that M. de Maurepas would let everything be lost.

Madame d'Adhémar recorded her conversation in the chapel with Saint Germain:

"In plain words, what do they want?" she asked Saint Germain.

"The complete ruin of the Bourbons; they will expel them from all the thrones they occupy, and in less than a century they will return to the rank of simple private individuals in their different branches."

"And France?"

"Kingdom, Republic, Empire, mixed Governments, tormented, agitated, torn; from clever tyrants she will pass to others who are ambitious without merit. She will be divided, parceled out, cut up; and these are no pleonasms that I use, the coming times will bring about the overthrow of the Empire; pride will sway or abolish distinctions, not from virtue but from vanity, and it is through vanity that they will come back to them. The French, like children playing with handcuffs and slings, will play with titles, honours, ribbons; everything will be a toy to them, even to the shoulder-belt of the National Guard; the greedy will devour the finances. Some fifty millions now form a deficit, in the name of which the Revolution is made. Well! under the dictatorship of the philanthropists, the rhetoricians, the fine talkers, the State debt will exceed several thousand millions!"

"You are a terrible prophet! When shall I see you again?"

"Five times more; do not wish for the sixth."

I confess that a conversation so solemn, so gloomy, so terrifying, inspired me with little wish to continue it. M. de St. Germain oppressed my heart like a night-mare, it is strange how much we change with age, how we look with indifference, even disgust, on those whose presence formerly charmed us. I found myself in this condition under present circumstances; besides, the immediate danger of the Queen preoccupied me. I did not sufficiently urge the Count, perhaps if I had entreated him he would have come to her; there was a pause, and then, resuming the conversation:—

"Do not let me detain you longer," he said; "there is already disturbance in the city. I am like Athalie, *I wished to see and I have seen*. Now I will take up my part again and leave you. I have a journey to take to Sweden; a great crime is brewing there, I am going to try to prevent it. His Majesty Gustavus III interests me, he is worth more than his renown."[39]

As Saint Germain left the chapel he disappeared. Madame d'Adhémar's confidential servant, who had been stationed at the door of the chapel, saw no one pass.

Madame d'Adhémar, stunned by Saint Germain's words, remained in the chapel for some time, deciding not to warn the Queen that day but to wait until the end of the week. By then it was too late. Saint Germain's prophecy came true. The next time she saw the master was at the Place de la Revolution, October 16, 1793, at the beheading of Queen Marie Antoinette.

Madame d'Adhémar's shock was typical among the French court and nobility. They had lived inside the "ancien régime"* with wealth, splendor, and a sense of entitlement from birth. They had no incentives to help them understand the consequences of their inertia. The problems for France were complex and involved structural and financial imbalances that had led to unprecedented state debt, inflation, and excessive taxation of a public that had no voice in their own government.

Both Britain and France had spent heavily on the Anglo-French War in North America from 1776 to 1783. But Britain's Parliament managed the interest on its debt more efficiently because it controlled both taxation and spending. In France, the monarchy did the spending and the fraudulent Estates-General did the taxing, unevenly and inconsistently, through hated private tax collectors. The King and Queen, finally alarmed by the increasing intensity of the Jacobin uprising, attempted to escape France but they were stopped, captured, and returned to Paris. By 1792 they and most of the royal family were imprisoned. King Louis XVI was guillotined on January 21, 1793.

Saint Germain did all in heaven's power to save the people from themselves, to save the good in the monarchy, to bring crucial reforms, and to save the nation from its shadow and karma. And the master is always there for the individual soul. Sorrowfully, Saint Germain could only stand by when Queen Marie Antoinette was beheaded, as he had prophesied, in October 1793. Esoteric teachings say that he then escorted her soul to the etheric retreat of the Master R

---

*ancien régime [French, "old regime"]: "a system or mode no longer prevailing" refers to the political and social system of France that the French Revolution overturned.

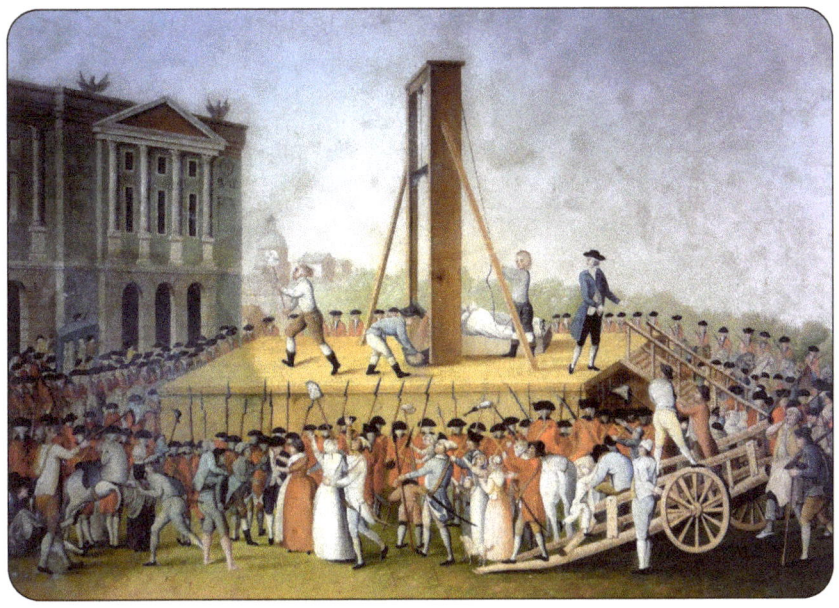

Marie Antoinette's execution in 1793 at the Place de la Révolution, artist unknown

in the Himalayas, where the healing angels tended her. Saint Germain had given his all to bring liberty to France, without bloodshed, but to no avail. The whirlwind engulfed France and then spread throughout Europe.

 ## The Reign of Terror

Saint Germain had attempted to advise Louis XV from 1743 and Louis XVI from 1775 on structural reform. During these decades, the master was aware of the growing momentum of what would become the Jacobins, an anti-monarchist association of more than half a million discontented people in France. Many were attracted to the movement by outwardly well-intended reforms, but they were led by deceptive individuals and financiers in a drive for revenge and power.

The Jacobin "reformers" found the whole of the clergy and the nobility guilty of counterrevolutionary activities, and France fell into brutal vengeance against the decadent elite. In the chaos, the deceivers of the people were lauded for their revolutionary virtue and became the de facto leadership of France. Saint Germain had foreseen it as "madness incredible."

Once in power, the Jacobins divided into two rival factions of violent radicals. Between them they guillotined each other and over seventeen thousand members of all three Estates nationwide, convicted mostly for counterrevolutionary crimes against the state. Tens of thousands more were lynched, drowned, shot, or died in captivity without record during the Reign of Terror. The violence and murders nearly destroyed France. The rest of Europe's nobility heard the news and shuddered.

The radicals' Committee of Public Safety called for conscription and war against most of the monarchies of Europe. Conditions became even worse for the public, and uprisings led to starvation and anarchy in many areas. The contrast with the relatively temperate teething pains of the new American republic could not have been clearer.

The Jacobin momentum of suspicion, accusation, betrayal, and violent zeal inspired the socialist, communist, fascist, and anarchist movements of the nineteenth and twentieth centuries. In the twenty-first century, the corrosive momentum continues through a more sophisticated global financial elite.

The Music of Freedom

As Saint Germain foresaw, people chose the path of violence by their free will. There were, however, students of liberty who chose to anchor the flame of freedom in culture and the arts.

Before mankind could even understand the meaning of a fiat of freedom, before the cycles were ready for the West to accept the mantras of the East or even the mantras of the teachers of the West, Saint Germain fed into the etheric, mental, emotional, and physical planes of the earth the momentum of the freedom flame of the seventh ray of God through the beautiful music of the Strauss waltzes, presaging the Aquarian age.

At the end of the eighteenth century, while France was falling to its own karma, this music of the flame of freedom was released by Saint Germain as the Wonderman of Europe, coming forth from the Rakoczy Mansion, an etheric retreat in the Carpathian Mountains, where the flame of freedom is anchored and blazes upon the altar there. The three-quarter time of the waltz has the rhythm of the heart—the rhythm of the fire within—the threefold flame of power, wisdom, and love.

Seen as revolutionary at the time of its release, the waltz radiates the joy of soul liberation and freedom. However, no greater music of freedom has ever been written than the nine symphonies of Beethoven. The power of the three-times-three was in these symphonies, the action of the Trinity multiplied by the power of three. Beethoven, another initiate of the Master R, lowered into manifestation the music of the flame of freedom.

Like Francis, Beethoven was interested in Eastern spiritual philosophies and held to many of the same moral foundations. His life philosophy can be found in his writings, "To do good wherever we can, to love liberty above all things, and never to deny truth though it be at the throne itself."[40] "The just man must be able also to suffer injustice without deviating in the least from the right course."[41] As these quotes of Beethoven echo Francis's own beliefs, it is not surprising that they share a spiritual teacher.

Beethoven's great work, "Ode to Joy," is the musical rendition of a poem by Schiller. For political reasons, Schiller did not use the word *freedom* in his title as he originally wanted to, but instead substituted it with the word *joy*. Beethoven understood this, so he sent forth the message of freedom of the soul as the "Ode to Joy."

Ludwig van Beethoven

For him the poem was an expression of spiritual freedom. It meant the emancipation of the soul, the freedom of the spirit from all physical and material limitations. It meant freedom to roam at will through the higher spiritual realms and to contact celestial beings who inhabit those realms. It meant for him the freedom to interact with the immortals, and to listen to the glorious music of the spheres. Flowing through Beethoven was the matrix of soul liberation that is played on earth and anchors the music of the spheres.

Even when people, through their own choices, create violence and chaos to gain the wished-for freedom, the Brotherhood continues to work for the good of all humanity, bringing true freedom closer with each heart that listens to their guidance.

A Farewell

In 1790 while Saint Germain visited with two of his fellow Rosicrucian friends in Vienna, he prophesied his final leave-taking from our physical world.

One evening during their discussions, one of the Rosicrucians wrote that Saint Germain grew still and withdrawn. When he came back to himself, he motioned with his hand as if signifying departure and spoke first of his traveling to Constantinople, then to England, and ending with a foretelling of his departure from Europe, saying:

> "I am leaving *(ich scheide)*; do not visit me. Once again will you see me. To-morrow night I am off; I am much needed in Constantinople; then in England, there to prepare two inventions which you will have in the next century—trains and steamboats. These will be needed in Germany. The seasons will gradually change—first the spring, then the summer. It is the gradual cessation of time itself, as the announcement of the end of the cycle. I see it all; astrologers and meteorologists know nothing, believe me; one needs to have studied in the Pyramids as I have studied. Towards the end of this century I shall disappear out of Europe, and betake myself to the region of the Himalayas. I will rest; I must rest. Exactly in eighty-five years will people

again set eyes on me. Farewell, I love you." After these solemnly uttered words, the Count repeated the sign with his hand. The two adepts, overpowered by the force of such unprecedented impressions, left the room in a condition of complete stupefaction. In the same moment there fell a sudden heavy shower, accompanied by a peal of thunder. Instinctively they return to the laboratory for shelter. They open the door. St. Germain is no more there. . . .[42]

Saint Germain's ascended twin flame, Portia, was with him in spirit throughout his decades as the Wonderman of Europe. She, as the Goddess of Justice, also withdrew her presence from the courts of Europe when he did. They went together to the second etheric focus of the Master R, the Cave of Light, in the interior of the Himalayas in India, there to consider what might be done for Europe in the remainder of the eighteenth century.

Portia left the etheric plane of this earth and returned to the Great Silence to hold the spiritual balance for her twin flame, while Saint Germain tried once more to save France from its own errors.

Hope for a United Europe

While the new American republic repaired and built its economy and generated a widely accepted and remarkable Constitution and Bill of Rights, France fell further into chaos. In 1789, due to self-inflicted internal and external threats, France was on the brink of complete destruction. The Jacobin devolution was on its way to creating a failed state with mass starvation, perpetual war in Western Europe, and the eventual breakup of France under foreign powers. Austria, Prussia, and Britain were ready to invade to stop the anti-monarchist Jacobin contagion before it affected them.

During Saint Germain's physical and etheric visits to European aristocracy from 1710 to the 1820s, his overarching goal had been to establish a broad consensus for a United States of Europe. A union of states had been established in America and set precedent that it *could* be done, along with a roadmap as to *how*.

As an ascended master, Saint Germain had physically stepped into the European arena from 1710 onward to extend mercy and offer wisdom. But even though his plan was rejected by every European monarch, and especially the Jacobins, he knew there could still be a way to protect France and spare millions from misery and even more violent conditions.

As the French Revolution reached the point of no return and France was embroiled in war with the major European monarchies, a certain junior artillery officer rose through the ranks.

Napoleon Bonaparte gained battlefield fame and a reputation as a man who spoke for the people. Saint Germain knew that Napoleon had a powerful momentum, both good and bad, as a national and military leader in previous lives. If Bonaparte agreed to serve the divine plan of the people of France, he could gain further attainment and balance the karma of past mistakes.

With a dispensation from cosmic hierarchy, Saint Germain offered Bonaparte an opportunity, at a soul level, for spiritual sponsorship, guidance, military counsel, inspiration for a fair legal code, and advice on political leadership, similar to his dispensation for advice to George Washington.

Napoleon Bonaparte
by Jacques-Louis David

If he could refuse tyranny, and if he could pass the test and not pursue or accept a crown, Bonaparte could bring France out of its deepening chaos and install an Enlightenment-era national legal code to replace France's corrupt feudal laws.

A true republic in France was yet possible. A phoenix could yet rise from the ashes. These changes could become a model for all of monarchical Europe, in which France could lead Europe toward the unity that had been achieved in America.

The master's sponsorship of Bonaparte began well. The Napoleonic Code released in early 1804 restored faith in law and order in France. The nation was pulled back from the brink of disaster. Beethoven wrote a symphony entitled *Bonaparte,* in honor of the revolutionary hero who fought for the rights of the common man and was righting the centuries-old wrongs committed by tyrants against the people.

An Initiation of Power

This time of hope for Europe, however, did not last. On May 18, 1804, Beethoven scratched out the title to his score—his great hero had failed the test of power. Napoleon Bonaparte succumbed to the temptation of misusing the loyal and disciplined army that followed him. He failed in service to his nation; where Washington had succeeded, Bonaparte crowned himself Emperor of France.

Bonaparte set out beyond his mandate from the master to wage wars of conquest in Europe and Egypt. Saint Germain warned Bonaparte away from any interference or invasion of Russia. As the Comte de Saint Germain, he had spent time in Russia and had ongoing plans for its future. Czar Alexander was known to have mystic beliefs and was idealistic about international brotherhood and reforms. He believed in national reform and freed the Russian serfs in 1861. He was in correspondence with President Abraham Lincoln who faced the same tests in America.

Russia had fought against France in the War of the Fourth Coalition, but they had become allies with the Treaties of Tilsit in 1807. However, in 1810, Czar Alexander pulled Russia out of the Continental System of 1806, in which Bonaparte had imposed a blockade against British trade.

Bonaparte continued to ignore Saint Germain's instruction, and in June 1812, he crossed the river Nieman from Poland and invaded Russia with a force of four hundred thousand men and cavalry.

Bonaparte expected an easy three-week victory and looked forward to gaining immense wealth and power from future peace negotiations with the Russian Czar. With that, his opportunity of national service to France under Saint Germain's guidance had ended.

What began in glory in Napoleon's imagination soon shifted. Mikhail Barclay de Tolly led the First Western Army, consisting only of 125,000 men. He knew that if he battled the French before the two other Russian armies reached him, he would be defeated. Though the move to wait was unpopular with the soldiers and the leader of the smaller Second Western Army, who was 160 km away, he ordered all Russian armies to avoid confrontation with the French force.

The smaller Russian imperial army baffled the brilliant military strategist's plans by limiting its exposure to a conclusive battle with the massive French force. The Russian troops burned the crops and took livestock as they retreated deeper into Russia. Though Barclay's retreat was weakening Napoleon's force, it did not sit well with the Russian soldiers and populace. They were not used to giving up ground without a fight.

At Smolensk, the army forced Barclay to stand and fight. They lost twelve thousand men and killed ten thousand of the French before Barclay ordered a retreat. Though the decision saved lives, Barclay lost his position due to nobles who were far from the bloody outcome of battle in Saint Petersburg.

The Russian army was put under the charge of Mikhail Kutuzov, who swore to die before letting the French enter Moscow. The Russian soldiers were elated. A young Russian Lieutenant, Radozhitsky, wrote:

> The moment of joy was indescribable: this commander's name produced a universal rebirth of morale among the soldiers.... The veterans recalled his campaigns in Catherine's time, his many past exploits such as the battle near Krems and the recent destruction of the Turkish army on the Danube: for many men all this was still a fresh memory. They remembered also his miraculous wound from a musket ball which passed through both sides of his temple. It was said that Napoleon himself long since had called Kutuzov the old fox and that Suvorov had said that "Kutuzov... can never be tricked."[43]

According to esoteric teaching, Kutuzov, too, received guidance from the master Saint Germain, who retained ties to the Russian court as well as the European courts and supported the Czar's societal and land-ownership reforms.

After the Battle of Borodino, the deadliest battle in the Napoleonic Wars, in which thirty-two thousand French and forty-five thousand Russians, including twenty-two generals, were killed in a matter of twelve hours, General Kutuzov chose to switch strategies. Moscow became the bait.

Portrait of Mikhail Kutuzov (1745–1813) artist unknown

The Russians continuously retreated in a straight line towards Moscow. General Kutuzov continued Barclay's scorched-earth strategy. They not only took the livestock with them but burned the crops and anything that would be of use to the oncoming French.

Kutuzov's decision saved the rest of the Russian army, and the sacrifice of Moscow won the war. The mayor of Moscow issued a call for the citizens to take their food stores, livestock, and treasures if possible, and evacuate. Kutuzov ordered that all remaining military stores be burned.

Napoleon entered the city expecting a Continental fanfare, the riches of Moscow, and the Czar's surrender. But instead, the time of starvation for Napoleon's troops began while fires spread throughout Moscow.

Napoleon and his army waited in deserted, burned-out Moscow for five weeks, expecting a note of surrender and an offer of peace negotiations from Czar Alexander. They never came. In October, Napoleon realized the onset of a Russian winter would soon overcome him, and made the belated decision to retreat.

Napoleon's retreat from Moscow, 1812
by Adolph Northen

The rested and well-fed Russian army flanked them and forced the French to retreat the way they had come, through burned fields and empty battlegrounds. On November 2, 1812, the bitter Russian snows began. The suffering of the French army was intense. They abandoned their loot as their horses died, their wagons broke down, and Russian cavalry put the snow-bound stragglers and the wounded to the sword. Bonaparte's retreat from Moscow is known as one of the worst military disasters in history.

The unchecked human ego can be a vicious tyrant. Outsmarted and outmaneuvered, Bonaparte abandoned the French Imperial Army on the snow-covered Russian steppes. He returned to Paris with only one aide. The people of France were shocked.

Only 9 percent of his four-hundred-thousand-man army ever returned to France. Beyond the hundreds of thousands of French soldiers who died under Bonaparte's command in Russia, somewhere between three and six million soldiers and civilians died during Bonaparte's unsanctioned wars in Egypt, Spain, Portugal, and across Europe.

Although Bonaparte raised his last imperial army in 1814, his open defiance and misuse of power meant the end of his tyranny in 1815 at the Battle of Waterloo in Belgium.

Although German and Italian territories consolidated into nations and several European governments instituted reforms toward equality, Napoleon failed to create Saint Germain's plan for a united and free Europe. But there was one flourishing example of representative government on the other side of the Atlantic. The United States was founded on divine principles and created a platform for the pursuit of happiness, liberty, and a spiritual path of personal Christhood open to all.

The last time Saint Germain was seen in Europe was in 1822. Just before her passing, he appeared to Countess d'Adhémar, who had survived the French Revolution.

The Force of Anti-Freedom

The new republic in America and the order of Freemasons did not escape the notice of those behind the Jacobin takeover of France and their plans for control. American Freemasons looked on in concern as European members began to fall for the philosophy of the Illuminati —an order of wealthy German intellectuals and lawyers who were expelled from the Kingdom of Bavaria in 1784.

Some of the Freemasons failed to see the vital and fundamental difference between the Illuminati philosophy and the one set forward by Francis Bacon. The latter wanted to change the world for the better through brotherhood and cooperation across national and religious lines. The former sought to control the world by dismantling and ruling over religion, commerce, and governments. Much like those who manipulated the French Revolution, this movement caught traction by masking its motives beneath words proclaiming enlightenment and "the greater good."

The founder of the Illuminati, Adam Weishaupt, was a professor of canon law at Ingolstadt University in Bavaria who became a Mason. At first, the order of the Illuminati was a secret one operating

Johann Adam Weishaupt

illegitimately within the Masonic framework. Because of the Illuminati's infiltration of Freemasonry, those involved had the opportunity to contact the best educated and the most influential people. They moved in on the association of the light-bearers. They couched their philosophy, which they called luminism or illuminism, in the terminology of Christ and religion. This way those who did not know their underlying schemes would be taken in by the "enlightened" wording and not understand the group's true goals.

Key Illuminati individuals had infiltrated Freemasonic groups in France prior to the French Revolution and provided the intellectual inspiration and rhetoric behind the madness of the Jacobins.

Dr. Wolfgang Riedel describes the Illuminati protocol: "Enlightenment takes place here, if it takes place at all, precisely *under* the direction of another, namely under that of the 'Superiors' [of the Order.]"[44] The expulsion of the Illuminati from Bavaria was assumed to be an effective rebuke and the end of the Order. But it simply went underground, becoming more secretive.

George Washington sent two letters, one on September 25 and one on October 24, 1798, to G. W. Snyder about the book *Proofs of a Conspiracy* by John Robison that Snyder had sent him. Though Washington did not think the American Freemasonic chapters were propagating the Illuminati tenets, he agreed that the movement was incredibly dangerous.

> Mount Vernon, September 25, 1798:
> I have heard much of the nefarious, and dangerous plan, and doctrines of the Illuminati, but never saw the Book until you were pleased to send it to me.[45]

Mount Vernon, October 24, 1798:
The idea that I meant to convey, was, that I did not believe that the Lodges of Free Masons in this Country had, as Societies, endeavoured to propagate the diabolical tenets of the first, or pernicious principles of the latter (if they are susceptible of separation). That Individuals of them may have done it, or that the founder, or instrument employed to found, the Democratic Societies in the United States, may have had these objects; and actually had a separation of the People from their Government in view, is too evident to be questioned.[46]

The Democratic Societies that Washington referred to were the Democratic-Republican societies that sprang up in the 1790s and which later influenced the party system that Washington had warned against. Four years earlier Washington had sent men to Pennsylvania to stop an insurrection started by these "self-created societies" who, he said, "assumed the tone of condemnation."[47]

These societies professed their support for the leaders of the French Revolution. Their public goals were to inform the populace and disseminate political information to support the equal rights of man. Through the battling between these societies and the Federalists, foreign powers and Jacobin philosophy entered the American political arena, both sides using founding members against one another.

On the one hand, there were the Federalists with Alexander Hamilton, unknowingly influenced by the international financiers who wanted to own the new representative government through a central bank. On the other hand, there were the Democratic-Republican Societies with Jefferson and Madison, unknowingly influenced by the Jacobian philosophies and those intent on destroying the new representative government. The early American government and her people were played between these forces that were controlled by the same interests.

In his farewell address to the people of the United States, Washington warned of the danger of societies such as these:

They serve to organize faction, to give it an artificial and extraordinary force—to put in the place of the delegated will of the nation the will of a party; often a small but artful and enterprising minority of the community; and, according to the alternate triumphs of different parties, to make the public administration the mirror of the ill concerted and incongruous projects of faction, rather than the organ of consistent and wholesome plans digested by common councils and modified by mutual interests. However combinations or associations of the above description may now and then answer popular ends, they are likely, in the course of time and things, to become potent engines by which cunning, ambitious, and unprincipled men will be enabled to subvert the power of the people and to usurp for themselves the reins of government, destroying afterwards the very engines which have lifted them to unjust dominion.[48]

The Illuminati principles and methods revolve around the battle for men's minds. They recognize that to control a man's mind is the best way to control him. They gain control over members' minds through a process of initiations proclaiming to free them from their prejudices. The promise of illumination is placed before the initiate who would free himself from prejudice. Lord Buddha spoke of the concept of illumination, which means illumined action. It is a sign of the development of the crown chakra. They have stolen the very words of the avatars so that when people hear them, they respond with trust and excitement.

So in every nation today the orders of the Illuminati cull the greatest minds. They take the best students from the best universities, from Harvard, Yale, Princeton. They draw them into their circle. They tell them that they are the ones that really have what it takes to rule the world. They send them to prestigious schools, such as the London School of Economics; they may get a Rhodes Scholarship or a Fulbright Scholarship. They are then educated according to the order's way of thinking.

The outer ring of novices support humanism and one-world government. Though accepted into the order, they are only told a few things—general humanitarian goals. The individuals in the outer rings are watched by the inner circle to see whether they are the ruthless ones, the dark seed. The ones who prove to have at their core an allegiance to the sinister forces are promoted to the inner circles. If, however, they are really souls of light, they are kept tied to this mandala in the outer rings. They never even know that there are inner rings. Each successive ring thinks that it is the highest. It has no awareness of who it is giving allegiance to beyond.

Like all those who do not have the light of the heart, Weishaupt had no creative force of his own, he could only subvert others' concepts. His order was a twisted version of what Francis had created. Whereas Francis used mystery to help humanity learn how to discover for themselves the secrets God has laid for us to find, Weishaupt used it to manipulate and control humanity. Francis believed that through seeking wisdom and acting with charity, one can grow to know God. In Weishaupt's writings he continually based one's level of morality on what "mental heights" they could achieve. For him, unimpeded mental activity was not the means to the end but rather the end itself. In his book *Diogenes' Lamp,* Weishaupt wrote:

> The question may arise: why would a person desire to become powerful or rich? You might even ask why someone would seek virtue and perfection. But is there no answer to the question of why people would want to be happy and enjoy existence? This goal is thus certainly the highest and final objective of humankind. Whoever achieves it is therefore perfect, because they have become what they are capable of becoming. It is actually impossible to be anything more, for whoever has unimpeded activity of the mind has everything....
>
> There are urges that, though they lead to pleasure, distinguish themselves by a sort of nobility and greatness. There are other urges the unimpeded and unlimited satisfaction of which brings people disgrace, dishonor, and disaster. Therefore, that which makes ambition and the thirst for power nobler than avarice, what elevates even greed itself above the tendency to gluttony, must also be considered the reason why ambition and the thirst for power are not the highest and noblest of all the

impulses. For why are they better than avarice or gluttony? Surely it is because they require a greater usage of reason, because they are the product of a more complete mental development. Reason and mental development thus determine the value; and any system in which the mind can develop the most will appear truer and more worthy of humanity than systems in which the mind develops less.[49]

It is possible to unravel the real origins of the Illuminati's secret society and philosophy, beyond its founding in Bavaria. The problem with the Illuminati title is that the word has been used throughout history by several societies, both good and evil. Illuminati means simply those who are illumined or luminous. The order of atheistic and power-hungry intellectuals that sought to control, and are still controlling, the destination of nations have called themselves Illuminati. However, certain secret orders of the Brotherhood of Light in history have also been called the Illuminati.

There has been an order of the darkest of the dark, the Luciferians, the laggards, all throughout history, organized in secret societies. In Babylon and in the Fertile Crescent at Byblos, there were terrible satanic practices of which there are records—sacrifices of virgins in the temples, terrible sexual abuses and practices. The Illuminati philosophy originally came out of those satanic practices.

There has been, however, simultaneously the order of the lightest of the light, the disciples of the ascended masters and of Christ, the Christian mystery schools, the Essene community, the Buddhist monks, and the high, high initiates in the secret temples.

Unfortunately, some people stumble onto incomplete research or are shown a small section of history; they then see all mystery schools as satanic. They mingle the two; they do not have discrimination. They look up the historical records and find glimpses of Saint Germain, glimpses of the Illuminati, and to them it is just one big hodgepodge. They decide that everything came from the same thing and thereby they are completely cut off from the real Saint Germain and the Brotherhood of the true light.

Both the divine right of kings and the divine rights of man are

God-given when anchored in the Christ consciousness. But when the sinister force infiltrates and takes over royal houses, causing corruption and tyranny, it becomes a tool of anti-freedom. When the divine rights of man are used as a defense for the rebellion of the human intellect and the human mind, it becomes Luciferianism. So, the pendulum swings between two extremes, all the while manipulated to strip people of their free will and place it in the hands of the few.

The Illuminati destroy economies and local governments while preaching democracy. They let "democracy" run its course for a couple hundred years. They sufficiently botch it up, attack it, tear it down, have selfish, corrupt people in government until the time comes when the people say, "Destroy the establishment. Rewrite the Constitution. It is too much red tape. We can't make our government work."

Then who has the right to rule? The people are manipulated into believing that their saviors—those who will save the planet through their wise governing—are the most educated people in the land. Thus, the people agree to have a rule of an intellectual elite.

How are people manipulated into this?

Through problems of ecology, they are taught to believe that the only way the earth will be a fit place to live is if a group of ecologists working with people in government form a one-world government. This way they can control the ecology of every nation on earth simultaneously. It becomes a dictatorship of the intellectual elite.

All forms of manipulated government and economy are instruments to get the people to be dissatisfied with the rule. War is another manipulation of the Illuminati to get us closer and closer to the time of a one-world government. They want humanity to scream for a one-world government because there is no other way to keep peace on earth. They launder the people's money through manufactured wars, with increasing violence and destruction until the people trade what is left of their liberty for peace.

If they could get the Middle East into a world conflagration with all the powers, the people would demand peace, and at the end of that war everybody, like sheep, would flock to a one-world government.

That is the whole goal of the Illuminati. And these Illuminati have been working for thousands of years.

This force of anti-freedom's reach for power and control can be seen throughout the United States' history. President Andrew Jackson and Congress defeated their lobbying for a central bank in 1820. The next generation of Wall Street bankers were known to President Abraham Lincoln during the Civil War as a more coercive and dangerous enemy than the Confederacy.

Their successors persisted in their ability to control and manipulate both political parties, making a huge breakthrough early in the twentieth century. In 1913 at a midnight congressional session with the minimum quorum on Christmas Eve, these successors of the Illuminati got their private monopoly on the money supply, deceptively calling it the Federal Reserve System instead of a central bank.

The Constitution was inspired by Saint Germain to keep the money supply accountable, in the hands of the peoples' representatives. But a bare quorum gave it away, and Congress has not yet rescinded the Federal Reserve Act. The national debt, owed by the people to the central bank network, is now so large that it can never be repaid. Unless the act is rescinded by the peoples' representatives, it will continue to be tolerated as a perpetual bondage. When too few are alert, when too few act to keep freedom alive for all, when too few pray for divine intercession, by cosmic law the master can only look on.

Karma, Destiny and Free Will

Saint Germain was aware of the long arc of the karmic history of our planet. Without a United States of Europe in place and a widely accepted Constitution designed to check and balance the stakeholders' competing interests, new Bonapartes would inevitably appear. The world was vulnerable to thousands of years of returning negative karma. It was a predictable repetition of previous cycles of history when tyrants would control the institutions of Germany, Spain, Italy, Russia, China, America, and many other nations.

Could Saint Germain, as an ascended master, not have seen the near impossibility of establishing a United States of Europe, founded on the rights of the individual? Why then did he try? Why did he place his trust, his flame, his mantle on Napoleon Bonaparte? Why did he bother going to the courts of Europe, patiently trying to convince individuals too superficial to understand his advice? Could he not have seen what would be the outcome and avoided failure by never sponsoring unpredictable or unprepared individuals?

Were it so, and had Saint Germain calculated his decisions based on the accurate computer of the mind of God, he would have stayed home for several centuries. But in so doing, he would have been the supreme denier of the free will of the individual to change the course of his destiny, to defy his stars, to rise up and to seize opportunity! He would have denied the freedom of God to go before certain fallen ones—and some of them were indeed fallen ones and some were children of the light playing their parts in adverse conditions. He would have denied the Almighty the opportunity to present himself in the person of the Comte de Saint Germain, as an ascended master with the full enlightenment and means of delivering humanity from the misuses of capitalism and World Communism and the violent collapse of the royal houses of Europe.

Should he have denied the free will of these individuals to change themselves when sacred alchemy is his gift to humanity? Should he have denied the Almighty One, whose freedom flame he represents, the opportunity once more to woo these souls in devotion to the divine cause? It is as Tennyson wrote,

> 'Tis better to have loved and lost
> Than never to have loved at all.[50]

Saint Germain is a master of love for all humanity. Imagine each one who has been touched by the master in each lifetime. Imagine all who met him as the Wonderman of Europe—and as the mystic Old Professor in the American colonies. Each soul has been lifted by contact with the heart of Saint Germain, who saw fresh opportunity for redemption instead of mere risk. Each person can change himself and his nation's history for the better because of that sacred heart contact.

Saint Germain, though he himself has met with disappointment for the density of those who choose the way of selfishness and ignorance, urges his keepers of the flame to stand and still stand. He enfires them not to be cynical, not to become hopeless. Those who seek to control have been the same gray, uninteresting compromisers with their infamous building of the hordes of darkness for thousands and thousands of years. In this age, their time is up and their day is done.

Just as Saint Germain stood with the American colonists at the signing of the Declaration of Independence and with George Washington as he led the American Revolution, so he stood with Simón Bolívar as he fought to liberate Venezuela, Colombia, Ecuador, Peru, and Bolivia. So he moved with José de San Martín as he fought to establish the independence of Chile, Peru, and Argentina. He was at the scene of their battles to liberate South America from Spanish rule, just as he was with the American colonists as they fought for their independence from the British.

Saint Germain comes to mankind not with a wrinkled brow of gloom, but rather as the practical man of action that he has always been. Those who serve the Great White Brotherhood and move among the nations have always had to deal with the knowns and with the possible. The fate and future of their plans is always dependent upon those in embodiment who have responded to be their helpers in action.

A New Cycle for Humanity

As Saint Germain had promised eighty-five years earlier, he returned to directly assist humanity in 1875. Saint Germain and other ascended masters could see the karmic vulnerabilities of the nations of Europe, and that they were facing what would become the bloodiest century in history. Germany's rapid invasion of France in 1870, stopping just short of Paris, was a prelude to the world wars that would follow. Saint Germain and the great mahatmas did not leave humanity to suffer without seeking to lift the veil of karmic blindness and bring illumination to their hearts.

The common understanding built off of Roman Christianity was

Himalayan mountain range

that Jesus had taken all believers' sins (their personal karma) on himself *for all time*. This vicarious atonement provided no answer as to why personal tragedies or global wars occurred.

Saint Germain had spent much of the 1800s in the etheric focus of the Himalayas with other ascended masters preparing to provide answers, to enlighten mankind, and to work closely with students of the original inner mysteries of the world's major religions. When the master became available again near the end of the nineteenth century, his new mission was not with governments but with people who were ready to learn. He is here to contact the hearts of fire.

In 1875 a new spiritual venture was founded—the Theosophical Society. The master Saint Germain was one of the spiritual sponsors for this new endeavor designed to change the spiritual and cultural paradigm for humanity. To counter the prevailing materialism of Western culture and to help millions of spiritual seekers, the Great White Brotherhood of unascended and ascended masters decided to release a new spiritual dispensation. The time had come to reveal secret and sacred teachings in order to help accelerate the soul evolution of mankind. These teachings revealed the deeper aspects of spiritual science leading to the awareness of the macrocosm, the microcosm, and even the existence of quantum energy.

The new spiritual awareness would have to come from a holy source outside of any established religious or philosophical organization, East or West. The new society would explain a hidden ancient wisdom that went further and deeper than even the secret Rosicrucian teachings.

The Masters of Wisdom

In 1877 an unusual book electrified the world. The Russian countess Helena Petrovna Blavatsky wrote *Isis Unveiled* with the support of American Civil War hero Colonel Henry S. Olcott. Blavatsky announced the existence of the unascended Brothers of the Himalayas and their ascended teachers to the outer world for the first time. These mahatmas had achieved the goal of human spiritual evolution and were offering to help mankind preempt or mitigate another series of man-made crises through shared wisdom on a global scale.

Helena Blavatsky was the masters' amanuensis, trained with the Brothers in Tibet and India to reveal, expound, and explain the secrets of soul evolution, karma and reincarnation, and the cosmic cycles of history on our planet. In her second book, *The Secret Doctrine,* she also unveiled the existence of the Divine Ego and eternal Monad that overshadow our spiritual evolution. These concepts were so new and profound to the majority of people in the West that their release brought about a spiritual revolution in the minds of many readers.

Blavatsky and Olcott in 1888. Theosophical Society.

The publishers, and Blavatsky herself, were stunned when the book sold millions of copies. The masters had sponsored this new dispensation, but not even the author knew what to expect. The release of the teachings caused a renaissance of learning in chemistry, physics, philosophy, literature, music, and religion. Helena, or HPB as she was called, was the "face" of this new revelation. She took no credit as author or teacher, but said she was simply a messenger and servant to the great ones on behalf of a needy humanity. She taught as she herself had been taught.

Two unascended masters El Morya (the Master M) and Kuthumi (the Master KH), with the support of their student Djwal Kul (the Master DK), stepped forward to see who among humanity would respond with interest to these teachings on cosmic law. These masters had deep inner connections to mystic Christianity and the inner teachings of Jesus. They were previously embodied as the three wise men: Balthazar, Caspar, and Melchior—the mysterious Magi, travelers from the East, who followed the sign of the star to find the infant Jesus after his birth. They had also lived as saints within Christianity, Buddhism, and Islam during the centuries that followed.

Portraits of Master Koot Hoomi and Master Morya
by Hermann Schmiechen

Saint Germain worked with the unascended adepts in the Himalayas, and the release of their teachings began a change in awareness of Western thought. The masters Morya and Kuthumi opened a window on these esoteric doctrines, long kept secret in the West. Theosophy dismantled the sacrosanct dogmas of orthodox Christianity, revealing their origins in ancient mystery religions and in the one universal wisdom-religion from which all major spiritual beliefs had descended. They also brought awareness of the Brotherhood itself, creating a revolution in spirituality.

As Ruth Drayer described it,

> The research of the Theosophical Society demonstrated the character, presence, and diffusion of this universal religion in every land. Blavatsky disseminated these teachings through her books *Isis Unveiled* and *The Secret Doctrine*. The books, crammed with the most comprehensive overview of esoteric wisdom ever to appear in print, exposed Westerners to the Eastern beliefs of reincarnation, karma, and the Hierarchy of Masters of Wisdom and Compassion, who lovingly guide the development of humankind on earth.[51]

The most unusual aspect of the Theosophical Society in its time was the insistence on a "Universal Fraternity and Brotherhood of Humanity." In the late 1800s, a brotherhood of humanity was a difficult pill for many to swallow. Yet, this revolutionary concept was one of the three foundational principles of Theosophy. The society "was open to people of all religions and its teachings encouraged investigation into the infinite...."[52] Though it went against the pervading feelings of the aristocracy, this openness and respect for all spiritual seekers attracted millions of readers and members throughout the world. The Theosophical Society's universal fraternity was for the global public—a natural extension of Francis Bacon's spiritual fraternities.

Blavatsky and other Theosophists were well aware of the great work of the Comte de Saint Germain, and knew him as a great initiate and adept, an agent of the Brotherhood in their present work.

Theosophical writer C. W. Leadbeater, previously a minister for the Church of England, described an encounter with "Master, the Comte de St. Germain":

> I met him under quite ordinary circumstances (without any previous appointment, and as though by chance) walking down the Corso in Rome, dressed just as any Italian gentleman might be. He took me up into the gardens on the Pincian Hill, and we sat for more than an hour talking about the [Theosophical] Society and its work; or perhaps I should rather say that He spoke and I listened, although when He asked questions I answered.[53]

An interesting connection between Saint Germain's work as the Wonderman of Europe and Helena Blavatsky is that the only copy that Isabel Cooper-Oakley could find of *Souvenirs de Marie-Antoinette* by the Comtèsse d'Adhémar, from which comes so much of what is known of the Comte de Saint Germain in France, was in "Odessa in the library of Madame Fadéef, the aunt and friend of Madame H. P. Blavatsky."[54] HPB stayed in the Château d'Adhémar in 1884 while visiting the family.

Isabel Cooper-Oakley was able to meet the Comtèsse d'Adhémar of her day who informed her that there are documents concerning the Comte de Saint Germain in their family papers.

In Theosophy, Kuthumi and Morya revealed that the soul is a ray, or emanation, of the Divine Monad/Divine Self and has evolved through vast cycles of development and evolution from higher dimensions down into the physical in order to acquire self-consciousness and mastery in the planes of matter. The soul follows the example of the Word and earns by degrees of wisdom an incremental return to the Divine, to eventually achieve God consciousness. This was and is the divine plan of the Logos for all humanity.

Darwin's evolutionary theory, which concerned itself with the physical evolution of man from lower life forms, was supplanted in Theosophy with a process of evolution that originated in spiritual realms—the soul descending into matter and ascending back to Spirit. Theosophy challenged Darwinian evolutionary theory, which was limited in scope to only what was physical.

The teachings given to Blavatsky by Kuthumi and Morya were based on ancient manuscripts and oral teachings from the adepts. The time had come to release certain teachings long kept hidden, solely for the enlightenment and upliftment of mankind. Some of these teachings included the seven principles or seven "bodies" of man, the highest of which is the Divine Self or Atman; the seven "rounds" or cycles of planetary incarnation comprising the lifetime of a planet, lasting over four billion years; the evolutionary journey of the monad (soul) through seven root races, and the out-breath (manvantara) and in-breath (pralaya) of the cosmos.

In a letter to A. P. Sinnett, master Morya wrote, "Europe is a large place but the world is bigger yet. The sun of Theosophy must shine for all, not for a part. There is more of this movement than you have yet had an inkling of, and the work of the T.S. [Theosophical Society] is linked in with similar work that is secretly going on in all parts of the world."[55]

The secret mission of Saint Germain was part and parcel of the mission of the Theosophical movement under the auspices of the same Brotherhood.

In another letter to Sinnett, master Kuthumi stated the purpose of the Theosophical Society:

> A genuine, practical Brotherhood of Humanity where all will become co-workers of nature, will work for the good of mankind. ... Plato was right: *ideas* rule the world; and, as men's minds will receive *new* ideas, laying aside the old and effete, the world will advance: mighty revolutions will spring from them; creeds and even powers will crumble before their onward march, crushed by the irresistible force. It will be just as impossible to resist their influx, when the time comes, as to stay the progress of the tide. But all this will come gradually on. ... The *Chiefs* want a "Brotherhood of Humanity," a real Universal Fraternity started; an institution which would make itself known throughout the world and arrest the attention of the highest minds.[56]

There could be no more apt description of the mission of Saint Germain, which began over a century earlier. The revolution that

Kuthumi speaks of is part of Francis's Great Instauration, the "Coming Revolution in Higher Consciousness."

Theosophy became a worldwide movement that had a profound and lasting effect on Western thinking. It was a tremendous and surprising challenge for many tied to an institutionalized Christianity. Mainstream Christian organizations attacked Blavatsky and never absorbed the great illumination dispensed by Theosophy. Yet, thousands and then millions of truth seekers were uplifted by the vast knowledge, unifying vision, and compelling story of the path of initiation that the masters taught. Many began to seek a personal connection with the masters and to walk the path of spiritual initiation—the path of personal development leading to integration with the Divine.

As the twentieth century began, World War I shattered Europe. Foreseeing the Second World War to come, the masters sought new ways to contact their students. Building on all that had gone before and teaching the ancient wisdom along with new revelations, they continued to build a universal brotherhood and brought new spiritual gifts, known as dispensations, to counter the oncoming wave of darkness.

Two of these new spiritual pathways were inaugurated during the early years of the twentieth century. Saint Germain's promise to return to help humanity was again coming to pass and entering the next spiral of evolution. One was born in the East and the second in the West. Each brought a beautiful new facet of divine truth and beauty. Each came from the Brotherhood of Light.

The Path of the Fiery Heart

Early twentieth century Russia was a country of immense change. Many of the upper class and intellectuals, especially the students in Moscow and St. Petersburg, rose to the call of universal truth, of government reformation, the mystical truths of Buddhism and Hinduism, and to the path of the saints and the mystics of the Orthodox Church, such as Saint Sergius.

Experimentation with new forms of art, music, dance, and philosophy were in vogue. "Dramatic changes were unfolding in Russia over the course of the reign of the last Russian Czar, Nicholas II; crises and wars, on the one hand, were accompanied by a period of economic growth and a flourishing of culture."[57]

Two young Russians, Nicholas and Helena Roerich, embodied this flowering of a new culture. Nicholas was a passionate archaeologist, scientist, historian, and above all an artist of rare vision, with a new take on the beauty of nature.

Helena was intelligent, beautiful, cultured, and wise. She was a linguist, spiritually sensitive, and an excellent pianist. Like Blavatsky before her, "Elena had read the entire collection of books in her grandfather's library and had progressed to studying the philosophies and traditions of the East, such as the Hindu Bhagavad Gita, the Mahabharata, and the three Vedas, the oldest existing works of literature."[58] At the age of six, she first met the "tall figure, dressed in white" and came to know him as a "Teacher of Light." Her family was distinguished and aristocratic. The composer Mussorgsky was her uncle, and the important historic figure and student of Saint Germain General Mikhail Kutuzov—who had commanded the victorious Russian forces opposing Napoleon in the War of 1812 and had been portrayed by Tolstoy in *War and Peace*—was her great-uncle.[59]

The inner tie to the ascended masters and Brothers of Light lay deep in the hearts and souls of Helena and Nicholas Roerich.

They were married in the fall of 1901 and began their life together in St. Petersburg. Two sons were born to them, and their family was happy. Their home was a haven for spiritual philosophy, and in addition to Theosophy they studied the teachings of Buddha, Vivekananda, the poet Rabindranath Tagore and the Vedas. They were uplifted and captivated by the ideas of universal brotherhood, enlightenment, beauty, and peace. These ideals were alive within them, and they became leading lights in the part of Russia that flourished during that time. Nicholas became the director for the Imperial Society for the Encouragement of the Arts and led sixty-three teachers and two thousand students.

At the same time as innovation in the arts and spiritual discovery flowered, the First World War and economic upheaval were causing great turmoil. Nicholas began to worry for his family and his country as Bolshevik revolutionary unrest swept the city. He was also weakened by illness. Doctors warned Nicholas that city life was harmful for his weak lungs and that he needed to breathe the clear air of the countryside to heal. Helena, the visionary, saw great hardship and chaos coming to the land they loved.

Sensing disaster for Russia, the Roerichs went against their relatives' strong disapproval and fled St. Petersburg

Nicholas Roerich painting at Isvara, 1897

late on December 17, 1916. They left their treasures of European art and archaeology behind. And wrapped in blankets against the extreme cold of the Russian winter night, they braved the unheated midnight train traveling across the border to Finland.

The coming Bolshevik revolution became an unexpected horror for most Russians and the rest of the world, yet the Roerichs foresaw its approach. Through the chaos of 1917, Nicholas was still able to travel from Finland to St. Petersburg whenever he was needed at the Academy. When the borders of Russia were suddenly sealed in May 1918, Nicholas and Helena and their sons were safe but exiled in Finland. By November 1918, the moderate reformers and their government fell, and the violent Bolsheviks took full power over the former Russian empire.

Mourning for their country and holding the inner flame for brotherhood, the Roerichs used their time in Finland to meditate and make the inner connection to the light and the masters. They were

Helena Roerich, passport photo, 1919

contacted directly by the master Morya. Their inner guidance directed them to England in 1919, then America, and finally the mountains of India. After exploring the Himalayas and parts of inner Asia, the Roerichs traveled back across Europe and America. Nicholas Roerich became a world-renowned artist, archaeologist, author, scholar, lecturer, costume and set designer, poet, mystic, and explorer. Whatever Roerich's pursuit, whether painting, writing or scientific studies, it always took on the quality of a quest.

Helena became an amanuensis for El Morya and other selected masters of the Great White Brotherhood, proclaiming the great mission of the Mother of the World for the coming Aquarian age. In the 1920s, Helena began releasing the teachings of the Great White Brotherhood through the Agni Yoga books. Agni Yoga is the synthesis of the previous yogas: karma, raja, jnana and bhakti. It comprises the essence of the whole of life. Agni Yoga means the way or path of fire. Morya describes it as "the perception and application in life of the all-embracing element of fire, which nourishes the seed of the spirit."[60] It is the path of self-sacrifice because to merge with the Real Self, one must identify and sacrifice the layers of the synthetic self that have been built, molded, and accepted as one's personality over many lifetimes.

Agni Yoga teaches the path of cooperation with the spiritual evolution of all life, the divine plan of the out-breath and in-breath of the cosmos over many trillions of years. In 1920 the Roerichs formed the first group devoted to the study and practice of Agni Yoga.[61]

Nicholas Roerich's art was just as much a part of their spiritual work for humanity as the books were. American poet Mary Siegrist wrote of his paintings, saying:

Song of Shambhala by Nicholas Roerich

Roerich's pictures are painted in flame. He follows no school or tradition, having in a sense absorbed and assimilated all cultures and gone on in paths of his own and in ways that his own genius directs.... The iridescence, the radiance of his canvases, is rather the product of spiritual awareness than of outward method. No man, woman or child can stand before these paintings without getting back "sounds of the infinite sea." To each one who listens with the inner ear, sees with the inner eye, they bring back some tidal wave of beauty.[62]

Critic Ivan Narodny writes of Roerich's work:

Somewhat similar to the early fresco painters, Roerich prefers the ecclesiastic blues and greens, the traditional colors of the transcendental distances of the sky and pure nature, in which one recalls the blues of the old Venetian masters, which they used for the garments of their madonnas and saints.

In the tradition of the ecclesiastic painters, blue is the tone of eternity, and the Byzantine Church Fathers explained it as a yearning for heavenly joys. Look at the blues of most of Roerich's works, and the greens of his mystic nature display, and you will find them similar to the lapis lazuli and the malachite—the stones that were used for the interiors of the temples and the altars of the holy shrines. His yellows are typical of the yellows of the lamaseries of the East. In fact all his colors are kept in the sombre major mode of the sky—vibrations of the celestial plane, which lead us into a world beyond—the hyper-nature of a higher dimension.[63]

Both Nicholas and Helena Roerich had an intense interest in Eastern philosophy and religion. In their travels through India and Tibet, they visited Buddhist monasteries, including one, Himis, at Ladakh, where monks showed them ancient documentary evidence of Jesus' travels to India in the years before his mission in Palestine.

Roerich wrote of his discovery of the legends of Jesus' journey to the East:

> Leh is a remarkable site. Here the legends connected the paths of Buddha and Christ. Buddha went through Leh northwards. Issa [Jesus] communed here with the people on his way from Tibet. Secretly and cautiously the legends are guarded. It is difficult to sound them because lamas, above all people, know how to keep silent. Only by means of a common language—and not merely that of tongue but also of inner understanding—can one approach their significant mysteries....
>
> Thus the legends of Asia weave such an image of Jesus, so ennobled and near to all nations. And Asia preserves in its mountains such legends. And it is not astonishing that the teachings of Jesus and Buddha are leading all nations into one family. But beautiful it is, that the light-giving idea of unity is expressed so clearly.[64]

The universal spiritual concepts of the sacred flame and soul perfection through service to humanity had special significance to the Roerichs. Nicholas once wrote:

> In the cults of Zoroaster there is represented the chalice with a flame. The same flaming chalice is engraved upon the ancient Hebrew silver shekels of the time of Solomon and of an even remoter antiquity. In the Hindu excavations of the periods from Chandragupta Maurya, we observe the same powerfully stylized image. Sergius of Radonega, laboring over the enlightenment of Russia, administered from the flaming chalice. Upon Tibetan images, the Bodhisattvas are holding the chalice blossoming with tongues of flame. One may also remember the Druid

chalice of life. Aflame, too, was the Holy Grail. Not in imagination; verily by deeds are being interwoven the great teachings of all ages, the language of pure fire!

It has long since been said, "Faith without deeds is dead." Buddha pronounced three paths: the long way of knowledge, the shorter way of faith, and the shortest way—through action. David and Solomon also glorify the strivings of labor. The Vedanta extols the manifestation of works. Verily, in the foundation of all covenants, action is placed foremost. This is the creative fire of the Spirit.[65]

Through many different paths, initiates find the same truths of God and what it means to *be* divine love in action, as the Roerichs and Francis Bacon were. In the opening letter of volume I of *The Letters of Helena Roerich,* her first two paragraphs hold echoes of Francis's Great Instauration. One can see the unbroken thread of the Brotherhood's help across diverse religions and cultures. In the previous lives of the masters and in all their work as ascended beings, they never cease to strive for humanity's spiritual evolution. Helena wrote:

From far-off India, the country of beauty, of achievements of the spirit, and of great thought, I send to you who are gathered in the name of the great labor and structure of the future—greetings of the heart! I call you to self-perfection and unlimited attainment.

The book of new discoveries and the light of daring is open before humanity, and you have already heard about the approach of the New Era. Every epoch has its Call, and the calling foundation of the New Era will be the power of thought. That is why we call you to understand the great significance of creative thought, and the first step in this direction will be the opening of consciousness, freedom from all prejudices and from all tendentiousness and forced concepts.[66]

The Roerich family permanently settled in the Kulu Valley in India in 1928 and founded the Urusvati* Himalayan Research Institute to study archaeology, linguistics, and botany. In several of her letters,

---

*Urusvati—"This is the name We have given to the star that is approaching the Earth with irresistible force. For long ages it has been a symbol of the Mother of the World, and the Epoch of the Mother of the World must begin when Her star has made an unprecedented approach to the Earth." El Morya, *Leaves of Morya's Garden II,* verse 138, p. 60.

Helena references the great master, the Comte de Saint Germain, and his mission in France:

> The publishing of the diary of the Countess d'Ademar, a lady-in-waiting to the unfortunate Marie Antoinette, revealed the fact that many warnings had been given to the Queen. The warnings were transmitted either by letter or through personal meetings arranged by this same countess. The message always emphasized that the country, the royal family and many friends were in danger. And every one of these warnings came from Count Saint-Germain, an envoy of the Himalayan Brotherhood. But all his salutary admonitions and advices were considered insulting and fraudulent. Saint-Germain was persecuted, and more than once was in danger of the Bastille. The tragic consequences of these rejections are quite well known.[67]

In *Agni Yoga,* Morya speaks of Saint Germain: "This age-old tradition of forewarning humanity, with each recurring century, is effected in full benevolence; in this lies its basic nature. Otherwise the role of the envoy would not be sincere and persuasive. St. Germain spoke to L. with good intent."[68]

El Morya recounts an interaction that exemplifies the consciousness of the nobles and Saint Germain's sense of humor balanced with his full awareness of world need.

> Once a French nobleman said to St. Germain, "I cannot even begin to understand the nonsense that surrounds you!"
>
> St. Germain answered, "It is not difficult to understand my nonsense if you will give it the same attention you give to your own, if you will read my reports with the same attention you give to the list of dancers at the court. But the problem is that the order of a minuet is of greater importance to you than the safety of the planet."
>
> In these words is contained the tragedy of our times. We find time without limit for all kinds of petty activities, but we do not find an hour for the most vital.[69]

El Morya spoke as well about the Russian General Kutuzov from the Turkish and Napoleonic Wars.

The "Green Laurel" about whom you have often spoken could combine leadership with sensitivity to the Counsels of the Brotherhood. He accepted the directions of Saint Germain with full confidence. In this lay his success. Perhaps Saint Germain came especially to prepare this future leader.

All over the world one can find established landmarks of Our Guidance. Some enlightened people accepted it, but some poor parodies of monarchs rejected Our Counsel and thereby plunged their countries into calamity. But even these situations We turned to good. You are acquainted with *Tactica Adversa*.[70]

Saint Germain and Francis Bacon's use of numerous pen names, as well as simple anonymity, is a method often used by the Great White Brotherhood. El Morya comments:

Compare the teachings of Pythagoras, the letters of Prester John, the activities of St. Germain, and the letters of the Mahatmas. You will find in all of them a concern for the purifying of humanity.

It matters not in which languages they were given or how they were adapted to each era. The fundamental ideas underlying all of them can be traced. Sometimes the writings were considered to be forgeries, but is it not obvious that the same thoughts lived throughout the ages? Many of the writings were attributed to particular individuals, but far more of them were anonymous. One can see how all of them found their following in various countries. This vast literature should be studied; it has never been fully collected, and the inner meanings of the many writings have not been adequately compared....

We do not see Our names as being of great importance. These names change often in Our long lives. We value the labor itself, and do not pay attention to whether the author's name can be found on the top or the bottom shelf.[71]

In one of her letters, Helena Roerich encourages the reader to understand how the Brotherhood of Light is often maligned by those writing history. Good people are persecuted and beneficial groups, such as Freemasonry, are co-opted. Her letter could have been written today about the same divide and conquer techniques used against sincere truth seekers. Helena Roerich writes in a letter dated 10 December 1936:

> And so, put aside the books on occultism, and do not burden yourself by criticizing them. In order to be able to criticize soundly, one has to know much. You write that certain people, or even some organizations, consider the book of the author you mentioned to be a Masonic work, moreover, "Jewish-Masonic." There is nothing new in this; it is the same old favorite formula of dull-witted and malicious ignorance. In the Middle Ages, all that brought Light was labeled with the seal of Satan, and now this stamp has only changed its name, that is all. Similar accusations, as well as the titles of "charlatan" and "spy" were, and still are bestowed upon many of the best minds and great workers for the General Good. Great is the assembly of the bearers of knowledge who have perished at the hands of ignorance! At one time, these honorable titles were bestowed upon the great Paracelsus and Comte Saint-Germain, and also on our compatriot, H. P. Blavatsky. Nowadays there are people who have labeled as "betrayers of their motherland" such great patriots as Subvorov, Golenishchev-Kutusov, Prince of Smolensk, Novikov, Lopukin, Prince Repnin, Karamzin, Prince Kurakin, Speranski, Pushkin, Griboyedov, and others, only because these people joined the highly cultural and progressive movement known at that time as Masonry. Take these minds from Russian culture, and what will be left? Let us not forget that even now a certain section of Russian society particularly traduces Tolstoy. Thus, in Harbin, it was forbidden to celebrate the centenary of his birth! Judge for yourself—can we, without deep shame before educated foreigners, face such a manifestation of medievalism? Not that I want to defend Masonry, since now, this movement has degenerated for the most part into mere trappings, clubs, etc. But it is only fair to admit that the original founders of Masonry in both the West and East were people of great intellect and high morality, and above all they were truly great patriots.[72]

Helena also mentions Comte de Saint Germain's time in Russia in her letter of 17 December 1936: "There is no doubt that Saint-Germain played a role in Russian history also. In international literature one comes across brief references to the prophecies he made while he was in the capital of Russia. The time has not yet come for making these public, but times change, and at the destined date we shall hear about these prophecies."[73]

It is clear that there is still much to discover concerning the benevolent intercession of Saint Germain and his great work to help humanity.

In the teachings of Agni Yoga, the masters gave deep personal instruction to their students in glyphs—in coded poetic thought—leading the students to make their own inner contact with the masters. The Agni Yoga books have an unworldly etheric vibration like the beauty of Roerich's paintings. The Roerichs published the word of the masters with the intention to reach both the Russian and American people at the same time with the energy and the enlightenment necessary to deter world tyranny. These works offer guidance as to how to accelerate our ability to live with a fiery heart, build harmonious communities and create true brotherhood. This is the culture of Light.

Nicholas Roerich with Sacred Casket (1928) by Svetoslav Roerich

The Magic Presence

Saint Germain directly inaugurated a parallel spiritual breakthrough in the West for the approaching Aquarian age in America. As a new cosmic cycle dawned, Saint Germain personally contacted humanity, intending to teach the wisdom and culture of Light to millions who were ready to listen. The ancient Occult Law of the Brotherhood, which for thousands of years had demanded secrecy to protect the integrity of spiritual science from being misused by the profane, had ended. This occult law had been put in place by necessity after the fall of Atlantis.

The teachings no longer needed to be in "code" or hidden in complexity; they could be published in simplicity and clarity. Saint Germain was determined to now reveal the most important secrets of life everlasting: the keys to accelerate our ability to transmute our karma, and the revelation of each one's own eternal divine identity, the I AM Presence, individualized. This was the open and simplified way to explain Jesus' allegorical teaching that each man would live under his own vine and fig tree.

Saint Germain's direct contact with his American students began at Mount Shasta in California in the 1920s. A mining surveyor named Guy Ballard was exploring the snowcapped mountain, trying to unravel the mysterious legends of the Great White Brotherhood that he had heard about. There he met an unusual stranger. The "mysterious young man" revealed himself to Guy Ballard as the master Saint Germain.

The master began by offering the surprised Ballard a golden elixir, with the teaching that God's intent for all his children is an abundance of every good and perfect thing.

"He created Perfection and endowed His children with exactly the same power. *They can create and maintain Perfection* also."[74] The master taught Ballard that the "personal self" of every individual must come to acknowledge the Great God Self within.

"The Eternal Law of Life is: 'What you think and feel you bring into form; where your thought is there you are, for you are your consciousness; and what you meditate upon, you become.'"[75]

This eternal truth is familiar to all who study the Buddha and the *Dhammapada*. Saint Germain gave his students the name of this Great God Self, the I AM THAT I AM who spoke to Moses, as the Magic Presence in each person.

In these simple yet profound teachings, Saint Germain brought the secret mystic teachings of the ancients into the everyday language of 1920s America. Through Guy Ballard, Saint Germain taught the secrets of spiritual alchemy again, as a lawful, personal re-creation of the human self into the true Divine Self. He reignited the ideals of the early phases of Francis's Great Instauration as universal enlightenment, available to all spiritual students in modern times, regardless of their religion or lack of religion.

The soul of Guy Ballard had been a student of Saint Germain for many lifetimes. In his previous lifetime, he was embodied as George Washington, first president of the United States, the indispensable leader and general who had worked alongside the "Old Professor" and received a celestial visitation at Valley Forge.

Guy Ballard

George Washington

Unveiled Mysteries

Saint Germain brought the ancient truths of the Brotherhood, as represented in the Hindu, Buddhist, and Theosophical concepts of the Atman and the Divine Monad, to the West and made these key teachings fresh and relevant to the students of today. The knowledge of and contact with the individual I AM Presence is the most amazing concept and gift of the ascended masters in this age. Each one of you has an I AM Presence that at this very moment is a permanent atom of being pulsating interconnecting spheres of energy—seven rings denoting seven vibrations, seven planes of consciousness, seven spheres of heaven. When in your heart you personify the flame and you adore the flame, the flame becomes the magnet which is the same magnet that is in the heart of your Presence. So the two become one, and you become the living awareness of God.

When God said, "Let there be light," and there *was* light, he implemented the expansion of the light by giving birth to individual spirit sparks. These drops of his cosmic identity were scattered throughout the universes as billions of seeds of light, each one with a unique destiny, yet each one an exact replica of the original Unity that was and is God. Separated in the time-space configuration, yet forever one with the Central Sun, or Centrosome of the Eternal, these sparks of the Divine Image were created that each soul might express an aspect of God. Although his Electronic Presence is multiplied billions of times for the purpose of his individualization in form, God is still one—one individed Whole. Just as one times one times one will always equal one, so God times God times God still equals God. This is the I AM Presence, the individuated God Presence of each one.

Saint Germain's teachings freed everyone to contact their own Magic Presence and begin an accelerated spiritual path of integration with the divine identity. He taught Guy Ballard the "Law of Life" and led him through amazing experiences inside the etheric as well as the physical retreats described in the classic spiritual books, *The I AM Discourses*, *The Magic Presence*, and *Unveiled Mysteries*.

In the foreword to *Unveiled Mysteries* (1939), Guy Ballard, under the pen name Godfré Ray King, wrote: "The purpose of putting this book into the hands of the public is to convey to the individual the encouragement and strength that will lift and sustain him through the transition period we are now in; and reveal something of the sane and sound Foundation upon which the future of Our Country and the coming age is, this hour, being built."[76]

This "sound foundation" was due to the visionary work of Saint Germain over centuries, and that which was being built was the all-encompassing Great Instauration, the universal enlightenment of humanity. Guy Ballard continues: "Its pages are a record of the way by which I was brought in touch with the Beloved Master, Saint Germain, and those other Great Ascended Masters who labor ceaselessly to assist the humanity of this earth, as it struggles on the path to Peace, Love, Light, and Everlasting Perfection."[77]

Succinctly stated—the path of the Great Instauration. Ballard further explained: "I was led step by step to realize and to accept the Mighty God 'Presence' within my own Being—the 'Light that lighteth every man that cometh into the world'—the 'Christ.' A way to make contact with the 'Light,' Its All-Knowing Omnipresence, and Unerring Activity was revealed to me, and I give it to the reader in these pages."[78]

The key to physical and spiritual attainment over outer conditions is the conscious use of the words "I AM." The sound of these syllables when spoken aloud transcends all languages and can be thought of as meaning, "God in me is..." In *The "I AM" Discourses,* Saint Germain explained:

> Life, in all Its Activities everywhere manifest, is *God in Action.*...
>
> The natural tendency of Life is Love, peace, beauty, harmony, and opulence, for Life cares not who uses It, but is constantly surging to pour more of Its Perfection into manifestation, always with that lifting process, which is ever inherent within Itself.
>
> "I AM" is the Activity of "That Life."...
>
> When you say, and feel "I AM," you release the spring of Eternal, Everlasting Life, to flow on Its way unmolested. In other words, you open wide the door to Its natural flow.

When you say, "I AM not," you shut the door in the face of this Mighty Energy.

"I AM" is the Full Activity of God.[79]

Saint Germain envisioned millions using the I AM name for positive transformation of themselves and the world. The teaching of the personal I AM Presence and how to access its divine power through attention and invocation is essential to the Great Instauration of humanity.

It was at this time that Saint Germain asked for a new spiritual dispensation regarding the ascension. Considering the intense manipulation of the souls of light on earth, the great spiritual beings who oversee earth's evolution determined to allow people to make the personal ascension with only 51 percent of their karma balanced. Souls could now ascend and work on the remaining balance of energy by serving life everywhere. This new spiritual law helped so many souls who otherwise would reach a high level of karmic balance and then fall back due to the severe impact of the "sinister force" and all the negative energies directed against them. Now many more people are able to reach the star of their personal ascension without incurring new negative karma under provocation and persecution. The bells of spiritual freedom began to ring in our time for people of light.

The Violet Transmuting Flame

The miraculous, personal spiritual alchemy of Saint Germain was also revealed at this time. Combined with the awareness of the I AM THAT I AM and the gift of requiring only 51 percent of karma balanced for the ascension, a third powerful dispensation was the revelation and scientific use of a powerful spiritual energy—the violet transmuting flame. Saint Germain created the opportunity for any soul to have access to this higher dimension of light that had been a closely held secret of the adepts and the mystery schools throughout history.

In the 1930s Saint Germain petitioned the cosmic councils for a solution to the oncoming wave of karma that mankind would face at the end of the Piscean age. These great masters granted the release of the ancient knowledge and ability to transmute energy with the violet flame through the sponsorship of Saint Germain.

As students of alchemy may know, transmutation means to change something common or base into a higher form. In the case of personal karma—the daily, God-given energy tied up in thoughts, feelings, speech, and actions that do not vibrate at the level of the heart and divine Reality—the records remain trapped within the lower emotional and unconscious realm within each person.

By cosmic law, this energy not aligned with divine Reality returns in kind to the sender, sometimes immediately and sometimes in a subsequent lifetime, centuries after the event. This law is how the schoolroom of earth helps to teach its students. "For whatsoever a man soweth, that shall he also reap."[80] Jesus taught us this long ago.

This was the collective weight of humanity's karma that Jesus as Saviour helped carry and set aside for every soul on earth, from the time of birth until the ending of the Piscean age. If the untransmuted karma of past ages had returned to each soul unmitigated, the consequences would have been dire. As with his effort to preempt the violence of the French Revolution, Saint Germain always seeks higher and more merciful ways for justice to be done. He and Portia gave the world the opportunity to transmute this trapped energy on a global scale.

Our Holy Brother offers us the ability to take personal responsibility for our own karma by invoking and visualizing the violet flame. This living, pulsating flame brings transmutation to levels upon levels of consciousness. The divine intelligence of the Holy Spirit discerns which unkind event in soul memory we are ready to surrender next. Our role as a soul seeking union with God is to invoke the violet flame at least once every twenty-four hours.

Saint Germain comes to tell us that we have the power to change the future and to make the Aquarian age a golden age. His cosmic purpose is to give everyone access to this transmutation aspect of the Holy Spirit. This dispensation could never have been granted for chelas to invoke this flame outside the retreats of the Great White Brotherhood had it not been for the fact that Saint Germain offered upon the altar of humanity the collateral of his own personal momentum and the energies of freedom garnered within his soul for thousands of years. For you see, when the Lords of Karma granted the dispensation through the intercession of this anointed one, they were fully aware that, given free will and given mankind's propensity to misuse that free will, it was altogether possible that certain numbers among mankind would misuse these sacred energies as they had done in the past in the days of ancient Lemuria and Atlantis. Were this to occur, someone would have to make up the difference.

Saint Germain understood this principle of cosmic law only too well. For the sake of the few and eventually the many who would make resplendent use of the violet flame, he was willing to forgo and to sacrifice that portion of his momentum that would be misused and to chalk up that misuse as a necessary expenditure in the laboratory of mankind's consciousness. He was thereby, in effect, underwriting the experiments not only of the alchemists of the sacred fire with whom he had personally worked through the centuries but also of the populace who would both use and misuse the alchemical fires ere coming into the enlightenment of the Christ mind and a centeredness in the Christ flame, which is necessary for the responsible use of the violet flame.

The violet flame is a physical flame. Of all of the rays, the violet flame is closest in vibratory action to the chemical elements and compounds of earth. And therefore, the violet flame can combine with any atom or molecule, any particle of matter, electron or light wave.

The application of the violet flame results in a specific action of a quality of the Christ in your body, soul, mind, and heart. When, as an act of your free will, you lovingly make the call to the violet flame and you surrender these unwanted, untoward conditions into the flame, the fire instantaneously begins the work of breaking down particles of substance that are part of the mass accumulation of hundreds and even thousands of incarnations.

The Power of the I AM

Saint Germain's revelations of a path toward karmic freedom ignited the hearts of many thousands of students of spirituality in the 1920s. The I AM Activity swelled to a membership of almost a million people, mostly in the United States, by 1938. Many were drawn by the revelation of the Magic Presence through Godfré's book *The Magic Presence,* the personal friendship of the masters, and the power of the karma-transmuting violet flame.

The I AM Presence was instantly accessible by prayer, invocation, and fiat. The mystical name I AM THAT I AM conveys the ancient hermetic idea of equivalent connected identity, as Above, so below. I AM THAT I AM can be written horizontally, indicating the brotherhood of God in humanity across the earth, or vertically, indicating that the same God who exists above in heaven simultaneously exists below on earth—in you.

The twin flames, Guy and Edna Ballard, acting as Saint Germain's carefully trained messengers, imparted the sacred mysteries of the Law and grace of the I AM, the knowledge of cosmic hierarchy, the invocation of the sacred fire, and the path to the ascension. Tested in multiple previous lives as representatives of Saint Germain, the Ballards were commissioned to remain the only messengers of the hierarchy of the Aquarian age until humanity should redeem a certain portion of their karma.

When Guy Ballard, the indispensable leader, was called to his ascension in 1939, the I AM Activity was capably led by Edna Ballard through the movement's most difficult years. Like her husband, the soul of Edna Ballard had served with Saint Germain for many lifetimes. The master revealed that in his life as Francis, she had been embodied as his mother, Queen Elizabeth I. Then, born as Benjamin Franklin, she had the opportunity to be Saint Germain's student and help him fulfill a vital step in his Great Instauration—the founding of the republic of the United States of America. One can see how the soul can recover from mistakes in previous lives through service to the light. Edna ascended at the close of her life and became the ascended lady master Lotus.

Queen Elizabeth I

Edna Ballard

Years ago while I was still searching for Saint Germain, I had the pleasure of meeting Mrs. Ballard. Having read the "I AM" books, I sought her out when I was traveling in Chicago. I was invited to lunch with her and her board of directors. She talked to me about many things—about Godfré, the movement, the youth, the world, and Saint Germain. I was thoroughly endued with the light and the presence of this wonderful person whose books I had read. She was overflowing with love and beauty to my heart and soul, and there was nothing but the great glory and beauty of love coming forth from her to me.

In the years since that time, I have heard the worst of the worst stories and gossip regarding Mrs. Ballard. It is shown to me as it was shown in the life of Thomas More, or Francis Bacon, that the persecution, gossip, and condemnation of the best of people that is carried on, repeated, and grows as it is repeated, ought never to weigh upon our hearts, but the contact with the light is what counts.

This is not to say that I could not acknowledge that she or I or anyone else representing the masters could have made mistakes, or that there may not have been times when, if I had seen her, I might have seen some aspect of the human side of things, because we all have it until we depart this world.

It was not in the sense that I had met a god, but I had met a woman who had dedicated her life to Saint Germain and made enormous sacrifices and given greatly of herself. The most important thing of all was not that I should judge that life, but that I was a witness to the light with which she was endowed—the Presence and the light of God that was in her and upon her. That Presence can be with us all in greater and greater measure daily, not because we are perfect human beings, but because God chooses to endow us with his light and with his mantle.

When World War II broke out, thousands of I AM students filled large auditoriums each night across the United States with vigils for the victory of freedom. The Soldier Field stadium in Chicago was at times filled with students led by Edna Ballard, invoking the Divine Presence and the violet flame for victory and peace. Because of the I AM movement and the students of the I AM, the war was not fought on American soil.

However, the forces of anti-freedom used both cooperative and unaware individuals to retaliate against Saint Germain's vehicle for humanity's freedom. The movement was sued by the United States Justice Department on an alleged violation of postal laws, alleging that they were mailing material fraudulently through the US mails. The I AM Activity had stated that Jesus and Saint Germain had appeared before the painter, whose portraits they mailed, and he had painted the likeness of the ascended masters, not just his idea of them. The Justice Department alleged that this was a fraudulent use of the mails, as they could not legally prove that the ascended masters were real.

The whole thing lasted close to a decade. It went to the Supreme Court three times, and they were convicted. Ultimately the case was reversed by the Supreme Court on the third appeal on the basis that women were being systematically excluded from the jury. That was the only thing they were finally released on. The case very seriously hampered the I AM Activity in its work. They were forced to defend themselves for years in fighting it.

Another factor behind the decline of the I AM Activity was the deep immersion in materialism that came with the post-war increase in manipulative advertising and the relentless focus on hedonism in popular mass media. It was funded by the same unsecured credit that had financed the world wars.

Saint Germain, together with the Darjeeling Council of the Great White Brotherhood, remained determined to continue to offer the teachings, even if it required a new platform for the public to find.

Keeping the Flame

The universe is governed by spiritual cycles. In 1956 Saint Germain was appointed to the office of Avatar and Hierarch of the Aquarian Age and received the spiritual authority from cosmic councils to inspire and direct the consciousness of humanity for the next two thousand years. Jesus held this same office during the previous two thousand years of the Piscean age. The authority to direct the consciousness of humanity by their free will was a continuation on a greater divine scale of what the master had initiated as Francis Bacon. His brilliant life as Francis Bacon, and all his previous lives, served as an extended training for this spiritual office. Jesus' previous lives had followed the same pattern of an ascending intensity in spiritual testing.

Consider the courage, vision, selflessness, and brotherliness of masters such as Jesus and Saint Germain who forgo the infinite paradise of the heavenly octaves and choose the difficult task of teaching wisdom to us. Much of humanity today is at best unaware and indifferent to their karmic condition, or to the definite timeline of their divine plan as co-creators with God. Many are hostile toward even the concept of a holy brotherhood who care about us as family and ask us to care about humanity.

There is a story in Buddhist scriptures of three men who are on a difficult journey through harsh terrain when they approach an impassable high wall. They sense there is something fantastic happening on the other side of the wall, so one of the men boosts another one up to see what is going on. When the man looks beyond the wall, he goes into bliss. He pauses, in speechless ecstasy. He climbs over the wall and, without saying anything, disappears from sight. The two other men left are dumbfounded. What is over the wall? So, the next man gets a boost from his friend. He looks amazed, and he too climbs over in bliss. Now the third man thinks, "Well, I'm going to find out what is going on, on the other side of this wall." He finds a way to climb up. When he looks over he sees the unexpected—the souls of beings who are liberated from any need to ever come back to his harsh side of the wall. They have been accepted into heaven. But he forgoes his liberation. He does not climb over the wall. He comes back, into that difficult terrain, to tell mankind what *is* on the other side of the wall.

The Great White Brotherhood is the company of ascended masters who have said: "We are not going on in the cosmos beyond and leaving our brothers and sisters behind. We will stay; we will tarry and explain the Way."

At the end of each two thousand years, there is an impetus of light whereby the door of the next level of wisdom-teaching opens, and cosmic law is presented for the next dispensation. The Galilean embodiment of Jesus was the last time that there was such an intense impetus of teaching about grace and love. Before that, at the beginning of the Mosaic dispensation, there were new revelations of the Law, the Ten Commandments, and the name of God revealed as I AM THAT I AM.

The Aquarian age is a time of cosmic abundance, a time when we can reap a harvest of spiritual fruit, win our victory, and climb over that wall after helping the rest of mankind over it too.

The masters named the plan for this cycle the Coming Revolution in Higher Consciousness—the time when the universal enlightenment prophesied and initiated by Francis Bacon would replace the density of materialism. It was the time for wonders of new spiritual teaching and a great awakening to arise. This is the path of Francis Bacon. It is the path of the Goddess of Truth, the Ancient Goddess of Wisdom, Pallas Athena, for she is the one who inaugurated the Coming Revolution in Higher Consciousness. She is in the front of the battle and stands with all those who love freedom and truth.

To fulfill this plan, the master El Morya, on behalf of Saint Germain, contacted an unascended initiate of the Brotherhood Mark L. Prophet in 1958 and asked him to found The Summit Lighthouse in Washington, D.C. As an initiate, Mark had been trained by Morya in this and prior lifetimes.

El Morya explained that "first and foremost, the greater cause of The Summit Lighthouse is the cause of divine love—love meeting the needs of people at every level, love that is understanding, love that, above all, is forgiveness."

My own introduction to Mark Prophet took place in 1961, when I was a student at Boston University, after I had been searching for contact with the master Saint Germain for a period of about five years. My calls to Saint Germain grew more and more fervent, and finally the compelling calls produced the answer of Mark Prophet journeying to Boston from Washington, holding a meeting and giving the first dictation that I ever heard, which was by Michael the Archangel.

At that time, I was very close to Saint Germain and had sensed this mission to which I had dedicated this life. As I was walking in a park in Boston, the master El Morya appeared to me and he said, "Go to Washington to be trained as a messenger. I have need of a feminine messenger." So I went and began my training in Washington in August 1961, three years after The Summit Lighthouse had begun.

Mark Prophet became the instrument of my training under El Morya and Saint Germain. The purpose of the training was to release the sacred scriptures for the Aquarian age—the two-thousand-year dispensation of the writing of the law of the flame of freedom, which had already been begun through the messengers Godfré Ray King and Lotus Ray King (Guy and Edna Ballard).

What Saint Germain went through with creating the I AM Activity, the dispensations necessary, the calling-together of a body of devotees, and what happened and transpired in their response to the flame of freedom, is a saga of souls—souls of freedom who have written an immortal page in the history of the planet.

In every age the Brotherhood has had those who are called the witnesses—those who write down the Law, who give the warning, and who give the prophecy to the people who are chosen. Those who are chosen are those who choose to listen and to identify with the flame of that which is real. God has never left mankind without messengers, without prophets. They have gone unrecognized, unheeded, and civilizations and karma have taken their course. But they have always been present—some known and some unknown.

I was ordained by the master Saint Germain to represent him and to complete the mission of beloved Godfré Ray King. I recall coming into incarnation in the year of his ascension, standing before the Lords of Karma and agreeing to continue the work of releasing the knowledge of the I AM Presence, the Real Self, and the violet flame.

Saint Germain and all ascended masters function at the plane of our I AM Presence. When we are one with the I AM Presence, we are one with the ascended masters. The messenger stands at the level of the Christ Self, or the Real Self, of mankind. The messenger is the one who assists the soul to make contact with the Christ Self so that the Christ Self can release to the soul and to the outer consciousness the teachings of the I AM Presence and the ascended masters. Hence the messenger stands representing the Christ Self until there is no longer any need for the messenger; and all mankind behold the I AM Presence and the ascended masters face-to-face.

So the dispensation of prophets and messengers is an intermediary dispensation. It is for that period when mankind cannot hear the voice of God. When they do, each man, each woman, sits under his own vine and fig tree. The vine is the crystal cord; the fig tree is your causal body—your own tree of life. And you, in meditation under your own vine and fig tree, commune with the Spirit of the Great White Brotherhood.

The Summit Lighthouse became the active platform of intensive spiritual teachings, the ascended masters making direct contact with their students through their two messengers. These teachings of the ascended masters are for each soul of light on earth, for the fulfillment of their individual divine plan. Some have made their personal ascension with the transfer of the engrafted Word through just one book. Others continue to walk their individual path to freedom, far ahead of where they would have been if no one who had felt the bliss of heaven had come back for them.

Shortly after the founding of The Summit Lighthouse, Saint Germain envisioned a fraternity, reminiscent of the group of "good pens," the loyal friends around Francis Bacon, continuing the ideal of the spiritual brotherhood of man taught in Theosophy.

In January 1961, Morya authorized the formation of the Keepers of the Flame Fraternity to be comprised of a devoted group of students who would make a commitment to Saint Germain. Morya did this in accordance with cosmic law, for Saint Germain had petitioned the Lords of Karma many times to offer the momentum of his causal body and to give of his energies for humanity's benefit, only for these to be abused and betrayed by certain individuals or ignored by mankind.

After the decline of membership in the I AM Activity, the Lords of Karma concluded that the betrayal of Saint Germain had been so continuous over many lifetimes that they determined to have a moratorium on dispensations that could be given to him. These cosmic masters chose to protect the divine energy investment of Saint Germain for a time. Understanding this, the eternal friends of Saint Germain came forward to support his great cause. El Morya and other masters of the Brotherhood offered their momentum to sponsor the new platform because Saint Germain effectively had his "wings clipped." For his own good, the Lords of Karma had stated, "Wait and see how mankind will respond to the dispensations that you have given through Godfré and Lotus."

So, the Keepers of the Flame Fraternity was authorized by El Morya and the Darjeeling Council, who took karmic responsibility for the conduct of the fraternity. Saint Germain became the head of the fraternity by the grace of other ascended masters who pledged their own attainment on his behalf.

In a letter dictated by Saint Germain to his students at the inauguration of the fraternity, he wrote:

Beloved Friends of Freedom,
 The requirements of the hour are constancy, harmony, and loyalty. For centuries men have tasted of the treasures of heaven; and for an equal time, they have debated, delayed, and strained at the proper use of those same treasures. The heaven that might

have manifested long ago upon earth has been delayed solely by man, and through no fault of the Father, whose kingdom is still in the process of coming....

As long as there are men and women of faith and goodwill who will lovingly band together with almost fierce loyalty under the Father's aegis and our right hand of fellowship, we will continue to provide the assistance from our level that is so necessary in carrying out upon earth the cosmic-purposed actions that fan the fires of freedom and keep aloft the torch of God-liberty.

Saint Germain created an extensive, written course of instruction for each member of the fraternity. He prepared in his lessons, and in all of his dictations through the messengers, a course of instruction whereby the individual may make the most progress and thereby be ready for any change, major or minor, conditioned by his own karma, written in his own astrology. He defined progress as the balancing of karma—the weight that keeps the soul from flying—thus his gift of the violet flame.

The greatest gift of Saint Germain and the ascended masters is the gift of themselves, their loving presence to their students. These teachers are not distant from us but reachable immediately through the Holy Spirit. The master-student relationship is the "place of great encounters." The ascended teacher holds the matrix, or immaculate vision, of your Divine Self as you climb the path of initiation, or testing, and gradually integrate with your I AM Presence.

 ## A Living Master

People have recognized Saint Germain in many guises as their paths have crisscrossed with his, lifetime after lifetime. Some have found him by "coincidence" as they studied ancient texts, not knowing what or whom they were looking for, but knowing they were looking for something or someone important.

Others know him through the Rosicrucians, the Rosicrosse Literary Society, the Freemasons, the Wonderman of Europe, Theosophy,

Agni Yoga, or the I AM Activity. Some know him through the story of his life as Francis Bacon, which he embedded in cipher in the Shakespeare plays. And for some, he is the spiritual master who has taught them in dreams.

You can feel the essence of this great adept in the teachings he has given for the I AM Race, which is composed of citizens of all nations who have the I AM Presence and the divine spark within them. Saint Germain said on May 3, 1981:

> In my final life as Francis Bacon, I endeavored to set forth, as I was able, those keys to the destiny of America that each and every one of you hold, as members of the I AM Race, within the nucleus of your heart in a very precious golden box that is upon the altar of your temple. There, in the heart of life, are the secrets of the ages and the mysteries which I have come to unveil.
>
> I AM indeed the one anointed as the seventh angel in this dispensation, come for the finishing of the mystery of God! Blessed ones, the unveiling of those mysteries through beloved Godfré and Lotus and through your own messengers has come to an hour of fulfillment for many—and to the hour of beginning for others among you....
>
> The dawn of freedom as an idea in the hearts of the people has come forth from our own twin flames and from many others who have gone before—the dawn of the idea of justice and of mercy....
>
> Realize, then, that the key to the liberation of souls upon earth is the prior acceptance, by millions of people, of the firstfruits of the Law. One by one, there is fulfilled that mosaic of life for every lifestream. For there is a magnificent mural—that is painted by each one's own Christ Self—of that which is the divine plan. And it is a mighty mural of life. And it is a mosaic that the soul may read—block by block, square by square—and thereby fill in that mosaic, as Above, so below.

Saint Germain continuously reaches the hearts of his students at inner levels and in everyday life.

My Own Story on Finding Saint Germain

I first learned about Saint Germain at the age of eighteen on one of the most memorable days of my life. I stood in my mother's library, and I offered this prayer to God. I said, "Dear God, I'm going away to school. I thank you for my parents, my home, my education, all that you have given me, but I'm leaving now and I won't be back. Is there anything you've placed in this home for me of which I have not availed myself?" And this resounding voice of God echoed in the chamber of my own temple almost unexpectedly and communicated to me that I should go to the bookcase and take up a book that I had seen there all my life that had been given to my mother when I was born, and I never quite had the courage to pick up that book. It had a forcefield of energy so intense that I feared it; I feared what it would do to my life. But I would walk by it, back and forth, looking at it, and so this day I said to myself, "Now you are in for it." I picked up the book; I sank down deep into an old leather chair with my legs over the arm, and I thought I would be there for hours pondering something that was imponderable. I opened it and what I saw first was a painting of the ascended master Saint Germain, the first time that I had ever seen him in my life.

I was electrified! It was no longer a painting, as I came to realize that ascended masters and the saints do use pictures of themselves to contact their disciples, and sometimes we can feel their very presence through a picture. And as I looked at him, the energy of it caused me to leap from this deep position in that chair to at least a foot in the air. I ran to the kitchen and I showed the picture to my mother and I said, "Mother, look—Saint Germain. I know him; I've got to find him. Do you know him?" She said, "Yes, I know him." I said, "You know him? Why didn't you ever tell me about him?" She said, "I wanted you to discover him for yourself." So I felt like every moment of my life for eighteen years had been wasted. Here was my mother, who had known about Saint Germain since I was born, had this book in her house, and it had taken me eighteen years to pick up the book.

Well, I set out to find Saint Germain for myself, and it took me five years to find him.

Here are a few other stories of life-changing encounters with Saint Germain.

From an Author

Alfred Dodd, the prolific biographer of Francis Bacon, wrote in *The Immortal Master* that he had no idea of the Bacon-Shakespeare controversy when he first visited the home of Shakespeare in Stratford-on-Avon. He completely believed the orthodox view of the matter until he happened to overhear a comment about Francis Bacon at the museum. He became transfixed by the idea that with enough research he could answer the authorship question for himself.

> "I will get to the bottom of this matter. I will find out for myself whether Francis Bacon is innocent or guilty of the crimes imputed to him. And I will find out whether he is connected with the Plays, too. I know where to find the Author: In the *Sonnets* . . . in his lyrics of personal emotion. . . . There or nowhere is he to be found.". . .
>
> Thus, I began the Quest.[81]

After days of reading, examining and analyzing, Dodd recounts that he fell asleep with the problem of authorship on his mind.

> I seemed to be roused in the middle of the night, for I found myself sitting up in bed. . . recalling a very vivid dream. I recalled this dream-experience over and over again.
>
> I was standing by the side of a large oblong table, looking at a number of square pieces of printed paper spread before me. As I looked at them I saw they were *Shakespeare's Sonnets*. They had been cut separately and set out perpendicularly in columns of ten in consecutive order. In my dream, I remember wondering who had cut up my Sonnet-book and the reason for it?
>
> As I was puzzling this out, I became conscious of the figure of a man standing by my right side. He was dressed in a dark cloak somewhat similar to the gown of a graduate. I felt his presence more than I saw it, for I was more interested in the Sonnets before me, too engrossed even to glance at the man's face who stood so close that his habit touched me.

I was still staring at them when the left hand and arm of the figure moved across the table—a delicate, aristocratic hand, long fingers, oval nails, flesh firm and white. It seemed to exude nervous energy, a-quiver with vitality; the hand of an artist, an idealist, stamped with culture and refinement.

The long index finger pointed at Sonnet number one, the first one in the first pile, and I heard the man's voice say, *"There is no number one. We will find it."* His finger ran down the column until it reached the Sonnet numbered nine. He whispered, *"Stop! This is the first half of the Canto."* He pushed away to the left, the column of nine Sonnets in their perpendicular consecutive order; then his finger travelled down the succeeding ones until it reached Sonnet eighteen. He again whispered, *"Stop! The end of the first Canto."* He placed these Sonnets in a second column, perpendicularly and consecutively, by the side of the first. I heard him murmur, *"The Key is in F. See the last page. F stands for Five as well as Francis and Freemasonry. Remember it is also the sixth letter."* His finger again travelled from Sonnet eighteen to twenty-three. He picked it up and said, *"Two and three are five: five divided by five equals ONE. This is the true ONE, the Prologue Sonnet."* He picked up "Sonnet 23" and placed it by itself before the other two columns with the remark, *"The Prologue."*

The shuffling and rearrangement went on steadily one by one, forming column after column.... Something seemed to tell me that the most important thing to remember was THE NEW ORDER, and the various COLUMNS, some with few Sonnets and some with many. I seemed to realize intuitively that each column represented a Canto.

Then, as is the way with dreams, as I was trying to burn into my very soul the lay-out of the table, and the New Order, there appeared at the head of each column a TITLE in large capitals.... And so I awoke, finding myself sitting up in bed with all the details stamped indelibly upon my outer consciousness until I was wide awake, my chief anxiety being whether I could recall the experience in the morning if I fell asleep. I remained awake some time pondering the dream and dozed off; but when I awoke in the morning, so vivid had been the impress that it all returned ... the lay-out of the irregular columns and the New Order.

I was certain I could rearrange the Sonnets as I had seen them. After breakfast I went to Philip, Son & Nephews, ... and purchased two Sonnet copies. I cut them up. I arranged them in accordance with the dream, making number "23" the Prologue Sonnet, and so on. I pasted them in Cantos under their Dream-Titles on sheets of paper.

The next day I began to study the Rearrangement.

By bedtime I was really ill through my own conflicting thoughts, and had to spend some days in bed; for the New Sonnet Order showed unmistakably that the writer was not the Stratford Actor but the impeached judge, Francis Bacon. As an ardent Stratfordian the revelation came to me as a very great shock.[82]

Dodd goes on to explain that it took some time for him to acknowledge that the dream figure who solved a three-hundred-year-old literary problem was, indeed, Francis Bacon. He began to feel sure that the truth had come to him in order to make it known. He wrote:

Finally, *I felt within my very soul that I could not and dare not be deaf to the voice speaking through the Rearranged Sonnets.* The determining factor that decided me were the Masonic Sonnets, and my research into the Masonic history which proved that Francis Bacon was the "St. Alban" of the Craft Legends, the writer of the Rituals, the Creator and Grandmaster of the Order. *He was my "Brother" in a very real sense,* and it was my duty as a Mason to listen to the prayer of Prospero....

"As you from CRIMES would pardoned be,
By your Indulgence SET ME FREE."[83]

Alfred Dodd went on to dedicate his life to setting the record straight about Francis Bacon as the actual Shakespeare author. Dodd's books are filled with brilliant, detailed research and an intense love for the master.

In *Immortal Master,* Dodd came to believe that he was the reincarnation of Robert Essex Tudor, and owed the soul of Francis Bacon his great efforts to redeem his past mistakes. He returned with his deep brotherly love to help the immortal cause of Francis.

From a Student

Sometimes people have an instantaneous recollection of knowing the master. A girl was accepted into an accelerated Shakespeare class in high school and was thrilled. She loved Shakespeare but had no idea about the authorship question or any of its mysteries. At the end of the first class, the professor was listing his demands for study and how his students could succeed in the class. Suddenly he raised his voice in anger, and said, "One more thing! I don't want anyone, ever, to bring up the question about authorship. Don't ever say that Francis Bacon wrote Shakespeare!" The girl's heart leapt at the name Francis Bacon, a name she had never heard before.

She then knew without the faintest doubt that Francis was the true author of the Shakespeare plays. That moment of soul recognition led her on a search to find out what happened to Francis Bacon, which ultimately brought her to the heart of the master Saint Germain.

A Surprise Meeting in a Pub

One young 21-year-old man was just beginning his spiritual search and had recently discovered the master Saint Germain. He was also spending some time with his brothers, sisters, and friends in a local pub.

One night as he was standing in the pub, he saw everything around him suddenly change, and instead of the wall of his local hangout, he was seeing, smelling, and experiencing a raucous Elizabethan pub. To his surprise he knew this place very well. The voice of a wise and wonderful man, just to his right and behind him, said, "In *that* time, you could have been great, but you let alcohol thwart you. You have *this* time now. You can stop drinking *now*, but if you wait it will be much more difficult."

The young man stopped any association with alcohol immediately.

A Dream

A professional psychologist who had studied many spiritual teachers and paths had a dream that affected him deeply.

He did not know Saint Germain—or rather he was not conscious of who he was even though later he realized the master had been speaking with him for some long while—until a few months ago when he had a dream in which he saw a tall, slender, well-dressed man with a mustache and beard. When he told a friend, she immediately recognized the description as Saint Germain.

The psychologist had never heard of this saint or master and began to search for his history. When he found the teachings in the book *Saint Germain On Alchemy*, he felt as if the master was teaching him directly.

 ## Light Is the Alchemical Key

The best way to use Saint Germain's gift of the violet flame is by giving decrees or mantras accompanied with visualization. A mantra is a worded formula expressing devotion to God. It is an energy matrix that sustains the qualities invoked by the science of sound and rhythm. It is a prayer, but it is also a dynamic decree and an affirmation. The prayer contains the pattern of that which you desire to manifest on earth by the authority of your God-given free will, by this divine spark in your heart, and by your I AM Presence. The science behind the devotional practice of this Word is both simple and vast.

You have a River of Life, which is called the silver or crystal cord. It descends from the heart of the Father (your individualized I AM Presence) through the heart of the Son (your individualized Christ Self) to your own heart chakra (containing the etheric threefold flame behind your physical heart).

This is your natural spiritual resource. It is the energy you use to live and move and have being—to put your ideas into action, to express your love, to do everything you do in a lifetime. Your spiritual resources may be used by you according to your free will because you have a divine spark—because when God gave you that threefold flame, he gave you the gift of himself, the gift of his power to create.

The threefold flame, which is also called the Holy Christ flame, is the focus in you of the consciousness of the Trinity—Father, Son, and Holy Spirit—which blossoms from the light of the Divine Mother. By that sacred fire of God glowing in your heart chakra, you are endowed with the universal Mind, you are a son or daughter of God and a co-creator with him.

A spoken decree, then, is an expression of your joy in God's flame in your heart. It is your joyous response to your Creator, affirming his Being where you are. When you decree, you are the instrument of God's Word. By the power of that Word you draw down, you import into your world, the infinite light that is sealed in your I AM Presence.

Saint Germain gave humanity this simple but profound decree, "I AM the Light of the Heart." It is a prayer of love to your God and to the God of your twin flame and can be easily remembered. Each line is a visualized spiritual concept, building on the meaning of the line before, an affirmation that the power of God exists in you as infinite love and victory over all barriers:

> I AM the light of the heart
> Shining in the darkness of being
> And changing all into the golden treasury
> Of the mind of Christ.
>
> I AM projecting my love
> Out into the world
> To erase all errors
> And to break down all barriers.
>
> I AM the power of infinite love,
> Amplifying itself
> Until it is victorious,
> World without end!

What this is saying is that God in me, the I AM THAT I AM, is the Light of my heart. It is an affirmation. When you affirm the Light of the I AM THAT I AM here below through the power of the spoken Word, which is the power to create, so it is done. So it does manifest.

We become enlightened by our love for the Christ in ourselves and in all of the saints of God. Our profound love for him makes us aware that experiences of hatred or mild dislike are misuses of God's daily flow of energy to us, for which we are responsible and ultimately accountable. We cannot hate any part of life, which is God, with impunity.

One may have an accumulation of that karma of hatred or another form of discord from previous embodiments. Sometimes you meet someone and you have an instantaneous dislike for that person, but you do not really know why. It might be that you had an altercation in a past life, and the sense of injustice and the energies tied up in it are still unresolved. You don't want to hate, and hate again, and pour out dislike again. Far better to release this balm of Gilead—the power of God's love—for change, for transmutation, for the dissolution by the sacred fire of this invisible but problematic record, this knot in your subconscious, or astral body.

Energy is neither created nor destroyed, but it may be transformed. Hatred is an overlay of negative vibration that people impose on God's pure energy, which must be transformed back to its original purity. Because we are God's children, his sons and daughters, he gave us the power to be co-creators with him. One can easily see the mess we have made of our world, but now and then we have also created bliss, which is pure, permanently retained energy. We have made our choices, and we live in the realms of our own creation. We can undo our past hatreds, discords, and dislikes before they return to our doorstep for our undoing.

The action of change is brought about by the violet flame. By the authority of the I AM Presence, the Holy Christ Self, and the threefold flame within us, we can give a decree that calls forth the violet flame from the heart of God and sends it into the cause and core of all conditions, known or unknown, conscious or unconscious, of hatred and the psychology of its nonresolution, arguments, anger—any and all problems we have ever had with anyone.

Everything from mild dislike to irritation to fear, which is also a perversion of love—all of this burdens the heart. It weighs down the heart chakra so that it does not spin with the vigor and purity of Christ light. This can eventually manifest as physical heart disease.

If we don't have a functioning heart in the physical octave, we leave this octave. We cannot make it without a heart, physically, and we cannot grow spiritually without a balanced and expanded heart flame allowing divine love to radiate from us.

Here is a simple invocation to God for the violet flame to come into your heart physically, emotionally, mentally, and spiritually through all of the various layers of your being, even to the subconscious levels, to purge you of the records and momentums of burdens, known or unknown.

While invoking the violet flame, recall in your heart any incidents in which you may have in any way misused divine love in this life, and visualize these moments transmuted, dissolved—all negative aspects withdrawn as the energy is reinstated to its divine essence. If you feel yourself hanging on to those incidents, think of Jesus' kind and wise advice, "What is that to thee? Follow thou me."[84] Self-condemnation is not the way of the Brotherhood.

If you would have the benefit of this miraculous energy, if you would be visited by the genie of the lamp of freedom, the master Saint Germain himself, you have but to make the call. For the fiat of Almighty God has gone forth, and it is a cosmic law: The call compels the answer! But the call is a very special call. It is not the demand of the human consciousness, but the command of your Real Self, your own true being, the mediator between the I AM Presence and the soul. Thus you declare:

Invocation example:

In the name of the Christ Self and in the name of the living God, I call forth the energies of the sacred fire from the altar within my heart. In the name of the I AM THAT I AM, I invoke the violet flame to blaze forth from the center of the threefold flame, from the white-fire core of my own I AM Presence, multiplied by the momentum of the blessed ascended master Saint Germain. I call forth that light to penetrate my soul and to activate my soul memory of freedom and the original blueprint of my soul's destiny. I call forth the violet transmuting flame to pass through my four lower bodies and through my soul consciousness to transmute the cause and core of all that is less than my Christ-perfection, all that is not in keeping with the will of God for my lifestream. So let it be done by the cloven tongues of the fire of the Holy Spirit in fulfillment of the action of that sacred fire, as Above, so below. And I accept it done this hour in the full power of the living God who even now declares within my soul, "I AM WHO I AM."

Decree example:
Violet fire, thou love divine,
Blaze within this heart of mine!
Thou art mercy forever true,
Keep me always in tune with you.

(repeat 3, 9, or 12 times)

This seemingly simple decree is calling for the action of the light that descends over the silver cord. It is a crystal clear River of Life, which as John saw it, proceeds "out of the throne of God [your I AM Presence] and of the Lamb [your Holy Christ Self]."[85]

This "pure river of water of Life" has no qualification. It is God's pristine energy that has not had the stamp of creation placed on it yet. When it reaches your temple, it passes through the top of the head and descends to the heart chakra, where the threefold flame fountain receives this light stream from its Source.

The author of Proverbs says, "Keep thy heart with all diligence; for out of it are the issues of life."[86] All that we do issues from the choices of our heart and our communion

with our conscience, our Christ Self. By the authority of that divine spark within us, we are commanding the light of God that is descending from his Presence into specific action.

Why do we repeat the decree? Why not say it only once? Is it a vain repetition of words?[87]

You are using the power of the spoken Word, and that Word in you is qualifying the never-ending flow of spiritual energy—the crystal clear light. It is a moving stream. As it passes through the nexus of the mind and heart, it is stamped with your fiat,* or decree. By this act of invoking the violet flame in giving this decree, you are spiritually coloring the stream violet and qualifying it with the vibration of divinity. You are extending your meditation on the master's holy affirmation as you intensify the visualization of violet light, all the while hidden within God's protection.

If you were standing by a stream and watching the flow, moment by moment new water would be passing by you. Decreeing is like putting dye in a stream—it colors the water violet, but that stream keeps moving. So if you want the whole stream to be violet, you have to qualify the next moment of water and the next.

So, the crystal water of Life is descending like Niagara Falls. The more we decree, the more we are charging the energy flowing over the silver cord with the violet flame.

First, this violet-flame stream charges our whole body and mind with a transmutative healing power. It flows through our chakras, purifying them along the way, to bless all whom we meet. This explains Jesus' Eastern teaching: "He that believeth on me, as the scripture hath said, out of his belly [the solar-plexus and seat-of-the-soul chakras] shall flow rivers of living water."[88]

Then your "lifestream" is stamped with the violet flame every time you decree. The repetition of the dynamic decree is for the intensification and the acceleration of God's light, scientifically, within you, qualifying your spiritual resources with the vibration and the purity of the Holy Spirit for the blessing of all life.

---

*fiat [Latin, "let it be done," from *fieri* "to become," "be done"]: a command or act of will that creates something without, or as if without, further effort. Fiats are exclamations of Christ-power, Christ-wisdom, and Christ-love consciously affirmed and accepted in the here and now.

This is not vain repetition but prayer with a purpose: the continuous re-creation of ourselves and our world in the image and likeness of God. Because the decree is expressing our will to confirm God's will "on earth as it is in heaven," the qualification of our energy and consciousness continues after the decree is given—so long as we hold the desire, the harmony, and the free will to have it so in our lives.

As the decree accelerates, you can hear it become fiery and intense because a decree is a command. God said to us, "command ye me." "Ask me of things to come concerning my sons, and concerning the work of my hands command ye me."[89] And the work of God's hands is everything that's happening in the physical universe. And the reason our souls descended into this physicality is to "work the works of him that sent me."[90] We are not only the handiwork of God, we are the instruments of God's work.

Creation is always by free will and by the spoken Word. God said in the Beginning, "Let there be light." It is written in Genesis, "and there was light."[91] He gave the spoken command, and the physical cosmos was created through all manifestations of himself—Elohim, archangels, elementals, and all the heavenly host.

But you yourself also have a world. It is your "little world," your microcosm. You make the same fiat: *Let there be light!* You are tired of the void of darkness and human nonsense in your physical, mental,

emotional, and memory bodies. You are tired of disease or being accident-prone or having problems with your job or your family. You want it to be consumed by the fire of God's will, so you make that creative fiat: *Let there be light!* You are so determined in your heart and soul and in your entire being that it becomes a command, on both the elements of nature and your causal body, and the light descends, and you are filled with that light—that Christ who personifies in you, and precipitates all of the light, energy, and consciousness of God in your being and aura.

You are the receiver of the light. The real decreer, the one who is really decreeing, is your own Holy Christ Self, who is your Real Self—the individual manifestation of that universal Christ where you are. So when you let yourself be the instrument of the decree, rather than trying to take it over, the light itself, as Christ in you, accelerates and increases its power over you.

Saint Germain teaches that this devotional science is for those who see their life's purpose in transcending the shallows of the mundane. Francis wrote the words of his vision in *Julius Caesar*, and as they were true for him, they are true for each of us: "There is a tide in the affairs of men, which taken at the flood, leads on to fortune. Omitted, all the voyage of their life is bound in shallows and miseries."[92]

When the violet flame is invoked, it loosens the dense substance and passes through and transforms that darkness into light. Since every human condition is the perversion of a divine condition, then, line for line and measure for measure, the human consciousness is changed into the divine, and the energy that was locked in pockets of mortality is freed to enter the sockets of immortality. And each time a measure of energy is freed, a measure of a man ascends to the plane of God-awareness.

As you begin to use the violet flame, you will experience feelings of joy, lightness, hope, and newness of life as though clouds of depression were being dissolved by the very sun of your own being. And the oppression of the very dark, dank energies of human bondage literally melts in the fervent heat of freedom's violet fires.

The devotional science of the spoken Word can become your

personal lifestyle, a lifelong daily commitment to our Holy Brother. In return, as friend, he gives you a never-ending promise to assist you to find your immortal freedom, as you determine never to give up and never to turn back.

 # The Inheritance

Helena Blavatsky, in *The Key to Theosophy*, traced a cumulative chronological pattern over many centuries of divine intercession and wisdom teachings from the ascended masters. The upward spiral of new dispensations can be seen, especially over the last six hundred years, as leading humanity toward greater understanding. In every century and every lifetime, individuals could choose by free will to rebel against the progressive revelations, ignore them, or accept the offered wisdom. Blavatsky wrote:

> During the last quarter of every hundred years an attempt is made by those "Masters," of whom I have spoken, to help on the spiritual progress of humanity in a marked and definite way. Towards the close of each century you will invariably find that an outpouring or upheaval of spirituality—or call it mysticism if you prefer—has taken place. Some one or more persons have appeared in the world as their agents, and a greater or less amount of occult knowledge and teaching has been given out. If you care to do so, you can trace these movements back, century by century, as far as our detailed historical records extend.[93]

If one researches history with this upward spiral in mind, the pattern offers great hope for the coming centuries of Aquarius.

1475—The Italian Renaissance

Artists such as Botticelli and Da Vinci exemplified the cultural wave that uplifted society in Europe. There was a reemergence of the wisdom of the Greek philosophers in the Platonic Academy of Florence, Italy. Dante Alighieri circumvented the corrupt elite of the Church when he published *The Divine Comedy*. In a time when books were rare and always censored, Dante's work was couched in deep

Crossing the Styx by Gustave Doré

spiritual symbolism in terms the Church could accept. *The Divine Comedy* shows a hero delving into the "underworld." The journey to the underworld is an exploration through our unconscious. Each spiritual student is a hero in the making, and no one can get beyond a certain point on the spiritual path until they deal with the contents of their unconscious and access the wisdom hidden there.

Dante's character Beatrice symbolizes the cosmic sense of grace. So cosmic consciousness, cosmic awareness, awareness of the potential in you—all of these things are in a very real sense the Angel of your Presence in your life. When the Angel of the Presence takes over, you have the quality of discrimination built in. Beatrice also characterizes the ascended twin flame, as well as the positive aspects of the anima, which is vital in putting a man's mind in tune with the right inner values and thereby opening the way into more profound inner depths.

1575—The English Renaissance

Brought about by Francis Bacon, the greatest mind that Western civilization has ever produced, the English Renaissance overflowed with literature that freed the minds and souls of the readers. Francis Bacon is the point that we look to and say, "I would like to evolve to that level of spirituality and a tremendous mind." The mind of Bacon is the mind of the New Age. Francis's Great Instauration taught the public that they were independent of superstition, free to explore science and learn from archetypal patterns of behavior through his plays. The plays became the parables of the New Age. Francis's secret societies were dedicated to keeping alive the ancient mysteries: the mysteries that came down not only from Jesus Christ but from the East, from Egypt; the mysteries that were taught to Moses that came down from the time of the Great Pyramid and from Ikhnaton, who founded the principle of the one God and monotheism. These pathways toward God answered the need of the public who were routinely condemned as miserable sinners by the clerical hierarchy.

1675—The Escape to America

The last quarter of the seventeenth century saw the rapid expansion of an immigrant society drawn mostly by free will from the feudal strictures of the Old World. Self-selecting waves of immigrants, spiritual pioneers, mystics, and even those tricked or pressed into slavery, yearned for the freedom to be a sovereign people under God, far from feudal tyrants and perpetual poverty. It was a vast new platform for self-starters, with far less control by the hierarchical elites of Church and State. Those sent from Africa and Europe as slaves and prisoners threw the need for freedom into sharp relief. The age-old practices needed to come to an end.

This was also an era of scientific and mathematical renaissance. The Royal Society was founded in England, and the world saw the works of Sir Isaac Newton and Descartes.

1775—The Independence of America

The rising belief in personal sovereignty and God-given rights triumphed over the violent reaction of the power elite, and an experimental republic was born whose constitution and growing abundance set precedents for the world.

1875—Theosophy

The founding of the first worldwide society to integrate the "perennial philosophy" with the ancient wisdom and mystic truths behind Eastern and Western spirituality dismantled the sacrosanct dogmas of orthodox Christianity. Theosophy revolutionized spirituality and culture by reintroducing the esoteric teachings of ancient wisdom and the concept of universal brotherhood to public awareness. It was also a great experiment, as it publicly presented the reality of unascended and ascended masters, who were not remote in heaven but caring and intimately involved with the well-being of all of humanity.

1975—The Summit Lighthouse

Following Theosophy, Agni Yoga, and the I AM Activity, the ascended masters added a spiral of progressively expansive teaching. By the last quarter of the twentieth century, The Summit Lighthouse had become a cornucopia of their teachings on cosmic law and the initiatory path toward personal Christhood. The teachings of the ascended masters are the teachings of the Divine Mother. They are soul-liberating and free the individual from institutionalized religious hierarchy.

2075—The Inheritance

The current cycle from 1975 to 2075 brings great risk but universal hope to humanity and the necessity for endurance through the end of a karmic age. People of light will ratify divine Reality on earth. A gradual purification process will unfold behind the headlines. New aspects of the Great Instauration will appear under the guidance of Saint Germain and will not be hindered as before. The period of opportunity to turn to the light for those who have controlled the people through fear, manipulation, war, and poverty is coming to an end.

A great decree has gone forth from the causal body of the Master R, reverberating the edict of Almighty God for the implementation of the golden age at hand. By the last quarter of the twenty-first century, certain among the seed of the wicked will no longer be allowed to reincarnate or propagate after their kind. Thus, with this removal of those who have perpetuated the great rebellion of Lucifer, there will come upon humanity such a dawning, such an awakening, that the children of light will no longer be bound by the workings of evil. Humanity may scarcely comprehend how the old order might pass and the new might begin. This dispensation will allow the founding principles of the golden age to become the new reality for our world.

The Great Instauration will expand in the centuries ahead toward

a culture of brotherhood. Humanity will experience firsthand through their own creativity the genius of the plan for a self-transcending golden age. The kindness of people toward nature and each other will approach a universal wisdom, where sainthood is accepted as normal behavior. This pure pattern held in the mind of God was long foreseen by that loyal servant of the brotherhood of man, Saint Germain.

The Age of the Seventh Angel

This age under the sign of Aquarius, is the age of the flame of freedom. Saint Germain embodies that flame of freedom and that awareness of God as freedom. In every lifetime he has lived, he has put on and internalized the light of freedom—freedom in science, in philosophy, alchemy and prophecy, in literature, and in government. Saint Germain comes in the seventh age, or the seventh cycle, which is the Aquarian age. He comes with a fulfillment of the message of Jesus Christ with the promised Comforter, the understanding of the Holy Ghost, and the baptism of the Holy Ghost with sacred fire.

It has been more than 450 years since Francis Bacon saw the need for a restoration of civilization to a golden-age level of abundance, peace, and creative freedom. Saint Germain now brings the message that sacred change is indeed the order of the day. The winds of Aquarius bring profound change, stripping from souls and body temples excess trappings and adornments until the individual is forced to look at himself in the cosmic mirror and say, "Is this what I am, or is there something more of me that I have not discovered?"

This change that is coming may be accepted in one of two ways by each of us: whether to ride the wave of light and to find oneself in a new age, at a new level of God-awareness, or to choose to deny it, to be inundated, as though watching the coming of a tsunami—not quite expecting that it will really come—and therefore to experience the vortex of returning karma.

The sine wave of the ages continues regardless of the comings and goings of humanity. It is irrevocable. It can no more be stopped than the rotation of the earth around the sun. But the course that humanity takes in the cycles of the night (the cycles of returning karma) and the cycles of the day (the cycles of opportunity to sow seeds of good karma and to balance negative karma) will determine how the ages are outplayed.

It is necessary for the wicked to outplay their hand, and for those that sleep to bear the fruit of their karma of ignoring both the Law and the dangers that are thrust against that Law. When all is outplayed and the harvest of all men and women is known, then mankind will understand that the judgment itself will sever night and day, Reality and unreality, and the dawn of a golden age shall appear.

In his own words, Saint Germain describes his reason for being as the personification of the divine quality of freedom, and then invites you to consider your own reason for being:

> I AM born to be free! I AM born to carry the torch of freedom! By free will I have elected to ensoul the flame that God, by freedom, has placed within me. And this is the convergence of the soul and the Spirit, the convergence of life, as Above, so below in the fiery destiny of life!

Would you meet your God? Then I say, run to greet your fiery destiny! Run into the threefold flame and there find the living Presence of the I AM THAT I AM, which has ordained that destiny from the Beginning, from the origin of cycles....

There are shrines of freedom, focuses of freedom, and masters who sponsor the flame of freedom in every nation. And nowhere upon Terra is there a nation or a people who have not the right, the opportunity, and the backing by the solar hierarchies to be free, to love freedom, and to love the light.

Your Own Holy Brother

Think now of the moment when you first heard or read the name Saint Germain. Was it in a book, or in a class, a dream, or from a conversation with a friend? Le Comte de Saint Germain—the name has been spoken in nation after nation. Think of the moment when *you* first heard it. Did it spark a fire to ignite your heart?

When you realize what Saint Germain has been through, and that what he has tried to do has met with adversity every step of the way, you realize that his love is an incomparable love, a love so intense, so zealous, so far-reaching.

So we understand that the greatest of adepts and masters of all ages have borne burdens such as we bear. We can count it, then, as a sign when we are persecuted, when our karma intensifies, that someone in heaven and at our side has called us apart and said, "I will be with you. I will walk with you. I will sponsor you in life and unto your *victory*. Simply receive what I give you of the Great Law and *apply* it. And come apart and enter the golden highway of light and the great spiraling staircase that leads to your I AM Presence, that leads to beings beyond, and to your beloved twin flame."

To become a student of Saint Germain, or any ascended master, one must set aside the human ego and connect with one's own heart and Christ Self. Saint Germain taught in *Unveiled Mysteries*:

> There is only one passport into the "Presence," of these Great Ones and that is enough Love poured out to one's own God Self,

and to Them, united with the determination to root out of the human all discord and selfishness. When an individual becomes determined *enough* to serve only the Constructive Plan of Life, he disciplines perfectly his human nature, no matter how unpleasant the task. Then, he will automatically draw to himself the attention of an Ascended Master, who will take note of his struggles and pour out courage, strength, and Love sustaining him, until he maintains the feeling of his permanent contact with the Inner God Self....

The attitude of one who wishes to work in conscious cooperation with the Ascended Host should not be, "I wish I could go to them for instruction," but rather, "I will so purify, discipline, and perfect myself, become such an expression of Divine Love, wisdom, and power that I can assist in Their work, then I will automatically be drawn unto Them. I will love so constantly, so infinitely, so divinely, that the very intensity of my own 'Light' will open the way for Them to accept me."...

There is a way for all to come into contact with the Ascended Masters, and that is to *think* upon them, *call unto them* and they will answer every call with their own "Presence" of Love, but the motive for the call must be, Love of the One Source, Love of the Light, Love of Perfection.

If this be real, determined, and steadfast, the student will receive greater and greater Light, for the "Light" knows Its own and gives of Itself, unceasingly, unconditionally, every moment. Ask and ye shall receive, knock and it shall be opened unto you, seek and ye shall find, call unto the "Light" and the Ascended Masters will answer you, for they are the "Light" of the world.[94]

Meditate on the heart of Saint Germain. Call forth his Electronic Presence over you through your own I AM Presence. The only way that an ascended master can enter your life is through your own free will and your God Presence. Saint Germain will never bypass your free will, never enter uninvited, never interfere with you. So if you want to work with a master, you can receive him. If you do not want to work with him, you can simply receive what you want from his teachings. So any level of contact or none at all is perfectly acceptable because the whole cosmos functions on free will.

Meditate on the beloved master any way you like.
Call to him.
Ask him to prove to you that he is real, that he exists.
Challenge him if you will.
Love him.
Ask him to help you with a problem, personal or planetary.

He is here as a brother to serve the light in you and help you make it as he has made it.

The Great White Brotherhood emphasizes the need for those who embark on the spiritual path to not be discouraged in well doing and in interior correction, for the weight of glory of the cause of freedom is beyond the span of mere mortal life. Yet, its rewards frequently come in moments of such beauty as to shatter the shell of mortality for humanity and give us glimpses beyond ourselves of that which God has prepared for all those who love him.

Saint Germain's heart is connected to the heart of every potential bearer of the cup, everyone who has sought the Holy Grail, everyone who may bear on behalf of humanity the strength, the foresight, and the leadership for that point of victory that is the point of the leader, in leading the hosts of the LORD.

The message of Saint Germain is one of the universe. It is a message of the revolutionaries of the spirit of East and West, of all ages. He teaches us how to fulfill our mission in this age, which is to establish freedom, peace, and enlightenment on earth and to prepare for the coming great golden age.

He is a greater friend than any friend we will ever know, or have known. His mind is so vast that I feel almost as a beggar to even attempt to be his messenger, to think that he has to put up with my vessel to get across what he wants to get across.

But he doesn't have to stop with me. All the marvelous advances in science and literature and culture that he has sparked can become your forte. You can become spokesmen for Saint Germain in a very detailed way through the technology that his scientific method has brought about. I think we should all dedicate ourselves to be spokesmen for Saint Germain, for he has so many, many, many talents and ideas in every field of human advancement that, even with all of us, he may not get it all said.

There is a tremendous sacred fire within all of us which, when united together, can truly stop what appears to be a downward spiraling of civilization, misuse of nuclear energy, and people not able to control the conditions of life, their circumstances, and forces of nature.

Saint Germain will not leave this planet in distress. Our beloved Holy Brother will not leave until every lifestream has had the opportunity to know the violet flame, to apply it, and to learn that the open door of the ascension is at hand.

Our Holy Brother is here to unveil the mysteries of God to each soul, in our time. He has not forgotten *his* time as Francis Bacon, where we began this journey, comfortable in his good company. Now, imagine your ongoing conversation with him, where he shares ancient memories and you finally understand that he is inviting you to join him, on earth and in heaven:

> But we who've been
> A part of earth
> And felt the lash
> Of tyrants bold,
> For freedom's sake
> We now do make
> A call to hearts of gold.[95]

APPENDICES

For a deeper understanding of the times and works of Francis Bacon, you can access the following appendices online at http://www.Summit UniversityPress.com/secrets-appendices.

- **APPENDIX A:** "The Timeline": See important dates at a glance of the life of Francis Bacon and the immortal works of Saint Germain.

- **APPENDIX B:** Delve into some of Saint Germain's past embodiments and learn what his soul has accomplished over thousands of years.

- **APPENDIX C:** Learn more about Francis writing the Shakespeare plays in this interview excerpt with the Baconian Scholar, Peter Dawkins. You can also explore Peter Dawkins's wealth of information on Francis Bacon at his website https://www.fbrt.org.uk.

- **APPENDIX D:** "Masks and Friends": See the breadth and width of Francis's literary work. What he did with his "Good Pens" is astounding.

- **APPENDIX E:** Learn more about those ciphers.

- **APPENDIX F:** Discover the names of those who have publicly doubted that the actor from Stratford wrote the Shakespeare plays. Some may surprise you.

- **APPENDIX G:** Find out about the Keepers of the Flame Fraternity and begin your journey with Saint Germain. Enjoy this gift of powerful decrees by Saint Germain and invoke the violet flame for yourself and the world.

NOTES

NOTE TO THE READER

1. Peter Dawkins, *Building Paradise* (Francis Bacon Research Trust, 2001), pp. xiv, 1, 4.

PART 1   A Sacred Mystery

1. Tycho Brahe, *Astronomiæ Instauratæ Progymnasmataor* ("Introduction to the New Astronomy"), Vol. 1 (1602).
2. Peter Dawkins, *The Great Vision* (Francis Bacon Research Trust, 1985), p. 70.
3. Alfred Dodd, *Francis Bacon's Personal Life-Story* (London, New York: Rider & Company, 1910, 1986), pp. 24–25.
4. Ibid., p. 26.
5. Ibid., p. 27.
6. Alfred North Whitehead, *Science and the Modern World:* Lowell lectures 1925 (London: Cambridge University Press, 1926), pp. 49–50.
7. Dawkins, *The Great Vision*, pp. 67–68.
8. For more information on Joseph of Arimathea in Britain, see *The Drama of the Lost Disciples,* George F. Jowett (Covenant Publishing, London, 1966).
9. Serenus de Cressy, *The Church History of Brittany from the Beginning of Christianity to the Norman Conquest...* (Printed by Rouen for the author, 1668), Book 2, chap. 1. p. 19, https://quod.lib.umich.edu/e/eebo/A34964.0001.001/1:7.2.1?rgn=div3;view=fulltext.
10. Dawkins, *The Great Vision*, p. 107.
11. Francis Bacon, *Government of England,* quoted in Dawkins, *The Great Vision*, p. 107.
12. Dawkins, *The Great Vision*, p. 108.
13. Ibid.
14. Ibid., p. 109.
15. Ibid.
16. Elizabeth Wells Gallup, *The Bi-Literal Cypher of Sir Francis Bacon* (Detroit, Michigan, Howard London, Gay & Bird, 1901), p. 90.
17. Orville Owen, *Sir Francis Bacon's Cipher Story Discovered and Deciphered by Orville W. Owen, M.D.*, Vol. 1 (Detroit and New York: Howard Publishing Company, 1893), p. 113.
18. Ibid., p. 108.
19. Dodd, *Francis Bacon's Personal Life-Story*, p. 16.

20. Sir Francis Bacon, Dr. William Rawley, *Resuscitatio* (3rd ed., printed by S.G. and B.G. for William Lee, London, 1671), *The Life of the Right Honourable Francis Bacon*, p. 2.
21. Dodd, *Francis Bacon's Personal Life-Story*, p. 50.
22. Virginia M. Fellows, *The Shakespeare Code* (Gardiner: Summit Publications, Inc., 2006), pp. 45–46.
23. William T. Smedley, *The Mystery of Francis Bacon* (London: Robert Banks & Son, 1912), pp. 78, 80.
24. Peter Dawkins, *Arcadia* (Francis Bacon Research Trust, 1988), p. 93.
25. Bacon, Rawley, *Resuscitatio, The Life of the Right Honourable Francis Bacon*, p. 9.
26. David Lloyd, *Statesmen and Favourites of Queen Elizabeth* (London, 1665).
27. Richard Ince, *England's High Chancellor* (London: Frederick Muller, 1935), pp. 18, 19–20.
28. The paper, "The Earliest Play Written By Francis Bacon When He Was Only Seven Years Old *Like Will To Like* One of Three Works Written in the Name of His Literary Mask Ulpian Fulwell and Their Links to His Shakespeare Plays"; https://aphoenix1.academia.edu/research#papers.
29. Francis Bacon, *Advancement of Learning, Second Book* (Oxford: Clarendon Press, 1880), p. 152.
30. James Spedding, *An Account of the Life and Times of Francis Bacon, Vol. 1* (Boston: Houghton, Mifflin and Company, 1880), pp. 4–5.
31. Francis Bacon, James Spedding, *The Works of Francis Bacon, Vol. V, Natural and Experimental History for the Foundation of Philosophy: or Phenomena of the Universe: Which Is the Third Part of the Instauratio Magna* (London: Longmans & Co., 1870), p. 132.
32. Francis Bacon, *The Advancement of Learning*, Edited with Introduction by G. W. Kitchin (London: J. M. Dent and Sons LDT, New York: E. P. Dutton and Co. Inc, 1915), pp. 6–8.
33. Francis Bacon, *Essays Civil and Moral: Advancement of Learning, Novum Organum, etc., Great Instauration* (London: Ward, Lock, Bowden, and Co., 1892), pp. 401–402.
34. Ibid., p. 407.
35. Dawkins, *The Great Vision*, p. 92.
36. Francis Bacon, "Of Truth" (London: Printed by John Haviland for Hanna Barret, and Richard Whitaker, 1625).
37. The essay, "Francis Bacon and his Authorship of Like Will To Like," p. 48, found at SirBacon.org. Quoting Roberta Buchanan, *Ars Adulandi, Or The Art Of Flattery By Ulpian Fulwell A Critical Edition Of The Author* (Institut Fur Anglistik Und Amerikanistik Universitat Salzburg A-5020 Salzburg Austria, 1984), p. 16.
38. Ibid., p. 74.

39. Dawkins, *The Great Vision*, p. 126.
40. Ibid., pp. 129–30.
41. Gallup, *The Bi-Literal Cypher of Sir Francis Bacon*, pp. 85–86.
42. Ibid., pp. 139–41.
43. Dawkins, *The Great Vision*, p. 15.
44. Ibid., p. 97.
45. Owen, *Sir Francis Bacon's Cipher Story*, Vol. 1, pp. 32–34.
46. Marguerite Valois, *Historic Court Memoirs of Marguerite de Valois* (New York: Printed for Merrill & Baker, 1800), p. 112.
47. Ibid., p. 108.
48. Ibid.
49. Ibid., p. 107.
50. Francis Bacon, *Mr. William Shakespeare's Comedies, Histories & Tragedies* (commonly called the First Folio), biliteral cipher, pp. 175–76; decoded in Dawkins, *The Great Vision*, p. 166.
51. Dawkins, *The Great Vision*, p. 170; decoded from the word cipher.
52. Bacon, *The New Atlantis*, 1627, biliteral cipher, p. 337, decoded in Dawkins, *The Great Vision*, p. 173.
53. Gallup, *The Bi-Literal Cypher of Sir Francis Bacon*, pp. 12–13.
54. Ibid., p. 79.
55. Dawkins, *The Great Vision*, p. 191.
56. Ibid., pp. 198–99.
57. Dodd, *Francis Bacon's Personal Life-Story*, p. 104.
58. Peter Dawkins, "The Bacon Brothers in France" (Francis Bacon Research Trust, 2015), quoting William T. Smedley, *The Mystery of Francis Bacon* (London: Robert Banks & Son, 1912), p. 135.
59. Dodd, *Francis Bacon's Personal Life-Story*, p. 106.
60. Ibid.
61. Dawkins, *The Great Vision*, p. 187.
62. Bacon, *Novum Organum*, biliteral cipher, p. 88; Dawkins, *The Great Vision*, p. 187.
63. Ibid., p. 122; Dawkins, *The Great Vision*, p. 188.
64. William Hepworth Dixon, *Personal History of Lord Bacon* (Boston: Ticknor and Fields, 1861), p. 14.
65. Smedley, *The Mystery of Francis Bacon*, p. 79.
66. Alfred Dodd, *Martyrdom of Francis Bacon* (London: Rider & Co., 1945), p. 37.
67. Gallup, *The Bi-Literal Cypher of Sir Francis Bacon*, p. 46.
68. Peter Dawkins, *Building Paradise* (Francis Bacon Research Trust, Warwickshire, UK, 2001), p. 13.
69. Dodd, *Francis Bacon's Personal Life-Story*, pp. 177–78.
70. Ibid., p. 120.
71. William Ralph Douthwaite, *Gray's Inn: Its History Associations* (London: Reeves and Turner, 1886), p. 59.

72. Spedding, *An Account of the Life and Times of Francis Bacon*, Vol. 1, pp. 109, 660.
73. James Spedding, *The Letters and the Life of Francis Bacon*, Vol. 3 (London: Longmans, Green, Reader, and Dyer, 1868), p. 301.
74. Dawkins, *Building Paradise*, p. 14.
75. Douthwaite, *Gray's Inn: Its History Associations*, p. 222.
76. Dodd, *Francis Bacon's Personal Life-Story*, pp. 154–55.
77. Ibid., pp. 155–56.
78. Ibid., p. 157; capitalization added by Alfred Dodd to emphasize Freemason symbolism.
79. Ibid., pp. 131–32.
80. John Aubrey, *Brief Lives, Chiefly of Contemporaries, Set Down by John Aubrey, Between the Years 1669 and 1696* (Oxford: At the Clarendon Press, 1898), ed. by Andrew Clark, pp. 311–12.
81. Bacon, Rawley, *Resuscitatio, The Life of the Right Honourable Francis Bacon*, p. 10.
82. Owen, *Sir Francis Bacon's Cipher Story*, Vol. 4, pp. 652, 655.
83. Ibid., p. 666.
84. Dawkins, *The Shakespeare Enigma*, p. 210.
85. Ibid., p. 212.
86. Margaret Barsi-Greene, *I, Prince Tudor Wrote Shakespeare* (Boston, Branden Press, 1973), p. 32.
87. Gallup, *The Bi-Literal Cypher of Sir Francis Bacon*, p. 37.
88. James Reeves, *A Short History of English Poetry, 1340–1940* (New York: E. P. Dutton, 1962), p. 61.
89. Dawkins, *The Great Vision*, p. 212.
90. Gallup, *The Bi-Literal Cypher of Sir Francis Bacon*, p. 365.
91. Dodd, *Francis Bacon's Personal Life-Story*, p. 111.
92. Dawkins, *The Shakespeare Enigma*, p. 137.
93. James Spedding, *An Account of the Life and Times of Francis Bacon* (Boston: Houghton, Osgood and Company, 1878), pp. 421–25.
94. Mrs. Henry Pott, *Francis Bacon and His Secret Society* (Chicago: Francis J. Schulte & Company, 1891).
95. Ibid., pp. 15–16.
96. Ibid., p. 51; *Promus*, 516.
97. Ibid., pp. 33–35.
98. Francis Bacon, "Of Gardens" (London: Printed by John Haviland for Hanna Barret, and Richard Whitaker, 1625).
99. Dixon, *Personal History of Lord Bacon*, pp. 75–76.
100. Dodd, *Francis Bacon's Personal Life-Story*, p. 176.
101. Dawkins, *The Shakespeare Enigma*, p. 259.
102. A replica of the manuscript can be found at https://SirBacon.org/NMANUSCR.HTM.

103. Images of the "Northumberland Manuscript" can be found in Dawkins, *The Shakespeare Enigma*, pp. 301–02.
104. See The Northumberland Manuscript (sirbacon.org).
105. Dawkins, *The Shakespeare Enigma*, p. 304.
106. Ibid.
107. Ibid.
108. Dodd, *Francis Bacon's Personal Life-Story*, p. 170.
109. Gallup, *The Bi-Literal Cypher of Sir Francis Bacon*, p. 28.
110. Fellows, *The Shakespeare Code*, p. 153.
111. Dodd, *Francis Bacon's Personal Life-Story*, p. 203.
112. Quoted from the most widely accepted version of the Tilbury speech found in a letter to the Duke of Buckingham from Leonel Sharp, the archdeacon of Berkshire.
113. Dawkins, *The Shakespeare Enigma*, p. 238.
114. Spedding, *An Account of the Life and Times of Francis Bacon*, pp. 52–53.
115. Gallup, *The Bi-Literal Cypher of Sir Francis Bacon*, pp. 209–10.
116. Dodd, *Francis Bacon's Personal Life-Story*, pp. 210–11.
117. Ibid.
118. Dixon, *Personal History of Lord Bacon*, pp. 91–92.
119. James Spedding, *The Letters and the Life of Francis Bacon*, Vol. 2 (London: Longman, Green and Roberts, 1862), p. 43.
120. Ibid.
121. Ibid., p. 40.
122. Dawkins, *The Shakespeare Enigma*, p. 267.
123. Spedding, *The Letters and the Life of Francis Bacon*, Vol. 3, pp. 149–50.
124. Dawkins, *The Shakespeare Enigma*, p. 270.
125. Dodd, *Francis Bacon's Personal Life-Story*, p. 273.
126. Agnes Strickland, *Lives of the Queens of England, from the Norman Conquest*, Vol. 7 (Philadelphia: Lea and Blanchard, 1844), p. 180.
127. Dodd, *Francis Bacon's Personal Life-Story*, p. 277.
128. Ibid., pp. 277–78; brackets added by Dodd.
129. Ibid., p. 278.
130. Ibid., p. 280.
131. Ibid.
132. Ibid., p. 287.
133. Fellows, *The Shakespeare Code*, p. 203.
134. Ibid., p. 205.
135. Dodd, *Francis Bacon's Personal Life-Story*, pp. 291–92.
136. Gallup, *The Bi-Literal Cypher of Sir Francis Bacon*, p. 160.
137. Ibid., p. 68.
138. Ibid., pp. 20, 22, 40–42, 178–79.
139. Peter Dawkins, "The Vestal Flame Portrait of Elizabeth I" essay.
140. Dodd, *Francis Bacon's Personal Life-Story*, p. 296.

141. Ibid., p. 337.
142. Ibid., p. 338.
143. Owen, *Sir Francis Bacon's Cipher Story,* Vol. 1, pp. 177–78.
144. Ibid., pp. 179–83.
145. Ibid., pp. 184–85.
146. Miguel Á. Granada, *The Nova of 1600 in Cygnus and the Christianization of the Constellations,* chapter 7 of *Kepler's New Star (1604): Context and Controversy,* Patrick J Boner, ed. (Koninklijke Brill NV, Leiden, The Netherlands, 2021), pp. 145–46.
147. Peter Dawkins, "Elias the Artist" essay (Francis Bacon Research Trust), www.fbrt.org.
148. Paracelsus, "De Mineralibus," ch. 1, Vol. II, Opera omnia medico-chemico-chirurgica, Geneva, 1658. As translated by Dawkins, "Elias the Artist" essay; bracketed words added by Dawkins.
149. Paracelsus, Arthur Edward Waite, *The Hermetic and Alchemical Writings of Aureolus Philippus Theophrastus Bombast, of Hohenheim, Called Paracelsus the Great* (London: James Elliott and Co. 1894), *The Economy of Minerals,* p. 104.
150. Ibid., *The Economy of Minerals,* pp. 96–97.
151. Dawkins, "Elias the Artist" essay.
152. Vries, Lyke de. "The Paracelsian Impetus." In *Reformation, Revolution, Renovation: The Roots and Reception of the Rosicrucian Call for General Reform,* Brill, 2022, p. 115; http://www.jstor.org/stable/10.1163/j.ctv29sfvg0.8.
153. Ibid., pp. 155–56; quoting Sperber, "Preface," *Von der höchsten Schätze;* bracketed ellipses in original.
154. Dodd, *The Martyrdom of Francis Bacon,* p. 154.
155. Dodd, *Francis Bacon's Personal Life-Story,* p. 563.
156. Ibid.
157. Wheeler, "Francis Bacon's Verulamium—the Common-Law Template of the Modern, in English Science and Culture" (1999), in *Angelaki* issue on "Judging the Law."
158. Dixon, *The Personal History of Lord Bacon,* p. 197.
159. Dawkins, *Building Paradise,* p. 2.
160. Alfred Dodd, *The Immortal Master* (London: Rider & Co., 1943), p. 33.
161. Dodd, *The Martyrdom of Francis Bacon,* p. 68.
162. Ibid.
163. Ibid.
164. Ibid.
165. Dawkins, *Building Paradise,* p. 31.
166. Dawkins, "Canonbury Place and Tower" essay (Francis Bacon Research Trust), www.fbrt.org.
167. Ibid.
168. Dodd, *Francis Bacon's Personal Life-Story,* p. 502.

169. Ibid.
170. Ibid., p. 503.
171. Ibid., p. 519.
172. Ibid.
173. Dodd, *The Martyrdom of Francis Bacon*, p. 79.
174. Ibid., p. 77.
175. Ibid., p. 86.
176. Ibid.
177. Ibid., p. 87, a letter from Nathaniel Brent to Sir Richard Beaumont.
178. Ibid., pp. 88–89.
179. Dodd, *The Secret History of Francis Bacon* (London: The C.W. Daniel Company, Ltd., 1942), pp. 26–27.
180. Dodd, *The Martyrdom of Francis Bacon*, p. 120.
181. Ibid., p. 119.
182. Ibid., p. 105.
183. Dodd, *The Secret History of Francis Bacon*, p. 151.
184. Ibid.
185. Dodd, *The Martyrdom of Francis Bacon*, p. 146 n. 16.
186. Dodd, *Francis Bacon's Personal Life-Story*, pp. 530–31.
187. Dawkins, "Rosicrucian Mysteries" lecture series; https://www.fbrt.org.uk/events/.
188. Ibid.
189. Granville C. Cuningham, *Bacon's Secret Disclosed in Contemporary Books* (London: Gay and Hancock Ltd., 1911), pp. 27–28.
190. Dawkins, *The Shakespeare Enigma*, p. 414.
191. Cuningham, *Bacon's Secret Disclosed in Contemporary Books*, p. 47.
192. *Baconiana* (Francis Bacon Society, 1917), vol. XV, July 1917, no. 59, p. 139.
193. William Smedley, *The Mystery of Francis Bacon* (San Francisco: J. Howell, 1851), p. 175; quoting Peter Boener's 'A Life,' 1647.
194. Francis Bacon, James Spedding, *Works of Francis Bacon*, vol. IV (London: Longmans & Co., 1883), *The Great Instauration*, p. 23.
195. Ibid., pp. 27–28.
196. Ibid., p. 29.
197. Dawkins, *Building Paradise*, p. 112.
198. Bacon, Spedding, *Works of Francis Bacon*, vol. IV, *The Great Instauration*, p. 31.
199. Dawkins, *Building Paradise*, p. 118.
200. Bacon, Spedding, *Works of Francis Bacon*, vol. IV, *The Great Instauration*, p. 31.
201. Ibid., p. 32.
202. Eccles. 3:11.
203. Dawkins, *Building Paradise*, p. 120.
204. Ibid., pp. 123–25.

205. Rev. 10:7.
206. "The forerunner of reuenge Vpon the Duke of Buckingham, for the poysoning of the most potent King Iames...", Frankfurt, 1626; in the digital collection Early English Books Online. https://name.umdl.umich.edu/a21195.0001.001. University of Michigan Library Digital Collections.
207. Dawkins, "Canonbury Place and Tower" essay; https://www.fbrt.org.uk/wp-content/uploads/2020/06/Canonbury_Place_Tower.pdf.
208. Dr. Rawley, *Manes Verulamiani, Sacred to the memory of The Right Honourable Lord Francis Baron Verulam, Viscount St. Albans* (London. From the Press of John Haviland, 1626). Translation can be found at https://home.hiwaay.net/~paul/bacon/manes/verulam.html.
209. Ibid.
210. Dodd, *The Martyrdom of Francis Bacon*, p. 132.
211. Dodd, *Francis Bacon's Personal Life-Story*, p. 545.
212. Ibid.
213. Dr. Rawley, *Manes Verulamiani*.
214. Dodd, *Francis Bacon's Personal Life-Story*, p. 545.
215. Dr. Rawley, *Manes Verulamiani*.
216. Ibid.
217. Dana Jalobeanu, *Natural History in Early Modern France* (Koninklijke Brill nv, leiden, 2018), pp. 180–81.
218. Dana Jalobeanu, *Bacon et Descartes: Genèse de la modernité philosophique*. Cassan, É. (Ed.) 2014. Lyon: ENS Éditions. Chapter VII, *The French Reception of Francis Bacon's Natural History in Mid Seventeenth Century*, doi:10.4000/books.enseditions.2571.
219. Gallup, *The Bi-literal Cypher of Sir Francis Bacon*, p. 208.
220. Charles Carlton, *The Experience of the British Civil Wars* (London: Routledge, 1992), pp. 211–14.
221. Henrietta Bernstein, *The Ark of the Covenant* (Marina del Rey: DeVorss & Co., 1998), p. 180.
222. Dawkins, *The Shakespeare Enigma*, p. 381.
223. Lindgren, Carl Edwin, *The Way of the Rose Cross: A Historical Perception, 1614–1620, Journal of Religion and Psychical Research*, Vol. 18, No. 3: 141–148, 1995.
224. From The Francis Bacon Society's video lecture *Did Francis Bacon Die in 1626 or Feign His Death with the Help of His Rosicrucian Brotherhood?*
225. Dodd, *The Secret History of Francis Bacon*, pp. 36–37.
226. James Spedding, *The Letters and the Life of Francis Bacon*, Vol 3, p. 228.

PART 2 A Holy Brother

1. Godfré Ray King, *Unveiled Mysteries* (Chicago: Saint Germain Press, 1939), pp. 134–36; quoting Saint Germain.
2. Rev. 10:7.
3. Isabel Cooper-Oakley, *The Comte de St. Germain* (Milano, G. Sulli-Rao, 1912), pp. 29–30.
4. Ibid., p. 31.
5. Karl, prince de Hesse, *Mémoires de mon temps, dictés par landgrave* (Copenhague Impr. de J.H. Schultz, 1861), p. 134; translated to English.
6. Cooper-Oakley, *The Comte de St. Germain*, p. 52, quoting Cornelis Ascanius van Sypesteyn, *Voltaire, Saint-Germain, Cagliostro, Mirabeau, in the Netherlands. History, memories from the eighteenth century*.
7. Ibid., p. 5.
8. Ibid., p. 51, quoting J. van Sypesteyn, *Historishe Herinneringen*.
9. Karl, prince de Hesse, *Mémoires de mon temps*, p. 135; translated to English.
10. Ibid., pp. 133–34; translated to English.
11. Cooper-Oakley, *The Comte de St. Germain*, p. 11.
12. Ibid., pp. 13–14, quoting Hezekiel.
13. Ibid., pp. 34–35; brackets added by Isabel Cooper-Oakley.
14. Du Hausset, *The Private Memoirs of Madame Du Hausset, Lady's Maid to Madame de Pompadour* (London: E. Wilson, 1825), pp. 101–102.
15. Ibid., p. 102.
16. Ibid., pp. 133–34.
17. Cooper-Oakley, *The Comte de St. Germain*, p. 43.
18. Elizabeth Wells Gallup, *The Bi-literal Cypher of Sir Francis Bacon* (Detroit: Howard Publishing Company; London: Gay & Bird), p. 58.
19. Henrietta Bernstein, *Ark of the Covenant, Holy Grail*, (Marina del Rey: Devorss & Company, 1998), p. 181.
20. George Lippard, *Legends of the American Revolution "1776" or Washington and His Generals* (Philadelphia: T.B. Peterson and Brothers, 1876), pp. 88–98.
21. Robert Allen Campbell, *Our Flag* (Chicago: H. E. Lawrence & Co, 1890), pp. 35–41.
22. Ibid., p. 46.
23. Ibid., pp. 47–48.
24. Ibid., p. 49.
25. Ibid., p. 61.
26. Ibid., pp. 61–62.
27. Peter Dawkins, *The Great Vision* (Francis Bacon Research Trust, 1985), p. 108.
28. Lippard, *Legends of the American Revolution*, p. 393.

29. Ibid., pp. 394–96.
30. Originally published by Wesley Bradshaw. Copied from a reprint in the *National Tribune*, Vol. 4, No. 12, December 1880. First published there in 1859.
31. Papers of Dr. James McHenry on the Federal Convention of 1787, *The American Historical Review*, Vol. 11, No. 3 (Apr. 1906), pp. 595–624; https://www.jstor.org/stable/1836024.
32. Cooper-Oakley, *The Comte de St. Germain*, p. 66.
33. Ibid., p. 67.
34. Ibid., p. 69.
35. Ibid., pp. 72–73.
36. Ibid., p. 76.
37. Ibid., pp. 78–80.
38. Ibid., pp. 86–87.
39. Ibid., pp. 89–91.
40. Herr Bocke, *Beethoven, the Man and the Artist: As Revealed in His Own Words* (New York: B. W. Huebsch, 1905), p. 76.
41. Ibid., p. 92. A letter from Beethoven to the Viennese magistrate.
42. Cooper-Oakley, *The Comte de St. Germain*, pp. 144–45; quoting Gräffer from H. P. Blavatsky, *The Theosophical Glossary*, pp. 136–62.
43. Dominic Lieven, *Russia against Napoleon* (Viking, 2010), p. 188.
44. Walter Müller-Seidel (Editor), Wolfgang Riedel (Editor) *Die Weimarer Klassic und ihre Geheimbuende*, 2001, p. 112.
45. A letter from George Washington to Rev. G. W. Snyder, September 25, 1798, Mount Vernon; a copy can be referenced in the Library of Congress, https://www.loc.gov/resource/mgw2.021/?q=Illuminati&sp=182&st=text.
46. A letter from George Washington to Rev. G. W. Snyder, October 24, 1798, Mount Vernon; a copy can be referenced in the Library of Congress, https://www.loc.gov/resource/mgw2.021/?q=Illuminati&sp=200&st=text.
47. Lance Banning, *Liberty and Order: The First American Party Struggle* (Indianapolis: Liberty Fund, Inc., 2004), p. 176, George Washington, "Message to the Third Congress 19 November 1794."
48. George Washington, *Washington's Farewell Address to the People of the United States of America: Published in September 1796* (https://www.senate.gov/artandhistory/history/resources/pdf/Washingtons_Farewell_Address.pdf), pp. 11–12.
49. Adam Weishaupt, *Diogenes' Lamp Or An Examination Of Our Present Day Morality And Enlightenment* (Regensburg, Montag and Weiss, 1804, republished by the Masonic Book Club, Bloomington, Illinois, 2008), pp. 111, 137.
50. Alfred, Lord Tennyson, *In Memoriam*, 27, stanza 4.
51. Ruth Adams Drayer, *Nicholas and Helena Roerich: The Spiritual*

Journey of Two Great Artists and Peacemakers (Quest Books Theosophical Publishing House, Wheaton, Illinois, Channai, India, 2005), Prologue, p. xxii.
52. Ibid.
53. C. W. Leadbeater, *The Masters and the Path Adyar* (Theosophical Publishing House, 1969), p. 8, brackets added.
54. Cooper-Oakley, *The Comte de St. Germain*, p. 53.
55. *The Mahatma Letters to A. P. Sinnett* (London: Rider and Company, 1926), Letter 47, Morya to Sinnett, March 3, 1882, p. 271.
56. *The Mahatma Letters,* Letter 6, Koot' Hoomi [K.H.] to Sinnett, December 10, 1880, pp. 23–24.
57. Renate Ulmer, "Russia 1900: Art and Culture in the Empire of the Last Tsar," *International Panorama,* Issue #3, 2008.
58. Drayer, *Nicholas and Helena Roerich,* p. 8.
59. Ibid., p. 7.
60. Morya, *Agni Yoga* (Agni Yoga Society. New York, First edition published 1928, sixth edition 1997), verse 185.
61. Jacqueline Decter, *Nicholas Roerich: The Life and Art of a Russian Master* (Rochester, Vt.: Park Street Press, 1989), pp. 106, 111, 107.
62. Mary Siegrist, "The Universe of Roerich," in *Himalaya* (New York: Brentano's, 1926), p. 38.
63. Ivan Narodny, "The Inner Meaning of Roerich's Art," in *Himalaya,* pp. 68, 70.
64. Nicholas Roerich, *Altai-Himalaya: A Travel Diary* (Brookfield, Conn.: Arun Press, 1929), pp. 120, 93.
65. Roerich, *Altai-Himalaya,* pp. 33–34.
66. *Letters of Helena Roerich, Volume I: 1929–1935* (New York: Agni Yoga Society, 1954); Letter 1 dated 1929.
67. Ibid., Letter from 25 March 1935.
68. Morya, *Agni Yoga,* verse 77.
69. Ibid., verse 451.
70. Morya, *Supermundane* (New York: Agni Yoga Society, 1938), verse 25.
71. Ibid., verse 539.
72. *Letters of Helena Roerich, Volume II: 1935–1939* (New York: Agni Yoga Society, 1967); letter dated 10 December 1936.
73. Ibid., letter dated 17 December 1936.
74. King, *Unveiled Mysteries,* p. 5.
75. Ibid., p. 6.
76. Ibid., p. viii.
77. Ibid., pp. viii–ix.
78. Ibid., p. ix.
79. Saint Germain, *The "I AM" Discourses* (Chicago: Saint Germain Press, 1940), pp. 2–3.
80. Gal. 6:7.

81. Alfred Dodd, *The Immortal Master* (London: Rider & Co., 1943), p. 47.
82. Ibid., pp. 47–49.
83. Ibid., p. 53.
84. John 21:22.
85. Rev. 22:1.
86. Prov. 4:23.
87. Matt. 6:7.
88. John 7:38.
89. Isa. 45:11.
90. John 9:4.
91. Gen. 1:3.
92. *Julius Caesar,* act 4, scene 3.
93. H.P. Blavatsky, *The Key to Theosophy: Being a Clear Exposition, in the Form of Question and Answer, of the ETHICS, SCIENCE, AND PHILOSOPHY for the Study of which The Theosophical Society has been Founded* (London; New York: Theosophical Pub. Co., 1888), pp. 228–29.
94. King, *Unveiled Mysteries,* pp. 141–45, quoting Saint Germain.
95. Excerpt of a poem by Saint Germain, as written down by Mark L. Prophet.

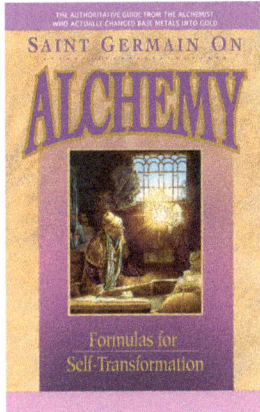

Saint Germain On Alchemy
Formulas for Self-Transformation

Voltaire called him the "man who never dies and knows everything." The Count Saint Germain turned base metals into gold, removed the flaws from diamonds and discovered the elixir of youth. In the eighteenth century, this "Wonderman of Europe" was the confidant of kings and a friend to the poor. Today the master Saint Germain shows that miracles are nothing more than the natural outgrowth of the practice of spiritual alchemy. In this greatest of all self-help books, he describes the principles of alchemy and how you can use them in your own life to bring about spiritual, mental, emotional and physical transformation.

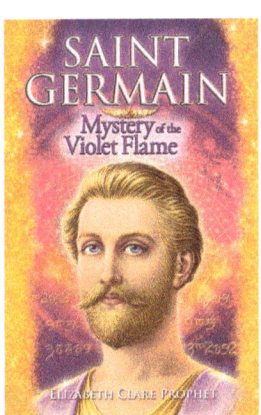

Saint Germain
Mystery of the Violet Flame

For millennia, mystics and alchemists have sought the keys to unlock secrets of life and eternity. Their discoveries were often veiled in esoteric symbolism—hiding their real knowledge from those who might use it for selfish ends. Saint Germain was one such seeker. Through many lifetimes as alchemist, adept and visionary, he found the priceless ancient formulas for self-transformation. In this day, he comes again, revealing some of that knowledge to those finally ready to receive it—mystics like you. Most importantly, he reveals the profound secrets of the violet flame—the key to personal and world transformation.

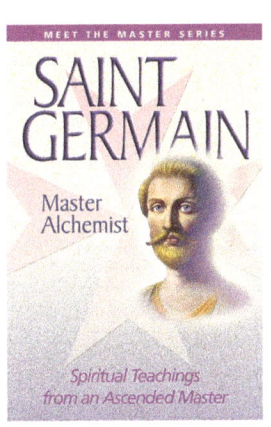

Saint Germain
Master Alchemist

In the 1700s he dazzled royal courts and became known as the Wonderman of Europe. Throughout history, the master Saint Germain has played many key roles. Today he is the immortal sponsor of the Aquarian age. Includes his priceless alchemical secrets for personal transformation.

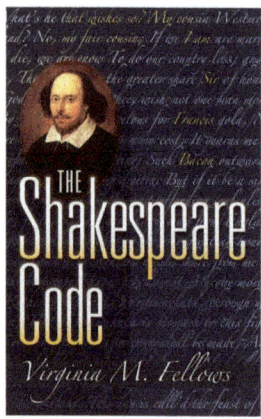

The Shakespeare Code

A true story! It reads like a Shakespearean tale, complete with mystery, villains, false identities and star-crossed lovers.

Author Virginia Fellows' fascinating and endearing tale weaves together the facts and history of the controversy, deception and mystery of Elizabethan England and the works of Shakespeare. She reveals Francis Bacon's own story as the rejected prince, son of the "Virgin Queen" Elizabeth, as encrypted in writings attributed to Shakespeare. Fellows' exhaustive research includes a 19th-century cipher wheel still in existence today.

See photos of the 100-year-old device and learn more about this book at ShakespeareCode.com.

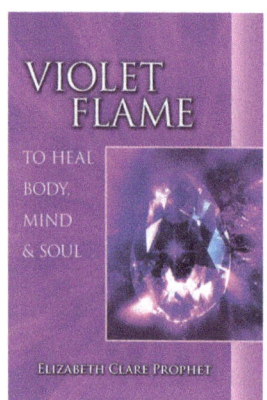

Violet Flame
To Heal Body, Mind and Soul

"The violet flame is a light that serves all spiritual heritages, that gives respect and dignity to all things. It gives us a way to connect with each other.... It's what really empowers you."
—Dannion Brinkley, author of *Saved by the Light*

Twentieth-century seer Edgar Cayce recognized the healing power of the violet light. Dannion Brinkley saw and experienced the violet flame in his near-death sojourns. Healers and alchemists have used this high-frequency spiritual energy to bring about energetic balance and spiritual transformation. Now you can learn how to apply the practical techniques in this book to create balance, harmony and positive change in body, mind and soul.

The Mystic's Path Home
Teachings of the Ascended Masters
Are you seeking Oneness with Divinity?

You are a Mystic. You walk the steeper path, but the high cliffs hold no fear for you who are drawn upward by the heart of the Divine Mother.

Whether you follow Buddha, Jesus, Krishna, Mother Mary, Saint Germain, Kuan Yin or others, this book shows you the inner path. Take their hand as they lead you Home.

About
The Summit Lighthouse

The Summit Lighthouse is an internationally recognized spiritual center for the advancement of inner awakening. Our international organization is a global family that is inspired, guided, and sponsored by those known as the ascended masters.

The ascended masters are the most beloved and trusted transcendent beings guiding our planet's material and spiritual evolution. Most of the world's religions are currently based on the revelations of one or more of these masters before their ascension. We openly embrace spiritual seekers from all paths of light, including the mystical traditions of the world's religions.

The ascended masters and their messengers have given us over fifteen thousand hours of invaluable inner wisdom and insightful instruction, and they have provided the means for our direct initiation into higher consciousness.

For the ascended masters . . . no subject is off limits! Their teachings contain amazing truths and awesome answers on spirituality, alchemy, astrology, sacred geometry, spiritual science, karma, reincarnation, ascension, archangels (and fallen angels), and even those issues that are considered taboo or "out of this world."

Primary Goals of the Teachings of the Ascended Masters

The ascended masters challenge us daily to be bold, to dare to be who we truly are, and to face adversity with courage, patience, perseverance, honesty, integrity, inner love, discipline, and discernment—all for a greater sense of inner peace, fearlessness, stillness and silence, harmony, self-mastery, compassion, and wisdom.

These teachings help our souls get back to the origin of their individualized inner source of True Self Love—the Higher Self, or I AM Presence. Our point of contact with our Higher Self is the "Spark of Life" or "Sacred Fire of the Heart," the place where our consciousness expresses its true divine nature of unconditional love and happiness, universal oneness, and an authentic desire to serve others.

How Our Teachings Came into Being

Our teachings were all released through highly trained and trusted messengers, Mark L. Prophet and Elizabeth Clare Prophet. Mark was contacted by the Ascended Master El Morya at the age of eighteen and received training from him for many years before he was instructed to establish The Summit Lighthouse in 1958 in Washington, D.C.

With his ascension in 1973, Mark passed the torch for the mission to his gifted wife, Elizabeth Clare Prophet, who continued her service until her retirement in 1999.

The dictations of the ascended masters were regularly given in public. The ascended masters also inspired thousands of lectures delivered by the messengers. The content of the dictations are, by most human standards, beyond the mind's ability to construct in real time. They carry very powerful frequencies of light, awakening us to the highest truths we've ever experienced.

We leave it up to you to decide the value for yourself.

Moving toward Your Victory

No matter what path of light you are on, spiritual freedom is attained using tools that have been passed down in wisdom teachings through the millennia: meditation, selfless service, devotional music, prayer, mantra, and the science of the spoken Word. The masters bring an accelerated understanding of these principles, especially suited for the challenges of the modern world, including dynamic decree work and the use of the violet flame.

Next Steps

We are genuinely excited to meet you on the path ... and hope you are too. We extend a warm welcome from everyone at The Summit Lighthouse, and we invite you to explore the teachings of the ascended masters at our website https://www.SummitLighthouse.org. Check out our free online lessons and hundreds of articles on a wide range of spiritual subjects. Browse through our online bookstore. And if you would rather talk to someone in person, please feel free to contact us today! Discover more about the Keepers of the Flame Fraternity at https://www.SummitLighthouse.org/keepers-of-the-flame/ and join Saint Germain's brotherhood of those who keep the Flame of Life.

ELIZABETH CLARE PROPHET is a world-renowned author, spiritual teacher, and pioneer in practical spirituality. Her groundbreaking books have been published in more than thirty languages and over three million copies have been sold worldwide.

Among her best-selling titles are *The Human Aura; The Science of the Spoken Word; Your Seven Energy Centers; The Lost Years of Jesus; The Art of Practical Spirituality;* and her best-selling Pocket Guides to Practical Spirituality series.

The Summit Lighthouse®
63 Summit Way
Gardiner, Montana 59030 USA
1-800-245-5445 / 406-848-9500

Se habla español.

info@SummitUniversityPress.com
SummitLighthouse.org

Printed in the USA
CPSIA information can be obtained
at www.ICGtesting.com
CBHW052139130624
9869CB00004B/3